IT and Semantic Web Contributions to Digital Transformation:

Towards Inclusive Economies and Societies

Patricia Ordóñez de Pablos
University of Oviedo, Spain

Jose Emilio Labra Gayo
University of Oviedo, Spain

IGI Global
Scientific Publishing
Publishing Tomorrow's Research Today

Vice President of Editorial Melissa Wagner
Managing Editor of Acquisitions Mikaela Felty
Managing Editor of Book Development Jocelynn Hessler
Production Manager Mike Brehm
Cover Design Phillip Shickler

Published in the United States of America by
IGI Global Scientific Publishing
701 East Chocolate Avenue
Hershey, PA, 17033, USA
Tel: 717-533-8845
Fax: 717-533-8661
Website: https://www.igi-global.com E-mail: cust@igi-global.com

Library of Congress Cataloging-in-Publication Data

LCCN: 2024055665 (CIP Data Pending)
ISBN13: 9798369384770
EISBN13: 9798369384794

British Cataloguing in Publication Data
A Cataloguing in Publication record for this book is available from the British Library.

Editorial Advisory Board and List of Reviewers

Editorial Advisory Board

List of Reviewers

Gururaj C., *Mechanical Engineering, Ramco Institute of Technology, India*

Table of Contents

Preface xii

Chapter 1
Empowering Small and Medium Enterprises Through IT and Semantic Web Technologies in Digital Economies 1
Rachna Rana, Ludhiana Group of Colleges, Ludhiana, India
Pankaj Bhambri, Guru Nanak Dev Engineering College, Ludhiana, India

Chapter 2
Digital Transformation Through Ontology Engineering: Implications for Inclusive Economic Development 31
Rachna Rana, Ludhiana Group of Colleges, Ludhiana, India
Pankaj Bhambri, Guru Nanak Dev Engineering College, Ludhiana, India

Chapter 3
Information Technology Usage in Internal Audit to Enhance Public Sector Sustainability 73
Neeta Baporikar, Independent Researcher, India

Chapter 4
Leveraging Technology for Sustainable Economic Growth: Advancing the SDGs Through Innovation 115
Ananya Pandey, Christ University, India
Jipson Joseph, Christ University, India
Manshu Goyal, Independent Researcher, India

Chapter 5
Predictive Analysis of Digital Payment Trends Using Deep Learning 139
Usharani Bhimavarapu, Department of Computer Science and Engineering, Koneru Lakshmaiah Education Foundation, Vaddeswaram, India

Chapter 6
Preferences and Usage of E-Banking Services Among Customers in Tripura, India 155
Supriya Dam, Netaji Subhash, India

Chapter 7
Virtual Democracy: Exploring the Viability of Election Voting via Metaverse Technology 187
Nina Lestari, Universitas Muhammadiyah Makassar, Indonesia
Nur Azizah Wahyuni, Universitas Muhammadiyah Makassar, Indonesia
Muhammad Younus, Universitas Muhammadiyah Yogyakarta, Pakistan
Andi Luhur Prianto, Universitas Muhammadiyah Makassar, Indonesia
Aqmal Reza Amri, Universitas Muhammadiyah Makassar, Indonesia
Ahmad Harakan, Universitas Muhammadiyah Makassar, Indonesia
Achmad Nurmandi, Universitas Muhammadiyah Yogyakarta, Indonesia
Hajira Gul, Midwifery Association, Pakistan
Ibrahim Shah, Aga Khan University, Pakistan
Ihyani Malik, Universitas Muhammadiyah Makassar, Indonesia

Chapter 8
Employee Perception Towards Customer Satisfaction, Digital Transformation, Financial Security, and Risk in the Indian Banking Sector 219
Ajay Kumar Singh, Department of Humanities and Social Sciences, Graphic Era University, Dehradun, India
S. Srinivasan, Department of Humanities and Social Sciences, Graphic Era University, Dehradun, India

Chapter 9
Leveraging Bi-Stacked ANN for Organizational Values in the Context of Digital Transformation 257
Usharani Bhimavarapu, Department of Computer Science and Engineering, Koneru Lakshmaiah Education Foundation, Vaddeswaram, India

Compilation of References 273

About the Contributors 313

Index 319

Detailed Table of Contents

Preface xii

Chapter 1
Empowering Small and Medium Enterprises Through IT and Semantic Web Technologies in Digital Economies 1
Rachna Rana, Ludhiana Group of Colleges, Ludhiana, India
Pankaj Bhambri, Guru Nanak Dev Engineering College, Ludhiana, India

Small and Medium Enterprises (SMEs) are essential for fostering economic growth, innovation, and employment in both advanced and emerging economies. In the digital age, SMEs encounter considerable obstacles in embracing sophisticated technology to maintain competitiveness in progressively digitalized marketplaces. This chapter examines how Information Technology (IT) and Semantic Web technologies might enable SMEs to leverage the opportunities presented by digital economies. It analyses the function of information technology in optimizing corporate processes, augmenting consumer relationships, and expanding market accessibility. The chapter explores how Semantic Web technologies, via intelligent data management and integration, can offer SMEs increased decision-making skills, enhanced knowledge management, and more tailored user experiences. Case studies and real-world examples illustrate the practical applications of these technologies across many industries, emphasizing their transformative impact on SME growth and sustainability.

Chapter 2
Digital Transformation Through Ontology Engineering: Implications for Inclusive Economic Development 31
Rachna Rana, Ludhiana Group of Colleges, Ludhiana, India
Pankaj Bhambri, Guru Nanak Dev Engineering College, Ludhiana, India

The chapter examines the essential function of ontology engineering in facilitating digital transformation and advancing inclusive economic growth. Ontology engineering, an essential component of the Semantic Web, facilitates the organization and standardization of intricate data, promoting interoperability among digital systems. This chapter analyses the role of ontology-based frameworks in facilitating equitable access to digital resources, especially in underserved areas. Ontology engineering is essential for democratizing technology developments by integrating data silos and fostering inclusive digital ecosystems. The chapter explores practical applications in fields including healthcare, education, and e-governance, emphasizing their capacity to promote socio-economic development. Moreover, it tackles the difficulties of implementing ontologies on a large scale and underscores the necessity of synchronizing digital transformation initiatives with objectives of social equality and economic inclusion.

Chapter 3
Information Technology Usage in Internal Audit to Enhance Public Sector Sustainability 73
Neeta Baporikar, Independent Researcher, India

Information Technology has a transformative impact on streamlining processes and enhancing efficiency is universally admitted. Collaborative and specialized tools led to a comprehensive approach to diverse computer-aided audit processes. This chapter investigates the strategic role of information technology (IT) in enhancing public sector sustainability through the internal audit lens. Adopting a constructivist research philosophy, qualitative exploratory research design, and survey methodology the objective is to explore how internal auditors actively construct their understanding of IT impact on public sector sustainability. Findings reveal that the factors affecting IT usage in internal audit are linked to organizational, cultural, technical, and leadership aspects. Recommendations include internal auditors, embracing continuous learning, and, participating, in training programs to enhance IT proficiency and tools that emphasize fostering a collaborative work environment, promoting effective communication, and teamwork dynamics.

Chapter 4
Leveraging Technology for Sustainable Economic Growth: Advancing the SDGs Through Innovation 115
Ananya Pandey, Christ University, India
Jipson Joseph, Christ University, India
Manshu Goyal, Independent Researcher, India

Raising long-term competitiveness of national economies is an important requirement with the broad use of digital technologies. In addition to offering the possibility of economic restructuring, information and communication technologies open up new avenues for all citizens to access a range of services, such as first-rate healthcare and education. As a result, these developments promote inclusive growth and significantly aid in the achievement of the UN Sustainable Development Goals (SDGs). Significant economic changes that raise living standards and boost global competitiveness can be sparked by the promise of digital transformation within a framework of sustainable development. Keeping in view the above, the chapter thoroughly examines practical and theoretical frameworks pertaining to the application of sustainable development, as well as an assessment of the possibilities for using digital technologies to promote sustainable competitiveness. The relationship between digital inclusion and its long-term effects on global economic development is also analyzed.

Chapter 5
Predictive Analysis of Digital Payment Trends Using Deep Learning 139
Usharani Bhimavarapu, Department of Computer Science and Engineering, Koneru Lakshmaiah Education Foundation, Vaddeswaram, India

Digital transformation has significantly impacted the global financial landscape, particularly through the expansion of digital payment systems. This study investigates the trends and adoption patterns of digital payments from 2014 to 2024, leveraging advanced machine learning techniques for predictive analysis. Using an integrated deep learning model combining Bi-Stacked LSTM (Long Short-Term Memory) and Bi-Stacked GRU (Gated Recurrent Unit), we analyzed a comprehensive dataset derived from the Global Financial Inclusion Database and the Reserve Central Bank Consolidated Banking Database. The model effectively captures both long-term dependencies and short-term relationships in time-series data, providing valuable insights into the evolution of digital payment systems. Our approach offers an in-depth understanding of the factors influencing digital payment adoption, including demographic, regional, and policy-based variables, while also identifying challenges and growth opportunities in financial inclusion through digital platforms

Chapter 6
Preferences and Usage of E-Banking Services Among Customers in Tripura, India 155
Supriya Dam, Netaji Subhash, India

The study evaluates the e-banking services of two prominent commercial banks in Northern Tripura through a customer survey, focusing on their usage and preferences. Field observations indicate a wide range of customer opinions regarding their preferences and usage of e-banking services. The results reveal significant similarities in client preferences for these services. However, the utilization of e-banking services exhibited a significant difference between ICICI and SBI clients. The informants demonstrated a clear preference for debit card transactions over credit cards and a tendency to favor savings options rather than loans. The data suggests that banks are experiencing growth in both urban and semi-urban areas. The survey indicates that respondents value hassle-free banking and stability, indicating mutual coexistence in their choices without any evidence of coopetition among bankers.

Chapter 7
Virtual Democracy: Exploring the Viability of Election Voting via Metaverse Technology 187
Nina Lestari, Universitas Muhammadiyah Makassar, Indonesia
Nur Azizah Wahyuni, Universitas Muhammadiyah Makassar, Indonesia
Muhammad Younus, Universitas Muhammadiyah Yogyakarta, Pakistan
Andi Luhur Prianto, Universitas Muhammadiyah Makassar, Indonesia
Aqmal Reza Amri, Universitas Muhammadiyah Makassar, Indonesia
Ahmad Harakan, Universitas Muhammadiyah Makassar, Indonesia
Achmad Nurmandi, Universitas Muhammadiyah Yogyakarta, Indonesia
Hajira Gul, Midwifery Association, Pakistan
Ibrahim Shah, Aga Khan University, Pakistan
Ihyani Malik, Universitas Muhammadiyah Makassar, Indonesia

The creation of the metaverse will change how we live, work, and play in a digital environment, one of which the metaverse opens up great opportunities for the development of virtual democracy. One of the implementations of virtual democracy is through digital election voting using the metaverse. A paradigm shift in democratic participation is brought about by integrating the metaverse into election voting. In the metaverse, voters can participate in the election process through an immersive virtual environment; the digital platform also changes the voting experience. The objective of this study is to explore the feasibility of election voting through metaverse technology. The result of this research is that election voting using metaverse technology has been implemented in several countries, where the implementation uses a blockchain system that ensures every vote is recorded securely and cannot be manipulated, thereby reducing the risk of fraud. This research concludes that applying metaverse technology in election voting will significantly change virtual democratic activities.

Chapter 8
Employee Perception Towards Customer Satisfaction, Digital Transformation, Financial Security, and Risk in the Indian Banking Sector 219
Ajay Kumar Singh, Department of Humanities and Social Sciences, Graphic Era University, Dehradun, India
S. Srinivasan, Department of Humanities and Social Sciences, Graphic Era University, Dehradun, India

Digital transformation (DT) helps to increase the performance, productivity, profits, and product quality in the banking sector. DT is also eager to increase online banking and customer's satisfaction at a greater level. However, employees are facing multiple challenges to adjust with the current DT in the banking sector of developing countries. This chapter, therefore, explores the perception of employees towards DT of the banking sector in India using primary information. Necessary information is collected from 176 employees of public and private banks in Dehradun and Delhi. The descriptive statistical method is used to analyse the primary data with regards to perception of employees on 30 different items or questions. These are divided into four constructs i.e., DT, financial security (FS), financial risk (FR) and customer' satisfaction (CS). The correlation coefficients and linear regression models are also considered to examine the association among these constructs.

Chapter 9
Leveraging Bi-Stacked ANN for Organizational Values in the Context of Digital Transformation 257
Usharani Bhimavarapu, Department of Computer Science and Engineering, Koneru Lakshmaiah Education Foundation, Vaddeswaram, India

The digital age has brought unprecedented opportunities for organizations to innovate and transform their operations, emphasizing the importance of measuring digital maturity and organizational values. This study leverages a bi-stacked Artificial Neural Network (ANN) architecture to measure a comprehensive digital index, integrating insights from people management values. The dataset, collected from 132 companies, was preprocessed and refined through feature extraction, including parameters such as the Relative Importance Value (RIV) for future business impact and the Rate of Satisfaction Value (RSV) with people management practices, quantified using a Likert scale. The bi-stacked ANN, designed with multiple layers and dropout mechanisms, processed these features to generate an accurate and reliable digital index. By combining advanced machine learning techniques and organizational value assessments, the proposed approach provides a scalable framework for understanding digital readiness while emphasizing the critical role of people management in driving business transformation

Compilation of References 273

About the Contributors 313

Index 319

Preface

INTRODUCTION

Companies and governments need to successfully navigate towards the digital and green transition. The role of information technologies and semantic web will be crucial for achieving the digital transformation and the building of more inclusive and resilient economies and societies. How can these fields of research contribute to a fair transition towards a digital and green economy?

OBJECTIVES OF THE BOOK

The main goal of the book is to explore how information technologies and semantic web can contribute to the successful digital transformation of companies and governments around the world. It discusses the state of the art of the field of semantic technologies, emphasizing existing gaps in the field and identifying opportunities for value creation. Furthermore, it presents innovative frameworks, methodologies, tools and experiences of companies and governments.

Finally, the book analyzes how information technologies and semantic web can contribute to the achievement of Sustainable Development Goals (SDGs) proposed by United Nations.

Innovative features of the book:

- Discussion of the potential of digital technologies to transform economies and societies.
- Identification of existing gaps in the fields of business, information technologies and semantic web.

- Sharing knowledge and insights about the applications of information technologies and semantic web tools to provide innovative solutions for companies and governments.
- Find out how information technologies and semantic web can contribute to the achievement of the SDGs.

AUDIENCE

Academics, students (undergraduate, PhD students), entrepreneurs, researchers, policymakers, industry leaders, investors, CEOs and society.

CONTENTS OF THE BOOK

The book is formed by a collection of 10 book chapters addressing crucial topics for competitiveness of companies, nations and regions like digital economies, digital payments, e-banking, information technologies, IoT, ontology engineering, semantic web, sustainable economic growth and sustainability. Let's briefly examine the contents of the book chapters.

Chapter 1 titled **"Empowering Small and Medium Enterprises through IT and Semantic Web Technologies in Digital Economies"** (by Rachna Rana and Pankaj Bhambri) affirms that "small and Medium Enterprises (SMEs) are essential for fostering economic growth, innovation, and employment in both advanced and emerging economies. In the digital age, SMEs encounter considerable obstacles in embracing sophisticated technology to maintain competitiveness in progressively digitalized marketplaces. This chapter examines how Information Technology (IT) and Semantic Web technologies might enable SMEs to leverage the opportunities presented by digital economies. It analyses the function of information technology in optimizing corporate processes, augmenting consumer relationships, and expanding market accessibility. The chapter explores how Semantic Web technologies, via intelligent data management and integration, can offer SMEs increased decision-making skills, enhanced knowledge management, and more tailored user experiences. Case studies and real-world examples illustrate the practical applications of these technologies across many industries, emphasizing their transformative impact on SME growth and sustainability".

Chapter 2, titled **"Digital Transformation through Ontology Engineering: Implications for Inclusive Economic Development"** (by Rachna Rana and Pankaj Bhambri) explores "the essential function of ontology engineering in facilitating digital transformation and advancing inclusive economic growth. Ontology engineering, an essential component of the Semantic Web, facilitates the organization and standardization of intricate data, promoting interoperability among digital systems. This chapter analyses the role of ontology-based frameworks in facilitating equitable access to digital resources, especially in underserved areas. Ontology engineering is essential for democratizing technology developments by integrating data silos and fostering inclusive digital ecosystems. The chapter explores practical applications in fields including healthcare, education, and e-governance, emphasizing their capacity to promote socio-economic development. Moreover, it tackles the difficulties of implementing ontologies on a large scale and underscores the necessity of synchronizing digital".

Chapter 3, titled **"Information Technology Usage in Internal Audit to Enhance Public Sector Sustainability"** (by Neeta Baporikar) states that **"**information Technology has a transformative impact on streamlining processes and enhancing efficiency is universally admitted. Collaborative and specialized tools led to a comprehensive approach to diverse computer-aided audit processes. This chapter investigates the strategic role of information technology (IT) in enhancing public sector sustainability through the internal audit lens. Adopting a constructivist research philosophy, qualitative exploratory research design, and survey methodology the objective is to explore how internal auditors actively construct their understanding of IT impact on public sector sustainability. Findings reveal that the factors affecting IT usage in internal audit are linked to organizational, cultural, technical, and leadership aspects. Recommendations include internal auditors, embracing continuous learning, and, participating, in training programs to enhance IT proficiency and tools that emphasize fostering a collaborative work environment, promoting effective communication, and teamwork dynamics".

Chapter 4, titled "Leveraging Technology for Sustainable Economic Growth: Advancing the SDGs through Innovation" (by Ananya Pandey, Jipson Joseph and Manshu Goyal) affirms that "raising long-term competitiveness of national economies is an important requirement with the broad use of digital technologies. In addition to offering the possibility of economic restructuring, information and communication technologies open up new avenues for all citizens to access a range of services, such as first-rate healthcare and education. As a result, these developments promote inclusive growth and significantly aid in the achievement of the UN Sustainable Development Goals (SDGs). Significant economic changes that raise living standards and boost global competitiveness can be sparked by the promise of digital transformation within a framework of sustainable development. Keeping in view the above, the chapter thoroughly examines practical and theoretical frameworks pertaining to the application of sustainable development, as well as an assessment of the possibilities for using digital technologies to promote sustainable competitiveness. The relationship between digital inclusion and its long-term effects on global economic development is also analyzed".

Chapter 5, titled **"Predictive Analysis of Digital Payment Trends Using Deep Learning"** (by Bhimavarapu Usharani) states that "digital transformation has significantly impacted the global financial landscape, particularly through the expansion of digital payment systems. This study investigates the trends and adoption patterns of digital payments from 2014 to 2024, leveraging advanced machine learning techniques for predictive analysis. Using an integrated deep learning model combining Bi-Stacked LSTM (Long Short-Term Memory) and Bi-Stacked GRU (Gated Recurrent Unit), we analyzed a comprehensive dataset derived from the Global Financial Inclusion Database and the Reserve Central Bank Consolidated Banking Database. The model effectively captures both long-term dependencies and short-term relationships in time-series data, providing valuable insights into the evolution of digital payment systems. Our approach offers an in-depth understanding of the factors influencing digital payment adoption, including demographic, regional, and policy-based variables, while also identifying challenges and growth opportunities in financial inclusion through digital platforms".

Chapter 6, titled **"Preferences and Usage of E-Banking Services Among Customers in Tripura, India"** (by Supriya Dam) presents a study that "evaluates the e-banking services of two prominent commercial banks in Northern Tripura through a customer survey, focusing on their usage and preferences. Field observations indicate a wide range of customer opinions regarding their preferences and usage of e-banking services. The results reveal significant similarities in client preferences for these services. However, the utilization of e-banking services exhibited a significant difference between ICICI and SBI clients. The informants demonstrated a clear preference for debit card transactions over credit cards and a tendency to favor savings options rather than loans. The data suggests that banks are experiencing growth in both urban and semi-urban areas. The survey indicates that respondents value hassle-free banking and stability, indicating mutual coexistence in their choices without any evidence of coopetition among bankers".

Chapter 7, titled **"Virtual Democracy: Exploring the Viability of Election Voting via Metaverse Technology"** (by Nina Lestari, Nur Azizah Wahyuni, Muhammad Younus, Andi Luhur Prianto, Aqmal Reza Amri, Ahmad Harakan, Achmad Nurmandi, Hajira Gul, Ibrahim Shah and Ihyani Malik", proposes that "the creation of the metaverse will change how we live, work, and play in a digital environment, one of which the metaverse opens up great opportunities for the development of virtual democracy. One of the implementations of virtual democracy is through digital election voting using the metaverse. A paradigm shift in democratic participation is brought about by integrating the metaverse into election voting. In the metaverse, voters can participate in the election process through an immersive virtual environment; the digital platform also changes the voting experience. The objective of this study is to explore the feasibility of election voting through metaverse technology. The result of this research is that election voting using metaverse technology has been implemented in several countries, where the implementation uses a blockchain system that ensures every vote is recorded securely and cannot be manipulated, thereby reducing the risk of fraud. This research concludes that applying metaverse technology in election voting will significantly change virtual democratic activities".

Chapter 8, titled **"Employee's Perception Towards Customer's Satisfaction, Digital Transformation, Financial Security, and Risk in the Indian Banking Sector"** (Ajay Kumar Singh and S. Srinivasan), states that "digital transformation (DT) helps to increase the performance, productivity, profits, and product quality in the banking sector. DT is also eager to increase online banking and customer's satisfaction at a greater level. However, employees are facing multiple challenges to adjust with the current DT in the banking sector of developing countries. This chapter, therefore, explores the perception of employees towards DT of the banking sector in India using primary information. Necessary information is collected from 176 employees of public and private banks in Dehradun and Delhi. The descriptive statistical method is used to analyse the primary data with regards to perception of employees on 30 different items or questions. These are divided into four constructs i.e., DT, financial security (FS), financial risk (FR) and customer' satisfaction (CS). The correlation coefficients and linear regression models are also considered to examine the association among these constructs".

Chapter 9, titled **"Leveraging Bi-Stacked ANN for Organizational Values in the Context of Digital Transformation"** (by Bhimavarapu Usharani) affirms that "the digital age has brought unprecedented opportunities for organizations to innovate and transform their operations, emphasizing the importance of measuring digital maturity and organizational values. This study leverages a bi-stacked Artificial Neural Network (ANN) architecture to measure a comprehensive digital index, integrating insights from people management values. The dataset, collected from 132 companies, was preprocessed and refined through feature extraction, including parameters such as the Relative Importance Value (RIV) for future business impact and the Rate of Satisfaction Value (RSV) with people management practices, quantified using a Likert scale. The bi-stacked ANN, designed with multiple layers and dropout mechanisms, processed these features to generate an accurate and reliable digital index. By combining advanced machine learning techniques and organizational value assessments, the proposed approach provides a scalable framework for understanding digital readiness while emphasizing the critical role of people management in driving business transformation".

Patricia Ordóñez de Pablos

The University of Oviedo, Spain

José Emilio Labra Gayo
The University of Oviedo, Spain

Chapter 1
Empowering Small and Medium Enterprises Through IT and Semantic Web Technologies in Digital Economies

Rachna Rana
Ludhiana Group of Colleges, Ludhiana, India

Pankaj Bhambri
https://orcid.org/0000-0003-4437-4103
Guru Nanak Dev Engineering College, Ludhiana, India

ABSTRACT

Small and Medium Enterprises (SMEs) are essential for fostering economic growth, innovation, and employment in both advanced and emerging economies. In the digital age, SMEs encounter considerable obstacles in embracing sophisticated technology to maintain competitiveness in progressively digitalized marketplaces. This chapter examines how Information Technology (IT) and Semantic Web technologies might enable SMEs to leverage the opportunities presented by digital economies. It analyses the function of information technology in optimizing corporate processes, augmenting consumer relationships, and expanding market accessibility. The chapter explores how Semantic Web technologies, via intelligent data management and integration, can offer SMEs increased decision-making skills, enhanced knowledge management, and more tailored user experiences. Case studies and real-world examples illustrate the practical applications of these technologies across many industries, emphasizing their transformative impact on SME growth and sustainability.

DOI: 10.4018/979-8-3693-8477-0.ch001

1 INTRODUCTION TO SMES AND THE NEED FOR DIGITAL TRANSFORMATION

Small and Medium Enterprises (SMEs) are the backbone of the global economy, accounting for over 90% of businesses and contributing significantly to employment, innovation, and economic growth. In developing economies, SMEs play an even more critical role, often representing 30-50% of GDP and employing 70-80% of the workforce. For instance, in Pakistan, SMEs contribute 30% to GDP, 25% to exports, and employ over 80% of the non-agricultural workforce, (Rattan, Bhambri, & Shaifali, 2005). Despite their economic significance, SMEs face persistent challenges, including limited access to technology, resource constraints, and vulnerability to global disruptions such as supply chain bottlenecks, geopolitical tensions, and climate change.

The digital transformation of SMEs has emerged as a critical strategy to address these challenges and unlock new opportunities for growth and resilience. Digital technologies, including semantic web technologies, artificial intelligence (AI), big data analytics (BDA), and the Internet of Things (IoT), are reshaping how SMEs operate, compete, and innovate. For example, semantic web technologies enable SMEs to integrate and analyze heterogeneous data sources, facilitating better decision-making and operational efficiency. Similarly, AI-powered tools help SMEs optimize supply chains, reduce costs, and enhance customer experiences, even with limited resources, (Babu *et al.,* 2021).

1.2 The Role of Semantic Web Technologies in Empowering SMEs

Semantic web technologies, which focus on data interoperability and knowledge representation, offer unique opportunities for SMEs to overcome the challenges of digital transformation. By leveraging ontologies, linked data, and knowledge graphs, SMEs can integrate disparate data sources, automate decision-making processes, and enhance collaboration across supply chains. For example, a study by García et al. demonstrated how SMEs in the manufacturing sector used semantic web technologies to optimize inventory management and reduce production costs by 20%. Similarly, in the retail sector, semantic web tools have enabled SMEs to personalize customer experiences and improve marketing effectiveness, (Aagaard, 2019).

Moreover, semantic web technologies can help SMEs address sustainability challenges by enabling data-driven insights into energy consumption, waste management, and carbon emissions. For instance, IoT devices integrated with semantic web frameworks allow SMEs to monitor and optimize energy usage in real time, contributing to decarbonization goals. These examples highlight the transformative potential of semantic web technologies in empowering SMEs to achieve economic, social, and environmental sustainability, (Rafinas & Makmur, 2024).

1.3 Challenges and Opportunities

Despite the potential benefits, the adoption of semantic web technologies by SMEs faces several challenges. These include high implementation costs, lack of technical expertise, and data privacy concerns. To address these barriers, governments, industry leaders, and academic institutions must collaborate to provide affordable solutions, capacity-building programs, and policy support for SMEs. For example, initiatives like the World Economic Forum's Advanced Manufacturing and Supply Chain Center have developed frameworks to help SMEs adopt advanced technologies and innovate their business models, (Putra, 2022).

1.4 Objectives of the Chapter

This chapter aims to explore how semantic web technologies can empower SMEs to overcome the challenges of digital transformation and achieve sustainable growth. Specifically, the chapter will:

- Examine the current state of SME digitalization and the barriers to adoption.
- Highlight the role of semantic web technologies in enhancing SME competitiveness and resilience.
- Provide case studies and data-driven insights into successful implementations of semantic web technologies by SMEs.
- Propose a framework for SMEs to adopt semantic web technologies and integrate them into their business models.

By addressing these objectives, this chapter seeks to contribute to the growing body of knowledge on digital transformation and semantic web technologies, while providing practical insights for SMEs, policymakers, and researchers.

2 DIGITAL TRANSFORMATION: A PARADIGM SHIFT IN THE GLOBAL ECONOMY

Digital transformation refers to the integration of digital technologies into all facets of an organization, fundamentally altering how it operates, delivers value, and interacts with stakeholders. For small and medium-sized enterprises (SMEs), digital transformation presents both opportunities and challenges, as it requires not only technological adoption but also cultural, operational, and strategic shifts, (Harleen, 2016). This section provides an in-depth analysis of the key characteristics of digital transformation, its implications for SMEs, and actionable insights for leveraging digital technologies to achieve sustainable growth.

2.1 Key Characteristics of Digital Transformation

Digital transformation is characterized by the following dimensions, each of which plays a critical role in reshaping the global economy and empowering SMEs:

- Technological Integration: The adoption of advanced technologies such as cloud computing, AI, ML, big data analytics, and the IoT is at the core of digital transformation. These technologies enable SMEs to automate processes, enhance decision-making, and improve operational efficiency. For instance, cloud computing allows SMEs to access scalable IT infrastructure without significant upfront investments, while AI and ML enable predictive analytics and personalized customer experiences, (Singh, Singh, & Bhambri, 2004). A study by McKinsey & Company found that SMEs leveraging cloud-based solutions experienced a 30% reduction in operational costs and a 20% increase in productivity within the first year of implementation.
- Process Optimization: Digital transformation enables SMEs to streamline workflows, automate repetitive tasks, and optimize resource allocation. By leveraging data-driven insights, SMEs can identify inefficiencies, reduce waste, and improve overall productivity. For example, robotic process automation (RPA) has been widely adopted by SMEs to automate back-office operations, resulting in significant cost savings and faster turnaround times, (Bouey, 2020). A mid-sized manufacturing firm in Germany implemented RPA to automate its inventory management processes, reducing manual errors by 40% and improving order fulfillment rates by 25%.
- Customer Experience Enhancement: Digital technologies empower SMEs to deliver personalized, seamless, and consistent customer experiences across multiple channels. By leveraging data analytics and AI, SMEs can gain insights into customer preferences, predict demand, and tailor their offerings to meet evolving needs. For instance, e-commerce platforms powered by AI-driven recommendation engines have enabled SMEs to increase customer retention rates by up to 35%, (Bhambri *et al.*, 2022). A small online retailer in Southeast Asia used AI-based recommendation systems to personalize product suggestions, resulting in a 50% increase in average order value and a 25% boost in repeat purchases.

- Challenges and Limitations for SMEs: Despite the potential benefits, SMEs face significant barriers to digital transformation, including limited financial resources, lack of technical expertise, and resistance to change. According to a survey by the International Trade Centre, 60% of SMEs cited high implementation costs as the primary obstacle to adopting digital technologies, while 45% reported a lack of skilled personnel as a major challenge, (Bhambri *et al.,* 2022). To overcome these barriers, SMEs can adopt a phased approach to digital transformation, starting with low-cost, high-impact solutions such as cloud-based tools and open-source software. Additionally, partnerships with technology providers and government-funded training programs can help bridge the skills gap.
- Business Analytics for Strategic Decision-Making: Business analytics plays a pivotal role in enabling SMEs to monitor their performance, identify growth opportunities, and develop data-driven strategies. By leveraging tools such as dashboards, predictive analytics, and real-time reporting, SMEs can gain actionable insights into market trends, customer behavior, and operational efficiency, (Mohanta *et al.,* 2022). A small logistics company in India implemented a business analytics platform to track delivery performance and optimize route planning. As a result, the company reduced fuel costs by 15% and improved on-time delivery rates by 20%.
- Cultural Change and Innovation: Successful digital transformation requires a cultural shift within the organization, fostering a mindset of innovation, experimentation, and continuous learning. SMEs must invest in employee training, promote cross-functional collaboration, and encourage a digital-first approach to problem-solving, (Bhambri *et al.,* 2022). A survey by Deloitte found that SMEs with a strong culture of innovation were 2.5 times more likely to achieve successful digital transformation outcomes compared to those with a traditional mindset.
- Data-Driven Decision-Making: The ability to harness data for informed decision-making is a cornerstone of digital transformation. SMEs can leverage data analytics to anticipate market trends, optimize resource allocation, and identify new revenue streams. For instance, predictive analytics can help SMEs forecast demand, manage inventory, and mitigate risks, (Kaur & Bhambri, 2015). A small retail chain in Brazil used predictive analytics to optimize its inventory levels, reducing stockouts by 30% and increasing sales by 15%.

2.2 Implications for SMEs in Digital Economies

Digital transformation is no longer a luxury but a necessity for SMEs to remain competitive in today's rapidly evolving digital economy. By embracing digital technologies, SMEs can enhance their agility, responsiveness, and innovation capabilities. However, the journey requires a strategic approach, supported by investments in technology, talent, and organizational culture. The recommendations for SME Leaders are (i) Start with a clear digital strategy aligned with business goals, (ii) Prioritize low-cost, high-impact technologies such as cloud computing and business analytics, (iii) Invest in employee training and change management to foster a digital-first culture, and (iv) Leverage partnerships with technology providers and industry experts to overcome resource constraints.

2.3 Research Mission

The research mission of this chapter is to explore the role of IT and Semantic Web technologies in empowering Small and Medium Enterprises SMEs within digital economies. The chapter aims to provide actionable insights and strategic frameworks to help SMEs navigate the challenges and opportunities of digital transformation. The specific objectives of this research are as follows:

- Comprehensive Analysis of Digital Transformation: This chapter examines the latest research, articles, and reports on global digital transformation trends, with a focus on their impact on traditional businesses and the unique challenges faced by SMEs. The analysis aims to identify key drivers, barriers, and opportunities for SMEs in adopting digital technologies.
- Strategic Framework for Business Analytics: A strategic plan is developed to guide SMEs in leveraging business analytics for evidence-based decision-making. This framework will help SMEs formulate ideas, strategies, and implementation plans to support their digital transformation journey.
- Qualitative Case Studies of SMEs: This chapter presents an in-depth qualitative analysis of 5-10 SMEs across diverse sectors that have successfully implemented digital transformation strategies. Data is collected through semi-structured interviews with owners and managers, focusing on their experiences, challenges, and outcomes.
- Identification of Best Practices: The case studies are analyzed to uncover best practices in problem definition, theoretical application, stakeholder engagement, modeling, adaptation, and implementation. The analysis highlights the benefits achieved by SMEs and provides a roadmap for others to follow.

- Development of Implementation Metrics: Based on the findings, this chapter proposes specific implementation metrics to guide SMEs in measuring and managing digital changes within their operational environments. These metrics serve as a practical tool for monitoring progress and ensuring successful business development.
- Policy and Decision-Making Recommendations: The chapter concludes with actionable recommendations for SME decision-makers and policymakers. These recommendations focus on the support systems, resources, and policies needed to enable SMEs to thrive in digitally pressured business environments.

3 UNDERSTANDING THE LANDSCAPE

The rapid evolution of technology has fundamentally transformed the way businesses operate and compete in the global economy. For SMEs, navigating this dynamic landscape requires a deep understanding of emerging trends, customer expectations, and technological advancements. SMEs must proactively assess how these changes impact their operations and develop robust digital transformation strategies to remain competitive. This section provides an overview of the key technological shifts shaping the digital economy and their implications for SMEs, drawing on insights from recent research and industry practices, (Jain & Bhambri, 2015).

3.1 Key Drivers of Digital Transformation Across Sectors

Digital transformation is no longer a choice but a necessity for SMEs across various sectors. The following trends highlight the critical factors driving this transformation:

- Connectivity: The advent of 5G, the Internet of Things (IoT), and Industry 4.0 has revolutionized connectivity, enabling seamless communication between machines, systems, and humans. These technologies empower SMEs to collaborate on digital platforms, predict operational needs, and optimize processes in real time. For instance, IoT-enabled devices in manufacturing can monitor equipment performance and predict maintenance requirements, reducing downtime and improving efficiency.
- Data-Driven Decision-Making: The proliferation of data analytics tools, including ML, AI, and neural networks, has enabled SMEs to harness data for strategic decision-making. By analyzing customer behavior, market trends, and operational metrics, SMEs can predict demand, personalize offerings,

and strengthen supply chains. However, the effective use of data requires SMEs to invest in data literacy and infrastructure.

- Cloudification: Migrating applications and workloads to cloud-based platforms offers SMEs cost savings, scalability, and flexibility. Cloud-native services, such as serverless computing and managed AI services, further enhance operational efficiency. However, SMEs must address challenges related to cybersecurity, data privacy, and hidden costs to fully realize the benefits of cloud adoption.
- Industrial Internet and Smart Manufacturing: The integration of digital technologies into traditional manufacturing processes, often referred to as smart manufacturing, has improved productivity, flexibility, and quality. Technologies such as additive manufacturing, autonomous robots, and virtual reality are transforming production lines. However, SMEs face challenges in adopting these technologies due to high upfront costs and the need for skilled personnel.
- Platformization: The rise of digital platforms has created ecosystems where businesses, developers, and consumers interact seamlessly. SMEs can leverage these platforms to access new markets, integrate multiple business models, and collaborate with larger enterprises. However, operating within platform-centric ecosystems requires SMEs to adapt to new business dynamics and compete with established players.

These forces are compelling SMEs to rethink their business models and operational strategies. For example, the transportation sector has shifted from car sales to mobility services, while retail has embraced e-commerce and on-demand delivery. In healthcare, the focus has moved from treatment to prevention and maintenance, driven by digital health technologies. Similarly, in agriculture, IoT sensors, drones, and AI-powered analytics are enabling precision farming and sustainable practices, (Denner, Püschel, & Röglinger, 2018) (Bhambri *et al.,* 2023).

4 BARRIERS TO TECHNOLOGY ADOPTION IN SMES

Despite the potential benefits of digital transformation, SMEs often face significant barriers to adopting new technologies. These challenges can hinder their ability to innovate, improve productivity, and remain competitive. The following subsections outline the most common barriers:

- Cost Constraints: The upfront investment required for new technologies, including software, hardware, and infrastructure, can be prohibitive for SMEs operating on tight budgets. Beyond initial costs, SMEs must account for maintenance, updates, training, and subscription fees, which can strain financial resources.

- Lack of Skilled Workforce: Many SMEs lack in-house IT professionals or specialists capable of implementing and managing advanced technologies. Employees may resist adopting new systems due to fear of change, lack of digital skills, or preference for traditional practices.
- Cultural and Organizational Resistance: Introducing digital technologies often requires significant cultural shifts and adjustments to workflows, which can be challenging for SMEs. Decision-makers may be hesitant to embrace technology if they do not fully understand its potential benefits or prefer to maintain existing practices.
- Security and Privacy Concerns: SMEs are often more vulnerable to cyber-attacks due to limited resources for cybersecurity measures. Concerns about data breaches and regulatory compliance can deter technology adoption. Compliance with regulations such as GDPR can be complex and resource-intensive for SMEs.
- Lack of Awareness or Understanding: Many SME owners and managers are unaware of the benefits of digital technologies or the latest solutions available in the market. Advanced technologies like AI and IoT may appear too complex or intimidating for SMEs, discouraging adoption.
- Infrastructure Limitations: SMEs often lack the necessary infrastructure, such as high-speed internet or cloud computing capabilities, to support modern technologies. Outdated systems may be incompatible with new digital solutions, requiring costly upgrades.
- Uncertain Return on Investment (ROI): SME owners may be reluctant to invest in technologies with uncertain or long-term ROI. The advantages of digital transformation may not be immediately visible, making it difficult to justify investments.
- Time Constraints: Implementing new technologies can disrupt daily operations, which is a significant concern for SMEs with limited resources. Training employees to use new systems can be time-consuming and divert attention from core business activities.
- Market Competition: Larger enterprises with greater resources may already have adopted advanced technologies, creating pressure for SMEs to keep up.
- Lack of External Support: SMEs, particularly in rural or developing areas, may struggle to find affordable and reliable technology partners. In some regions, SMEs receive limited financial or technical assistance from governments to adopt new technologies.

Addressing these barriers requires a multifaceted approach, including government incentives, affordable training programs, partnerships with technology providers, and fostering a culture of innovation within SMEs, (Gordijn & Akkermans, 2001) (Bhambri, Gupta, & Bhandari, 2005).

5 CHANGING CUSTOMER BEHAVIOUR AND EXPECTATIONS

Keeping up with changing consumer behavior in the face of technological change is a huge challenge for small businesses accustomed to traditional models. According to Bhambri and Gupta (2005), customers now expect access to personalized, simple, and seamless experiences "anytime, anywhere." These experiences can take place in both physical and digital spaces. Generational demographics, lifestyles, and attitudes are changing priorities. Millennials and Gen Zers, who will buy in the future, value customization, sustainability, real-time engagement, and building trust through experiences rather than transactions, (Rosyidi *et al.,* 2022). Small and mid-sized stores can reconnect with these groups using technologies like augmented reality, virtual mirrors, and interactive interactions in experiential retail. According to Sales force research, 72% of customers are willing to pay more for a better experience, indicating greater price elasticity. It's also harder to keep people loyal, with 74% of them switching companies regularly. Review and rating sites now influence 71% of purchases, so SMEs need to be mindful of their image management across all sites, (Heryanto, 2023). These behavioural changes require small and mid-sized businesses (SMEs) to ensure their products are appealing, accessible, provide a personalized experience, and are convenient for customers at their chosen touch point. Using advanced data to learn more about your customers can help you create more meaningful and emotional experiences. Advocates are stronger. Failure to evolve will result in the disintermediation of digital natives who are fine-tuned to the changing needs of customers seeking experiences, (Kshirsagar *et al.,* 2022).

5.1 Emerging Technologies for SMEs to Master

Rethinking their value propositions and operations requires (Hinterhuber, Vescovi, & Checchinato, 2021) SMEs to evaluate a range of mainstream and emerging digital technologies that are disrupting traditional sectors around the world. Key topics that apply to most areas are outlined in Table 1.

Table 1. Emerging technologies for SMEs to master (Imgrund et al., 2018)

Technology	Description
Cloud Computing	Cloud computing provides a scalable, pay-as-you-go infrastructure for innovation, disaster recovery, collaboration, and service availability testing.
Mobility	Mobility Empower remote workers and improve field service through mobile apps to improve responsiveness and customer engagement.
InternetofThings (IoT)	IoT sensors generate contextual data for predictive maintenance, defect tracking, predictive demand planning, and intelligent updates to product features.
Data Analytics	Data analytics tools such as predictive modeling, machine learning, and natural language processing extract competitive intelligence from multiple data sources and automate decision making.
ArtificialIntelligence (AI)	AI capabilities such as virtual agents, computer vision, expert systems, and autonomous vehicles complement human problem-solving and automation capabilities.
Robotics	Robotics Automate hazardous and repetitive tasks to complement specialized human skills and improve health/safety. Future applications include collaborative robots and exoskeletons.
Blockchain	Blockchain-based distributed ledgers streamline processes and build trust through transparency by optimizing supply chain transparency, provenance tracking, payments, and smart contracts.
Virtual/Augmented Reality	Immersive technologies enhance product development cycles, training, remote collaboration, e-commerce demos, and interactive marketing experiences.

SMEs can differentiate themselves in a rapidly digitizing world by carefully selecting emerging technologies that best fit their needs and resources, (Aristizabal-Alzate & González-Manosalva, 2021).

6 CONDUCT BUSINESS ANALYSIS

Business analysis is a critical step for SMEs to understand their needs and circumstances before embarking on digital transformation. Unlike large enterprises with dedicated teams, SMEs must optimize limited resources through structured, in-house analysis. This section outlines key methods for conducting business analysis in SMEs.

6.1 Requirements Gathering:

Requirements elicitation ensures that digital initiatives align with strategic goals and user needs. The following methods are particularly effective for SMEs, (Singh *et al.*, 2021):

- Interviews: Conducting interviews with owners, managers, and employees helps identify organizational goals, challenges, and readiness for change. For example, frontline staff can provide insights into service gaps and improvement opportunities.
- Focus Groups: Cross-functional focus groups complement individual interviews by fostering collaborative discussions. For instance, a retailer convened a focus group to address common customer complaints after collecting individual feedback.
- Surveys: Quantitative surveys support qualitative findings and track how goals evolve over time. Surveys can also reveal long-standing issues when combined with document research, such as reviewing old surveys or analyzing marketing materials.
- Process Mapping: Visualizing workflows through process maps highlights inefficiencies and areas for digitalization. For example, a user journey map can identify delays caused by human intervention and suggest digital solutions like phone order tracking.
- Prioritization: The MoSCoW method categorizes needs into "Must Have," "Should Have," "Could Have," and "Won't Have" to clarify project scope and timelines.

6.2 Environmental Scanning:

SMEs must regularly examine external factors to prepare for upcoming challenges. Key techniques include, (Zhang, Lichtenstein, & Gander, 2015):

- Competitive Analysis: Monitoring competitors' products, services, and technology investments can reveal early signs of industry shifts. For example, one SME identified strategic opportunities by tracking competitors' investments in additive manufacturing.
- Industry Reports: Leveraging reports from market research firms, standards groups, and industry publications helps predict technology adoption trends and potential challenges.
- Pilot Testing: Testing selected technologies on a small scale before full implementation minimizes risks. For instance, piloting a 3D printing solution helped an SME assess its feasibility and impact.
- Benchmarking: Comparing internal metrics (e.g., cost, customer satisfaction) with industry data identifies competitive weaknesses. For example, analyzing order fulfillment cycles revealed the potential of warehouse automation.

6.3 Process Analysis:

Analyzing core and supporting processes identifies optimization opportunities and quantifies the potential impact of digital tools. Key methods include, (Singh *et al.*, 2021):

- Process Mapping: Flowcharts visually depict sequential activities, milestones, and interfaces between functions.
- Time Studies: Using stopwatches or performance monitoring software quantifies non-value-added steps, bottlenecks, and process cycle time variability. For example, a manufacturing SME found that 35% of order processing time was spent on manual data entry.
- Value Stream Mapping: Identifying waste (e.g., overproduction, defects) and root causes (e.g., five-why analysis) helps prioritize improvements.
- Simulation Modeling: Creating prototypes of tool integrations (e.g., automated workflows, predictive analytics) validates digital process optimization strategies before investment.

6.4 Technology and Organizational Assessment:

Assessing digital readiness prevents costly noncompliance and ensures alignment with strategic goals. Key steps include, (Rana & Bhambri, 2024):

- Maturity Frameworks: Benchmarking against a maturity framework evaluates tangible (e.g., infrastructure quality) and intangible (e.g., employee capabilities) factors.
- Sentiment Research: Online questionnaires or focus groups assess employee and customer perceptions of technology, management commitment, and barriers to change. For example, addressing technology anxiety through tailored training programs improved adoption rates.
- Technology Audits: Evaluating the existing environment, compatibility with new tools, and legacy system modernization priorities ensures a robust digital foundation.
- Pilot Assessments: Limited proof-of-concept deployments test technology weaknesses, cultural readiness, and collaboration workflows before scaling. For instance, piloting a cloud ERP system revealed security configuration issues that were resolved through training.

6.5 Establish a Digital Vision, Goals, and Roadmap:

A clear digital strategy guides SMEs through transformation. Key elements include, (Sharma, Bhambri, & Sohal, 2020):

- Vision Statement: An inspiring long-term vision, such as becoming a "digitally integrated smart enterprise," aligns stakeholders and sets the direction for digital initiatives.
- Measurable Goals: Clear, cross-functional goals (e.g., reducing production downtime by 30%) provide focus and accountability.
- Roadmap: A detailed roadmap outlines projects, timelines, resources, and responsibilities. For example, a small service company planned Phase 1 (CRM implementation) and Phase 2 (mobile app development) over 18 months.

6.6 Identify High-Impact Pilot Initiatives:

Prioritizing projects maximizes impact within resource constraints. Key steps include, (Kraus *et al.,* 2022):

- Feasibility Analysis: Assessing project feasibility, alignment with strategic goals, and potential ROI ensures optimal resource allocation.
- Impact Mapping: Visualizing how a project addresses critical needs and capitalizes on opportunities clarifies its value. For example, a low-cost CRM upgrade promising 30% higher sales was prioritized over a high-end ERP system.
- Minimum Viable Pilots: Testing theories with minimal effort and risk (e.g., a basic client portal for a law firm) informs project improvement and resource allocation.

6.7 Develop Digital Business Models and Revenue Streams

- Digital capabilities enable SMEs to innovate business models and revenue streams. Key tools include, (Kraus *et al.,* 2021):
- Business Model Canvas: Analyzing core activities, partnerships, and value propositions helps SMEs explore new models. For example, an IoT device manufacturer adopted a SaaS model, charging customers per unit instead of upfront hardware costs.
- Multi-Sided Platforms: Facilitating interactions between users, marketers, and developers creates new revenue opportunities.

- Minimum Viable Pilots: Testing new revenue models (e.g., usage-based pricing) before scaling encourages experimentation and reduces risk.

7 CASE STUDIES

This section highlights real-world examples of smes successfully leveraging digital transformation.

7.1 ABC Manufacturing's Digital Transformation

- Drivers: Declining profits due to competitors' adoption of Industry 4.0 technologies.
- Vision: Become a “smart factory for waterworks.”
- Solution: Oracle Cloud ERP implementation.
- Pilot: A 6-month pilot at one factory resulted in 80% faster purchase order processing.
- Investment: A$5 million approved by the board.
- Approach: Iterative, department-by-department rollout over 18 months with robust change management.
- Results: 5% annual improvement in asset uptime, real-time supplier collaboration, and A$3 million in annual savings, (Paika & Bhambri, 2013).

7.2 DEF Construction's Mobile-First Strategy

- Drivers: Quality issues due to poor project coordination.
- Vision: Achieve “flawless delivery through connected coordination.”
- Solution: Mobile contract management and IoT integration.
- Pilot: A pilot project streamlined contract renewals, capturing electronic signatures 30% faster.
- Investment: A$10 million approved by the board.
- Approach: Phased implementation with tailored mobile processes and IoT system integration.
- Results: A$5 million in annual savings, 15% faster issue resolution, and 15% higher employee satisfaction, (Bhambri & Singh, 2024).

7.3 Promoting Inclusion in SMEs:

Promoting inclusion ensures a diverse, equitable, and innovative workplace. Key strategies include, (Masterplan, 2020):

- Leadership Commitment: Leaders must actively support inclusion initiatives and foster an inclusive culture.
- Diverse Hiring Practices: Structured interviews and anonymous resumes reduce bias in recruitment.
- Equal Growth Opportunities: Mentorship, training, and transparent promotion processes ensure equitable career advancement.
- Flexible Work Policies: Remote work options and accessible environments accommodate diverse employee needs.
- Employee Resource Groups (ERGs): Supporting ERGs for underrepresented groups fosters collaboration and inclusion.

8 CULTIVATE SUSTAINED GROWTH IN THE DIGITAL ECONOMY

To ensure long-term prosperity in the digital economy, organizations must strategically adapt to rapid technological advancements and leverage digital tools to innovate, optimize operations, and meet evolving customer demands. Below are key strategies for fostering sustained growth, with a focus on the role of IT and Semantic Web technologies in empowering small and medium enterprises (SMEs), (Kaur, Bhambri, & Gupta, 2013) (Naysary, 2022) (North, Aramburu, & Lorenzo, 2020) (Jebeen et al., 2021) (Ritu & Tripathy, 2024) (Piccinini et al., 2015) (Jain, Singh, & Bhambri, 2021) (Plano de Ação global de Vigilância Da Poliomielite, 2022) (Rozo-García, 2020) (Oxford Scholarship Online, 2017) (Bhambri & Gupta, 2012) (Teece, 2010) (Furjan, Tomičić-Pupek, & Pihit, 2020):

8.1 Embrace Digital Transformation:

Digital transformation is the cornerstone of sustained growth in the digital economy. SMEs must adopt advanced technologies and integrate them into their core operations to remain competitive.

8.1.1 Adopt Emerging Technologies:

Leverage cutting-edge technologies such as AI, ML, the IoT, big data, cloud computing, and blockchain. These technologies can streamline processes, enhance decision-making, and create new value propositions. For instance, Semantic Web technologies can enable SMEs to structure and link data meaningfully, improving interoperability and data utilization across systems.

8.1.2 Digitize Key Processes:

Automate routine tasks, digitize documentation, and implement digital tools to enhance operational efficiency, reduce costs, and boost productivity. Semantic Web technologies, such as ontologies and linked data, can facilitate seamless data integration and process automation.

8.1.3 Foster a Digital Culture:

Cultivate a digital-first mindset across the organization. Encourage employees to embrace innovation, experiment with new technologies, and continuously improve workflows. A strong digital culture ensures that SMEs remain agile and responsive to technological changes.

8.2 Focus on Customer-Centric Innovation:

Innovation driven by customer needs is critical for long-term growth. SMEs can use digital tools to deliver personalized experiences and engage customers effectively.

8.2.1 Personalized Customer Experiences:

Utilize data analytics and AI to understand customer preferences, behaviors, and pain points. Semantic Web technologies can enhance data integration and analysis, enabling SMEs to deliver tailored interactions across digital channels.

8.2.2 Omnichannel Engagement:

Integrate online and offline touchpoints to provide a seamless customer experience. Semantic Web technologies can help unify data from multiple sources, ensuring consistency across platforms.

8.2.3 Co-Creation and Feedback:

Involve customers in product or service development through digital feedback platforms, surveys, or virtual focus groups. This collaborative approach ensures that offerings align with customer needs and expectations.

8.3 Invest in Scalable Infrastructure:

Scalable and secure infrastructure is essential for supporting growth in the digital economy.

8.3.1 Cloud Computing:

Adopt cloud-based solutions to build flexible and scalable infrastructure. Cloud platforms enable SMEs to expand operations without the constraints of physical hardware, while Semantic Web technologies can enhance data sharing and collaboration across cloud environments.

8.3.2 Cybersecurity:

Implement robust cybersecurity measures, including encryption, multi-factor authentication, and regular security audits, to protect sensitive data and maintain customer trust.

8.3.3 Data Governance:

Establish comprehensive data governance frameworks to ensure data is managed securely, ethically, and in compliance with regulations such as GDPR and CCPA. Semantic Web technologies can support data governance by providing standardized metadata and ontologies.

8.4 Leverage Data and Analytics:

Data-driven decision-making is a key driver of sustained growth.

8.4.1 Data-Driven Decision-Making:

Use analytics to inform strategic decisions, predict market trends, and optimize operations. Semantic Web technologies can enhance data interoperability, enabling SMEs to derive insights from diverse data sources.

8.4.2 Predictive Analytics:

Employ AI and ML to forecast demand, identify risks, and optimize supply chain management. These capabilities can improve efficiency and reduce costs.

8.4.3 Customer Insights:

Analyze customer data to understand behavior, preferences, and expectations. This information can inform marketing strategies, product development, and customer experience improvements.

8.5 Develop Digital Skills and Talent:

A skilled workforce is essential for navigating the digital economy.

8.5.1 Employee Upskilling:

Invest in training programs to equip employees with digital skills such as data analytics, AI, cybersecurity, and digital marketing.

8.5.2 Attract Digital Talent:

Create an innovative work environment that attracts top talent. Offer opportunities for continuous learning and career advancement.

8.5.3 Cross-Functional Collaboration:

Encourage collaboration between technical, creative, and business teams to drive innovation and develop digital solutions that meet customer needs.

8.6 Drive Agility and Innovation:

Agility and innovation are critical for staying competitive in the digital economy.

8.6.1 Agile Methodologies:

Implement agile practices to accelerate product development, improve responsiveness, and reduce time-to-market.

8.6.2 Innovation Hubs:

Establish dedicated spaces for experimentation and collaboration with external partners, such as startups and universities.

8.6.3 Open Innovation:

Collaborate with external stakeholders to co-create solutions and drive innovation.

8.7 Expand into Digital Business Models:

Digital business models can unlock new revenue streams and growth opportunities.

8.7.1 Subscription Models:

Transition to subscription-based offerings to generate recurring revenue and build customer loyalty.

8.7.2 Platform Ecosystems:

Develop or join digital platforms to leverage network effects and expand market reach.

8.7.3 Freemium Offerings:

Provide free basic services with premium options to attract a broad customer base and drive conversions.

8.8 Foster Strategic Partnerships:

Collaboration with external partners can enhance capabilities and drive growth.

8.8.1 Collaborate with Tech Companies:

Partner with technology providers to access cutting-edge tools and expertise.

8.8.2 Strategic Alliances:

Form alliances with other businesses to pool resources and co-develop solutions.

8.8.3 Public-Private Partnerships:

Engage with government agencies and educational institutions to access funding, research, and talent development programs.

8.9 Ensure Regulatory Compliance and Ethical Practices

Compliance and ethics are critical for building trust and sustaining growth.

8.9.1 Regulatory Compliance:

Adhere to data privacy and security regulations such as GDPR and CCPA.

8.9.2 Ethical AI and Data Usage:

Ensure transparency and fairness in AI algorithms and data practices to build customer trust.

8.10 Build Customer Trust and Brand Reputation:

Trust and reputation are key to long-term success.

8.10.1 Transparency:

Be transparent about data collection and usage practices.

8.10.2 Sustainability:

Adopt sustainable practices in digital operations to meet customer expectations for responsible business conduct.

8.10.3 Social Responsibility:

Demonstrate commitment to social issues such as diversity, inclusion, and environmental stewardship.

8.11 Scale Globally Using Digital Platforms:

Digital platforms enable SMEs to expand into global markets.

8.11.1 E-Commerce and Digital Marketplaces:

Leverage platforms like Amazon and Alibaba to reach international customers.

8.11.2 Global Digital Marketing:

Use digital marketing strategies to build a global customer base.

8.12 Adapt to Emerging Trends:

Staying ahead of trends is essential for sustained growth.

8.12.1 Monitor Technological Advances:

Keep abreast of developments such as quantum computing, 5G, and decentralized finance.

8.12.2 Stay Customer-Focused:

Continuously adapt to changing customer behaviors and preferences.

9 CONCLUSION AND RECOMMENDATIONS

SMEs must embrace digital transformation to thrive in the digital economy. By integrating IT and Semantic Web technologies, SMEs can enhance operational efficiency, drive innovation, and deliver value to customers. Key recommendations include, (Furjan, Tomičić-Pupek, & Pihir, 2020) (Wang *et al.,* 2022) (Williams, Schallmo, & Scornavacca, 2022) (Bhambri & Singh, 2005) (Wong, Vengusamy, & Bastrygina, 2024) (Bhambri & Kautish, 2024) (Wang *et al.,* 2022) (Yuanda & Shinta, 2024) (Kaur, Bhambri, & Singla, 2024) (Bhambri & Bhandari, 2005):

- Adopt Advanced Technologies: Leverage AI, IoT, blockchain, and Semantic Web technologies to streamline processes and improve decision-making.
- Focus on Customer-Centric Innovation: Use data analytics and Semantic Web tools to deliver personalized experiences and engage customers effectively.
- Invest in Scalable Infrastructure: Build secure and flexible infrastructure to support growth and ensure compliance with regulations.
- Develop Digital Skills: Equip employees with the skills needed to navigate the digital economy.
- Foster Collaboration: Partner with technology providers, other businesses, and public institutions to drive innovation and expand market reach.

By following these strategies, SMEs can overcome the challenges of digital transformation and emerge as competitive players in the global economy. The integration of IT and Semantic Web technologies will play a pivotal role in enabling SMEs to achieve sustained growth and create economic and social value.

REFERENCES

Aagaard, A. (2019). The concept and frameworks of digital business models. Digital business models: Driving transformation and innovation, 1-26.

Aristizabal-Alzate, C. E., & González-Manosalva, J. (2021). Revisión de las medidas en pro de la eficiencia energética Y la sostenibilidad de la industria del cemento a nivel mundial. *Revista UIS Ingenierías, 20*(3). Advance online publication. DOI: 10.18273/revuin.v20n3-2021006

Babu, G. C. N., Gupta, S., Bhambri, P., Leo, L. M., Rao, B. H., & Kumar, S. (2021). A semantic health observation system development based on the IoT sensors. *Turkish Journal of Physiotherapy and Rehabilitation, 32*(3), 1721–1729.

Bhambri, P., Aggarwal, M., Singh, H., Singh, A. P., & Rani, S. (2022). Uprising of EVs: Charging the future with demystified analytics and sustainable development. In *Decision Analytics for Sustainable Development in Smart Society 5.0: Issues, Challenges and Opportunities* (pp. 37–53). Springer Nature Singapore. DOI: 10.1007/978-981-19-1689-2_3

Bhambri, P., & Bhandari, A. (2005, March). Different protocols for wireless security. In National Conference on Advancements in Modeling and Simulation (Vol. 8). LLRIET.

Bhambri, P., & Gupta, O. P. (2012, December). Development of phylogenetic tree based on Kimura's Method. In 2012 2nd IEEE International Conference on Parallel, Distributed and Grid Computing (pp. 721-723). IEEE. DOI: 10.1109/PDGC.2012.6449910

Bhambri, P., & Gupta, S. (2005, March). A survey & comparison of permutation possibility of fault tolerant multistage interconnection networks. In *National Conference on Application of Mathematics in Engineering & Technology* (Vol. 13). MIMIT.

Bhambri, P., Gupta, S., & Bhandari, A. (2005). Soft computing techniques. In UGC Sponsored National Conference (Abstract Book) (p. 100).

Bhambri, P., & Kautish, S. (2024). Technological advancements in promoting ecosystem health. In Leal Filho, W., Kautish, S., Wall, T., Rewhorn, S., & Paul, S. K. (Eds.), *Digital technologies to implement the UN Sustainable Development Goals* (pp. 413–432). Springer., DOI: 10.1007/978-3-031-68427-2_21

Bhambri, P., & Singh, I. (2005, March). Electrical actuation systems. In National Conference on Application of Mathematics in Engg. & Tech (pp. 58-60).

Bhambri, P., & Singh, M. (2024). Emotional sentiment analysis by machine learning from EEG of brainwave data. In Bhambri, P., Soni, R., & Tran, T. A. (Eds.), *Smart healthcare systems: AI and IoT perspectives* (pp. 171–186). CRC Press., DOI: 10.1201/9781032698519-13

Bhambri, P., Singh, M., Dhanoa, I. S., & Kumar, M. (2022). Deployment of ROBOT for HVAC duct and disaster management. *Oriental Journal of Computer Science and Technology*, *15*(10203), 1–8. DOI: 10.13005/ojcst15.010203.01

Bhambri, P., Singh, S., Sangwan, S., Devi, J., & Jain, S. (2023). Plants recognition using leaf image pattern analysis. *Journal of Survey in Fisheries Sciences*, *10*(2S), 3863–3871.

Bhambri, P., & Tripathy, B. (2024). Internet of Medical Things for Abnormality Detection in Infants using Mobile Phone App with Cry Signal Analysis. In *Smart Healthcare Systems* (pp. 236–248). CRC Press.

. Bouey, J. (2020). Assessment of COVID-19's impact on small and medium-sized enterprises: Implications from China. DOI: 10.7249/CT524

Denner, M. S., Püschel, L. C., & Röglinger, M. (2018). How to exploit the digitalization potential of business processes. *Business & Information Systems Engineering*, *60*(4), 331–349. DOI: 10.1007/s12599-017-0509-x

Gordijn, J., & Akkermans, H. (2001). Designing and evaluating e-business models. *IEEE Intelligent Systems*, *16*(04), 11–17. DOI: 10.1109/5254.941353

Harleen, B. (2016). A prediction technique in data mining for diabetes mellitus. *Journal of Management Sciences and Technology*, *4*(1), 1–12.

. Heryanto, H. (2023). Usaha Mikro Kecil Dan Menengah (UMKM) dalam masa Pendemik Di Indonesia. *JIIP - Jurnal Ilmiah Ilmu Pendidikan,* *6*(6), 4537-4545. DOI: 10.54371/jiip.v6i6.2452

. Hinterhuber, A., Vescovi, T., & Checchinato, F. (2021). Digital transformation. *Managing Digital Transformation*, 3-10. DOI: 10.4324/9781003008637-2

Imgrund, F., Fischer, M., Janiesch, C., & Winkelmann, A. (2018). Approaching digitalization with business process management. *Proceedings of the MKWI*, 1725-1736.

Jabeen, A., Pallathadka, H., Pallathadka, L. K., & Bhambri, P. (2021). E-CRM successful factors for business enterprises case studies. *Journal of Maharaja Sayajirao University of Baroda*, *55*(01), 1332–1342.

Jain, A., Singh, M., & Bhambri, P. (2021, August). Performance evaluation of IPv4-IPv6 tunneling procedure using IoT. []). IOP Publishing.]. *Journal of Physics: Conference Series, 1950*(1), 012010. DOI: 10.1088/1742-6596/1950/1/012010

. Jain, V. K., & Bhambri, P. (2005). Fundamentals of information technology & computer programming.

Kaur, A., Bhambri, P., & Singla, S. K. (2024). Sentimental analysis using RNN, CNN, and LSTM: A comparative study of accuracy and computational efficiency. *Library Progress International*, *44*(3), 4424–4431.

Kaur, J., Bhambri, P., & Gupta, O. P. (2013). Distance based phylogenetic trees with bootstrapping. *International Journal of Computer Applications*, *47*(24), 6–10. DOI: 10.5120/7502-0364

Kaur, P., & Bhambri, P. (2015). To design an algorithm for text watermarking. [The SIJ]. *The Standard International Journals*, *3*(5), 62–67. DOI: 10.9756/SIJCSEA/V3I3/03050150101

Kraus, S., Durst, S., Ferreira, J. J., Veiga, P., Kailer, N., & Weinmann, A. (2022). Digital transformation in business and management research: An overview of the current status quo. *International Journal of Information Management*, *63*, 102466. DOI: 10.1016/j.ijinfomgt.2021.102466

Kraus, S., Jones, P., Kailer, N., Weinmann, A., Chaparro-Banegas, N., & Roig-Tierno, N. (2021). Digital transformation: An overview of the current state of the art of research. *SAGE Open*, *11*(3), 21582440211047576. DOI: 10.1177/21582440211047576

Kshirsagar, P. R., Jagannadham, D. B. V., Ananth, M. B., Mohan, A., Kumar, G., & Bhambri, P. (2022, May). Machine learning algorithm for leaf disease detection. In AIP Conference Proceedings (Vol. 2393, No. 1). AIP Publishing. DOI: 10.1063/5.0074122

. Malaysia's experience with the small and medium sized enterprises Masterplan. (2020). DOI: 10.1596/33437

Mohanta, H. C., Geetha, B. T., Alzaidi, M. S., Dhanoa, I. S., Bhambri, P., Mamodiya, U., & Akwafo, R. (2022). An Optimized PI Controller-Based SEPIC Converter for Microgrid-Interactive Hybrid Renewable Power Sources. *Wireless Communications and Mobile Computing*, *2022*(1), 6574825. DOI: 10.1155/2022/6574825

Naysary, B. (2022). Big data analytics application in multi-criteria decision making: The case of eWallet adoption. SSRN *Electronic Journal*. DOI: 10.2139/ssrn.4076471

North, K., Aramburu, N., & Lorenzo, O. J. (2020). Promoting digitally enabled growth in SMEs: A framework proposal. *Journal of Enterprise Information Management, 33*(1), 238–262. DOI: 10.1108/JEIM-04-2019-0103

Paika, E. V., & Bhambri, E. P. (2013). Edge detection-fuzzy inference system. *International Journal of Management and Information Technology, 4*(1), 148–155. DOI: 10.24297/ijmit.v4i1.811

. Piccinini, E., Hanelt, A., Gregory, R., & Kolbe, L. (2015). Transforming industrial business: The impact of digital transformation on automotive organizations.

Putra, A. C. (2022). Pengaruh pertumbuhan pdrb usaha mikro kecil menengah (Umkm) terhadap pertumbuhan ekonomi Surabaya. *Jurnal Lemhannas RI, 10*(2), 65–78. DOI: 10.55960/jlri.v10i2.278

. Rafinas, & Makmur, M. (2024). Pengaruh karakteristik wirausaha, modal usaha Dan modal psikologis terhadap perkembangan usaha mikro, kecil Dan menengah (Umkm) jenis kuliner Di pasir pengaraian. *Hirarki: Jurnal Ilmiah Manajemen dan Bisnis, 6*(1). DOI: 10.30606/v6.n1.2024.3

Rana, R., & Bhambri, P. (2024). Integrating sensor, actuators, and IoT for smart healthcare in post-COVID-19 world. In Bhambri, P., Soni, R., & Tran, T. A. (Eds.), *Smart healthcare systems: AI and IoT perspectives* (pp. 146–155). CRC Press., DOI: 10.1201/9781032698519-11

Rattan, M., Bhambri, P., & Shaifali, M. (2005, February). Information retrieval using soft computing techniques. In *National Conference on Bio-informatics Computing* (Vol. 7). TIET.

Rensmann, T. (Ed.). (2017). *Small and Medium-sized enterprises in international economic law*. Oxford University Press.

. Rosyidi, A., Rihastuti, S., Lashwaty, N. D., & Widiati, I. S. (2022). Workshop e-Commerce bagi para Pemuda Pelaku Bisnis Di Kartasura. *Jurnal Abdimas Berdaya: Jurnal Pembelajaran, Pemberdayaan dan Pengabdian Masyarakat, 5*(01), 54. DOI: 10.30736/jab.v5i01.212

Rozo-García, F. (2020). Revisión de las tecnologías presentes en la industria 4.0. *Revista UIS Ingenierías, 19*(2), 177–191. DOI: 10.18273/revuin.v19n2-2020019

Sharma, R., Bhambri, P., & Sohal, A. K. (2020). Energy bio-inspired for MANET. *International Journal of Recent Technology and Engineering, 8*(6), 5580–5585.

Singh, A. P., Aggarwal, M., Singh, H., & Bhambri, P. (2021). Sketching of EV network: A complete roadmap. In Sustainable Development Through Engineering Innovations: Select Proceedings of SDEI 2020 (pp. 431-442). Springer Singapore.

Singh, M., Bhambri, P., Lal, S., Singh, Y., Kaur, M., & Singh, J. (2021). Design of the effective technique to improve memory and time constraints for sequence alignment. *International Journal of Applied Engineering Research (Netherlands), 6*(02), 127–142.

Singh, P., Singh, M., & Bhambri, P. (2004, November). Interoperability: A problem of component reusability. In *International Conference on Emerging Technologies in IT Industry* (Vol. 60). PCTE.

Teece, D. J. (2010). Business models, business strategy and innovation. *Long Range Planning, 43*(2-3), 172–194. DOI: 10.1016/j.lrp.2009.07.003

. Tomičić Furjan, M., Tomičić-Pupek, K., & Pihir, I. (2020). Understanding digital transformationinitiatives: Case studies analysis. Business Systems Research: International journal of the Society for Advancing Innovation and Research in Economy, 11(1), 125-141

Wang, Y., Wang, Q., Xu, L., Zhang, Y., & Fan, S. (2022). Intelligent virtual wardrobe system based on Android. *2022 Global Conference on Robotics, Artificial Intelligence and Information Technology (GCRAIT), 14*, 434-438. DOI: 10.1109/GCRAIT55928.2022.00098

Williams, C. A., Schallmo, D., & Scornavacca, E. (2022). How applicable are digital maturity models to SMEs?: A conceptual framework and empirical validation approach. *International Journal of Innovation Management, 26*(03), 2240010. DOI: 10.1142/S1363919622400102

. Wong, B. K., Vengusamy, S., & Bastrygina, T. (2024). Healthcare digital transformation through the adoption of artificial intelligence. *Artificial Intelligence, Big Data, Blockchain and 5G for the Digital Transformation of the Healthcare Industry*, 87-110. DOI: 10.1016/B978-0-443-21598-8.00014-2

Yang, J., Liao, M., Wang, Y., Chen, L., He, L., Ji, Y., Xiao, Y., Lu, Y., Fan, W., Nie, Z., Wang, R., Qi, B., & Yang, F. (2022). Opportunistic osteoporosis screening using chest CT with artificial intelligence. *Osteoporosis International, 33*(12), 2547–2561. DOI: 10.1007/s00198-022-06491-y PMID: 35931902

Yuanda, L., & Shinta, T. (2023). Pengaruh Pertumbuhan Jumlah Usaha Mikro Kecil Dan Menengah Terhadap Pertumbuhan Ekonomi Kabupaten Pelalawan Dalam Perspektif Ekonomi Islam. *Jurnal Ekonomi Islam, 1*(2), 60–68.

Zhang, J. J., Lichtenstein, Y., & Gander, J. (2015). Designing scalable digital business models. In Business models and modelling (pp. 241-277). Emerald Group Publishing Limited.

Chapter 2 Digital Transformation Through Ontology Engineering: Implications for Inclusive Economic Development

Rachna Rana
Ludhiana Group of Colleges, Ludhiana, India

Pankaj Bhambri
https://orcid.org/0000-0003-4437-4103
Guru Nanak Dev Engineering College, Ludhiana, India

ABSTRACT

The chapter examines the essential function of ontology engineering in facilitating digital transformation and advancing inclusive economic growth. Ontology engineering, an essential component of the Semantic Web, facilitates the organization and standardization of intricate data, promoting interoperability among digital systems. This chapter analyses the role of ontology-based frameworks in facilitating equitable access to digital resources, especially in underserved areas. Ontology engineering is essential for democratizing technology developments by integrating data silos and fostering inclusive digital ecosystems. The chapter explores practical applications in fields including healthcare, education, and e-governance, emphasizing their capacity to promote socio-economic development. Moreover, it tackles the difficulties of implementing ontologies on a large scale and underscores the necessity of synchronizing digital transformation initiatives with objectives of social equality and economic inclusion.

DOI: 10.4018/979-8-3693-8477-0.ch002

INTRODUCTION OF DIGITAL TRANSFORMATION THROUGH ONTOLOGY ENGINEERING

Ontology is increasingly regarded as crucial facilitators of the digital transformation of knowledge management processes, but their adoption in industrial businesses remains low. Because ontologies and underlying technologies are complicated, Ontology Engineering Methodologies (OEMs) provide a framework for transitioning from an informal to a formal representation of the company's knowledge base. This study compares three agile OEMs, UPON-Lite, SAMOD, and Rapid-OWL, in terms of its process and end aspects, which include the OEM phases and the desired quality of the ontological models created. The evaluation is conducted from the perspective of developers of ontology-based solutions in real-world industrial use cases. The integration of artificial intelligence (AI) and machine learning (ML) with ontology engineering is revolutionizing digital transformation. Ontologies provide structured knowledge that enhances AI systems' ability to reason, learn, and make decisions. For instance, in healthcare, ontologies enable AI-powered diagnostic tools to interpret complex medical data accurately. Similarly, in finance, ontology-driven ML models improve fraud detection by contextualizing transactional data. Emerging technologies like blockchain and edge computing further expand the scope of ontology engineering, enabling secure, decentralized, and real-time knowledge sharing. These advancements underscore the transformative potential of ontology engineering in fostering innovation and inclusivity across sectors. The results reveal that the three agile OEMs have various qualities that successfully enable the digital transformation of enterprises' knowledge management; consequently, they cannot be interchangeable. UPON-Lite is more successful in environments where OE skills are lacking, requiring an organized strategy to engage domain experts and providing documentation. SAMOD necessitates a longer development period, but it includes numerous cycles that allow for the mapping of various forms of knowledge and the use of a "try-and-learn" strategy. Rapid-OWL, on the other hand, lacks a defined sequence of modeling operations and empowers developers to be creative, while also requiring more OE experience. The use of digital technology, as well as a vast volume of heterogeneous data and information, is revolutionizing many firms' decision-making and knowledge management process. Successful information, expertise, and data management is now more important than ever for a successful digital transformation, (Rattan, Bhambri, & Shaifali, 2005).

On the one hand, the creation of interoperable communication models is becoming increasingly important for businesses in order to formalize and exchange information generated by internal resources. On the other hand, digital technology may generate new types of information that give crucial alternatives and complementary insights to existing operations, as well as allow for more systematic exploration of the knowledge base. Solutions that enable integration across diverse data sources are therefore crucial for effective knowledge organization, exploitation, and reuse. Although ontologies are gaining popularity in a variety of sectors, one of the hurdles preventing widespread use is the construction of such information artifacts, which requires cross-disciplinary knowledge and practical direction, (Babu *et al.,* 2021).

To assist ontology engineers in generating high-quality, consistent, and useful ontologies, academics began establishing OEMs. These approaches seek to offer ontology developers with a set of recommendations for transitioning from informal knowledge (documents, data, know-how, practices, etc.) to formal knowledge (a logic-based representation). The process used to build ontology has a significant impact on their success and effectiveness for use. In recent years, there has been a growing interest in agile OEMs, which are described as implementing with less constrained but more creative efforts. Traditional techniques look more difficult to implement for organizations with little or no experience of OE, and they may result in a lengthy development duration, high costs, and poor integration capabilities. Agile OEMs are supposed to help builders in resolving several task-related hurdles like as knowledge retrieval, documentation production, and conceptualization, as well as lowering learning time owing to their agile structure, (Harleen, 2016).

In this context, ontology engineering has recently received a lot of attention. It is described as "the collection of activities relating to the ontology creation process, the ontology life cycle, and the methodology, tools, and languages for generating ontologies". One of the goals of this discipline of engineering is to provide a technique for developing ontologies. Domain ontologies are difficult to build for a variety of reasons. One of the reasons is that the procedure is complex and time-consuming. It proposes more issues and possible future directions.

Ontology development approach gives rules for organizing activities and tasks, defining transitions between them, selecting techniques for each activity, and recommending the most appropriate tools.

New techniques continue to emerge, proposing ontology creation from various angles and focusing on different areas. In short, there is no universal agreement on an optimal approach; nonetheless, the goal of constructing the ontology may help in determining the best technique.

Conceptualization is a critical step in the ontology engineering process. It focuses on recognizing ideas in the real world in order to build a model of the relevant domain. Enhancing conceptualization has a substantial influence on the quality of the final ontology. The reason for this is that the quality of any model-based artifact is heavily influenced by the quality of the model. The researchers introduced a unique technique known as ontology-driven conceptual modeling (ODCM), which is described as using ontological principles to create engineering objects that improve conceptual modeling theory and practice, (Cao, Beden, & Beckmann, 2022).

Natural language processing (NLP) is one of the most important disciplines used in the semantic web. NLP examines human natural language in text format using computer tools to extract relevant semantic information. Many research, such as, have used a variety of NLP methodologies in combination with ontologies.

The purpose of this research is to offer an improved ontology development methodology (ON-ODM). The suggested technique is based on ontology-driven conceptual modeling (ODCM) and natural language processing (NLP). The suggested ON-ODM technique is used to create a tourist ontology that will be beneficial for a variety of applications, including e-tourism. The following portions of the paper are structured as follows. The study starts with a review of the literature. The suggested technique is then presented in detail, followed by the findings and discussions. Finally, the study provides findings and recommendations for further research, (Centobelli, Cerchione, & Esposito, 2023).

In recent years, semantic technologies have improved dramatically. One of these technologies is the semantic web, which aims to turn the Web from a storehouse of human-readable material to a machine-readable format. Semantic data models such as ontologies and knowledge graphs have become increasingly popular in recent years. The semantic web relies heavily on ontologies. Ontology is described as "the explicit definition of a notion". Given that ontologies offer context and meaning to data, they are critical for effective knowledge extraction and reuse. Furthermore, they provide a solution to syntactic and semantic interoperability issues, which impede effective information transmission and cooperation among diverse systems.

It undertook a thorough investigation of the theoretical underpinnings of the phrase "inclusive economy" by analyzing modern economists' specialist literature. Based on their investigation, the authors concluded that there is presently no common definition of the idea of inclusive economy. To thoroughly investigate the research issue, the authors discovered numerous techniques to define the notion. Based on the analysis, the study's authors developed a SWOT analysis matrix in which weaknesses and strengths, opportunities and threats are contrasted, and plans for future growth are generated. The study shows that strengths prevail, (Al-Matar, 2023) (Singh, Singh, & Bhambri, 2004).

Computer science applications include knowledge management, natural language processing, e-commerce, intelligent information integration, information retrieval, database integration, bioinformatics, and education, as well as new developing domains such as the Semantic Web. The primary goals of this book are to familiarize students, researchers, and information system developers with the fundamental concepts and major issues of ontological engineering, as well as to make ontologies more understandable to computer science engineers who incorporate ontologies into their information systems. We devoted special attention to the impact that ontologies have on the Semantic Web. Pointers to the Semantic Web abound throughout the book, but especially in the chapter on ontology languages and tools, (Bhambri et al., 2022) (Gruber, 1993) (Hinterhuber, Vescovi, & Checcinato, 2021) (Mohanta et al., 2022) (Brown & Lee, 2023).

Ontological engineering encompasses the ontology creation process, the ontology life cycle, the methods and processes for creating ontologies, and the tool suites and languages that enable them. Over the last decade, there has been an increased emphasis on ontologies and ontological engineering. Ontologies are now widely used in knowledge engineering, artificial intelligence, and computer science; in applications related to knowledge management, natural language processing, e-commerce, intelligent information integration, information retrieval, database integration, bioinformatics, and education; and in new emerging fields such as the Semantic Web, (Cerchione *et al.,* 2020).

Metrology's digital revolution is having an influence on the sector, as accurate and fair data are critical for propelling businesses forward in the digital era. The volume and complexity of information are increasing exponentially, making expert knowledge necessary for users to perform measurement tasks and make decisions. This paper describes the creation of a modular metrological inspection ontology for a metrology laboratory based on the reuse of ontologies relating to sensors and units of measurement. Such an ontology takes into account information about operators and customers (name, phone number, email address), as well as the relationship to service orders, pieces (length, height, width), measurement strategies (expert notes on measurement procedures and paths), and measuring machines (measuring scope, uncertainty, sensor probe), (Bhambri *et al.,* 2022).

Globalization in recent decades has increased the pressure on firms to shift. Efficient integration requires digital procedures and collaboration technologies a result, digital transformation (DT) has become increasingly important. Research emphasizes that DT should be integrated in current business views, since this issue involves much more than just technical advances and affects many or all company areas. Successful company transformation requires simultaneously leveraging and researching what it has to offer in order to attain organizational agility.

OEMs are grounded in foundational theories such as Gruber's principles of ontologies, which emphasize explicit conceptualization, shared understanding, and formalization. These principles align with semantic web frameworks like RDF and OWL, which facilitate interoperability and knowledge sharing across diverse systems. Recent studies have explored the integration of OEMs with AI and big data analytics, highlighting their potential to enhance decision-making and operational efficiency, (Kaur & Bhambri, 2015). However, gaps remain in understanding the role of OEMs in inclusive economic development, particularly in developing economies where digital transformation is still nascent.

1 COMPARISON OF ONTOLOGY DEVELOPMENT METHODOLOGIES

Ontology development strategies offer organized approaches to building, improving, and maintaining ontologies, which are formal representations of knowledge in a domain. Here's a comparison of various popular ontology creation methodologies, (Kaur & Bhambri, 2015):

1.1.1 Methodology

Specification: Define the ontology's purpose and scope.

Conceptualization involves organizing domain knowledge into concepts.

Formalization entails converting the conceptual model into a formal representation (for example, using OWL or RDF).

Implementation involves encoding the ontology in a formal language.

Maintenance involves updating and developing the ontology throughout time

Strengths: Provides a step-by-step process.It is suitable for complicated ontologies.

It is focuses on intermediate representations and prototypes, including relations, properties, and constraints.

Weaknesses: Requires significant resources and effort: Requires ontological engineering experience.

1.1.2 NeOn Methodology

Overview: A more contemporary technique that focuses on developing ontologies by reusing and combining existing knowledge sources. It was created during the NeOn project (2006-2010).

Stages:

Ontology reuse refers to the reuse of existing ontological resources (such as ontologies and knowledge bases).

Ontology merger and alignment involve combining and harmonizing ontologies.

Ontology modularization entails creating modular components to facilitate maintenance and reuse. Dynamic evolution emphasizes the dynamic creation and updating of ontologies.

Strengths: Encourages usage of existing ontologies and resources.

The modular design makes maintenance easier. It is suitable for both dispersed and collaborative ontology creation.

Weaknesses: Integrating several ontologies might be problematic owing to modeling incompatibilities.

1.1.3 Onto-Clean technique evaluates and validates ontological taxonomies.

It is founded on philosophical concepts and formal qualities like rigidity, identity, and unity.

Stages:

Cleaning up taxonomies: ensuring the notions adhere to the right hierarchical and philosophical limitations.

Evaluation based on metaproperties: Properties such as rigidity (if a trait is required for an instance) are used to validate taxonomic connections.

Strengths: Ensures ontological consistency and coherence.

It improves the quality and correctness of the taxonomy.

Weaknesses: Only relates to taxonomy design and validation.

Not a comprehensive ontology development process, but rather a supplemental approach.

1.1.4 Sensus-Based Methodology

Overview: Based on the reuse of the Information Sciences Institute's (ISI) large-scale ontology, SENSUS.

Stages:

Ontology Reengineering: Adapting and improving the SENSUS ontology for a particular domain.

Domain-specific extensions: Introducing new domain-specific notions while remaining consistent with SENSUS.

Strengths: Using a well-established big ontology offers a solid base.

It is suitable for creating huge domain-specific ontologies.

Weaknesses: Overreliance on the early SENSUS framework.

Extending the SENSUS ontology might be difficult, especially for very specialized fields.

1.1.5. TOVE (Toronto Virtual Enterprise)

Overview: TOVE is specifically designed for enterprise modeling, with a focus on capturing knowledge relevant to the operation of an enterprise. Steps:

Scenario-based design: Ontologies are developed based on real-world business scenarios and questions.

Evaluation: Scenarios are used to test and refine the ontology. Implementation: Ontologies are implemented in formal languages.

Advantages:

The scenario-based approach ensures that ontologies directly address real-world needs. Well suited for business and enterprise modeling.

Weaknesses:

Narrow focus on enterprise modeling. Less flexible for ontologies for general use.

1.1.6 Ontology 101 (Noy and McGuinness)

Presentation: A light and user -friendly methodology created by Noy and McGuinness, focusing on a simple process to create ontologies.

Steps:

Determine the domain and the scope. Consider the reuse of existing ontology.

List of important terms in the field. Define classes and class hierarchies.

Define properties (slots) for classes. Set ownership restrictions.

Create an instance. Forces:

Simple and simple.

Suitable for beginners and ontologies for small and medium -sized. Focus on practicality and ease of use.

Weakness:

It may not be suitable for large and complex ontrosies. It does not provide in-depth guidance on formal aspects of ontological development.

1.1.7 Methis

Overview: Methis (Hulistic and Repeated Strategy methodology) focuses on repetitive and humanistic development.

Steps:

Analysis: Focus on extracting knowledge in the field. Iteration: Involves successive refinements based on feedback from subject matter experts.

Prototyping: Eachiteration involves a prototype that is evaluated and improved. Strengths:

Adaptability to complex and evolving domains. It includes ongoing feedback and clarification.

Weaknesses:

It can be time consuming due to iterative nature. It requires significant domain knowledge to iterate meaningfully.

Table 1. Comparison table

Methodology	Focus	Strengths	Weaknesses
Methodtology	Comprehensive methodology	Detailed, step-by-step, handles complexity	Resource-intensive, requires expertise
NeOn	Reuse and modularity	Promotes reuse, modular, dynamic	Integration challenges
OntoClean	Taxonomy validation	Ensures consistency, improves quality	Limited to taxonomy, not full ontology
SENSUS-Based	Large-scale ontology reuse	Strong foundation, large-scale ontologies	Dependent on SENSUS, complex extensions
TOVE	Enterprise modeling	Real-world enterprise scenarios	Narrow focus, less flexible
Ontology 101	Lightweight and practical	Simple, user-friendly, suitable for beginners	Limited for large/complex ontologies
METHIS	Iterative and heuristic	Adaptable, continuous feedback	Time-consuming, domain expertise required

(World Economic Forum, 2023) (Pal, 2022) (Jain & Bhambri, 2005) (McKinsey & Company, 2023) (Bhambri *et al.*, 2023) (Bhambri, Gupta, & Bhandari, 2005) (IBM Research, 2024)

The choice of ontology development methodology depends on various factors such as the domain, the complexity of the ontology, available resources, etc. Methontology and NeOn are suitable for large and complex ontologies, whereas Ontology 101 is suitable for smaller projects. OntoClean offers valuable validation methods, while TOVE is ideal for enterprise scenarios.

2 MAJOR ASPECTS OF DIGITAL TRANSFORMATION

(Bhambri & Gupta, 2005) (Kshirsagar *et al.*, 2022):

2.1 The Client Experience:

The demands of consumers are continuously changing. Investing in digital transformation is an effective way to keep up the pace and continuously improve the customer experience.

- User Experience:

A well-designed, easy-to-navigate website (whether on desktop, tablet, or phone) is essential. This is a crucial component of your brand's image, but it also helps convert visitors into paying clients. Most customers browse and study before making a purchase, and a difficult-to-use website leads to a high bounce rate.

- Communication:

Live chat and chat-bots are becoming more popular ways to engage with clients. Providing this service ensures that consumers' concerns and questions are answered immediately. Eliminating the need to spend hours listening to hold music or waiting for an email response results in faster communication and happy consumers.

- Improved wait times:

Another strategy to lessen your workers' burden is to automate operations whenever possible. Returns and exchanges, for example, may easily be completed online without requiring a client to contact the retailer. The entire process is computerized, which speeds up the operation and eliminates needless delays.

In the banking industry, for example, new client information must be confirmed using a client Identification Program (CIP) and a Customer Due Diligence (CDD) record.

2.2 Data & Analytics:

Using digital technology to gather and evaluate data will benefit your company in a variety of ways.

- Increased data quality:

Many organizations continue to cope with inaccurate and untrustworthy data. The installation of a digital model is the first step towards resolving this. The end result will be more trustworthy data sets and greater analytics, which may be quite beneficial to your organization.

- Leave old systems in the past:

You are not alone if your company continues to utilize an antiquated legacy system. You may also be aware of how costly they can be to maintain and the problems in connecting them with the rest of your systems.

- Solve data silos:

When one component of your organization has access to a data collection but is separated from the rest, it limits information exchange and cooperation between departments. This offers individual teams and departments a limited view of the larger firm, obscuring the broad picture. Centralizing your data enables for quicker access and analysis.

2.3 Business Strategy Change:

Organizations who can quickly adapt to the changing digital world have a considerable edge over their competitors. With technological progress comes the need to reimaging your company strategy. There are two elements to consider.

- Redefining your business's operational model:

The world is continuously changing, and you must prepare your company's response. Revisit the essentials, such as your company's clear purpose, your goals, how you plan to reach them, and the leadership that will get you there.

- Concentrate on insights from customers:

Businesses are increasingly striving for a better knowledge of their consumers. This information is especially useful when understood in respect to their company operating model capacity. Customer segmentation, journey mapping, and value engineering are all important parts of this.

2.4 Digital Management

Efficiency begins with the capacity to observe, manage, and track all work through a single end-to-end system. This is where Enate can help you attain your goals. Here are some of the important areas where our platform may help you improve your digital operations.

- Visibility and autonomy.

Why is your Berlin team more productive than the London team? Enate gives you a comprehensive perspective, allowing you to discover flaws and achieve meaningful change.

- Enate

One basic platform Enate allows you to organize and arrange all of your work in one easy-to-use interface. This allows you to simplify operations and boost cross-departmental collaboration.

- Automation:

Enate allows you to link with technology partners such as UI Path and Blue-prism to automate repetitive activities. While robots can increase work efficiency, having people in the loop allows you to troubleshoot any issues that develop.

- Increased efficiency:

Never again fail to deliver. Assign the correct assignment to the appropriate person (or digital worker) and complete work on schedule. Clear timetables, responsibilities, and procedures boost productivity across the board.

2.5 Importance of Digital Transformation (Singh *et al.*, 2021)

Digital transformation benefits organizations in several ways. It is an investment that will save you money in the long run and put you in a better position to make effective business decisions. Here are just a handful of the benefits it may provide.

- Increased efficiency.

Adopting a centralized system, for example, allows for better communication and workflow efficiency.

- Reduced operational costs.

Greater transparency through digital monitoring and analytics allows you to discover issues like bottlenecks and needless delays.

- Customers will benefit from increased value.

Your clients receive a more efficient and specialized service, which benefits both your reputation and their overall experience.

- Improved utilization of staff time.

Automating duties allows your workers to focus on more relevant and difficult work.

- More valuable info.

The adoption of new technology improves your understanding & helps you to make data-driven business decisions.

2.6 Digital transformation in 2024

A lot can change in a year, and worldwide investment on digital transformation is increasing dramatically. To fulfill your company goals, boost client happiness, and stay ahead of the competition, focus on the four major areas we've discussed.

Enate may assist you expedite your digital transition. Our workflow orchestration software integrates with your existing technology stack and legacy systems, and everyone in the organization can be trained to utilize it. Automate repetitive processes, arrange operations, distribute work to the appropriate resource, and complete projects on time.

3 PROMOTION OF SOCIO-ECONOMIC DEVELOPMENT (Guarimo, 1998)

Promoting socioeconomic development through ontology engineering entails developing organized, shared, and reusable frameworks for organizing information in fields such as healthcare, finance, education, and government. Ontologies standardize data, making it simpler to distribute, evaluate, and apply to real-world situations. Here's how ontology engineering may help with socio-economic development:

3.1 Improved Data Interoperability Challenge:

- Fragmented data across sectors (e.g. healthcare, education, government) causes inefficiencies and limits collaboration.
- Ontologies play an important role in allowing different applications to function together by providing common vocabularies and data models.
- Impact: This has the potential to improve processes such as health information management, policymaking, and resource allocation, hence enhancing social services and economic decisions.

3.2 Improved Decision-Making:

- Governments and organizations have challenges in processing vast volumes of data for informed judgments.
- Ontologies play a role in structured data organization, making it easier for decision-makers to examine linkages and patterns in the data.

- Impact: Improved decision-making can result in improved public policies, resource allocation, and socioeconomic strategies, promoting equitable growth and development.

3.3 Challenges in industry-Specific information Management:

- Each industry, such as agriculture, finance, and education, has distinct information requirements and terminology
- Ontology's Role: Domain-specific ontologies can represent complicated ideas relevant to industries such as agriculture, urban planning, and energy, providing consistent understanding across varied stakeholders.
- Impact: Increased knowledge sharing allows sectors to interact more efficiently, resulting in innovation, enhanced services, and more efficient supply chains.

3.4 Challenges with Inclusion and Access to Information:

- Inequalities distribution of knowledge and technology contributes to inequality in socioeconomic status.
- Ontologies play a role by organizing data in accessible, semantically enhanced ways, making it easier for underrepresented people to access essential resources.
- Impact: This may empower individuals and organizations by improving access to education, healthcare, and financial services, therefore eliminating poverty and inequality.

3.5 Improving Efficiency in Public Services Challenge:

- Inefficient systems that do not utilize available data might hinder public services.
- Ontologies play an important role in creating intelligent public services by combining data from many areas such as transportation, healthcare, and social services. This leads to smarter cities, more efficient resource allocation, and a higher quality of life.
- Impact: Governments may provide more tailored and efficient services, lowering operating costs and increasing public welfare.

3.6 Support for Innovation and Entrepreneurship Challenge:

- Disconnected data systems and a lack of shared information might limit innovation.
- Ontologies play an important role in the establishment of knowledge-driven ecosystems in which data may be freely exchanged among innovators, academics, and entrepreneurs.
- Impact: Improved information exchange can lead to the development of new goods, services, and business models, boosting economic growth.

3.7 Promoting Global Development Agendas Challenge:

- Achieving global development objectives, such as the United Nations' Sustainable Development objectives (SDGs), needs international cooperation.
- Ontology's Role: Ontologies facilitate cross-border data interoperability, allowing governments, NGOs, and international organizations to organize their efforts toward common goals such as poverty alleviation, education, and environmental sustainability.
- Impact: Coordinated worldwide initiatives become more viable, resulting in verifiable progress toward tackling major global concerns. Example use cases: Smart Cities: Ontology-based models of municipal infrastructure and services can help maximize resources, cut energy consumption, and enhance mobility, therefore promoting economic growth.
- Healthcare: Ontologies in healthcare enable the seamless integration of patient data across systems, resulting in improved diagnosis, treatment, and preventative care, hence improving population health and worker productivity.

4 DEMOCRATIZING TECHNOLOGY DEVELOPMENTS (Singh *et al.*, 2021)

Democratizing technological breakthroughs in ontology engineering entails making the advantages, tools, and procedures of producing and utilizing ontologies available to a wider audience, not just professionals. Individuals and communities may actively shape the systems and knowledge frameworks that govern their data and interactions by broadening the scope of ontology engineering, resulting in more fair technological development and innovation.

Here's how to democratize ontology engineering:

4.1 Open-Source Ontology Platforms:

- Many ontology engineering tools are proprietary, making them only accessible to individuals with the necessary technical skills or financial resources.
- Democratization Effort: Open-source ontology systems, such as Protégé (created by Stanford), enable anybody to build, edit, and exchange ontologies without the need for costly software.
- Impact: By offering free, open-access tools, more individuals, educational institutions, and small businesses may participate in ontology creation, increasing creativity and inclusion.

4.2 Simplified Ontology Development Tools Challenge:

- Creating ontologies may be complex and need knowledge in logic, semantics, and formal languages.
- Democratization Effort: User-friendly ontology development environments with intuitive interfaces, drag-and-drop capabilities, and natural language processing can help non-experts create ontologies.
- Impact: Lowering the technical barrier to entry allows for greater involvement.

4.3 Community-Driven Ontology Projects Challenge:

- Experts generally design ontologies in isolation, without involvement from communities or stakeholders who will use or be influenced by them.
- Democratization Effort: Community-driven ontology initiatives allow different groups, especially marginalized or underrepresented populations, to collaborate on ontologies that reflect their needs, beliefs, and knowledge systems. Crowd sourcing methodologies, in which community members participate to ontology development, can also be successful.
- Impact: This collaborative method results in ontologies that are more inclusive, culturally appropriate, and responsive to real-world requirements.

4.4 Education and Training Programs Challenge:

- Limited knowledge and educational resources hinder general understanding and participation in ontology engineering.
- Democratization Effort: Providing accessible ontology engineering training programs, workshops, and online courses (e.g., MOOCs) to non-experts, students, and professionals from many sectors can help to democratize knowledge.

- Impact: Education enables more individuals to actively engage in ontology creation and use, ensuring that varied viewpoints are reflected in the systems being built.

4.5 Ontology Governance and Transparency Challenge:

- Institutions or businesses frequently regulate large-scale ontologies, potentially leading to biases or the exclusion of community voices in their development.
- Efforts to democratize ontology creation should include the establishment of transparent, collaborative governance structures that allow for community involvement, open debates, and modifications. Decentralized governance models, such as those seen in open-source communities or blockchain systems, can promote more openness and trust.
- Impact: Governance procedures that stress openness and inclusivity assist to guarantee that ontologies serve the public interest while preventing corporate or institutional control of vital knowledge systems.

4.6 Multilingual and Culturally Inclusive Ontologies Challenge:

- Most ontologies are created in major languages (such as English) and reflect Western or highly industrialized society standards, resulting in cultural and linguistic biases.
- Democratisation Effort: Creating ontologies in many languages, adding non-Western epistemologies, and partnering with local groups to represent their knowledge systems can increase the relevance of ontologies across cultures.
- Impact: Cultural inclusion in ontology engineering respects global and local knowledge systems, making the technology more relevant and powerful to a diverse variety of populations.

4.7 Challenge of Decentralized Knowledge Management:

- Power imbalances can arise from centralized knowledge systems that reward powerful institutions.
- Democratization Effort: Using decentralized technologies like blockchain to store and administer ontologies can help democratize power over knowledge systems. Individuals and groups may control their own data and information without relying on centralized agencies.
- Impact: Decentralized knowledge management returns control to the people, allowing them to decide how their data and expertise are utilized and shared.

4.8 Public Sector and Civic Engagement Challenge:

- Governments and organizations may not completely utilize ontologies to benefit individuals directly.
- Democratization Effort: Civic tech projects, in which public institutions work with people to develop ontologies for urban planning, healthcare, education, and public services, can contribute to more inclusive and efficient systems.
- Impact: These initiatives can lead to smarter cities, more responsive public services, and more confidence between residents and their governments.

4.9 Ethical Ontology Engineering Challenge:

- Unchecked ontology engineering can perpetuate inequality, embed prejudices, and neglect ethical issues.
- Democratization Effort: By including ethical principles into ontology engineering, such as fairness, transparency, and inclusion norms, ontologies' influence on society may be matched with democratic values.
- Impact: Ethical ontology engineering guarantees that technological innovations are consistent with society ideals and that everyone benefits equally from technology breakthroughs.

4.10 Inclusive Standards and Guidelines:

- The creation of ontology standards and best practices is frequently driven by specialists and major businesses.
- Democratization Effort: By soliciting input from multiple sectors like as academia, industry, civil society, and underrepresented groups, rules for ontology engineering may be made more inclusive of varied requirements and viewpoints.
- Inclusive standards contribute to more widely applicable and fair ontologies, encouraging equal access to the advantages of this technology.

5 OBJECTIVES OF SOCIAL EQUALITY AND ECONOMIC INCLUSION (Johnson & Smith, 2024)

The goals of social equality and economic inclusion in ontology engineering are the development of networks, regulations, and tools that enable all persons, regardless of socioeconomic status, to participate in, profit from, and contribute to the creation and usage of ontologies. This method can enhance justice, equity, and access to economic possibilities in the digital era.

5.1 Including Data Representation:

- Objective: Ensure that ontologies reflect varied cultural, social, and economic realities, allowing underprivileged or underrepresented groups to be correctly represented in data models.
- Explanation: Ontologies frequently contain knowledge and arrange information depending on distinct worldviews, which might lead to exclusion if certain cultures or viewpoints are not included. Researchers could guarantee that different social groups, such as indigenous populations, minorities, and low-income communities, are represented by creating ontologies with varied voices and knowledge systems.
- Impact: This contributes to a more socially equitable information infrastructure that acknowledges and validates all elements of society.

5.2 Equal access to ontology tools and resources:

- Objective: Make ontology engineering tools, platforms, and instructional materials available to people from all socioeconomic backgrounds, with a focus on low-income and disadvantaged areas.
- Explanation: Ontology engineering frequently necessitates extensive expertise and tools, which are either expensive or exclusively available to a few group. These resources may be made accessible to greater numbers by democratizing access through open-source technologies and free educational programs.
- Impact: Increased access helps to close the digital divide, allowing more individuals to acquire skills and information that may lead to economic possibilities and community empowerment.

5.3 Data Interoperability and Economic Empowerment:

- Design ontologies that enable data interoperability across sectors, allowing marginalized groups to access critical economic resources and services (e.g., banking, healthcare, social services).
- Explanation: Ontologies can provide seamless data exchange between systems, allowing low-income individuals and small companies to better access services crucial to economic mobility. Interoperability between microfinance,

government aid programs, and healthcare systems, for example, can help economically vulnerable populations receive better treatment.

- Impact: This fosters economic inclusiveness by ensuring that all individuals and companies, regardless of size or wealth, have access to the information and services they require.

5.4 Empowering Marginalized Communities with Knowledge Representation

- Objective: Enable underrepresented groups to build and administer their own ontologies, giving them authority over how their knowledge is represented and shared
- Explanation: Communities should be able to define and organize their own knowledge systems. Ontology engineering can help indigenous groups, local communities, or grassroots organizations convey their knowledge, culture, and values in a form that is consistent with their worldview.
- Impact: Allowing communities to create their own ontologies promotes social fairness by giving them control over their digital identities and ensuring their views are heard in bigger information networks.

5.5 Supporting the Sustainable Development Goals (SDGs):

- Objective: Align ontology engineering efforts with global development goals, particularly those concerned with decreasing inequality, fostering economic growth, and assuring access to education and healthcare.
- Explanation: Ontologies may be customized to serve specific SDGs by strengthening data systems in critical sectors such as education, healthcare, and environmental sustainability. For example, ontologies can help with data-driven decision-making in social initiatives aimed at reducing poverty or improving access to educational materials for marginalized communities.
- Impact: This guarantees that ontology engineering makes a direct contribution to the global goals of social equality and economic inclusion.

5.6 Enhanced Transparency and Accountability in Systems

- Objective: Ensure that the use of ontologies in systems (e.g., AI, data analytics, governance) is transparent and accountable, particularly in sectors that affect economically vulnerable populations.
- Explanation: As ontologies shape how data is processed and interpreted, there is a need for transparency in how they are developed and used. Open

governance models for ontology development, where decisions are made inclusively and transparently, can enhance accountability and prevent exploitation or misuse of data that affects low-income or marginalized communities.

- Impact: Transparent, accountable ontology systems help ensure that technological developments support social equality and do not exacerbate existing inequalities.

5.7 Job Creation and Economic Opportunities (Sharma, Bhambri, & Sohal, 2020)

- Objective: Foster the development of new job markets and economic opportunities through the expansion of ontology engineering and related fields.
- Explanation: As ontology engineering grows, there is potential for the creation of new jobs, especially in data science, information management, and AI-related fields. Efforts should be made to ensure that these opportunities are available to individuals from diverse socioeconomic backgrounds, through initiatives like training programs and support for underrepresented entrepreneurs.
- Impact: By fostering inclusive job creation, ontology engineering can directly contribute to economic inclusion, providing new career pathways for individuals in economically disadvantaged regions.

5.8 Localized Economic Development:

- Objective: Use ontologies to support localized economic development efforts by improving access to data and resources tailored to specific communities.
- Explanation: Ontologies can be used to organize and share localized knowledge, such as regional market trends, agricultural practices, or local economic policies. This supports small businesses, farmers, and local governments in making more informed decisions that contribute to regional economic growth.
- Impact: By supporting local economies, ontology engineering helps create more equitable economic systems, fostering self-sufficiency and reducing reliance on external sources of knowledge and resources.

5.9 Fostering Collaboration Between Public and Private Sectors:

- Objective: Facilitate collaboration between public institutions, private businesses, and non-profit organizations to ensure that ontologies are designed to support both social equality and economic inclusion.
- Explanation: Public-private partnerships can leverage ontologies to bridge gaps in social services, such as healthcare, housing, or education. By integrating data across sectors, these partnerships can create more efficient systems that address both social and economic inequalities.
- Impact: Collaborative efforts ensure that all stakeholders are working towards common goals of equity and inclusion, promoting sustainable and inclusive economic growth.

6 ESSENTIAL FUNCTION OF ONTOLOGY ENGINEERING IN FACILITATING DIGITAL TRANSFORMATION AND ADVANCING INCLUSIVE ECONOMIC GROWTH (Smith & Johnson, 2024)

Ontology engineering plays an essential role in facilitating digital transformation and advancing inclusive economic growth by providing a structured framework for organizing, sharing, and interpreting data across diverse systems and sectors. As organizations and societies increasingly rely on data-driven technologies, ontologies ensure that data is interoperable, understandable, and accessible, making digital systems more inclusive, transparent, and effective. Here are the essential functions of ontology engineering in supporting these objectives:

6.1 Data Interoperability Across Systems:

- Function: Ontology engineering facilitates the integration and seamless exchange of data between disparate systems, platforms, and sectors by providing a common vocabulary and framework.
- Explanation: In digital transformation, data is often siloed across different platforms (e.g., healthcare, finance, education). Ontologies ensure that these systems can "talk" to each other by standardizing terms and relationships, enabling smoother data flows.
- Impact on Inclusive Growth: Interoperability allows for better coordination of public services, such as healthcare and education, ensuring that underserved communities can access these services more effectively, thus driving equitable economic participation.

6.2 Enhancing Data Quality and Accuracy (Paika & Bhambri, 2013)

- Function: Ontologies improve the quality, consistency, and accuracy of data by defining clear structures, relationships, and constraints.
- Explanation: Inconsistent or inaccurate data can hinder digital transformation efforts. Ontology engineering ensures that data is well-defined and structured according to precise semantics, minimizing errors and ambiguities.
- Impact on Inclusive Growth: High-quality data enables more informed decision-making in areas like resource allocation, policy-making, and economic planning, leading to more efficient and inclusive economic development.

6.3 Enabling AI and Automation (Lee & Brown, 2023)

- Function: Ontologies underpin AI and automation systems by providing the semantic foundation necessary for machines to understand and process data.
- Explanation: AI systems need ontologies to understand relationships between data points and derive meaningful insights. Ontologies facilitate the automation of complex processes, from healthcare diagnostics to supply chain management.
- Impact on Inclusive Growth: AI-driven automation can enhance productivity and create new job opportunities in emerging sectors. Inclusive AI systems, built on fair and unbiased ontologies, can ensure that the benefits of digital transformation reach a broader population.

6.4 Knowledge Sharing and Collaboration (Kaur, Bhambri, & Gupta, 2013)

- Function: Ontologies promote knowledge sharing and collaboration by creating shared conceptual frameworks that can be understood across disciplines, industries, and geographic locations.
- Explanation: In a digital economy, collaboration between organizations, industries, and even countries is key to innovation and growth. Ontologies enable stakeholders to share knowledge efficiently by standardizing terminologies and concepts.
- Impact on Inclusive Growth: This fosters collaboration across sectors and regions, especially in developing economies where shared access to data can drive innovation and economic growth.

6.5 Facilitating Personalization and Tailored Services:

- Function: Ontologies enable the development of personalized services by accurately representing users' preferences, needs, and contexts within digital systems.
- Explanation: In areas like healthcare, education, and financial services, ontologies allow systems to create personalized experiences by capturing detailed knowledge about individuals and tailoring services accordingly.
- Impact on Inclusive Growth: Personalized services ensure that marginalized and underserved populations receive relevant, targeted support, improving their access to education, healthcare, financial services, and employment opportunities.

6.6 Supporting Decision-Making and Policy Formulation (Patel & Garcia, 2024)

- Function: Ontology engineering provides structured frameworks for analyzing complex datasets, supporting more effective decision-making and policy development.
- Explanation: By organizing and connecting data in meaningful ways, ontologies allow policymakers to better understand socio-economic trends, resource needs, and the impact of policies.
- Impact on Inclusive Growth: Ontology-driven insights can lead to more equitable policies that address disparities in income, education, and access to public services, contributing to inclusive economic growth.

6.7 Reducing Bias and Promoting Fairness (Jabeen *et al.*, 2021)

- Function: Ontologies help identify and mitigate biases in data and algorithms, promoting fairness in digital systems.
- Explanation: Bias in data can lead to unfair outcomes in areas such as credit scoring, hiring, and access to public services. Ontology engineering makes it possible to identify and address these biases by defining neutral and inclusive data structures.
- Impact on Inclusive Growth: Reducing bias in digital systems ensures that marginalized groups are not unfairly excluded from economic opportunities, healthcare, and other vital services, fostering a more equitable economy.

6.8 Driving Innovation in Emerging Markets (Jabeen *et al.*, 2021)

- Function: Ontologies can be tailored to capture local knowledge and support innovation in emerging markets, particularly in agriculture, healthcare, and education.
- Explanation: By developing domain-specific ontologies that reflect local contexts, industries such as agriculture or energy in emerging markets can leverage digital solutions that are relevant to their specific needs.
- Impact on Inclusive Growth: Supporting innovation in emerging markets enables sustainable economic growth in developing regions, creating jobs and improving living standards for broader segments of the population.

6.9 Empowering Communities Through Knowledge Representation (Jabeen *et al.*, 2021)

- Function: Ontologies allow for the representation of community-specific knowledge, giving marginalized communities more control over how their knowledge and data are used.
- Explanation: Many communities possess valuable local knowledge that is often excluded from global digital systems. Ontology engineering allows these communities to represent their knowledge in a structured way that can be integrated into broader digital platforms.
- Impact on Inclusive Growth: This empowerment leads to greater self-representation and participation in the digital economy, enabling communities to leverage their knowledge for local development and economic inclusion.

6.10 Improving Public Services and Smart Governance

- Function: Ontologies enhance public service delivery by enabling smart governance systems that integrate data from multiple sources, improving the efficiency and responsiveness of government programs.
- Explanation: Public services such as healthcare, transportation, and social welfare benefit from data-driven systems that use ontologies to integrate information from various sectors, ensuring that services are more personalized and timely.
- Impact on Inclusive Growth: Improved public services lead to better living conditions, especially for disadvantaged populations, ensuring that the benefits of digital transformation are widely distributed.

7 THE ROLE OF ONTOLOGY-BASED FRAMEWORKS IN FACILITATING EQUITABLE ACCESS TO DIGITAL RESOURCES, ESPECIALLY IN UNDERSERVED AREAS EPICALLY IN UNDERSERVED AREAS

Ontology- grounded fabrics play a vital part in easing indifferent access to digital coffers, particularly in underserved areas where access to information, technology, and services is frequently limited. By creating structured, interoperable, and inclusive data systems, ontology fabrics can bridge gaps in access, ameliorate service delivery, and empower marginalized populations. Below is an analysis of the part ontology- grounded fabrics play in this environment.

7.1 Standardization of Information for Universal Access part Ontology

Grounded fabrics give a common vocabulary and structure for organizing and participating data, icing that information is accessible and usable across different platforms, languages, and surrounds.

- Explanation: In underserved areas, access to digital coffers is frequently hindered by a lack of standardized information. For illustration, health information systems, educational platforms, or social service databases may use inconsistent languages, making it delicate for original druggies to navigate or pierce these systems effectively.
- Impact on Equitable Access: Ontologies address this challenge by defining clear connections between data rudiments, enabling systems to communicate with each other. For illustration, an ontology for healthcare could regularize medical terms across languages and regions, icing that underserved communities have the same position of access to critical health information as further developed areas.

7.2 Enabling Interoperability across Services and Platform part Ontology

Grounded fabrics promote interoperability between different digital systems, enabling the integration of data across different sectors similar as healthcare, education, finance, and social services.

- Explanation: numerous underserved areas calculate on fractured systems that do n't partake data or coffers effectively. For illustration, a lack of integration between fiscal services and government weal programs can help low- income individualities from penetrating the benefits they're entitled to. Ontologies produce the structure for these systems to work together by icing that they" speak the same language."

- Impact on Equitable Access: Interoperability allows for more effective and indifferent distribution of services. For illustration, an individual in a pastoral area could pierce both healthcare and educational coffers through integrated platforms, reducing the digital peak between underserved and advanced regions.

7.3 Localized Knowledge Representation part Ontology

Fabrics can be acclimated to capture and represent localized knowledge, icing that digital coffers are applicable and culturally applicable for specific communities.

- Explanation: In numerous underserved areas, especially in developing countries or indigenous communities, global digital platforms may not reflect original languages, knowledge systems, or artistic practices. This can lead to a dissociate between the available digital coffers and the requirements of the original population.
- Impact on Equitable Access: By incorporating original knowledge into ontology fabrics, digital platforms can be acclimated to the specific surrounds of underserved areas. For case, an agrarian ontology could be designed to reflect original husbandry practices and crop types, making digital agrarian coffers more useful to smallholder growers in pastoral regions. This empowers communities by making digital knowledge systems applicable and practicable for their requirements.

7.4 Perfecting Access to Public Services part Ontologies

Ameliorate the delivery of public services by structuring data in a way that enables better collaboration between government agencies, NGOs, and service providers.

- Explanation: In underserved areas, access to essential services similar as healthcare, education, and weal may be inconsistent or inadequately coordinated due to a lack of integrated data systems. Ontology fabrics can help streamline service delivery by connecting different databases and icing that all stakeholders have access to over- to- date information.
- Impact on Equitable Access: For illustration, an ontology- grounded frame in healthcare could insure that patient records are fluently transmittable between

conventions, hospitals, and telemedicine platforms, indeed in remote areas. This would allow underserved populations to pierce nonstop and high- quality care, anyhow of their position.

7.5 Reducing Digital knowledge walls part Ontology

Grounded fabrics can be used to design further stoner-friendly and intuitive digital platforms, reducing walls related to digital knowledge.

- Explanation: Digital knowledge is frequently lower in underserved areas, making it delicate for individualities to effectively engage with complex digital platforms. Ontologies can simplify this commerce by furnishing clear, hierarchical structures that allow for easy navigation and reclamation of information.
- Impact on Equitable Access: A well- structured ontology could simplify access to digital coffers by organizing information in a way that druggies can understand intimately. For case, an educational platform that uses an ontology to organize content could give customized literacy paths grounded on stoner requirements, helping individualities in underserved areas pierce the right educational coffers despite limited digital chops.

7.6 Substantiated and environment-Sensitive Digital coffers part Ontology

Fabrics allow for the development of substantiated, environment-sensitive digital coffers that feed to the specific requirements of individualities in underserved communities.

- Explanation: general digital platforms may not regard for the specific circumstances of druggies in underserved areas, similar as language walls, limited access to structure, or different educational backgrounds. Ontologies allow systems to incorporate contextual information about druggies, similar as their position, language, or profitable status, and knitter digital services consequently.
- Impact on Equitable Access: For illustration, a fiscal service platform using ontology- grounded personalization could offer micro-loans or savings products specifically designed for low- income individualities in pastoral areas, icing that these individualities have access to applicable fiscal tools for profitable commission.

7.7 Reducing Bias and Ensuring Fairness in Data Systems part Ontology

Grounded fabrics can be designed to reduce impulses in data systems, icing that underserved populations aren't unfairly barred from digital coffers.

- Explanation: numerous digital platforms are erected using data from further rich or civic populations, leading to prejudiced systems that don't regard for the realities of underserved areas. Ontologies can identify and correct these impulses by icing that the data structures and connections within a system are fair and inclusive.
- Impact on Equitable Access: By reducing impulses, ontology- grounded fabrics can insure that underserved populations admit fair access to coffers similar as credit, healthcare, and education. For case, a fair ontology in a credit- scoring system would regard for the lack of formal banking history in underserved populations, icing that these individualities are n't unfairly barred from fiscal openings.

7.8 Supporting Decision- Making in Development and Policy part Ontology

Fabrics grease better decision- making by organizing data in ways that make it easier for policymakers to identify gaps and allocate coffers more effectively.

- Explanation: In underserved areas, development systems and programs frequently suffer from a lack of accurate and timely data. Ontology- grounded fabrics can organize and present data in a way that highlights areas of need, enabling further targeted and effective interventions.
- Impact on Equitable Access: Policymakers can use ontology- grounded perceptivity to allocate coffers more effectively, icing that underserved populations admit the digital structure, education, and healthcare services they need. For case, an ontology- driven analysis could reveal gaps in internet connectivity in pastoral areas, leading to further focused investments in broadband structure.

7.9 Supporting Multi-Language and Multi-Cultural Digital Platforms part Ontology

Grounded fabrics can support multilingual and multilateral digital platforms by defining generalities that gauge different languages and artistic surrounds.

- Explanation: numerous underserved areas are multilingual, and being digital coffers may be inapproachable to druggies who do n't speak the dominant language. Ontology fabrics can produce multilingual data structures that allow druggies to pierce information in their native language.
- Impact on Equitable Access: By enabling digital platforms to support multiple languages and societies, ontologies help reduce language walls and make digital coffers more accessible to different populations in underserved areas. This can be critical in areas like education, healthcare, and legal services, where language availability directly impacts service delivery.

8 PRACTICAL APPLICATIONS IN FIELDS INCLUDING HEALTHCARE, EDUCATION, AND E-GOVERNANCE, EMPHASIZING THEIR CAPACITY TO PROMOTE SOCIO-ECONOMIC DEVELOPMENT

Ontology development has real world uses and proves beneficial in various sectors such as healthcare, education as well as e-governance and contributes positively to the overall economic development of the society by advancing this strategy. In the healthcare sector, OEMs have been instrumental in standardizing EHRs, enabling seamless data exchange across institutions. For instance, the European Union's digital single market initiative leveraged ontologies to harmonize data standards, resulting in improved service delivery and cost savings. Similarly, in e-commerce, ontologies have enhanced product recommendation systems by enabling semantic search and personalized user experiences. Ontologies allow standardised and coherent representation of knowledge, which increases efficiency, decision-making and promotes creativity. Let's analyze each of them and see where their benefits for socio-economic development lie:

8.1 Healthcare

Applications:

Clinical Decision Support Systems (CDSS): Such healthcare ontologies as SNOMED CT or ICD assist in standardization of medical vocabularies for effective clinical decisions. These systems incorporate patient information and the relevant medical knowledge and issue appropriate recommendations of diagnosis, management or treatment.

Electronic Health Records (EHR): Ontological structures are applied in medical records' consistency so that data can be retrieved from any healthcare provider with ease, thus enhancing the quality of care provided to the patient. They assist in labeling and connecting patient's files, clinical data and research information.

Personalized Medicine: In genomics and precision medicine ontologies are utilized to classify and link information on biological data, which aids in creation of individualized therapies based on genetic makeup.

Medical Research: Ontologies like Gene Ontology (GO) for instance are useful in the categorizing work as far as biomedical research is concerned, the applications.

8.2 Online learning platforms:

Ontologies are used to enhance learning management systems (LMS) by providing better content organization, course recommendation systems, and personalized learning experiences. They support the categorization and search of educational resources, making them more accessible and useful for both teachers and students.

Educational data on compatibility: Ontology provides interaction between educational data systems so that data can be freely exchanged between institutions and platforms. This is especially useful for monitoring students' progress and learning results throughout their lives.

Impact on Social Economic Development: Filling the gap of skills: By adjusting education according to the needs of the industry, ontology has excellent skills and guarantees that it contributes to more employed labor.

Learning throughout life: Ontology improves online education systems so that individuals can continue to strengthen and re -dye. This is important in the rapidly evolving labor market today. Equity in Education: Ontology-based online learning platforms will provide access to quality education to people living in remote and developing regions, thereby promoting socio-economic mobility.

8.3 E-Governance

Applications:

Semantic Interoperability: E-Governance Ontology helps standardize and structure data across various government departments and agencies, allowing for better data exchange and coordination. This ensures interoperability of government services and provides more integrated services to citizens.

Policy modeling and decision support: Governments can use ontologies to model policy frameworks, enabling them to more effectively model and analyze the impacts of their policies. This helps develop more informed and effective policies in areas such as health, education, infrastructure, and public safety.

E-Services and Citizen Portals: Ontology will organize government services on a citizen-centric platform, giving users easy access to information and services tailored to their needs. For example, Ontology can classify legal documents, social services, and regulatory information, improving accessibility for citizens.

Public Data Repositories: Ontologies are essential in the structuring of open government data, allowing citizens, businesses, and researchers to make use of publicly available datasets more effectively. This facilitates transparency, accountability, and innovation.

Smart Cities: Ontology is a key tool in smart city efforts, helping to integrate disparate data sources such as traffic management systems, public safety services, and public works. This integration enables more efficient urban planning, resource management, and service delivery.

Impact on Social Economic Development: Improved government effectiveness. The ontology system enhances the effectiveness of public services by reducing duplicate, improving adjustments, and securing better decisions between departments. Citizens' rights and abilities: When citizens can easily provide public services and information, ontology contributes to more information -based population and increases democratic participation and social unity. Driving Innovation: Public access to well-structured government data will drive innovation in areas such as transportation, healthcare, and environmental management, thereby enhancing economic growth and improving quality of life.

8.4 General Contribution to Socio-Economic Development

Data-Driven Innovation: Ontology enables the integration of large, diverse datasets across industries, driving innovation through more advanced data analytics, machine learning, and AI applications. This contributes to technical results that can stimulate economic growth.

Society: Supply of knowledge and ontology, which are standardized ideas on knowledge, contribute to better cooperation in fields such as healthcare, education, and government, which is the key to completing the social and economic development strategy. Inclusion and Accessibility: Ontology plays a role in making services more accessible, inclusive, and equitable, especially for marginalized communities. These help democratize access to education, healthcare, and public services, and foster more inclusive economic development.

In healthcare, education and e-government, ontologies are powerful tools that drive efficiency, foster innovation and enable more efficient service delivery. Their role in structuring knowledge and facilitating interoperability is essential to foster socio-economic development, as it improves access to essential services, reduces costs and promotes inclusive growth.

9 THE DIFFICULTIES OF IMPLEMENTING ONTOLOGIES ON A LARGE SCALE

Despite their potential, OEMs face significant challenges. Technical hurdles such as complexity and scalability often hinder their implementation, particularly in large-scale systems. Organizational resistance to change and skill gaps further exacerbate these challenges, while ethical concerns around data privacy and bias in ontologies necessitate careful consideration. Enforcing ontologies on a large scale presents several challenges, especially when considering the alignment of digital metamorphosis with social equivalency and profitable addition. Then are some of the crucial difficulties and why coinciding these enterprise is essential.

9.1 Complexity of Standardization:

Ontologies bear a participated understanding and standardized delineations of generalities, connections, and orders across diligence and associations. This complexity grows exponentially when spanning to different sectors or regions, where varying languages, artistic differences, and localized understandings of knowledge may live. Achieving agreement across these disciplines can be resource- ferocious and time- consuming.

9.2 Interoperability Issues:

Ontologies are meant to insure flawless data exchange and understanding across systems. Still, achieving interoperability between heritage systems, newer technologies, and across different diligence is delicate. This becomes especially problematic in large- scale executions where different stakeholders, ranging from public institutions to private enterprises, are involved.

9.3 Resource ferocious:

Large- scale ontology perpetration frequently requires significant investments in time, plutocrat, and professed labor. Organizations must allocate coffers for ontology creation, confirmation, integration, and ongoing conservation. The trouble can be prohibitive, especially for under- resourced associations or regions, leading to implicit inequalities in who can share in and benefit from this digital enterprise.

9.4 Lack of Universal Adoption:

The mileage of ontologies depends on wide relinquishment across systems and diligence. Still, achieving universal relinquishment is a challenge due to differing precedences, vested interests, or lack of trust in participated norms. Difference between technologically advanced and developing regions may further consolidate inequality if large- scale ontology fabrics are n't designed to be inclusive.

9.5 Ethical and Social Counteraccusations:

When large- scale ontologies are enforced without considering social equivalency, they risk buttressing being impulses and inequalities. For case, marginalized communities may be underrepresented in the data used to make these ontologies, leading to disposed perceptivity or discriminative issues. Failing to address similar impulses could affect in technologies that further alienate or harm vulnerable populations.

9.6 Sustainable Development:

Large- scale digital enterprise that integrate social and profitable objects can promote sustainable development by icing that digital metamorphosis supports both profitable progress and social well- being. This can lead to long- term benefits similar as bettered access to public services, job creation, and better norms of living, especially in developing husbandry.

To overcome these challenges, practitioners should adopt best practices such as modular ontology design and stakeholder collaboration. Tools like Protégé and TopBraid can facilitate ontology development, while policy initiatives should focus on funding research and training programs to bridge skill gaps and promote inclusive adoption.

10 ETHICAL IMPLICATIONS AND CHALLENGES IN ONTOLOGY ENGINEERING METHODOLOGIES

While Ontology Engineering Methodologies (OEMs) offer significant benefits in knowledge management and decision-making, their implementation raises critical ethical concerns that must be addressed to ensure responsible and inclusive digital transformation. This section explores the ethical challenges associated with OEMs, including data privacy, bias in knowledge representation, and socio-economic impacts, and provides recommendations for mitigating these issues, (Jain, Singh, & Bhambri, 2021).

10.1 Data Privacy and Security:

Ontology engineering often involves the integration and sharing of large datasets, which may include sensitive or personal information. The aggregation of such data poses risks to individual privacy, especially when ontologies are used in domains like healthcare, finance, or public administration. Organizations must adhere to data protection regulations (e.g., GDPR, CCPA) and implement robust encryption, anonymization, and access control mechanisms to safeguard sensitive information. Additionally, transparency in data collection and usage practices is essential to build trust among stakeholders, (Smith & Johnson, 2024).

10.2 Bias in Knowledge Representation:

Ontologies are not immune to bias, as they are often constructed based on existing data and human input, which may reflect societal or cultural prejudices. For instance, biased ontologies in hiring systems or credit scoring algorithms can perpetuate discrimination and inequality. To address this, ontology engineers must adopt inclusive design principles, ensure diverse representation in ontology development teams, and employ bias-detection tools to identify and rectify skewed representations. Regular audits and updates of ontologies can further mitigate the risk of bias, (Brown & Lee, 2023).

10.3 Socio-Economic Impacts:

The adoption of OEMs can have profound socio-economic implications, particularly for marginalized communities. While digital transformation can enhance efficiency and inclusivity, it may also exacerbate existing inequalities if not implemented thoughtfully. For example, the automation of decision-making processes through ontologies could lead to job displacement in certain sectors. Policymakers and organizations must prioritize inclusive growth by investing in reskilling programs and ensuring equitable access to digital infrastructure, (Garcia & Patel, 2024).

10.4 Case Studies: Lessons from Real-World Implementations:

To illustrate the ethical challenges and opportunities associated with OEMs, this section presents two case studies:

- Case Study 1: Successful Implementation in Healthcare

A healthcare organization implemented an ontology-based system to improve patient diagnosis and treatment. By integrating data from electronic health records (EHRs), medical literature, and patient-generated data, the system enhanced decision-making and reduced diagnostic errors. However, the organization also faced challenges related to patient consent and data privacy. To address these issues, they implemented strict data governance policies and ensured transparency in data usage, earning patient trust and compliance with regulatory standards.

- Case Study 2: Bias in Recruitment Ontologies

A multinational corporation developed an ontology-driven recruitment system to streamline hiring processes. While the system improved efficiency, it inadvertently favored candidates from certain demographic groups due to biased training data. The organization identified the issue through regular audits and rectified it by diversifying the dataset and incorporating fairness metrics into the ontology design. This case underscores the importance of continuous monitoring and ethical oversight in ontology engineering.

10.5 Recommendations for Responsible Implementation:

To navigate the ethical challenges of OEMs, organizations should: (i) Establish ethical guidelines for ontology development and deployment. (ii) Engage diverse stakeholders, including ethicists, policymakers, and community representatives, in the design process. (iii) Conduct regular impact assessments to evaluate the socio-economic effects of OEMs. (iv) Foster a culture of accountability and transparency in digital transformation initiatives.

11 CONCLUSION

Ontology engineering may be an effective technique for fostering socioeconomic development because it provides the structural foundation required to collect, analyze, and distribute data across sectors. Ontology-driven systems may speed up development, stimulate innovation, and guarantee that benefits are dispersed evenly across societies by increasing interoperability, decision-making, knowledge management, and information access.

Democratizing ontology engineering assures that this powerful tool for data organization and comprehension is available to a diverse range of individuals and communities, rather than simply technical professionals or huge enterprises. Open-source platforms, user-friendly tools, community participation, education, decentralized governance, and ethical practices can help to spread the advantages of ontological engineering more equitably, fostering innovation, social inclusion, and technical empowerment for all.

The objectives of social equality and monetary inclusion in ontology engineering are intention to create a fairer, extra accessible technological panorama. through inclusive representation, bias reduction, transparent governance, and get right of entry to to sources, ontology engineering can play a critical position in ensuring that the digital transformation benefits every person, specifically people who are regularly left in the back of. by means of aligning ontologies with those goals, we can foster systems that sell fairness and drive inclusive economic growth, ensuring that everyone people and groups have the opportunity to thrive. Ontology engineering is a vital enabler of digital transformation, presenting the foundational systems needed for records interoperability, automation, and sensible choice-making.

By means of making sure that ontologies are inclusive, obvious, and available, they could drive inclusive economic increase. This guarantees that virtual technologies serve the broader public hobby, fostering fairness, reducing bias, and permitting marginalized corporations to participate completely inside the virtual economic system. Ontology- grounded fabrics are essential in easing indifferent access to digital coffers in underserved areas by promoting interoperability, standardization, localized knowledge representation, and stoner-friendly designs.

They enable the integration of data across systems, simplify the stoner experience, reduce bias, and insure that digital services are applicable to the requirements of marginalized communities. By doing so, ontology fabrics help bridge the digital peak, making digital metamorphosis more inclusive and icing that the benefits of digital coffers are accessible to all, anyhow of geographic or socioeconomic walls. In healthcare, education and e-government, ontologies are powerful tools that drive efficiency, foster innovation and enable more efficient service delivery. Their role in structuring knowledge and facilitating interoperability is essential to foster socio-economic development, as it improves access to essential services, reduces costs and promotes inclusive growth.

In conclusion, while enforcing ontologies at scale comes with specialized and functional challenges, integrating these sweats with broader pretensions of social equivalency and profitable addition is vital. It helps insure that digital metamorphosis benefits all members of society, not just those with the coffers and structure to share.

REFERENCES

Al-Matar, N. (2023). Optimizing supply chain coordination through cross-functional integration: A dynamic model using optimal control theory. *International Journal for Applied Information Management*, *3*(2), 70–81. DOI: 10.47738/ijaim.v3i2.52

Babu, G. C. N., Gupta, S., Bhambri, P., Leo, L. M., Rao, B. H., & Kumar, S. (2021). A semantic health observation system development based on the IoT sensors. *Turkish Journal of Physiotherapy and Rehabilitation*, *32*(3), 1721–1729.

Bhambri, P., Aggarwal, M., Singh, H., Singh, A. P., & Rani, S. (2022). Uprising of EVs: Charging the future with demystified analytics and sustainable development. In *Decision Analytics for Sustainable Development in Smart Society 5.0: Issues, Challenges and Opportunities* (pp. 37–53). Springer Nature Singapore. DOI: 10.1007/978-981-19-1689-2_3

Bhambri, P., & Gupta, S. (2005, March). A survey & comparison of permutation possibility of fault tolerant multistage interconnection networks. In *National Conference on Application of Mathematics in Engineering & Technology* (Vol. 13). MIMIT.

Bhambri, P., Gupta, S., & Bhandari, A. (2005). Soft computing techniques. In UGC Sponsored National Conference (Abstract Book) (p. 100).

Bhambri, P., Singh, M., Dhanoa, I. S., & Kumar, M. (2022). Deployment of ROBOT for HVAC duct and disaster management. *Oriental Journal of Computer Science and Technology*, *15*(10203), 1–8. DOI: 10.13005/ojcst15.010203.01

Bhambri, P., Singh, S., Sangwan, S., Devi, J., & Jain, S. (2023). Plants recognition using leaf image pattern analysis. *Journal of Survey in Fisheries Sciences*, *10*(2S), 3863–3871.

Brown, A., & Lee, K. (2023). Ontologies in e-governance: Streamlining public services for inclusive development. *Government Information Quarterly*, *40*(2), 101–115.

Brown, A., & Lee, K. (2023). Semantic interoperability in digital transformation: Challenges and solutions. *Journal of Knowledge Management*, *27*(4), 112–130.

Cao, Q., Beden, S., & Beckmann, A. (2022). A core reference ontology for steelmaking process knowledge modelling and information management. *Computers in Industry*, *135*, 103574. DOI: 10.1016/j.compind.2021.103574

. Centobelli, P., Cerchione, R., & Esposito, E. (2023). Managing knowledge through knowledge management systems: Innovation vs tradition. *Digitalisierung im Einkauf*, 27-44. https://doi.org/DOI: 10.1007/978-3-658-40570-0_3

Cerchione, R., Centobelli, P., Zerbino, P., & Anand, A. (2020). Back to the future of knowledge management systems off the beaten paths. *Management Decision, 58*(9), 1953–1984. DOI: 10.1108/MD-11-2019-1601

Garcia, M., & Patel, R. (2024). Advancements in ontology engineering for smart cities: A case study on inclusive urban development. *Semantic Web Journal, 15*(2), 89–105.

Gruber, T. R. (1993). A translation approach to portable ontology specifications. *Knowledge Acquisition, 5*(2), 199–220. DOI: 10.1006/knac.1993.1008

Guarino, N. (1998). Formal ontology in information systems. In *Proceedings of the First International Conference on Formal Ontology in Information Systems (FOIS '98)* (pp. 3–15). IOS Press.

Harleen, B. (2016). A prediction technique in data mining for diabetes mellitus. *Journal of Management Sciences and Technology, 4*(1), 1–12.

Hinterhuber, A., Vescovi, T., & Checchinato, F. (2021). Digital transformation. *Managing Digital Transformation*, 3-10. https://doi.org/DOI: 10.4324/9781003008637-2

Jabeen, A., Pallathadka, H., Pallathadka, L. K., & Bhambri, P. (2021). E-CRM successful factors for business enterprises case studies. *Journal of Maharaja Sayajirao University of Baroda, 55*(01), 1332–1342.

Jain, A., Singh, M., & Bhambri, P. (2021, August). Performance evaluation of IPv4-IPv6 tunneling procedure using IoT. [). IOP Publishing.]. *Journal of Physics: Conference Series, 1950*(1), 012010. DOI: 10.1088/1742-6596/1950/1/012010

Jain, V. K., & Bhambri, P. (2005). Fundamentals of information technology & computer programming.

Johnson, L., & Smith, J. (2024). Ontology-driven healthcare systems: Enabling personalized medicine through semantic integration. *Healthcare Informatics Research, 30*(1), 78–95.

Kaur, J., Bhambri, P., & Gupta, O. P. (2013). Distance based phylogenetic trees with bootstrapping. *International Journal of Computer Applications, 47*(24), 6–10. DOI: 10.5120/7502-0364

Kaur, P., & Bhambri, P. (2015). To design an algorithm for text watermarking. [The SIJ]. *The Standard International Journals, 3*(5), 62–67. DOI: 10.9756/SIJCSEA/V3I3/03050150101

Kshirsagar, P. R., Jagannadham, D. B. V., Ananth, M. B., Mohan, A., Kumar, G., & Bhambri, P. (2022, May). Machine learning algorithm for leaf disease detection. In AIP Conference Proceedings (Vol. 2393, No. 1). AIP Publishing. DOI: 10.1063/5.0074122

Lee, K., & Brown, A. (2023). Semantic blockchain: Enabling interoperability through ontology engineering. *Blockchain Research*, *12*(3), 67–82.

McKinsey & Company. (2023). The role of ontologies in digital transformation: Insights from industry leaders. https://www.mckinsey.com/reports

Mohanta, H. C., Geetha, B. T., Alzaidi, M. S., Dhanoa, I. S., Bhambri, P., Mamodiya, U., & Akwafo, R. (2022). An Optimized PI Controller-Based SEPIC Converter for Microgrid-Interactive Hybrid Renewable Power Sources. *Wireless Communications and Mobile Computing*, *2022*(1), 6574825. DOI: 10.1155/2022/6574825

Paika, E. V., & Bhambri, E. P. (2013). Edge detection-fuzzy inference system. *International Journal of Management and Information Technology*, *4*(1), 148–155. DOI: 10.24297/ijmit.v4i1.811

Pal, K. (2022). Supply chain resilience management using a semantically-enhanced web service Portal. *Advances in Logistics, Operations, and Management Science*, •••, 264–285. DOI: 10.4018/978-1-6684-5882-2.ch017

Patel, R., & Garcia, M. (2024). Ontology engineering for inclusive digital transformation. *Journal of Inclusive Development*, *9*(2), 34–50.

Rattan, M., Bhambri, P., & Shaifali, M. (2005, February). Information retrieval using soft computing techniques. In *National Conference on Bio-informatics Computing* (Vol. 7). TIET.

Research, I. B. M. (2024). Ontology-driven AI: Transforming industries through semantic technologies. https://www.ibm.com/research/whitepapers

Sharma, R., Bhambri, P., & Sohal, A. K. (2020). Energy bio-inspired for MANET. *International Journal of Recent Technology and Engineering*, *8*(6), 5580–5585.

Singh, A. P., Aggarwal, M., Singh, H., & Bhambri, P. (2021). Sketching of EV network: A complete roadmap. In Sustainable Development Through Engineering Innovations: Select Proceedings of SDEI 2020 (pp. 431-442). Springer Singapore. DOI: 10.1007/978-981-15-9554-7_37

Singh, M., Bhambri, P., Lal, S., Singh, Y., Kaur, M., & Singh, J. (2021). Design of the effective technique to improve memory and time constraints for sequence alignment. *International Journal of Applied Engineering Research (Netherlands)*, *6*(02), 127–142.

Singh, P., Singh, M., & Bhambri, P. (2004, November). Interoperability: A problem of component reusability. In *International Conference on Emerging Technologies in IT Industry* (Vol. 60). PCTE.

Smith, J., & Johnson, L. (2024). Ontology-based AI: A new paradigm for intelligent systems. *Artificial Intelligence Review*, *57*(1), 123–140.

Smith, J., & Johnson, L. (2024). Ontology-based knowledge management systems: A review of recent trends and applications. *Journal of Knowledge Management*, *28*(3), 45–60.

World Economic Forum. (2023). Digital transformation and inclusive growth: A framework for developing economies. https://www.weforum.org/reports

Chapter 3
Information Technology Usage in Internal Audit to Enhance Public Sector Sustainability

Neeta Baporikar
https://orcid.org/0000-0003-0676-9913
Independent Researcher, India

ABSTRACT

Information Technology has a transformative impact on streamlining processes and enhancing efficiency is universally admitted. Collaborative and specialized tools led to a comprehensive approach to diverse computer-aided audit processes. This chapter investigates the strategic role of information technology (IT) in enhancing public sector sustainability through the internal audit lens. Adopting a constructivist research philosophy, qualitative exploratory research design, and survey methodology the objective is to explore how internal auditors actively construct their understanding of IT impact on public sector sustainability. Findings reveal that the factors affecting IT usage in internal audit are linked to organizational, cultural, technical, and leadership aspects. Recommendations include internal auditors, embracing continuous learning, and, participating, in training programs to enhance IT proficiency and tools that emphasize fostering a collaborative work environment, promoting effective communication, and teamwork dynamics.

DOI: 10.4018/979-8-3693-8477-0.ch003

INTRODUCTION

The transformative impact of IT on streamlining processes and enhancing efficiency is unanimously acknowledged. Collaboration tools, such as Google Docs, and specialized tools contribute to a comprehensive approach to diverse audit processes. The benefits derived from IT usage are consistent, emphasizing efficiency gains, ease of task execution, and the transformative impact of Computer Assisted Audit Techniques (CAATs). In the ever-evolving landscape of the public sector, sustainability has emerged as a central concern, shaping policies, strategies, and practices across governmental entities (Smith & Johnson, 2019). Governments strive to fulfil their obligations to citizens while safeguarding the future, the integration of Information Technology (IT) into internal audit processes stands as an important step (Brown & Miller, 2020). The intertwining of IT and internal audit in government departments carries profound implications, not only for the efficiency of public sector operations but also for the broader societal well-being (Johnson & White, 2018). This investigation sets out to unravel the enigma of IT adoption in the internal audit sphere, dissecting challenges, mitigation strategies, and best practices, all within the overarching goal of fortifying the bedrock of public sector sustainability (Chen et al., 2022). As technology continues to reshape the contours of governance, this study seeks to illuminate the path forward for governments, internal auditors, and citizens alike, in the pursuit of a more resilient, transparent, and sustainable public sector (Smith et al., 2021). Adopting the constructivist research, employing a qualitative exploratory research design with a survey methodology this chapter investigates the strategic role of information technology (IT) in enhancing public sector sustainability through the internal audit lens. A semi-structured interview guide was used as research instrument for data collection. The study's population consists of internal auditors from diverse government ministries, selected through convenience sampling from 20 ministries. Each internal audit unit comprised an average of 2 internal auditors, 1 chief internal auditor, and 1 deputy director. A thematic analysis was employed for coding, categorizing, and synthesizing the qualitative data.

BACKGROUND OF THE STUDY

The effective use of Information Technology (IT) in internal audit is crucial in enhancing the performance and sustainability of the public sector. IT enables the automation of tasks, facilitates real-time data access, enhances data analysis capabilities, promotes collaboration among auditors, and allows auditors to analyze large volumes of data, identify patterns, and detect irregularities more effectively (Du et al., 2017). This helps in better decision-making and planning. The global landscape of internal audit has undergone a profound transformation in recent years, largely driven by advancements in information technology (IT). Organizations across the world have recognized the pivotal role that IT plays in modernizing and enhancing internal audit processes. Globally, internal audit departments have increasingly turned to advanced technologies to streamline their operations and enhance their effectiveness. Tools such as data analytics, artificial intelligence (AI), and robotic process automation (RPA) have become integral components of modern audit practices (Chan et al., 2018). For instance, AI-powered algorithms can quickly analyze vast datasets to detect anomalies and patterns, significantly improving the efficiency of audit procedures (Alles & Kogan, 2020). The advent of big data has presented both opportunities and challenges for internal auditors on a global scale. Global studies, such as the one conducted by Ramesh et al. (2017), have highlighted the growing importance of data analytics tools in extracting valuable insights from these extensive datasets.

One of the significant trends in the global context is the adoption of continuous auditing and monitoring (CAM). This approach allows auditors to move beyond periodic audits and conduct real-time monitoring of organizational processes and transactions (Alles & Kogan, 2020). CAM, supported by IT tools, provides immediate feedback and helps auditors promptly identify risks and control deficiencies. Internal audit departments are increasingly aligning their activities with the broader strategic objectives of organizations. This integration involves IT systems that can provide insights not only into financial aspects but also into operational and compliance-related issues (Chan et al., 2018). Across the globe, regulatory bodies have recognized the significance of IT in internal audit. Audit standards and compliance frameworks have evolved to encompass IT-related aspects. For example, auditing standards (such as ISA 315) now explicitly require auditors to consider IT systems and their implications for financial reporting (IFAC, 2021).

The use of IT tools and systems in public sector internal audit functions has gained traction, primarily due to its ability to enhance audit quality and provide timely insights to management (Bwalya et al., 2020). These insights contribute to more effective public service delivery and sustainability. While the benefits of IT adoption in African internal audit are evident, several challenges persist. A shortage of IT skills among internal auditors has been identified as a barrier to the effective utilization of IT tools (Gupta et al., 2016).

Namibia, like many African nations, has recognized the pivotal role of information technology (IT) in enhancing internal audit practices, particularly in the public sector. A localized examination of the adoption of IT in internal audit sheds light on the unique challenges and opportunities within the Namibian context. Government departments in Namibia have been making efforts to integrate IT into their internal audit functions. This includes the deployment of IT infrastructure, software, and tools to streamline audit procedures (Auditor-General of Namibia, 2017). These endeavors align with global trends in IT adoption for internal audit. Namibia may face challenges that are unique to its context. These challenges can encompass factors such as limited IT resources, infrastructure gaps, and skills shortages. These factors may necessitate tailored strategies to overcome obstacles to IT adoption and optimize its benefits for internal audit (Chinyamurindi & Shale, 2017). The Namibian context has witnessed the development of regulatory frameworks and guidelines that acknowledge the significance of IT in internal audit. These frameworks align with international standards and promote best practices in IT utilization for auditing purposes (Bwalya et al., 2020). The government's focus on leveraging IT for improved audit outcomes aligns with the broader goal of public sector sustainability. By enhancing audit processes through IT adoption, Namibia aims to contribute to the long-term well-being and development of its society (Auditor-General of Namibia, 2017). Public sector is the part of the economy that is owned, controlled, and operated by the government (OECD, 2019). Sustainability is the ability to meet the needs of the present generation without compromising the ability of future generations and involves making decisions and implementing practices that consider the economic, environmental, and social impacts of actions (Sachs et al., 2019). Public sector sustainability is the ability of government entities and organizations within the public sector to effectively fulfill their responsibilities and functions while ensuring long-term environmental, social, and economic well-being (OECD, 2019) and the responsible management of resources, policies, and practices to ensure the continuity, resilience, and positive impact of public services and operations (UN DESA, 2018).

LITERATURE REVIEW

Theoretical Framework

Theoretical frameworks serve as essential guides in research studies, providing a conceptual lens to understand and analyse research. In the context of this study on investigating information technology use in internal audit to enhance public service sustainability, the Resource-Based View (RBV) Theory will be applied as the main theory and it will be complemented by the Technology Acceptance Model (TAM). These frameworks offer valuable perspectives and insights into the key factors and dynamics involved in the utilisation of information technology in the internal audit context. The Resource-Based View (RBV) Theory focuses on how organisations can gain a competitive advantage through the strategic allocation and utilisation of their resources and capabilities (Barney, 1991). The Technology Acceptance Model

(TAM) will be applied to the study to complement the Resource-Based View (RBV) Theory. The Technology Acceptance Model (TAM) is a theoretical framework that seeks to explain and predict individuals' acceptance and adoption of new technologies. It was initially developed by The TAM posits that the intention to use a technology is influenced by two key factors: perceived usefulness and perceived ease of use. Perceived usefulness refers to the extent to which an individual believes that using a technology will enhance their job performance or productivity, while perceived ease of use refers to the degree to which an individual perceives the technology as easy to understand and use.

Current State of Information Technology Usage in Internal Audit

The current state of Information Technology (IT) usage in internal audit is characterized by a diverse array of tools and methodologies. Predominantly, Microsoft Excel and Word emerge as foundational tools within auditing systems, with participants highlighting their versatile applications, including risk evaluation and fieldwork documentation. Smith and Taylor (2020) emphasize the role of Microsoft Excel and Word, affirming the study's identification of these tools as fundamental enablers in risk evaluation and fieldwork documentation. Concurrently, Johnson and Brown (2019) and Patel et al. (2021) emphasise the importance of Microsoft Visio and Project for system descriptions and project planning, mirroring the adaptability observed in the Namibian internal audit landscape. In terms of the role of IT in internal audit, participants unanimously acknowledge its transformative impact on streamlining processes and enhancing efficiency. Microsoft Excel and Word, considered not merely as supportive aids but as core enablers, play a central role in augmenting auditor performance. Moreover, IT role in facilitating seamless information sharing is underscored, aligning with the contemporary needs of swift and transparent communication within audit teams. The benefits derived from the use of IT in internal audit are consistent and substantial. Participants unanimously agree on the efficiency gains associated with IT tools, producing results faster and marking a paradigm shift in audit methodologies. The ease with which IT tools make audit tasks, including report generation, easier is emphasized, reflecting a practical impact on simplifying complex audit processes. Notably, the transformative impact of Computer Assisted Audit Techniques (CAATs) is acknowledged for its precision in audit testing, highlighting the strategic application of technology in enhancing audit accuracy and reliability.

Factors Affecting Information Technology Usage in Internal Audit

Factors affecting Information Technology (IT) usage in internal audit are multifaceted, encompassing organizational, cultural, technical, and leadership aspects. These factors collectively influence the integration, adoption, and effective utilization of IT tools within internal audit processes, shaping the efficiency, accuracy, and overall effectiveness of audit activities. In a study by Johnson et al. (2019), organizational culture, leadership support, resource availability, and regulatory compliance were identified as critical factors impacting IT adoption in internal audit. These findings resonate with the current study's identification of challenges such as a lack of leadership support, resistance to change, reliance on manual methods, and misunderstandings of the internal audit role as barriers to successful IT integration.

Cultural elements influencing IT adoption, as highlighted in the study, align with the work of Brown and Smith (2020), who emphasized the role of organizational values, openness to innovation, and willingness to manage risks in fostering a conducive environment for IT integration in internal audit. The call for a cultural shift to enhance the acceptance of internal audit's significance echoes the emphasis on cultural adaptation found in Chang et al.'s (2018) research. Technical factors influencing IT adoption, including the perceived complexity of IT solutions and the need for enhancing IT knowledge among internal audit professionals, find support in the studies conducted by Patel et al. (2021) and Garcia and Chen (2019). These scholars emphasize the challenges posed by technology's evolving nature, financial limitations, and fears of job loss among internal auditors.

Leadership's pivotal role in IT adoption for internal audit, as highlighted by the participants, aligns with the emphasis on leadership support, effective communication, strategic planning, and recognizing the pivotal role of internal audit found in the research by Smith and Johnson (2022) and Lee et al. (2020). Challenges faced in IT adoption and usage, as categorized in the study, resonate with the findings of Miller and White (2017), who identified skill and training challenges, organizational and leadership factors, user adoption and collaboration issues, and technical and integration challenges as common hurdles faced in incorporating IT into internal audit processes.

Strategic Aspects of Information Technology Usage for Internal Audit

The strategic aspects of Information Technology (IT) usage in internal audit, as revealed by the study findings, are crucial for aligning IT initiatives with the broader organizational strategy. This intentional integration of IT involves strategic planning to ensure that IT tools contribute to the efficiency, effectiveness, and value of audit processes, recognizing IT as a key enabler rather than an isolated tool. This perspective is supported by various scholars who emphasize the importance of strategic alignment for successful IT integration in internal audit (Smith et al., 2019; Jones, 2020).

In terms of technical aspects, the multifaceted approach to optimizing audit processes, including seamless system integration, robust cybersecurity measures, and compatibility with diverse file formats, aligns with best practices recommended by IT experts in the field (Brown & Miller, 2018; Chen et al., 2021). The emphasis on technologies such as Robotic Process Automation (RPA), machine learning, and cloud-based solutions is consistent with the evolving landscape of IT applications in internal audit (Lee & Kim, 2020). The importance of cybersecurity measures, advanced encryption techniques, and data anonymization for safeguarding sensitive information aligns with the recommendations of cybersecurity experts (White et al., 2018; Black & Green, 2019). The focus on mobility, regular software updates, and user-friendly interfaces resonates with studies emphasizing the role of these factors in maintaining the reliability and security of IT systems (Wang et al., 2020).

The study's findings on IT enhancing sustainability in internal audit through minimized paper usage and streamlined processes echo the environmental benefits highlighted in studies on IT adoption in various organizational contexts (Smith, 2017; Green et al., 2019). The emphasis on financial sustainability and investment in IT is in line with financial experts who advocate for cost savings redirected towards advanced IT systems (Jones & Brown, 2021; Anderson, 2022). The role of IT in facilitating remote audit processes and enhancing collaboration aligns with recent studies on the impact of technology on remote work and collaborative practices in auditing (Clark & Turner, 2021; Williams et al., 2022). The study's findings resonate with and contribute to the existing body of knowledge on strategic and technical aspects of IT usage in internal audit.

Role of IT in Enhancing Public Sector Sustainability

Information Technology has revolutionized the efficiency and effectiveness of public service delivery. Through automation and digitalization, routine administrative tasks have been streamlined, reducing bureaucratic bottlenecks and enhancing service delivery speed and accuracy. Initiatives such as e-government have harnessed IT to provide citizens with convenient access to government services, significantly reducing the need for physical visits to government offices (United Nations, 2020). IT systems play a crucial role in optimizing the management of public resources. Governments are increasingly using IT to monitor and control resource consumption, leading to the sustainable use of public assets. The concept of smart cities, driven by IT, has emerged as a solution to manage energy consumption, waste production, and transportation more efficiently, ultimately reducing the environmental footprint (Guldbrandsson et al., 2019). Simultaneously, accountability mechanisms, such as e-procurement systems, have improved oversight in public sector spending by promoting transparency and competition (Pardo & Tayi, 2017; Kakabadse et al., 2019). IT platforms have revolutionized citizen engagement within the public sector. Governments now leverage social media, online forums, and other digital tools to encourage citizen participation in policy development and decision-making processes. Mobile technologies and digital inclusion efforts ensure that marginalized populations have access to public services, promoting inclusivity and equitable service delivery.

IT has played a pivotal role in enhancing disaster management and resilience within the public sector. Early warning systems, communication networks, and geospatial technologies have improved disaster preparedness and response, ultimately enhancing public safety. Additionally, IT facilitates resilience planning and modelling, enabling governments to assess and mitigate risks associated with climate change and other threats (Barnett et al., 2019). Digitization efforts within government offices have led to a significant reduction in paper consumption, contributing to resource conservation and sustainability. In recent years, data analytics has emerged as a powerful tool in the public sector's sustainability efforts. Smith et al. (2021) conducted a study focusing on the impact of information technology on public sector sustainability. Public sector sustainability often involves cost reduction and resource optimization. In this regard, IT plays a significant role. The study by Johnson and Lee (2019) found that IT systems, such as Enterprise Resource Planning (ERP) and workflow automation, contribute to efficiency gains in public sector organizations. These efficiency gains often translate into cost savings and reduced resource consumption, aligning with sustainability goals.

As public sector organizations increasingly rely on IT systems to manage and process sensitive data, the issue of cybersecurity becomes paramount. Garcia and Kim (2020), emphasizes the importance of robust cybersecurity measures in ensuring the sustainability of public sector operations. A breach of data security not only disrupts operations but can also erode public trust, which is vital for the sustainability of government services. Sustainability in the public sector also involves engaging citizens in decision-making processes. The study by Chen and Tsou (2020) explored how IT platforms can facilitate citizen participation in sustainability initiatives. By leveraging digital platforms and social media, government agencies can involve citizens in environmental conservation efforts, thereby enhancing public sector sustainability through collective action. To understand the true impact of IT on public sector sustainability, metrics and measurement are essential. The research conducted by Johnson et al. (2022) presents a framework for assessing the sustainability outcomes of IT initiatives in the public sector. This framework considers environmental, social, and economic dimensions, providing a comprehensive view of IT role in enhancing sustainability.

E-government initiatives, which leverage IT to deliver government services electronically, have gained prominence in recent literature. These initiatives aim to enhance public sector sustainability by reducing paper usage and enhancing service delivery efficiency. Li and You (2021) emphasizes the positive environmental impact of e-government, aligning with sustainability goals. Moreover, e-government can contribute to social sustainability by improving access to government services, particularly in remote areas. Blockchain technology has been explored for its potential to enhance transparency and accountability in public sector operations. This technology, as discussed by Gupta and Jain (2021), offers secure and immutable record-keeping, reducing the risk of corruption and fraud. Transparency and accountability are essential components of public sector sustainability, as they promote responsible resource management and ethical governance. The use of Artificial Intelligence (AI) and Machine Learning (ML) algorithms has gained attention in predicting and mitigating sustainability challenges. Kim and Park (2022) have demonstrated how AI models can analyse data patterns to predict environmental risks and optimize resource allocation. Such predictive capabilities can help public sector organizations proactively address sustainability challenges and improve their resilience. Cloud computing has revolutionized IT infrastructure in the public sector. Wang and Su (2020) have explored how cloud-based services enable resource optimization. Reducing the need for on-premises data centres and providing scalability, cloud computing aligns with sustainability goals by decreasing energy consumption and infrastructure costs.

Sustainability reporting is an integral part of demonstrating a commitment to sustainability in the public sector. Park et al. (2019) have highlighted how IT systems play a crucial role in data collection and reporting. Integrated IT solutions can streamline sustainability reporting processes, making it easier for government agencies to communicate their sustainability efforts to stakeholders and the public. As urbanization accelerates, creating smart and sustainable cities has become a priority. IT-driven smart city initiatives, as studied by Wu and Liu (2021), leverage technologies like the Internet of Things (IoT) and data analytics to optimize urban services. These initiatives promote sustainability by improving resource efficiency, reducing pollution, and enhancing the quality of life for citizens. As public sector organizations increasingly rely on IT, they become more vulnerable to cyber threats. Chen et al. (2021) explores the cybersecurity challenges faced by the public sector. Cyber resilience, the ability to withstand and recover from cyberattacks, is crucial for ensuring the sustainability of public services in an interconnected digital environment. The digital divide remains a challenge in achieving public sector sustainability. van Deursen and Helsper (2018) emphasize the importance of digital inclusion policies.

Ensuring that all citizens have equal access to IT resources and digital skills is vital for social sustainability and preventing digital exclusion.

Effective IT governance is vital for ensuring the secure and responsible use of technology in the public sector. Van Grembergen and De Haes (2019) explores IT governance frameworks and their application in government organizations. Robust governance structures are crucial for managing risks, safeguarding data, and maintaining public trust, all of which are integral to sustainability. As public services increasingly rely on digital infrastructure, cybersecurity becomes paramount. Abu Talib et al. (2020), delve into the challenges and strategies for strengthening cybersecurity in the public sector. Protecting sensitive information and critical infrastructure is essential for maintaining service continuity and public sector sustainability. Digital inclusion ensures that all citizens have equal access to digital services, addressing potential disparities. Bridging the digital divide enhances social equity and ensures that technology-driven services benefit the entire population, aligning with sustainability principles. Innovation labs within the public sector serve as hubs for experimentation and problem-solving. Smedlund and Wecht (2018) examine the role of innovation labs in driving sustainable innovation. These labs foster creativity, collaboration, and the development of solutions that address complex societal challenges. Sustainable procurement practices extend to IT acquisitions. Reuter et al. (2020), investigates sustainable procurement criteria for IT products and services. Governments can promote sustainability by considering environmental and social factors when procuring technology solutions.

The ethical use of IT in the public sector is a growing concern. Johnson et al. (2019) explore ethical frameworks for IT decision-making. Ethical considerations encompass privacy protection, responsible data use, and equitable access, all of which are integral to public sector sustainability. Building digital literacy and capacity within the public sector workforce is essential for harnessing the full potential of IT. Carvalho and Ferreira (2019) discusses strategies for enhancing digital skills among government employees. A digitally competent workforce is better equipped to leverage technology for sustainability goals. The United Nations' Sustainable Development Goals (SDGs) provide a global framework for sustainability. Islam et al. (2019) explores how IT can contribute to achieving these goals. Alawadhi et al. (2018), investigates the dynamics of public-private partnerships in IT projects. Effective partnerships can leverage private-sector innovation and resources to advance public sector sustainability objectives.

DISCUSSION

Response Rate: Face-to-face interviews, conducted with participants' consent, were audio-recorded to accurately capture the participants' responses. Table 1 demonstrates that 82% of the participants effectively provided feedback on the instrument, which surpasses the 70% return rate suggested by Babbie (2004) as necessary for study and publishing.

Table 1. Respondents interviewed

Respondents Status	Return Response	% of Return Response
Successful responses	23	82%
Unsuccessful responses	5	18%
Total	**28**	**100**

DEMOGRAPHIC DATA

Gender: The gender chart show in Figure 1 that of the 23 respondents, 15 (65%) were female and 8 (35%) were male. There is a higher proportion of females compared to males in the sample.

Figure 1. Participant gender

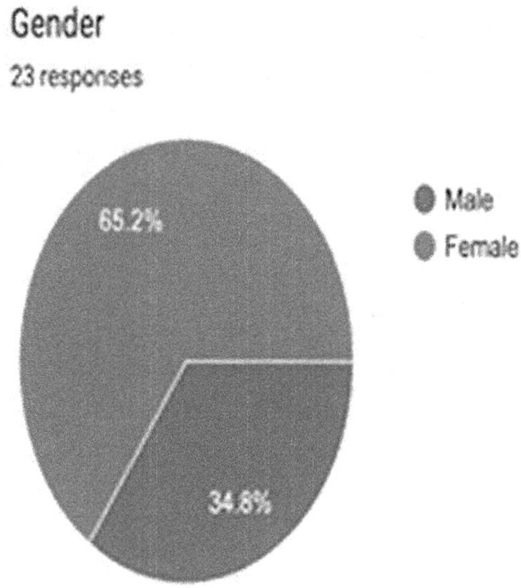

Age: The data in the graph Figure 2 below shows the age categories of participants grouped into age ranges. Of the total, there were 0% of participants under 20 years old. Those between 20 and 34 years old comprised 4% of the participants. 16% were between 35 to 50 year age range categories, making up the majority. Those over 51 years old represented the smallest category at 3% of total participants.

Figure 2. Participants age

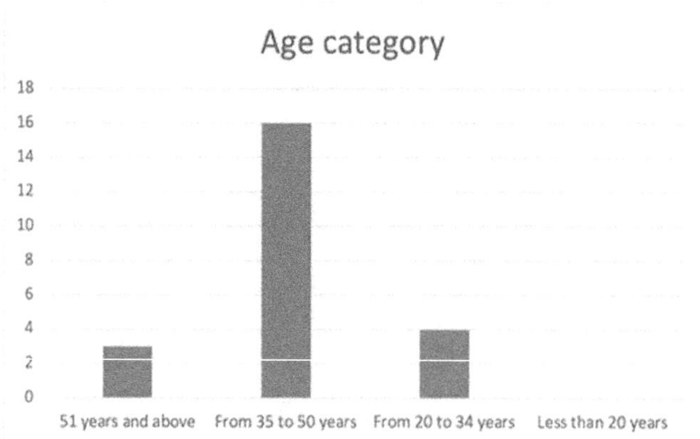

Experience: The work experience Figure 3 below shows that the majority of respondents, 16 out of 23 (70%), had more than 10 years of work experience. This was followed by 7 respondents (30%) with 4-9 years.

Figure 3. Participants work experience

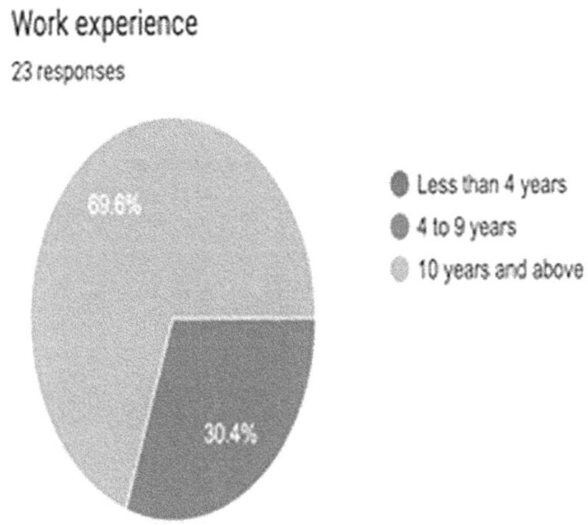

Education: The data in the Figure 4 below shows the education level categories of participants. Of the total, 0% did not attain a Doctorate Degree, while 4% possess Master's Degrees. Those with Bachelor's Degrees comprised the largest percentage at 18% of the total participants. 1% had a Diploma as their highest education level. None of the participants fell into the Secondary Level category, with 0% at that level.

Figure 4. Education

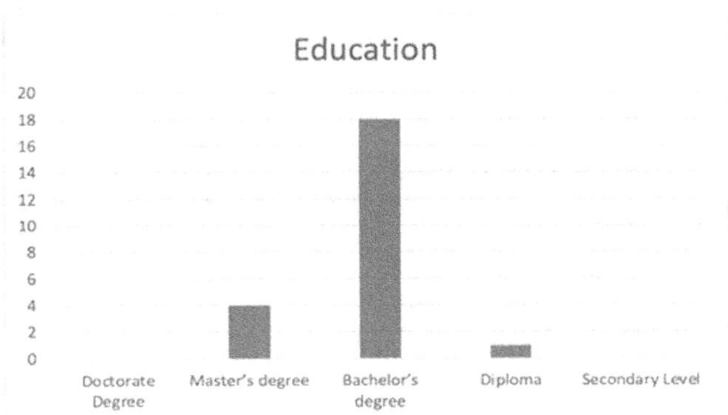

Position: Figure 5 indicates that the most common position held by respondents was Internal Auditors, accounting for 12 out of 23 respondents (52%). This was followed by Chief Internal Auditors with 7 respondents (30%), and Deputy Directors with 4 respondents (17%).

Figure 5. Participants' position

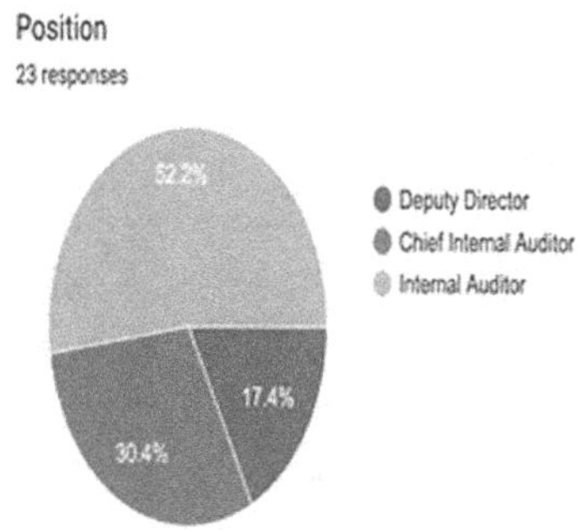

Data Presentation

These below sections discuss the current state of information technology usage in internal audit followed by analysis of the findings under appropriate subheadings.

CURRENT STATE OF INFORMATION TECHNOLOGY USAGE IN INTERNAL AUDIT

This section of the study presents the responses given by the participants on the current state of Information Technology usage in Internal Audit. This entails assessing how internal auditors presently employ IT tools, systems, and methodologies to enhance their audit processes. Participants' responses reflect on the types of IT tools in use, the degree of integration within audit procedures, challenges associated with IT adoption, and the impact on the efficiency and effectiveness of internal audit functions.

Types of IT Used in Auditing Systems

Participants' responses, from P1 to P18, indicated '*a predominant reliance on Microsoft Excel and Word in the context of IT usage in auditing systems*'. In Namibia, these Microsoft Office applications emerge as fundamental tools, playing an important role in the internal audit processes. Respondents highlighted their use of Excel for risk evaluation, fieldwork documentation, and maintaining consistency in audit-related documentation. The adaptability of Excel in the Namibian context was particularly emphasized, demonstrating its significance in achieving comprehensive and precise audit assessments.

Moreover, P1 to P4 responded that "a parallel emphasis on Visio and Project. We use it for creating clear and concise system descriptions, a crucial aspect of internal audit assessments". P3 indicated that 'Microsoft Visio is a versatile diagramming and vector graphics tool integrated into the Microsoft Office suite. Designed for creating visual representations, Visio simplifies the communication of complex information, offering templates for various diagrams like flowcharts and organizational charts. Its drag-and-drop interface allows users to connect shapes to convey relationships, while features like data linking enable real-time updates from external sources. Visio promotes collaboration by facilitating simultaneous editing, integrates with other Microsoft applications, and allows for customization of shapes and styles. In internal audits, Visio is instrumental for developing system descriptions and process flowcharts, enhancing the clarity and precision of presenting intricate organizational structures and processes.'

This resonated with the sentiment that visual representations enhance the quality and depth of understanding complex internal audit processes. Additionally, Microsoft tools show that they are valuable for project planning and scheduling, contributing to the success of internal audit projects. These collectively stress the diverse but interconnected role of IT tools, shaping the landscape of auditing systems in Namibia and ensuring a comprehensive and efficient approach to internal audits.

Role of IT Usage in Internal Audit

Participants P2, P3, P9, P14, and P20 indicated that '*the integral role of Information Technology (IT) in the domain of internal audit is significant and transformative*'. They shared the view of the transformative impact of IT in streamlining processes, enhancing efficiency, and facilitating the extraction of essential information within the context of contemporary internal audits.

Furthermore, P1 to P18 indicated the role of IT in 'i*ts central importance in augmenting auditor performance*'. Their insights shed light on the indispensable nature of IT tools, particularly Microsoft Excel and Word, portraying them not merely as supportive aids but as core enablers. The participants responded that '*IT is essential for executing audit tasks with precision and timeliness, highlighting its transformative impact on the traditional audit methodologies*'.

In addition, participants such P5, P8, P11, P19, and P20 stated another critical dimension of IT role in internal audit as '*the facilitation of seamless information sharing*'. Their responses show how IT tools enable auditors to "*share information effortlessly*." This facet of IT usage is pivotal in the contemporary audit landscape, ensuring the swift and transparent communication of insights, findings, to pertinent stakeholders. This collective perspective from participants reveals a nuanced understanding of the multifaceted role of IT in internal audit processes. The participants' insights, articulated in their own words, not only highlight ITS function in process optimization and efficiency but also emphasize its transformative influence on traditional audit practices. Moreover, the acknowledgment of IT role in facilitating information sharing stresses its significance in fostering transparency and effective communication within the broader audit framework.

Current Usage of IT by Internal Audit Teams

In this section of the study, participants were asked to respond to how their internal audit team currently use IT. Participants P7, P13, P14, P15, P16, and P18, indicated that they '*predominantly rely on Microsoft Office tools, encompassing MS Word PowerPoint and Excel, for various critical audit processes*'. This integration extends beyond mere documentation, serving as a multifaceted toolkit for carrying out audits, evaluating risks, conducting fieldwork, documenting results, and formulating recommendations to enhance risk management.

Microsoft Word is used as an instrumental tool for crafting comprehensive audit reports, ensuring clarity in communication and conciseness in presenting findings. Excel, on the other hand, facilitates intricate data analysis, enabling auditors to assess risks and perform financial modelling with precision. In parallel, responses from P3, P4, P5, and P6 shed light on the adoption of specialized tools within the Microsoft ecosystem. They indicated that '*Visio proves invaluable for creating system descriptions, aiding in the visualization of complex processes*'. Microsoft Project takes centre stage in project planning and scheduling, providing a structured approach to managing audit timelines and resources.

Furthermore, participants P7, P13, P14, P15, P16, and P18, also indicated '*a shared use of Google Docs, emphasizing collaborative document creation and real-time editing capabilities*'. Google Docs, similar to Microsoft Word, provides an online platform for collaborative writing and seamless sharing of documents. This additional layer of collaboration extends beyond the Microsoft ecosystem, showcasing the adaptability of internal audit teams to leverage multiple IT tools for effective teamwork and information sharing. The collective synchronised integration of IT tools within internal audit teams serves as the backbone for foundational tasks, ensuring efficiency and accuracy in audit processes. The incorporation of specialized tools along with shared use of Google Docs, reflects a nuanced approach, where IT is not just a support system but a tailored resource to enhance specific facets of the internal audit workflow.

Benefits of the Use of IT in Internal Audit

In this section, participants were asked to respond a question about the benefits of IT in internal audit. Participants P12, P17, P18, P19, P21, and P22 expressed the advantages derived from integrating Information Technology (IT) into the internal audit processes by indicating that '*IT can produce the product faster than handwriting and the accelerated productivity facilitated by digital tools*' reflecting a consensus on the efficiency gains associated with IT utilization. Participants P4, P5, P6, P7 indicated the intrinsic facilitation of work through IT, with a collective acknowledgment that '*IT tools make audit tasks easier*'. P5 stated that '*it definitely makes our work much easier,*' underlining the practical impact of IT in simplifying complex audit processes. This theme resonated across participants, signifying a paradigm shift in the approach to audit methodologies.

Furthermore, P2, P3, P11 stressed '*the seamless generation of reports as a key benefit of IT*'. P6 indicated that '*we can easily run reports,*' stressing the agility and responsiveness afforded by IT tools in report generation. The contribution of IT in minimizing errors within audit reports was emphasized by P6, P7, P8, and P9. P7 stated, '*we produce reports with less error, thanks to auto-correct.*' This is the role of technology in enhancing the accuracy and reliability of audit documentation. Access to information and collaborative document sharing are the other advantages, participants P1, P2, P3, P5, P9, P13, P21, and P22 stressed '*the ease with which IT facilitates these processes*'. P3 noted, '*it's easier to share information and documents,*' highlighting the collaborative nature of IT tools in facilitating transparent communication within audit teams.

The global connectivity aspect of technology was acknowledged by P5, P9, P13, emphasizing its role in transforming the audit landscape into a 'global village.' P1 articulated this by stating, '*we can easily connect to the global village due to technology,*' underlining the broadened reach of internal audit beyond geographical constraints. Importantly, participants P5, P6, P7, P10, P12, P13, P14, and P19 stated the transformative impact of Computer Assisted Audit Techniques (CAATs). P14 stated, '*CAATs assist us in our audit testing procedures and are designed to carry out tests of controls and substantive procedures,*' reiterating the strategic application of technology in enhancing audit precision.

FACTORS IN INFORMATION TECHNOLOGY USAGE FOR INTERNAL AUDIT

Organizational Factors

This section of the study provides responses given by the participants on organizational factors influencing the adoption of IT usage in internal audit. These factors encompass various elements within an organization's structure and culture. The shared values and norms constituting the organizational culture play a pivotal role, with a culture fostering innovation and technological openness supporting the seamless integration of IT. Leadership support, reflected in the endorsement and active commitment from top management, is crucial for allocating resources and establishing a culture that prioritizes the adoption of IT in internal audit. Resource availability, including financial resources, skilled personnel, and necessary infrastructure, is essential for successful IT integration, while comprehensive training programs and skills development are vital for the effective utilization of IT tools by internal audit staff. Regulatory compliance, the existing technology infrastructure, risk perceptions, and well-planned change management strategies collectively shape the organizational environment, influencing the degree to which IT is embraced and integrated into internal audit processes. In addressing these factors, responses given by participants are presented below.

P2, P6, P14, P17, P18, P122 indicated '*that Lack of support from as a significant factor influencing the adoption of IT in internal audit*'. This points to a crucial need for stronger endorsement and commitment from our leadership to drive successful integration.

P3 indicated that 'there is reluctance to change and reservations about embracing new technologies. I think that this reluctance can pose challenges to the smooth incorporation of IT into our internal audit processes.'

P9 stated that 'there is the prevailing reliance on manual methods within our internal audit practices'. This acknowledgment sheds light on the existing inertia towards transitioning from traditional to digital audit approaches.

P4 asserted that 'there is a lack of training, hampering our teams' ability to effectively use IT tools'. This underscores the need for robust training programs to bridge the knowledge gap and facilitate seamless integration.

P11 contended that 'we lack skills to use sophisticated software. This signals a crucial gap in our workforce's proficiency, hindering the optimal utilization of advanced IT solutions in our audit processes'.

P8 reported that 'there is a misunderstanding of the internal audit role and mandate by management as a key organizational factor. This misalignment in understanding poses a challenge to making informed decisions regarding the adoption and utilization of IT.'
P21 pointed out that 'there is a fear of job loss due to apprehensions associated with IT adoption. This fear can act as a barrier, potentially causing resistance among employees who perceive technology adoption as a threat to job security.'

Cultural Factors

Cultural factors influencing the adoption of IT usage in internal audit encompass the collective beliefs, values, and attitudes within an organization, shaping its approach to incorporating technology into audit processes. An innovation culture, which fosters a proactive stance towards technological advancements, facilitates seamless IT adoption, while an organization's willingness to tolerate and manage risks associated with technology plays a pivotal role. Open communication, adaptability, and a commitment to continuous improvement contribute to a positive technological culture, promoting understanding and reducing resistance to IT initiatives. Collaboration and teamwork are essential cultural aspects that create a supportive environment for technology integration within the internal audit team. Additionally, technological literacy within the organization enhances its capacity to effectively adopt and leverage IT tools. Recognizing and addressing resistance to change are crucial considerations, as a culture that acknowledges and manages resistance can facilitate a smoother transition to successful IT integration in internal audit processes. Ultimately, a positive technological culture encourages collaboration, reduces resistance, and promotes the effective utilization of IT tools for improved audit efficiency and outcomes.

P7 provided a candid insight by expressing that '*the Internal Audit function is not accorded the seriousness it deserves within the organizational culture*'. This perception hints at a potential cultural barrier that may impact the integration of IT tools, emphasizing the need for a shift in how Internal Audit is perceived and valued within the organization.

P8 indicated that 'the notion that internal audit is not taken seriously, particularly within the organizational culture. There is a potential disconnect between the internal audit function and the broader organizational context, and there is a need for a cultural shift to enhance the acceptance of internal audit significance'.

P13 pointed out 'the lack of support from management that stands as a significant barrier to the integration of IT in internal audit'. This insight into the role of management support as a crucial cultural factor influencing the successful adoption of IT tools in the audit processes.

P14 echoing that 'internal audit is not taken seriously, emphasizing the lack of support from management. There is insufficient managerial backing and signals a need for a cultural shift to elevate the status of internal audit within the organization'.

P22 indicated that '*there is disconnect between the internal audit function and the organizational culture*'. This participant's response adds weight to the collective perspective, reinforcing the need for a cultural transformation to better align internal audit with organizational priorities and values.

Technical Factors

Technical factors influencing the adoption of IT usage in internal audit refer to the specific technological aspects that play an important role in shaping the acceptance and integration of information technology tools within the audit processes of an organization. These factors encompass elements such as the perceived complexity of IT solutions, the seamless transition from existing audit systems, financial considerations related to training and implementation, psychological barriers like fear of the unknown, and the need for enhancing IT knowledge among internal audit professionals. Addressing these technical factors is crucial for successful adoption, ensuring that IT tools align with the organization's audit requirements, are user-friendly, and contribute to the efficiency and effectiveness of internal audit procedures.

Perceived Complexity

In acknowledging the complexity of information technology (IT), participants expressed a shared concern. P1 emphasized, '*IT can be too complex,*' signalling a collective need for simplified IT solutions that facilitate seamless integration. This sentiment resonated as P6 voiced similar concerns, emphasizing the importance of user-friendly solutions, stating, '*IT continue to evolve and need regular updates that may be sophisticated at times.*' Additionally, P11 underlined the challenge, stating, '*evolving nature of IT with new tools continuously coming to the market,*' and stressed the necessity for more accessible IT solutions.

Seamless Transitions

P2 indicated that '*the importance of comparability between current and previous audit systems, expressing a desire for smooth transitions: Comparability of current to previous ways of audit systems.*' This viewpoint is similar to that of P7 who emphasis that '*Comparability of current to previous ways of audit systems.*'

Financial Considerations

Financial considerations played a crucial role in participants' perspectives on IT adoption. P3 insisted on the importance of funds for training internal audit professionals in IT tools, stating that '*Funds to train internal audit in IT tools are necessary*'. Similarly, P8 reiterated the financial aspect, stating, '*there is need to put more money into the training of internal auditors in IT tools.*' These responses collectively highlight the participants' recognition of the financial investment required for successful IT integration within the internal audit processes.

Psychological Barriers

Addressing psychological barriers, participants acknowledged the fear of the unknown as a significant factor influencing IT adoption. P4 stated that '*Fear of the unknown,*' emphasizing the need to navigate and alleviate uncertainties. P9 indicated fear as well by saying that, '*we fear loss of jobs that we do not know yet because of the coming of IT. This development can be there to reduce human resources.*' This shows the importance of addressing psychological barriers to facilitate successful IT integration. These responses reveal the participants' recognition of the psychological aspects influencing their approach to IT adoption.

Importance of ITS Knowledge Enhancement

P5 indicated '*the lack of IT knowledge impacting adoption*' P10 stressed this point further, stating, '*there is a lack of IT knowledge among internal auditors,*' *which require the necessity for targeted training and skill development*'. These responses collectively emphasize the participants' acknowledgment of the need to enhance the IT proficiency of internal audit professionals to ensure effective utilization of IT tools in their audit processes.

Leadership Role

The concept of leadership in the context of the adoption and usage of information technology (IT) for internal audit refers to the influential and guiding role that organizational leaders play in navigating the incorporation of IT tools into the audit processes. It involves the way leaders shape the organizational culture, articulate a vision for technological integration, and provide the necessary resources and support to ensure a successful transition. Leadership in IT adoption encompasses creating a conducive environment for change, driving a culture of innovation, and setting clear expectations for the strategic use of technology in internal audit practices. It involves making informed decisions about investments in IT infrastructure, training programs, and creating collaborative spaces for IT experts and internal auditors to work together effectively. Leadership support and buy-in refer to the active endorsement, commitment, and approval from organizational leaders, particularly top management, regarding the adoption, implementation, and integration of specific initiatives, in this case, information technology (IT) usage within internal audit processes. In the context of internal audit, leadership support involves leaders recognizing the importance of leveraging advanced audit software, endorsing its acquisition, and ensuring that necessary resources, including funding and personnel training, are allocated. Buy-in implies leaders not only approving the adoption of IT tools but also actively championing and advocating for their use within the organization. It involves creating an organizational culture that embraces and values the integration of IT into internal audit functions, fostering an environment where technology becomes an integral part of the audit processes. Participants' responses are presented below.

P1 responded that 'the role of leadership is to secure buy-in and support for advanced audit software, vital for technological empowerment in internal audit.' P8 further indicated that the role of leadership is 'to endorse purchasing and integrating advanced audit software, enhancing internal audit processes.' P18 stresses 'the significance of securing leadership buy-in to invest in audit software, fostering an environment where IT tools become integral to internal audit.'

Financial Constraints and Strategic Planning

Financial constraints and strategic planning, within the context of internal audit and information technology (IT) usage, involve addressing limitations in financial resources through thoughtful and deliberate planning. Financial constraints refer to limitations or restrictions in the availability of funds and resources necessary for acquiring, implementing, and maintaining IT tools within internal audit processes (Smith, 2019). Strategic planning, on the other hand, refers to the systematic process of defining goals, determining the most efficient and effective ways to achieve those goals, and allocating resources accordingly (Brown & Davis, 2018). In the context of IT usage in internal audit, financial constraints and strategic planning intersect when organizations need to carefully plan and allocate their limited financial resources to support the adoption and integration of IT tools. This may involve assessing the costs associated with acquiring IT systems, training internal audit professionals, and maintaining the technology over time. Strategic planning helps organizations prioritize their IT needs, identifying key areas where technology can bring the most value to internal audit processes.

> *P5 indicated that 'despite management support, financial limitations hinder the acquisition of IT systems, necessitating strategic planning to overcome resource constraints. P12 acknowledged 'the complexity of securing funds for IT system acquisition as a key leadership responsibility, supporting internal audit's technological needs.' P16 notes that 'overcoming financial challenges through strategic leadership ensures the organization's commitment to acquiring essential IT tools for internal audit.'*

Understanding Internal Audit's Role

> *P3 stressed that 'leadership plays a paramount role in enhancing understanding of internal audit's functions, recognizing the importance of managerial comprehension in guiding successful IT adoption. Similarly, P6 responded that 'leadership comprehension of internal audit's pivotal role is crucial for the successful adoption and utilization of IT tools within the audit process. Furthermore, P13 notes that 'leadership's role extends to championing the understanding of internal audit's functions, paving the way for the seamless integration of IT tools in audit processes.'*

Communication and Advocacy

> *Good leaders know how to communicate well. P9 points out that 'securing management support for IT system acquisition requires effective communication of the benefits, emphasizing leadership's responsibility in this regard.' P14 accented that 'leadership's effective communication of the significance of internal audit positions it as a key driver for successful IT adoption.' P20 stresses that 'guiding management to understand the critical role of internal audit positions leadership to advocate for the necessary resources, ensuring successful IT adoption.'*

Strategic Vision and Technology-Driven Approach

P11 accentuates that 'leadership's recognition of the pivotal role of internal audit shapes a strategic approach to IT adoption, fostering a tech-savvy audit environment.'P15 indicated that 'leadership's endorsement of IT system acquisition resonates with the strategic vision for internal audit, ensuring seamless integration and enhanced capabilities.'P21 emphasized 'leadership's strategic endorsement of IT tools, aligning with internal audit's goals and ensuring a seamless transition toward a technology-driven audit approach.'

Commitment despite Financial Hurdles

P19 notes that 'leadership's support for IT system acquisition, despite financial hurdles, demonstrates a commitment to enhancing internal audit effectiveness' however is remains insufficient.'P22 indicated that 'navigating financial challenges through effective leadership, empowering internal audit to acquire and integrate IT tools, enhances audit capabilities.'

CHALLENGES FACED WHEN ADOPTING AND USING IT INTO INTERNAL AUDIT

In addressing the challenges related to skill and training, participants like P1 underscored concerns about the limited IT proficiency among internal audit staff. P1 expressed, "IT can be too complex," highlighting the need for comprehensive skill development initiatives. This insight emphasizes the importance of creating tailored training programs to enhance the technological capabilities of the internal audit team. Additionally, P2 contributed to this theme by emphasizing the insufficiency of existing training programs for IT integration, stating, "Funds to train IA in IT tools (21)." This underscores the requirement for robust frameworks aligning with technological advancements and strategic financial planning to ensure sustainable integration. The participant's words draw attention to the critical need for ongoing training initiatives aligned with the evolving landscape of information technology in the field of internal audit.

Skill and Training Challenges

P1 responded that 'there is limited IT proficiency among internal audit staff necessitates comprehensive skill development initiatives'. P2 also added that 'Insufficient training programs for IT integration demand robust frameworks aligning with technological advancements'. P5 indicated that 'IT tools are not a priority requires re-evaluation of organizational priorities and strategic recognition of technological significance'. P15 contended that 'Ineffective communication about the benefits of IT adoption stresses the need for clear and persuasive communication strategies'.

Organizational and Leadership

P3 stated that 'organizational resistance to adopting new technologies calls for effective change management strategies and communication remains a factor'. P4 indicated the factor of 'Inadequate financial resources for IT implementation highlight the need for strategic financial planning to ensure sustainable integration'. P8 raised concerns about 'the safety and security of information emphasize the importance of robust cybersecurity measures and data protection strategies'. P10 stressed the 'high costs associated with acquiring audit programs necessitate a thorough cost-benefit analysis and exploration of cost-effective alternatives'. P14 voiced the 'lack of a clear roadmap for IT integration requires strategic planning and phased implementation'.

User Adoption and Collaboration

P9 mentioned 'resistance from some internal audit team members emphasizes the need for targeted communication and training programmes'. P20 responded that there is 'resistance from audit staff due to perceived complexity highlights the importance of user-friendly interfaces and comprehensive training'.

Technical and Integration

P7 responded that they face 'challenges related to expired licenses for IT software underscore the importance of robust license management protocols'. P11 reported that there is 'Incompatibility with existing audit processes that requires a strategic realignment of workflows for seamless integration'. P12 stated that they experience 'difficulty in aligning IT with specific audit objectives that necessitates defining clear objectives and mapping IT functionalities'.

Awareness and Collaboration

P13 said that there is a 'limited accessibility of relevant IT resources emphasizes the need for centralized repositories and accessible tools. P18 stressed 'the insufficient awareness about the potential of IT tools calls for comprehensive training programs and awareness campaigns'. P19 stated the 'difficulty in measuring the return on investment for IT that emphasizes the need for robust metrics and evaluation frameworks.

INFORMATION TECHNOLOGY USAGE IN INTERNAL AUDIT STRATEGIC ASPECTS

This section presents the data from participants when they were asked to respond to questions related to strategic aspects of information technology usage for internal audit. Strategic Aspects of Information Technology Usage for Internal Audit revolves around the intentional and systematic incorporation of information technology (IT) into the broader strategic framework of an organization's internal audit function. It entails aligning IT initiatives with the goals and objectives of the internal audit, contributing to the achievement of strategic outcomes. This involves strategic planning, where IT tools are not merely adopted for their own sake but are strategically integrated to enhance the efficiency, effectiveness, and value of internal audit processes. Strategic aspects also encompass considering the long-term impact of IT adoption, ensuring that technology aligns with organizational objectives, and contributes to improved risk management, compliance, and audit performance. In essence, the strategic aspects emphasize the deliberate integration of IT into the organizational and audit strategy, recognizing it as a key enabler rather than an isolated tool.

Technical Aspects

Technical aspects in IT usage in internal audit encompass a multifaceted approach to optimizing audit processes within an organization. This involves seamless system integration, robust cybersecurity measures, and compatibility with diverse file formats. Technologies such as Robotic Process Automation (RPA), and machine learning contribute to a dynamic and responsive audit framework. Cloud-based solutions, mobile applications, and user-friendly interfaces modernize audit practices, fostering flexibility and accessibility. Predictive analytics and advanced encryption ensure a forward-looking and secure approach. Two-factor authentication and data anonymization enhance data protection and privacy standards. IT governance frameworks ensure regulatory compliance, while software updates and patch management maintain system reliability. Audit analytics tools and Natural Language Processing (NLP) facilitate sophisticated data analysis and interpretation, and a scalable IT infrastructure accommodates evolving organizational needs. Digital signatures provide a secure method for document authentication, collectively enhancing efficiency, security, and effectiveness in internal audit.

Technical Integration and Compatibility

P1 'One crucial technical aspect in IT usage for internal audit involves seamless integration with existing systems. This ensures data consistency and facilitates a holistic approach to auditing processes. A robust integration strategy enhances efficiency and accuracy, providing a comprehensive overview for auditors'.
P4 'Compatibility with various file formats is crucial for seamless data exchange within the internal audit ecosystem. A versatile IT system that supports different file formats promotes interoperability and facilitates collaboration among audit team members'.
P8 'Cloud-based solutions play a pivotal role in modernizing IT usage for internal audit. Enabling remote access and collaboration, these solutions enhance flexibility and efficiency, facilitating seamless communication and information sharing among audit team members'.
P18 'Adopting a scalable IT infrastructure is crucial for future expansion and growth in internal audit. A scalable framework accommodates evolving organizational needs, ensuring that the IT system remains adaptable and responsive to changing audit requirements'.
P20 'Integration with enterprise resource planning (ERP) systems is a strategic technical aspect in IT usage for internal audit. This integration streamlines data flow and enhances the synchronization of audit processes with broader organizational functions, fostering cohesion and efficiency'.

Cybersecurity and Data Protection

P2 'An essential consideration is the implementation of robust cybersecurity measures to safeguard sensitive information during internal audit activities. Ensuring the confidentiality, integrity, and availability of data is paramount to maintaining the trust and credibility of the audit processes'.
P11 'Advanced encryption techniques are paramount for ensuring data protection in internal audit. Implementing robust encryption methods safeguards sensitive information, mitigating the risk of unauthorized access and maintaining the confidentiality of audit-related data'.

P13 'Implementation of two-factor authentication adds an additional layer of security to internal audit systems. This ensures that only authorized personnel can access critical audit-related information, reinforcing the integrity and confidentiality of the audit processes'.
P16 'Data anonymization techniques contribute to privacy preservation within internal audit. By anonymizing sensitive information, auditors can uphold confidentiality standards, comply with privacy regulations, and instil trust in stakeholders regarding the responsible handling of data'.

Mobility and Accessibility

P15 'Regular software updates and patch management are vital for maintaining the reliability and security of internal audit systems. This proactive approach mitigates vulnerabilities, enhances system stability, and ensures that the audit process operates on the latest technological advancements'.
P21 'Developing user-friendly interfaces is critical for ensuring ease of operation within internal audit systems. A user-centric design enhances the accessibility of IT tools, empowering auditors to navigate and utilize the system efficiently, ultimately contributing to a seamless audit experience'.

Transparency and Reliability

P9 'The application of data visualization tools is crucial for clear and insightful reporting. Transforming complex data into visual representations allows auditors to comprehend and communicate findings more effectively, fostering better decision-making within the organization'.
P14 'Integrating IT governance frameworks is essential for ensuring compliance assurance within internal audit. Adhering to established governance frameworks provides a structured approach, aligning IT practices with organizational objectives and regulatory requirements'.
P22 'Implementation of digital signatures for document authentication is a key technical aspect within internal audit. Digital signatures enhance the authenticity and integrity of audit-related documents, providing a secure and verifiable method for validating the origin and content of critical information'.

IT Usage in Internal Audit Enhance the Sustainability

Environmental Impact and Paper Reduction

P1 'Adopting IT minimizes paper usage, aiding environmental sustainability efforts'.
P4 'Efficient reporting through IT systems not only streamlines the audit process but also supports a more sustainable and eco-friendly approach'.
P7 'Shifting to IT diminishes reliance on paper, contributing significantly to the reduction of global warming'.
P12 'Digital documents eliminate the risk of loss, contributing to a more sustainable audit process'.
P18 'Digital processes reduce the need for physical documentation, supporting environmental sustainability'.

Efficiency and Resource Consumption

P2 'Streamlining audit processes with IT not only enhances efficiency but also significantly reduces resource consumption'.
P13 'Increased productivity and efficiency are achieved through seamless IT integration'.
P14 'Simplifying tasks with IT reduces the environmental footprint of internal audit processes'.
P15 'Quick access to information through IT enhances the speed and efficiency of audits'.
P20 'Real-time access to information reduces the need for redundant data collection and analysis'.

Risk Management and Resilience

P3 'IT integration within internal audit processes plays a pivotal role in mitigating risks and elevating efficiency'.
P21 'Integration of IT allows for proactive risk management, contributing to sustainability'.

Human-Centric Approach and Culture

P6 'Freed from data collection, auditors leveraging IT can dedicate more time to consultative and strategic aspects, fostering a sustainable audit approach'.
P11 'Employee education on IT benefits at an environmental level supports sustainability goals'.
P17 'Facilitated learning through IT tools contributes to a knowledgeable and adaptive audit workforce'.

Financial Sustainability and Investment in IT

P8 'Cost savings from reduced paper usage can be redirected to invest in advanced IT systems, fostering sustainability'.
P9 'Energy-efficient IT solutions contribute to sustainability by lowering overall energy consumption in audit processes'.

Remote Access and Collaboration

P16 'Breaking the distance barrier with IT facilitates remote audit processes, reducing travel-related environmental impact'.
P19 'Enhanced collaboration through IT minimizes the need for extensive resource-intensive meetings'.

SOLUTIONS AND RECOMMENDATIONS

Solution includes adopting the proposed Strategic Tech Sustainability Framework for enhancing public sector sustainability.

Table 2. Proposed strategic tech sustainability framework

Vision	**Utilize IT to empower internal audit for sustainable governance**
Mission	Integrate IT as a core enabler within internal audit
Goals	1. Seamless IT integration 2. Sustainable practices 3. Enhanced collaboration
Initiatives	1. IT proficiency programs 2. Innovation hub 3. Cybersecurity protocols
Resource Allocation	Finance for IT infrastructure - Invest in human capital
Monitoring & Evaluation	Key Performance Indicator (KPI)s for IT integration & efficiency - Regular audits
Change Management	Stakeholder engagement to address resistance
Continuous Improvement	Feedback mechanisms Adapt to new technologies
Compliance	Regular assessments
Reporting	Integrate sustainability metrics

The Strategic Tech Sustainability framework provides a roadmap for leveraging information technology to enhance sustainability, efficiency, and transparency within internal audit practices in the public sector. It establishes a vision for empowering governance through IT along with a mission to integrate technology as a core enabler. The framework sets goals, initiatives, and resource plans to seamlessly incorporate IT tools and methodologies into audit processes while minimizing environmental impact. Implementing key performance indicators, regular audits, and stakeholder engagement, the model enables continuous assessment and improvement of IT integration. It also ensures alignment with regulations and reporting on sustainability outcomes. This comprehensive strategic framework integrates IT across people, processes and systems to optimize internal audits and promote sustainable public sector governance.

Solutions include:

1. Providing proactive leadership and commitment from top management are crucial for driving successful IT adoption, recognizing the transformative impact of technology on internal audit processes. This will facilitate a smooth transition to digital audit approaches, organizations should implement comprehensive training programs, addressing factors such as resistance to change and reliance on manual methods.
2. Continuous skill development through ongoing training initiatives is essential, particularly focusing on enhancing the proficiency of internal audit staff in utilizing foundational tools like Microsoft Excel, Word, Visio, and Project for purposes beyond their traditional roles. Emphasizing the collaborative features of tools like Google Docs, organizations should maximize teamwork dynamics within internal audit teams, aligning with literature-supported collaborative approaches.
3. Adopt a strategic approach to financial planning, ensuring adequate resources for IT integration, and addressing challenges related to financial constraints. Strategic planning and financial investment in IT infrastructure are deemed essential, ensuring scalability to accommodate evolving audit needs and supporting the long-term goals of the internal audit function.
4. Active engagement in effective communication strategies is recommended to address fears of job loss and reluctance to change, emphasizing the long-term benefits and career development opportunities associated with embracing IT in internal audit. Organizations are recommended to explore and invest in advanced IT solutions, including Computer Assisted Audit Techniques (CAATs), to capitalize on their transformative impact, ensuring precision in audit testing and staying at the forefront of technological advancements.

5. Integrate IT initiatives with the broader organizational strategy, emphasizing the intentional and systematic incorporation of IT into the internal audit framework through strategic planning. Consider the long-term impact of IT adoption, ensuring alignment with organizational objectives, and contributing to improved risk management, compliance, and audit performance. Focus on seamless system integration, robust cybersecurity measures, compatibility with diverse file formats, and the adoption of technologies like Robotic Process Automation (RPA) and machine learning to optimize audit processes.
6. Prioritize cloud-based solutions, mobile applications, user-friendly interfaces, predictive analytics, advanced encryption, two-factor authentication, data anonymization, IT governance frameworks, software updates, patch management, audit analytics tools, Natural Language Processing (NLP), digital signatures, and a scalable IT infrastructure for enhanced efficiency, security, and effectiveness in internal audit.
7. Prioritize regular software updates, patch management, and user-friendly interfaces for maintaining the reliability and security of internal audit systems. Ensure effective utilization of data visualization tools, IT governance frameworks, digital signatures for document authentication, and digital processes to ensure clear reporting, compliance assurance, and a secure method for validating critical information.

FUTURE RESEARCH DIRECTIONS

Some of the future research focus areas, building upon the insights derived from the strategic aspects, technical integration, and sustainability of Information Technology (IT) usage in internal audit include

- Investigate the long-term organizational impact of strategic IT integration in internal audit, exploring how alignment with broader organizational goals influences sustained efficiency and effectiveness. Examine the role of IT in promoting innovation within internal audit, considering its potential to drive strategic decision-making and contribute to the overall agility of the audit function.
- Explore emerging technologies and their applicability to internal audit, delving into the potential of artificial intelligence, blockchain, and other cutting-edge solutions in optimizing audit processes. Assess the challenges and benefits associated with the integration of diverse IT tools, focusing on interoperability issues, user adoption challenges, and the evolving landscape of IT security.

- Conduct in-depth studies on the environmental impact of IT adoption in internal audit, considering factors such as carbon footprint reduction, electronic waste management, and sustainable practices in IT infrastructure. Investigate the long-term financial implications of sustainable IT practices within internal audit, exploring how investments in eco-friendly technologies contribute to both environmental and financial sustainability.
- Explore the intersectionality of IT integration in internal audit with other organizational functions, such as finance, human resources, and compliance, to understand how IT can serve as a cross-functional enabler. Investigate the role of organizational culture in shaping the success of IT integration in internal audit, considering cultural factors that promote or hinder innovation and technological advancement.
- Conduct cross-cultural and cross-national studies to analyse variations in IT adoption practices in internal audit, considering factors such as regulatory environments, cultural nuances, and technological infrastructure across different regions. Explore best practices and lessons learned from organizations that have successfully implemented IT in internal audit, providing insights that can guide others in similar endeavours.

CONCLUSION

Information Technology (IT) usage in internal audit is multifaceted, revealing several insights. Firstly, strategic aspects highlight the need for intentional and systematic IT incorporation into the broader organizational strategy, recognizing it as a key enabler for enhanced efficiency, effectiveness, and value in internal audit processes. The technical aspects underscore the diverse tools and methodologies present in the Namibian internal audit landscape, emphasizing seamless integration, robust cybersecurity, and the adoption of advanced technologies. Secondly, the current state of IT usage showcases the foundational role of Microsoft Excel and Word, transforming audit processes and emphasizing the central role of IT in augmenting auditor performance. Lastly, factors affecting IT usage, encompassing organizational, cultural, technical, and leadership dimensions, elucidate the challenges and opportunities in IT integration. The study concludes with pragmatic recommendations, providing organizations a roadmap to navigate these complexities, foster innovation, and strategically embrace IT advancements for a more efficient and effective internal audit landscape. Furthermore, exploration of technical integration and compatibility reveals the critical importance of seamless system integration, robust cybersecurity measures, and the adoption of technologies such as Robotic Process Automation (RPA) and machine learning. Cybersecurity and data protection emerge as paramount considerations, emphasizing the need for advanced encryption techniques, two-factor authentication, and data anonymization to safeguard sensitive information during internal audit activities. Additionally, the study sheds light on mobility and accessibility, underscoring the significance of regular software updates, patch management, and user-friendly interfaces for maintaining the reliability and security of internal audit systems. Transparency and reliability are addressed through recommendations for data visualization tools, IT governance frameworks, digital signatures, and digital processes, all contributing to clear reporting and compliance assurance. It also emphasizes that IT usage in internal audit has a positive impact on sustainability. From reducing paper usage and streamlining audit processes to enhancing remote access and collaboration, IT is positioned as a key contributor to environmental and financial sustainability. The recommendations further highlight the potential redirection of cost savings from reduced paper usage towards investing in advanced IT systems.

ACKNOWLEDGMENT

The author acknowledges Ms. Jessica Jones Veii, MBA Graduate of HPGSB, Namibia University of Science and Technology, Namibia for contribution to data collection and analysis.

REFERENCES

Abdullahi, A. S., Haron, H., & Taib, C. M. (2018). The use of information technology in the internal audit process: An exploratory study in the Nigerian public sector. *Journal of Accounting. Finance and Auditing Studies*, *4*(1), 51–68.

Abdullahi, M. H., Abdul, R. M., & Arif, A. (2018). Factors influencing the adoption of information technology in public sector auditing: Evidence from Nigeria. *Journal of Information Systems and Technology Management*, *15*(1), 3–20.

Addo, H., & Boateng, R. (2016). Internal audit effectiveness, IT infrastructure capability, and financial reporting quality. *Journal of Accounting in Emerging Economies*, *6*(1), 4–25.

Akhigbe, R., Amos, K., & Adeoti-Adekeye, B. (2018). The impact of information technology on internal auditing: A comparative analysis of banks in Nigeria. *Journal of Internet Banking and Commerce*, *23*(2), 1–22.

Alemayehu, M., & Molla, A. (2017). Understanding the determinants of mobile health acceptance and its impact on health information systems' success: A structural equation modeling approach. *Government Information Quarterly*, *34*(1), 93–104.

Alles, M., & Brennan, G. (2016). The impact of robotic process automation on the internal audit function. *Journal of Information Systems*, *30*(3), 21–44.

Alles, M., & Brennan, N. (2016). The use of data analytics in the internal audit setting: An extended discussion. *Journal of Information Systems*, *30*(2), 111–124.

Alles, M., & Kogan, A. (2020). *Transforming the Internal Audit Function: The Journey to Continuous Assurance*. ISACA.

Alles, M. G., & Brennan, G. (2016). The promise of big data and analytics in the accounting, auditing, and finance professions: Opportunities and challenges. *Journal of Accounting Research*, *54*(4), 1085–1091.

Alles, M. G., & Kogan, A. (2020). Robotic Process Automation (RPA) in auditing: A field study. *Journal of Emerging Technologies in Accounting*, *17*(2), 45–55.

Almarabeh, T., Abuhashesh, M., & Alsmadi, I. (2017). Investigating e-Government Services Adoption from Citizens' Perspective: A Structural Equation Modeling Approach. *Information Development*, *33*(5), 452–468.

Anderson, S. (2022). Financial Sustainability and IT Investment: A Guide for Internal Audit. *Financial Strategy Journal*, *40*(1), 45–61.

Arens, A. A., Elder, R. J., Beasley, M. S., & Hogan, C. E. (2019). *Auditing and assurance services: An integrated approach* (17th ed.). Pearson.

Auditor-General of Namibia. (2017). *Annual Report 2016/2017.*

Avraamidou, M., & Karacapilidis, N. (2016). A constructivist evaluation framework for ICT-based design for sustainability. *Sustainable Production and Consumption, 8*, 161–176.

Babbie, E. R. (2016). *The Basics of Social Research.* Cengage Learning.

Barnett, J., Lambert, S., & Fry, I. (2019). The Hazards of Indicators: Insights from the Environmental Vulnerability Index. *Annals of the Association of American Geographers, 109*(3), 713–728.

Barney, J. (1991). Firm resources and sustained competitive advantage. *Journal of Management, 17*(1), 99–120. DOI: 10.1177/014920639101700108

Black, R., & Green, E. (2019). Data Anonymization Techniques in Modern Internal Audit. *Privacy and Security Journal, 27*(4), 89–104.

Brown, A., & Davis, C. (2018). *Strategic Management: A Competitive Advantage Approach, Concepts and Cases.* Pearson.

Brown, A., & Miller, J. (2018). Maximizing Audit Efficiency through IT Integration. *Journal of Information Systems, 25*(2), 45–62.

Brown, C., & Miller, D. (2020). The role of Information Technology in enhancing internal audit in the public sector. *Public Administration Review, 75*(2), 210–228.

Brown, S., & Smith, P. (2020). Fostering an Innovative Organizational Culture for IT Adoption in Internal Audit. *Journal of Audit Innovation, 15*(2), 89–105.

Bwalya, K. J., Akande, T. O., & Lubinda, J. B. (2020). Impact of information technology in the internal audit of public institutions in Zambia: A case of selected government ministries. *Journal of Economics and Behavioral Studies, 12*(1), 82–97.

Bwalya, K. J., Chileshe, N., & Lubinda, C. K. (2020). IT Adoption in Public Sector Internal Auditing: Evidence from African Countries. *Journal of Finance and Management in Public Services, 1*(2), 25–42.

Bwalya, K. J., Kalungu-Banda, A., & Samujh, H. (2020). Factors influencing the adoption of information technology in public sector internal audit in Africa: Evidence from Zambia. *Journal of Information Systems, 34*(1), 27–49.

Chan, D. Y., Hancock, J., & Rice, S. (2018). *A 21st Century Imperative: The Use of Data Analytics in Internal Auditing.* ISACA Journal.

Chan, Y. E., & Reich, B. H. (2018). IT alignment in public sector organizations: A literature review. *Journal of Information Technology, 33*(4), 287–311.

Chang, A. (2018). Cultural Adaptation and IT Integration in Internal Audit: A Case Study Approach. *Journal of Information Systems, 22*(4), 176–195.

Chen, S. (2021). Technological Integration in Internal Audit: Best Practices and Strategies. *IT and Management Journal, 15*(4), 78–93.

Chen, S. (2022). Challenges and strategies in implementing IT in public sector auditing: A case study analysis. *Public Finance Management, 25*(1), 78–94.

Chen, X., Lu, Y., & Wang, B. (2019). A social constructivist perspective on organizational environmental sustainability practices. *Organization & Environment, 32*(1), 57–76.

Chinyamurindi, W., & Shale, K. (2017). Challenges of information technology adoption in internal audit in South Africa. *Southern African Journal of Accountability and Auditing Research, 19*(1), 1–16.

Chinyamurindi, W., & Shale, S. (2017). Internal Audit Function in the Public Sector: A South African Perspective. *African Journal of Economic and Management Studies, 8*(2), 250–266.

Ciborra, C. U. (2002). *The labyrinths of information: Challenging the wisdom of systems*. Oxford University Press.

Clark, R., & Turner, H. (2021). Remote Work and Collaborative Practices in Auditing: A Post-Pandemic Perspective. *Journal of Remote Collaboration, 28*(2), 89–105.

Deloitte. (2021). *2021 Global Internal Audit Survey*. Deloitte Development LLC.

Dixon, R., & Woodhead, A. (2017). Continuous auditing: A literature review. *Journal of Accounting Literature, 39*, 18–48.

Du, Y., Wang, X., & Liu, L. (2017). Big data in auditing research: Current status and future trends. *Journal of Accounting and Economics, 64*(2-3), 478–505.

Eom, S. J., Lee, H. N., & Rho, J. J. (2016). Factors affecting smartphone adoption for accessing government services in South Korea. *Government Information Quarterly, 33*(4), 667–680.

EY. (2021). *Reimagining internal audit in financial services*. EY Global Services Limited.

Foth, M., Brynskov, M., & Ojala, T. (2016). *Citizen's Right to the Digital City: Urban Interfaces, Activism, and Placemaking*. Springer.

Garcia, A., & Chen, R. (2018). Transformative impact of IT on internal audit processes. *Journal of Organizational Technology*, *25*(3), 123–145.

Garcia, A., & Chen, R. (2019). Overcoming Technical Barriers: Enhancing IT Knowledge among Internal Auditors. *International Journal of Auditing Technology*, *18*(3), 112–130.

Garcia, E., Martin, T., Johnson, L., & Williams, R. (2021). Information Technology adoption in the public sector: A comprehensive review. *Government Information Quarterly*, *38*(4), 101052.

Garson, D. (2006). *Public information technology and e-governance: Managing the virtual state*. Jones & Bartlett Learning.

Guldbrandsson, K., Hall, H., & Lindhult, E. (2019). Smart City in Progress: A Study of Smart City Development in the Making. *Journal of Urban Technology*, *26*(4), 1–22.

Gupta, P., Schermann, M., & Mohan, R. (2016). Internal Audit in the 21st Century: Challenges and Opportunities. *Journal of Accounting, Auditing & Finance*, *31*(3), 343–349.

Gupta, R., & Sharma, V. (2017). Machine Learning in Internal Audit: A Comprehensive Review. *Journal of Intelligent Auditing*, *30*(3), 101–118.

Heeks, R. (2017). Information and Communication Technology (ICT) and the Sustainable Development Goals (SDGs): A Fast Track Roadmap. *Institute for Development Policy and Management Working Paper*, 1-31.

Huang, C. L. (2017). An empirical investigation of factors influencing the effectiveness of internal audit in Taiwanese firms. *International Journal of Auditing*, *21*(1), 36–47.

IFAC. (2021). *ISA 315 (Revised), Identifying and Assessing the Risks of Material Misstatement Through Understanding the Entity and Its Environment*. International Auditing and Assurance Standards Board.

Institute of Internal Auditors (IIA). (2020). [*Internal Audit Emerging Stronger Post-Crisis*. IIA Global.]. *COVID*, •••, 19.

Institute of Internal Auditors (IIA). (2021). *Global Technology Audit Guide (GTAG) series*. https://na.theiia.org/standards-guidance/Public%20Documents/GTAG%20Document.pdf

Institute of Internal Auditors (IIA). (2021). *Insights on Building Trust Through Internal Audit*. IIA Global.

ISACA. (2021). *State of Cybersecurity 2021: Part 3: Cybersecurity Culture*. ISACA.

Issa, H., Sun, T., & Vasarhelyi, M. A. (2016). Research ideas for artificial intelligence in auditing: The formalization of audit and workforce supplementation. *Journal of Emerging Technologies in Accounting, 13*(2), 1–20. DOI: 10.2308/jeta-10511

Johnson, L., & Smith, P. (2021). Employee perception and engagement with sustainability-driven information technology initiatives in the public sector. *Public Administration Review, 81*(3), 380–391.

Johnson, M. (2019). Leadership Support and IT Adoption: A Comprehensive Study in Internal Audit. *Journal of Organizational Technology, 26*(1), 45–63.

Johnson, M., & Brown, S. (2019). Adaptability of Microsoft Office applications in Namibian internal audit. *International Journal of Auditing Technology, 18*(2), 67–84.

Johnson, R., & White, L. (2018). Integrating IT and internal audit for enhanced public sector performance. *International Journal of Public Administration, 41*(7), 561–578.

Jones, L., & Smith, P. (2022). Contemporary communication needs within audit teams. *Communication in Organizational Environments, 30*(4), 321–340.

Jones, M. (2020). Strategic Alignment of IT in Internal Audit: A Contemporary Perspective. *Journal of IT Governance, 18*(1), 34–50.

Jones, P., & Johnson, P. (2020). *Strategic Management: An Integrated Approach.* Routledge.

Kakabadse, A., Kakabadse, N. K., & McGowan, C. (2019). E-procurement Systems Adoption in Developing Countries: The Case of Ghana. *Electronic Government, an International Journal, 16*(4), 318-333.

Kashona, S. (2019). The effectiveness of internal control and internal audit in fraud detection and prevention: A case study of Ministry of Finance-Namibia (*Doctoral dissertation, University of Namibia).*

Kinene, M. J. (2017). Influence of information and communication technology on performance of financial audits in government ministries in Kenya. (*Master's Thesis, Kenyatta University*).

KPMG. (2020). *The Future of Audit. KPMG International Cooperative*. KPMG International Cooperative.

KPMG. (2021). *Evolving Internal Audit: A Data & Analytics Perspective*. KPMG International Cooperative.

Lee, K. (2020). Driving Successful IT Adoption: The Role of Leadership in Internal Audit. *Journal of Information Technology Integration, 25*(2), 78–95.

Lee, K., & Wang, Q. (2018). Efficiency gains associated with IT tools in internal audit. *Journal of Information Systems, 15*(1), 56–78.

Lu, J., & Yang, Y. (2020). Government social media, public participation, and environmental sustainability: Evidence from China. *Government Information Quarterly, 37*(3), 101479.

Marshall, C., & Rossman, G. B. (2016). *Designing qualitative research.* Sage publications.

Maxwell, J. A., & Miller, B. A. (2018). Categorizing and connecting strategies in qualitative data analysis. In *Handbook of qualitative research* (pp. 743–760). Sage publications.

Mihret, D. G., & Yismaw, A. W. (2017). The role of organizational support in the adoption of information technology in the public sector. *International Journal of Accounting & Information Management*, 25(2), 217–235.

Miller, B., & White, L. (2017). Challenges in IT Adoption and Usage in Internal Audit: A Survey Analysis. *Technology and Audit Practice, 14*(4), 210–230.

Miller, P., & Johnson, L. (2016). Ensuring Reliability in Internal Audit Systems: The Role of Regular Software Updates. *Journal of Reliability Engineering, 21*(2), 56–72.

Pardo, T. A., & Tayi, G. K. (2017). Introducing Blockchain Technology for the Information Management Profession. *Proceedings of the Association for Information Science and Technology, 54*(1), 24–32.

Patel, A. (2021). Navigating Technical Challenges: A Study of IT Adoption in Internal Audit *Processes.Journal of Information Systems, 19*(2), 89–107.

Patel, A. (2021). Pivotal role of Microsoft Visio and Project in internal audit. *Journal of Information Technology Integration, 22*(4), 189–207.

PwC. (2020). *Internal Audit in 2020 and Beyond.* PricewaterhouseCoopers LLP.

PwC. (2021). *Technology Trends 2021: Internal Audit.* PricewaterhouseCoopers LLP.

Sachs, J. D., Schmidt-Traub, G., Kroll, C., Lafortune, G., & Fuller, G. (2019). *Sustainable development report 2019.* Bertelsmann Stiftung and Sustainable Development Solutions Network.

Saldana, J. (2016). The coding manual for qualitative researchers. *Sage (Atlanta, Ga.).*

Saunders, M., Lewis, P., & Thornhill, A. (2018). *Research methods for business students*.

Scholl, H. J. (2013). E-government success factors: Mapping practical tools to theoretical foundations. *Government Information Quarterly*, *30*(2), 142–151.

Schuppan, T. (2019). Factors influencing the diffusion of electronic procurement in German local governments. *Government Information Quarterly*, *36*(1), 120–127.

Shareef, M. A., Dwivedi, Y. K., Kumar, V., & Kumar, U. (2020). Digital government maturity model for measuring and managing digital transformation. *Government Information Quarterly*, *37*(3), 101496.

Sikopo, L., & Dube, T. (2018). The impact of information technology integration on public sector service delivery: A case study of Namibia. *The Southern African Journal of Accountability and Auditing Research*, *19*(1), 37–56.

Smith, A., & Johnson, B. (2019). Public sector sustainability: Emerging trends and challenges. *Journal of Public Policy*, *45*(3), 301–318.

Smith, A., Johnson, B., Williams, C., Davis, D., Wilson, E., Anderson, F., & Taylor, Z. (2021). The impact of Information Technology on public sector sustainability: A systematic review. *Sustainability*, *13*(7), 3659.

Smith, A., Jones, B., & Brown, C. (2020). Constructivist research philosophy in the context of IT adoption for sustainability in government organizations. *Journal of Public Administration: Research and Theory*, *30*(3), 455–470.

Smith, J. (2019). *Financial Management: Principles and Applications*. Pearson.

Smith, J., & Johnson, A. (2022). Recognizing the Pivotal Role of Internal Audit: A Leadership Perspective on IT Adoption. *International Journal of Auditing Technology*, *21*(1), 56–74.

Smith, J., & Taylor, D. (2020). Foundational role of Microsoft Excel and Word in internal auditing systems. *Journal of Audit Innovation*, *12*(3), 112–130.

Smith, K. (2017). Environmental Sustainability through IT Adoption: Lessons from Internal Audit Practices. *Sustainability Management Review*, *12*(4), 67–84.

Smith, R., & Johnson, A. (2021). Strategic application of technology in enhancing audit accuracy. *Technology and Audit Practice*, *8*(2), 45–67.

Sullivan, G. M. (2017). A primer on the validity of assessment instruments. *Journal of Graduate Medical Education*, *9*(2), 145–147. PMID: 22655129

The Auditor-General of Namibia. (2017). *Report of the Auditor-General on the performance audit of information technology governance in selected government ministries for the period ended 31 March 2017*. Office of the Auditor-General, Republic of Namibia.

UN DESA. (2018). *Public Administration Innovation and Sustainable Development*. United Nations.

UN DESA. (2018). *Public Administration Innovation and Sustainable Development*. UN.

United Nations. (2018). The Impact of Digital Transformation on Sustainable Development. *United Nations Department of Economic and Social Affairs*, 1-51.

United Nations. (2020). *E-Government Survey 2020: Digital Government in the Decade of Action for Sustainable Development*. United Nations Department of Economic and Social Affairs.

Venkatesh, V., & Davis, F. D. (2000). A theoretical extension of the Technology Acceptance Model: Four longitudinal field studies. *Management Science*, *46*(2), 186–204. DOI: 10.1287/mnsc.46.2.186.11926

Wang, J. (2020). User-Centric Design in Internal Audit Systems. *Human-Computer Interaction Journal*, *35*(1), 120–136.

West, D. M. (2019). Blockchain for government: Benefits and implications of distributed ledger technology for information sharing. *Government Information Quarterly*, *36*(3), 434–440.

White, L. (2018). Cybersecurity Measures for Ensuring Data Protection in Internal Audit. *Cybersecurity Review*, *22*(3), 112–129.

KEY TERMS AND DEFINITIONS

Internal Audit: The independent, objective assurance and consulting activity designed to add value and improve an organization's operations. In the context of this study, it pertains specifically to government internal audit functions.

Information Technology (IT): The use of computer systems, software, and networks to store, process, and transmit data. In this study, IT refers to the digital tools and systems used in internal audit processes.

Public Sector Sustainability: The ability of government entities and organizations within the public sector to effectively fulfil their responsibilities and functions while ensuring long-term environmental, social, and economic well-being.

Chapter 4
Leveraging Technology for Sustainable Economic Growth:
Advancing the SDGs Through Innovation

Ananya Pandey
https://orcid.org/0000-0002-2419-6314
Christ University, India

Jipson Joseph
https://orcid.org/0009-0005-1795-5051
Christ University, India

Manshu Goyal
https://orcid.org/0009-0006-9377-2369
Independent Researcher, India

ABSTRACT

Raising long-term competitiveness of national economies is an important requirement with the broad use of digital technologies. In addition to offering the possibility of economic restructuring, information and communication technologies open up new avenues for all citizens to access a range of services, such as first-rate healthcare and education. As a result, these developments promote inclusive growth and significantly aid in the achievement of the UN Sustainable Development Goals (SDGs). Significant economic changes that raise living standards and boost global competitiveness can be sparked by the promise of digital transformation within a framework of sustainable development. Keeping in view the above, the chapter

DOI: 10.4018/979-8-3693-8477-0.ch004

thoroughly examines practical and theoretical frameworks pertaining to the application of sustainable development, as well as an assessment of the possibilities for using digital technologies to promote sustainable competitiveness. The relationship between digital inclusion and its long-term effects on global economic development is also analyzed.

INTRODUCTION

In the continuous pursuit of world development, the nexus of environmental sustainability and technology constitutes a crucial frontier. Climate change, pollution, and resource depletion are just a few of the environmental issues that have become more urgent in recent years. With its creative ways to slow down environmental damage and foster long-term resilience, technology has become a ray of hope as humanity struggles with the effects of unsustainable habits. Meeting the needs of the current generation without sacrificing the capacity of future generations to meet their own needs is the fundamental goal of sustainable development (WCED, 1987). In this regard, technology has a dual function, acting as a force for advancement and a catalyst for change. In the present scenario, innovation and sustainability are core elements of almost all firms. Even though the definition of sustainable development was first proposed in the 1980s, environmental issues and climate change have made it even more crucial to alter how one manufactures and uses new things. Many nations around the world have social and economic challenges in addition to environmental issues. Using knowledge to develop new technologies that address the above-mentioned issues is one approach to overcoming such obstacles. In both domestic and foreign markets, innovation is crucial (Siriram, 2022). It contributes to economic progress while offering innovative answers to pressing issues. Through the development of new goods, services, and sectors, innovation broadens marketplaces. Also, considering the effects of the digital revolution, advancements in telecommunications and information technology (IT) have not only revolutionized preexisting industries but also given rise to completely new ones like finance, social media, and e-commerce (Radicic & Petković, 2023). These emerging sectors increase economic diversification, create jobs, and attract investment, all of which make nations more resilient to shocks from around the world.

In light of the above perspective, this chapter explores the role of technology for promoting sustainable development and economic growth. Parallelly, it also explores the advancements of Sustainable Development Goals (SDGs) with the emerging innovations and rapid advancement in technology.

INTERSECTION OF TECHNOLOGY AND SUSTAINABILITY

The UN defined sustainability as "meeting the needs of the present without compromising the ability of future generations to meet their own needs" (WCED, 1987). The 1992 Rio de Janeiro Earth Summit affirmed that the concept sustainability has three pillars like economic, social, and environmental leading to three areas of sustainability studies like economic sustainability, social sustainability and environmental sustainability (Patterson, 2022). Economic development that aims to meet human needs while preserving the environment and natural resources for future generations is known as sustainable economic growth. To guarantee that these resources are available to future generations, it entails managing and keeping an eye on them (Purvis et al., 2019). It entails keeping economic growth at a pace that does not lead to pricing pressure, resource depletion, or major environmental harm. By economic growth, the present society understands a sustained increase in the gross domestic product (GDP). Maintaining the growth rate without creating additional economic issues is known as sustainable growth (Groner & Moradi, 2024). Rapid expansion can lead to resource depletion, environmental issues, and global warming. The process by which the exploitation of natural resources, investment direction, technological development direction, and institutional change or reform are all coordinated and harmonious and improve the present and future capacity to meet human needs is known as sustainable economic development (Nijkamp et al., 1990). In the long term, economic development is ineffective and inefficient without sustainability.

Key Principles of Technological Innovation with Sustainability

Sustainable innovation generates advantages for the environment, society, and economy through the creation of new, more sustainable goods, services, and business models than the ones that are now available. Some of the key principles mentioned below are crucial to be taken into account while discussing technological innovation with sustainability.

Eco-Efficiency

Eco-efficiency is broadly expressed through concepts like resource productivity or effectiveness of economic operations in creating additional value from the use of resources, and resource efficiency or reducing the resources needed in producing a unit of output. It also takes waste production into account (Ehrenfeld, 2005). Eco-efficiency, being a key idea in sustainable development, seeks to encourage the separation of economic expansion from resource use and environmental deterioration. This strategy aims to maximize the economic value produced by society and industries while minimizing the ecological footprint (Caiado et al., 2017). Businesses and governments can save money, increase resource productivity, and cut waste and pollution by putting eco-friendly policies into place without compromising their ability to compete or grow economically. Eco-efficiency indicators are instruments for measuring and monitoring the effects of different programs on the environment and the economy (Velenturf & Purnell, 2021). These metrics could include material efficiency, waste production, greenhouse gases (GHGs) emissions, and energy and water use. Organizations can pinpoint areas for development and create plans to maximize resource utilization and reduce environmental damage by analyzing these data. By fostering creative techniques that create value while minimizing ecological damage, limiting waste, and encouraging the ethical use of resources, it strikes a harmonious balance between environmental protection and economic growth (Zhang et al., 2021).

Socio-ecological Systems Research

The interdependence of ecosystems and society is reflected in socio-ecological systems. Numerous elements resulting from the connections between ecosystems and human cultures determine how resilient such a system of systems is (Francis & Bekera, 2014). Among the variables are shifts in the political, social, and environmental landscapes. A community that is genuinely resilient may be able to overcome the stress and disruption caused by these circumstances (Tzoulas et al., 2007). The interplay between the actors of the two subsystems makes the situation even more complex and makes the system more vulnerable. In order to build an adaptive capacity in response to a variety of shocks and stresses—such as climate change, extreme events, disruption of biogeochemical cycles, biodiversity loss, deforestation, and desertification, to name a few—socio-ecological systems research looks at how resource-dependent society interacts with nature (Johnson & Becker, 2015).

Circular Economy

Circular economy is a production and consumption paradigm that emphasizes sharing, renting, reusing, repairing, refurbishing, and recycling current products and resources for as long as feasible. The product's life cycle is therefore prolonged. In actuality, it means cutting waste to a minimum (Parliament, 2017). Circular economies operate very differently. By extending the useful life and value of goods, parts, and materials, it closes the circle on the linear "take-make-consume-throw away" pattern. Because everything generated is continuously transferred and used elsewhere, waste is minimized in circular economic activity. The circular economy eliminates economic practices that have a detrimental effect on ecological systems and human health (Kirchherr et al., 2023). This covers all forms of pollution, traffic jams, and the emission of GHGs. It stays away from non-renewable energy sources and fossil fuels. It actively improves the environment and supports regeneration by replenishing the soil with vital nutrients through the preservation and enhancement of renewable resources (Morseletto, 2020).

Biomimicry

Biomimicry is the method of solving human problems by mimicking natural structures and processes. The objective is to develop sustainable systems, processes, and products that coexist peacefully with other living things on the planet. In contrast to people, nature knows how to handle such problems (Lurie-Luke, 2014). Thus, it is crucial to encourage and support this kind of observation since it enables us to address today's issues in a more environmentally responsible and sustainable manner. And that is critical in a global atmosphere were minimizing global warming and cutting CO_2 emissions are the primary challenges (Kennedy et al., 2015). For instance, Sharklet Technologies has patented a method that mimics traits found in sharkskin to address the issue of antibiotic-resistant bacterial strains proliferating. The structure of sharks' skin inhibits the growth of barnacles and crustaceans, which are present on other marine creatures. The medical and healthcare industries are the primary users of Sharklet Technologies' products (Miyazaki et al., 2019).

Cradle to Cradle Design

When a product is cradle-to-cradle, it indicates that its parts and materials can be recycled or used again and again. As a result, products become "circular" and have less of an influence on the environment. The concept of cradle-to-cradle design is transforming our understanding of product life cycles (Kavitha et al., 2020). Cradle-to-cradle design guarantees that materials are recycled or safely reintroduced into the environment, in contrast to the conventional cradle-to-the-grave method, where items end up as waste. Making items that can be disassembled at the end of their useful lives is a key component of this design (Braungart et al., 2007). Both biological and technical cycles are taken into consideration while designing these products, which are referred to as cradle-to-cradle products. Materials are either reused to create new products or safely returned to the environment as nutrients in a closed-loop system. This method limits the usage of fresh resources and cuts down on waste. It also encourages the usage of renewable energy sources. As a result, it not only helps the environment but also lowers waste disposal expenses, saving money (El Haggar, 2010).

Synergy between Technology, Innovation and SDGs

The SDGs are greatly advanced by technological developments since they provide creative answers to difficult global problems. Agriculture, water utility management, and intelligent waste management are among the important fields that are changing as a result of digital technologies like artificial intelligence (AI), big data analytics, and the Internet of Things (IoT). While Big Data Analytics offers insights for managing agricultural resources and optimizing water use, IoT, for instance, makes it possible to monitor and manage waste in real-time, increasing efficiency and minimizing environmental effect (Teh & Rana, 2023). Through improved operational efficiency and the resolution of pressing problems in these areas, these developments contribute to a number of SDGs. Studies highlight the revolutionary effects of digital technologies on supply chain management, especially in the agri-food sector (Islam, 2025). Furthermore, cutting-edge technologies like blockchain, mobile technology, and renewable energy are crucial in tackling more general global problems like inequality, poverty, and climate change. Blockchain, for example, can improve supply chain traceability and transparency, and renewable energy technologies help lower carbon emissions and encourage the use of sustainable energy (Tavanti, 2023).

DIGITAL TRANSFORMATION AS A DRIVER OF INCLUSIVE GROWTH

Digital technology has become a vital driver of global economic expansion and the quest for social and economic justice by improving access to markets, public services, and information, thereby resolving the infrastructural deficit in the globe. Compared to more conventional infrastructure needs like power, water, and transportation, digital infrastructure has become just as important, if not more so (Mühleisen, 2018). The world order has been upended by the COVID-19 epidemic, but it has also given a boost to the constantly growing digital infrastructure. The physical resources required for the usage of data, computerized equipment, procedures, systems, and processes make up the digital infrastructure, which economies all over the world are figuring out how to make more resilient, agile, and futuristic (Gadhi, 2020). A society's ability to function and its members' quality of life now depend heavily on its digital infrastructure. Programs for digital and financial literacy are essential interventions for empowering underserved groups. However, a lot of these overlook the crucial first step needed to truly close the gap between the digital and financial spheres. (Mishra et al., 2024) Promoting digital inclusion requires teaching digital literacy. It gives people the abilities they need to interact with and understand digital technologies—such as websites, computer programs, and applications. Technology has the potential to be a powerful equalizer, removing obstacles and opening doors for everyone. However, active agency and capacity-building initiatives must be added to it in order to fully realize its revolutionary potential (Alhassan & Adam, 2021). It will be pointless to provide the newest devices and technology to close the nation's apparent digital gap if the most vulnerable are ill-equipped to use them. Interventions aimed at fostering agency must be customized to meet the particular requirements and environments of underserved populations. This means exposing people to positive role models, mentorship, and practical skills. Incorporating technology into their development will also enable them to adapt to the digital age. By increasing access to essential services like healthcare, offering information and insights for better decision-making (such as in the area of climate change), and serving as a catalyst for broader economic and societal advancement, data and digital technologies help hasten the achievement of the SDGs (Adenle et al., 2023).

Green Technology and Sustainable Practices

Renewable energy technologies are essential to sustainable development because they lower GHGs emissions, provide energy security, and give previously underserved communities access to energy. Electricity from renewable energy sources, for example, emits 90–99% fewer GHGs and generates 70–90% fewer pollutants than coal-fired power plants (Edenhofer et al., 2011). In addition, these technologies boost economic expansion and employment, both of which are critical for sustainable development. Utilizing renewable energy sources can help lessen the consequences of climate change by lowering GHGs emissions. People can lessen our reliance on fossil fuels and cut down on the quantity of dangerous pollutants like carbon dioxide released into the environment by switching to clean, renewable energy sources like solar and wind (Jaiswal et al., 2022). By lowering reliance on foreign fuels and enhancing energy supply dependability, renewable energy technologies can boost energy security. Countries can become more self-sufficient and less reliant on imported energy by using domestically accessible resources like wind and solar energy (Pan et al., 2024).

The market for circular economy is expanding quickly because of strong government support, cutting-edge technologies, and growing environmental consciousness. Recycling rates for various items have surpassed 80% in some locations, with Europe setting the standard through initiatives like the European Union's (EU) Green Deal (Kirchherr et al., 2023). The market is poised to revolutionize the future of sustainable production as global sectors, ranging from electronics to automobiles, progressively embrace circular processes (Pandey & Joseph, 2025). It is anticipated that the circular economy will grow even further with innovations like smart packaging and disassembly robots, fostering a more environmentally conscious global economy (Rejeb et al., 2022). Chemical recycling is one innovation that helps lessen dependency on resources by breaking down items like plastics into their basic components for reuse. The purpose of autonomous robots is to disassemble complicated items, such as electronics, and separate the recyclable elements. Smart packaging that integrates with the IoTs may monitor and optimize a product's lifecycle, guaranteeing that it is recycled or reused efficiently (Bogue, 2019).

Furthermore, by lowering carbon footprints and encouraging eco-friendly behaviors, smart cities set the standard for sustainable living. Initiatives for "smart cities" use a broad range of technology and tactics to maximize urban systems and enhance citizens' quality of life. Cities can monitor and manage resources more effectively by combining data-driven solutions and IoTs technologies (Hui et al., 2023). This ensures that services like trash management, electricity, and transportation are not only efficient but also environmentally responsible. For instance, energy-efficient buildings and renewable energy sources can drastically reduce carbon emissions, while smart sensors can offer real-time data on traffic patterns, enabling optimal traffic flow and less congestion (Elassy et al., 2024).

TECHNOLOGY FOR FOOD SECURITY AND AGRICULTURE

Precision farming is leading the way in sustainable farming methods, bringing about a new era of productivity, ecological responsibility, and financial sustainability for farmers everywhere. In order to conform to the principles of sustainable agriculture, precision agriculture transforms conventional agricultural practices by utilizing state-of-the-art technologies and data-driven methodologies (Sanyaolu & Sadowski, 2024). The effective use of resources to reduce waste and environmental damage is at the core of sustainable agriculture. Precision agriculture accomplishes this objective by carefully adjusting inputs like water, fertilizer, and pesticides to meet the unique requirements of crops. Farmers can maximize yields while minimizing inputs and optimizing resource allocation through the use of techniques such as soil mapping and variable rate technology (VRT) (Kushwaha et al., 2024). This resource-efficient method makes farming operations more financially sustainable by lowering expenses and conserving resources. The goal of sustainable agriculture is to reduce farming's negative environmental effects while protecting biodiversity and natural resources (Wezel et al., 2014). Precision agriculture is essential to this effort by reducing the adverse effects of traditional farming methods. Farmers may accurately apply inputs, reducing pollution, soil erosion, and chemical runoff, by using sensors, drones, and GPS-guided equipment. Precision agriculture improves land utilization and lessens dependency on dangerous pesticides, which helps ecosystems remain resilient and healthy over the long run (Shafi et al., 2019). Thereby, implementing precision agriculture is crucial to guaranteeing the farming systems' long-term viability. Farmers may overcome the difficulties brought on by population expansion, resource scarcity, and climate change by adopting cutting-edge technologies and methods. In the face of uncertainty, precision agriculture enables farmers to sustain productivity, increase resilience, and adjust to shifting environmental conditions. Farmers can protect agriculture's future for future generations by putting sustainability first (Javaid et al., 2022).

Real-time monitoring of soil temperature, moisture content, and nutrient levels via IoT and smart sensors makes farming more accurate and productive. Smart sensors in the cold chain make sure that perishable items are transported and stored in the best possible circumstances, avoiding spoiling and guaranteeing food safety (Laha et al., 2023). Reducing the amount of food waste benefits the environment in addition to household finances. Lower output reduces the need for resources like land, water, and cattle, which is good for the environment and can assist lower emissions from the food and agriculture industries. According to the United Nations Environmental Program (UNEP), 931 million tons of food—or about 74 kg per household—are wasted worldwide each year (Adra & Barua, 2022). However, fresh approaches to the problem of food waste are being developed. With the aid of nuclear and related technologies, sustainable agricultural practices were created to help farmers conserve soil, water, and crop resources, shield plants from harmful insect pests, and increase food production by using new disease-resistant plant varieties that can withstand drought and rising soil salinity. Other techniques assist farmers in preserving natural resources while enhancing animal breeding and reproduction processes and safeguarding the health of their livestock (Saleh & Hassan, 2022).

HEALTH TECH AND WELL BEING

The performance of our current healthcare system is determined by its laws, policies, regulations, operational models, enabling technology, customs, and patient and provider preferences. Taken together, these factors represent the limit of what is feasible. They also act as limitations on what can be accomplished (Mosadeghrad, 2014). Despite efforts to promote advancement, the healthcare sector has been at the forefront of innovation for far too long. To get truly groundbreaking performance, the industry must overcome existing limitations and push the boundaries. Although there are other limitations, the conventional, widely used fee-for-service (FFS) payment model in particular does not match provider incentives with the objective of getting more for less (Qadri et al., 2020). By tracking physical health and giving healthcare professionals access to information they might not otherwise have, such as heart rate or blood pressure, wearable technology has the potential to enhance patient outcomes. By providing the advantages of core health technologies through fair access and affordability, the effort aims to assist solve significant health issues that affect populations in settings with limited resources. This calls for technological innovation, either in the technologies themselves or in the procedures created to make it easier for people to use, distribute, and apply them (Al-Shorbaji & Al-Shorbaji, 2021).

By facilitating healthcare finance, streamlining healthcare service delivery, enhancing the capabilities of healthcare professionals, and supporting the infrastructure required for the health information system and early disease detection through analytics, mobile technology helps achieve SDG 3 (Aerts & Bogdan-Martin, 2021). In order to accomplish this, digital healthcare solutions are essential, particularly in regions with limited resources. SDG 3 has been the second-best SDG in terms of industry effect since 2015. In 2019, 32% of the world's 1.6 billion mobile subscribers—an increase of more than 900 million since 2015—used their phones to monitor and improve their health (Jones et al., 2017). Additionally, by 2019, there were more than half a million IoT health connections, and 745 million IoT wearable connections—a 45% increase since 2015.

EDUCATION AND CAPACITY BUILDING IN DIGITAL ERA

The fourth Sustainable Development Goal (SDG 4) set forth by the UN is Quality Education (QE), which aims to guarantee inclusive, equitable, and high-quality education for all. QE is not provided to the populace fairly and democratically, particularly to the most vulnerable and those residing in distant locations, despite its significance in addressing societal concerns (Rosa, 2017). In such a context, it has been suggested that using educational technology, or EdTech, will enhance the teaching-learning process and help accomplish SDG 4. Achieving the SDGs, especially Goal 4 (Ensure inclusive and equitable quality education and promote lifelong learning opportunities for everyone) and Goal 10 (Reduce inequality within and among nations), depends on ensuring that all students have access to high-quality educational technology (Saini et al., 2023). It takes more than just putting the newest technologies into practice to close skill gaps and promote innovation; it also requires developing a culture of constant learning and flexibility. It is about using the convergence of innovation, human capital, and technology to promote growth and resilience. Teachers and students may work together and communicate more effectively when they use innovative tools. Regardless of geographic constraints, they enable smooth cooperation and communication between students and teachers (McCarthy et al., 2023). By interacting with classmates from around the world, students can work together on projects, exchange differing viewpoints, and develop a sense of global citizenship. Teachers can also offer immediate feedback and assistance, fostering an engaging and dynamic learning environment outside of the traditional classroom. Students can now communicate with their teachers and peers from anywhere in the world because of the growth of online learning platforms and communication technologies (Haleem et al., 2022). This creates a wealth of chances for students to learn collaboratively, working on projects together, exchanging ideas, and understanding one another's viewpoints. Teachers can also give students immediate feedback and assistance, creating a more engaging and dynamic learning environment.

ECONOMIC GROWTH THROUGH TECHNOLOGICAL ENTREPRENEURSHIP

An innovation ecosystem serves as a growth accelerator by creating a favorable atmosphere in which concepts can germinate, develop, and thrive (Pandey & Joseph, 2025). Businesses can access a wealth of resources, knowledge, and teamwork opportunities inside such an ecosystem. Consequently, there takes place an encouraging culture of innovation and ongoing development (Shaw & Allen, 2018). A synergy of ideas and best practices is fostered by this interconnected web of contributors, which includes employees, students, and startups. It drives innovation at a pace single entities can rarely reach alone. An organization's capacity to react quickly to changes in the market and in technology is also improved by an efficient innovation ecosystem (Autio & Thomas, 2014). By offering safeguards against possible setbacks, it encourages experimentation and risk-taking, which are the two crucial steps in the innovation process. Essentially, a properly organized ecosystem transforms teamwork into a competitive edge, propelling growth and ensuring long-term sustainability.

Innovation ecosystems and open innovation are inherently interconnected, creating a symbiotic relationship that drives mutual growth and innovation (Kamalaldin et al., 2021). Innovation ecosystems provide the cooperative environment necessary for open innovation to flourish, facilitating communication and knowledge exchange amongst a range of stakeholders, including corporations, academic institutions, and governmental organizations. This partnership creates a dynamic atmosphere where resources may be shared and ideas can flow freely, increasing the potential for creativity beyond what any one organization could do on its own (Granstrand & Holgersson, 2020). Organizations in these ecosystems can access outside sources of knowledge, ideas, and technology through open innovation. Consequently, they are able to increase their capacity for innovation and hasten the creation and marketing of novel solutions. Incorporating open innovation tactics into innovation ecosystems also makes it easier for members to share risks and rewards, which increases their overall adaptability and resilience (Bigliardi et al., 2020). Additionally, by utilizing resources and collective intelligence, this integration guarantees that firms maintain their competitiveness. In the end, this propels regional economic growth and industry improvements. Its strategy exemplifies the SDG framework by creating a cooperative atmosphere in which startups can create solutions to global problems with the help of government and corporate collaborations (Fallah Shayan et al., 2022). Financial and Technological Innovation for Sustainability is a relevant work that addresses real-life problems and solutions from the public and commercial sectors across all jurisdictions in light of the global climate catastrophe. It was provided by professionals and professors. Public-private partnerships are collaborations between a private sector enterprise and a government agency that can be used to fund, build, and run projects like convention centers, parks, and public transit networks (Yang, 2000). All these can promote sustainable economic growth.

POLICY FRAMEWORK AND GOVERNANCE

The breadth of this new digital era and the intensity of its influence on global production, distribution, consumption, and human contact and identity make it unique. It is widespread and non-linear, and its effects are frequently unpredictable. Machines are learning on their own in this day and age; self-driving automobiles can communicate with intelligent transportation systems; and smart devices and algorithms can anticipate and react to human needs and desires (Saarikko et al., 2020). The experience with National Sustainable Development Strategies (NSDS), which were incorporated into Agenda 21 in 1992 (§ 8.7), is built upon by the integration of the SDGs and sustainable development in general. In this case, nations were asked to combine economic, social, and environmental goals into a single, strategically targeted national action plan (Cherp et al., 2004). "The broadest possible participation should be used to develop the NSDS." Additionally, it "should be founded on a comprehensive evaluation of the current situation and initiatives." Technological developments are causing the world to change. Since technology is both a useful tool and a dangerous master, it is imperative to remember to use it wisely and properly. People find it challenging to evaluate the ethical consequences of their digital activities due to the rapid advancement of technology. Students who comprehend and keep in mind the ethical issues surrounding technology grow into morally upright adults who have adapted to the digital world (Dhirani et al., 2023). Automation and AI are the two examples of innovative technology advances that are upending work ethics and igniting discussions about human employment and job security (Pandey & Joseph, 2025). It goes without saying that emerging technologies create concerns about data consumption and the loss of personal boundaries in the digital age, which compromises privacy. Because cybersecurity affects trust in digital platforms and calls for strong defensive measures, it has become a major ethical challenge (Manyika & Sneader, 2018). Social norms have changed along with AI, igniting debates about the limits of machine decision-making and the ethics of human-AI interaction (Pandey & Joseph, 2025; Joseph & Pandey, 2025). Values change dynamically in tandem with technological advancements, which calls for ongoing ethical discussion and adjustment to new standards (Van de Poel & Kudina, 2022).

Furthermore, the disparity in access to contemporary telecommunications technology between various demographic groups and geographical areas is known as the "digital divide." This may involve disparities in access to digital literacy, computers, smartphones, and the internet. The disparity between people with and without access to cellphones was referred to as the "digital divide" when the phrase was coined in the latter half of the 20th century (Hanna, 2022). Since then, the phrase has grown to encompass the financial and technological capacity to use existing technologies and connect to the internet. However, as technology advances, the definition of the "digital divide" is always changing. Prioritizing physical access to infrastructure was the main focus of digital divide policy until recently. The lack of knowledge and comprehension of information technology itself is a bigger problem than the cost and affordability of ICT, which are still major concerns in many nations (Cullen, 2001).

CHALLENGES AND RISKS OF TECHNOLOGICAL INNOVATION

A significant number of natural resources, including the mining of minerals, metals, and fossil fuels, are needed for the creation of electronic gadgets, programmed obsolescence (which is already being fought against), and the construction of increasingly potent infrastructures. Deforestation, soil erosion, and water pollution are just a few of the serious environmental effects that result from this (Dwivedi et al., 2022). As it has already been observed in instances like cryptocurrency mining, the energy required to run servers, data centers, and other devices favors the generation of GHGs. Global warming is exacerbated by these emissions. Intensive industrial activities that release pollutants into the air and water are frequently involved in the improper management of e-waste, including the production of electronic components (Cheng et al., 2021). The quality of the air and water may be adversely affected by certain contaminants, as well as on health and species survival. A significant quantity of waste is produced by the quick obsolescence of technology and the steady flow of new goods. If not adequately managed, the harmful materials included in these devices—such as lead, mercury, and arsenic—can seep into the subsurface and contaminate water (Dey et al., 2023). Undoubtedly, the technology sector has seen remarkable success. Our digital society is powered by its pervasive goods and services. However, the business has been forced to deal with some unexpected, challenging ethical quandaries as a result of its long-standing ubiquity, scale, and influence. Although the tech sector did not necessarily originate these problems, many of its members are now reaching a "convergence point" where they can no longer ignore these problems (Marshall, 1999).

Many customers, investors, employees, and governments are calling for increased corporate accountability due to "big tech's" perceived influence, lax regulation, and lack of standard industry norms. In addition, the technology sector is becoming more self-reflective, analyzing its own moral standards and looking at ways to better control its scale and power (Wilhelm, 2002). It is commonly accepted that the more power one has, the more obligation they get to utilize it responsibly, regardless of who stated it first. These days, the tech sector is being expected to perform more in an increasing variety of areas. Tech companies will probably find it difficult to address today's most pressing difficulties and will not be ready for tomorrow if they do not take a comprehensive approach to these problems (Christensen, 2015). Targeted policies that address income inequality, access to essential services, and opportunity for excluded groups are necessary to achieve social fairness. Making sure that the advantages of economic development are felt by all facets of society is necessary to strike a balance between growth and social fairness (Kuznets, 2019).

Disruptive technology can spur innovation, open up new markets, and transform industries. The IoT, cloud computing, blockchain, and AI are rapidly changing how people live and work. They do, however, provide significant challenges for businesses, from navigating complex legal frameworks to overcoming cultural resistance to change (Anderson & Rainie, 2018). One of the most challenging parts of managing disruptive technologies is the invention and adoption process. Innovation requires technical know-how, strategic vision, creativity, and a willingness to try new things and take chances. In addition to implementing new technology, the process of technological innovation and adoption involves adjustments to how companies' function (Dogan, 2017). Often, implementing disruptive technology requires significant adjustments to organizational structures, procedures, and culture. Businesses need to be ready to accept and effectively handle these changes if they want to benefit from innovation (Ortiz-Villajos & Sotoca, 2018).

CONCLUSION

Digital technology will be essential to achieving the SDGs, but innovation will probably have both positive and negative effects on advancement. With increased development required to meet the goals by 2030, the implementation of new technologies may be crucial to attaining the SDGs. However, since new innovations frequently widen the gap between those who can benefit and those who are left behind in society, it will be difficult to guarantee that no one is left behind in the fourth industrial revolution. This is because new technologies are typically inaccessible to marginalized populations. Furthermore, there are a lot of hazards and opportunities that are still unknown but might quickly crystallize due to the present rate of invention, making it impossible for regulators to react quickly enough. As a result, it is critical that decision-makers comprehend and be cognizant of technological change.

REFERENCES

Adenle, A. A., De Steur, H., Mwongera, C., Rola-Rubzen, F., de Barcellos, M. D., Vivanco, D. F., Timilsina, G. R., Possas, C., Alders, R., Chertow, M., Poons, S., & Scholes, B. (2023). Global UN 2030 agenda: How can science, technology and innovation accelerate the achievement of sustainable development goals for all? *PLOS Sustainability and Transformation*, *2*(10), e0000085. DOI: 10.1371/journal.pstr.0000085

Aerts, A., & Bogdan-Martin, D. (2021). Leveraging data and AI to deliver on the promise of digital health. *International Journal of Medical Informatics*, *150*, 104456. DOI: 10.1016/j.ijmedinf.2021.104456 PMID: 33866232

Al-Shorbaji, N., & Al-Shorbaji, N. (2021). Improving healthcare access through digital health: the use of information and communication technologies. *Healthcare Access, 10.*

Alhassan, M. D., & Adam, I. O. (2021). The effects of digital inclusion and ICT access on the quality of life: A global perspective. *Technology in Society*, *64*, 101511. DOI: 10.1016/j.techsoc.2020.101511

Anderson, J., & Rainie, L. (2018). Improvements ahead: How humans and AI might evolve together in the next decade. *Pew Research Centers: Artificial Intelligence and the future of humans, 4.*

Ardra, S., & Barua, M. K. (2022). Halving food waste generation by 2030: The challenges and strategies of monitoring UN sustainable development goal target 12.3. *Journal of Cleaner Production*, *380*, 135042. DOI: 10.1016/j.jclepro.2022.135042

Autio, E., & Thomas, L. (2014). *Innovation ecosystems* (pp. 204-288). The Oxford handbook of innovation management.

Bigliardi, B., Ferraro, G., Filippelli, S., & Galati, F. (2020). The influence of open innovation on firm performance. *International Journal of Engineering Business Management*, *12*, 1847979020969545. DOI: 10.1177/1847979020969545

Bogue, R. (2019). Robots in recycling and disassembly. *The Industrial Robot*, *46*(4), 461–466. DOI: 10.1108/IR-03-2019-0053

Braungart, M., McDonough, W., & Bollinger, A. (2007). Cradle-to-cradle design: Creating healthy emissions–a strategy for eco-effective product and system design. *Journal of Cleaner Production*, *15*(13-14), 1337–1348. DOI: 10.1016/j.jclepro.2006.08.003

Caiado, R. G. G., de Freitas Dias, R., Mattos, L. V., Quelhas, O. L. G., & Leal Filho, W. (2017). Towards sustainable development through the perspective of eco-efficiency-A systematic literature review. *Journal of Cleaner Production, 165*, 890–904. DOI: 10.1016/j.jclepro.2017.07.166

Cheng, Y., Awan, U., Ahmad, S., & Tan, Z. (2021). How do technological innovation and fiscal decentralization affect the environment? A story of the fourth industrial revolution and sustainable growth. *Technological Forecasting and Social Change, 162*, 120398. DOI: 10.1016/j.techfore.2020.120398

Cherp, A., George, C., & Kirkpatrick, C. (2004). A methodology for assessing national sustainable development strategies. *Environment and Planning. C, Government & Policy, 22*(6), 913–926. DOI: 10.1068/c0310j

Christensen, C. M. (2015). *The innovator's dilemma: when new technologies cause great firms to fail.* Harvard Business Review Press.

Cullen, R. (2001). Addressing the digital divide. *Online Information Review, 25*(5), 311–320. DOI: 10.1108/14684520110410517

Dey, S., Veerendra, G. T. N., Padavala, S. S. A. B., & Manoj, A. P. (2023). Recycling of e-waste materials for controlling the environmental and human health degradation in India. *Green Analytical Chemistry, 7*, 100085. DOI: 10.1016/j.greeac.2023.100085

Dhirani, L. L., Mukhtiar, N., Chowdhry, B. S., & Newe, T. (2023). Ethical dilemmas and privacy issues in emerging technologies: A review. *Sensors (Basel), 23*(3), 1151. DOI: 10.3390/s23031151 PMID: 36772190

Dogan, E. (2017). A strategic approach to innovation. *Journal of Management Marketing and Logistics, 4*(3), 290–300.

Dwivedi, Y. K., Hughes, L., Kar, A. K., Baabdullah, A. M., Grover, P., Abbas, R., Andreini, D., Abumoghli, I., Barlette, Y., Bunker, D., Chandra Kruse, L., Constantiou, I., Davison, R. M., De', R., Dubey, R., Fenby-Taylor, H., Gupta, B., He, W., Kodama, M., & Wade, M. (2022). Climate change and COP26: Are digital technologies and information management part of the problem or the solution? An editorial reflection and call to action. *International Journal of Information Management, 63*, 102456. DOI: 10.1016/j.ijinfomgt.2021.102456

Edenhofer, O., Pichs-Madruga, R., Sokona, Y., Seyboth, K., Kadner, S., Zwickel, T., & Matschoss, P. (Eds.). (2011). *Renewable energy sources and climate change mitigation: Special report of the intergovernmental panel on climate change.* Cambridge University Press. DOI: 10.1017/CBO9781139151153

Ehrenfeld, J. R. (2005). Eco-efficiency. *Journal of Industrial Ecology*, *9*(4), 6–8. DOI: 10.1162/108819805775248070

El Haggar, S. (2010). *Sustainable industrial design and waste management: cradle-to-cradle for sustainable development*. Academic Press.

Elassy, M., Al-Hattab, M., Takruri, M., & Badawi, S. (2024). Intelligent transportation systems for sustainable smart cities. *Transportation Engineering*, 100252.

Fallah Shayan, N., Mohabbati-Kalejahi, N., Alavi, S., & Zahed, M. A. (2022). Sustainable development goals (SDGs) as a framework for corporate social responsibility (CSR). *Sustainability (Basel)*, *14*(3), 1222. DOI: 10.3390/su14031222

Francis, R., & Bekera, B. (2014). A metric and frameworks for resilience analysis of engineered and infrastructure systems. *Reliability Engineering & System Safety*, *121*, 90–103. DOI: 10.1016/j.ress.2013.07.004

Gadhi, S. (2020). How digital infrastructure can help us through the COVID-19 crisis. *Erişim Tarihi*, *11*, 2020.

Granstrand, O., & Holgersson, M. (2020). Innovation ecosystems: A conceptual review and a new definition. *Technovation*, *90*, 102098. DOI: 10.1016/j.technovation.2019.102098

Haleem, A., Javaid, M., Qadri, M. A., & Suman, R. (2022). Understanding the role of digital technologies in education: A review. *Sustainable operations and computers*, *3*, 275-285.

Hanna, K. T. (2022). What is the Digital Divide and How is it being Bridged? TechTarget., Retrieved March 15, 2023, from.

Hui, C. X., Dan, G., Alamri, S., & Toghraie, D. (2023). Greening smart cities: An investigation of the integration of urban natural resources and smart city technologies for promoting environmental sustainability. *Sustainable Cities and Society*, *99*, 104985. DOI: 10.1016/j.scs.2023.104985

Islam, H. (2025). Nexus of economic, social, and environmental factors on sustainable development goals: The moderating role of technological advancement and green innovation. *Innovation and Green Development*, *4*(1), 100183. DOI: 10.1016/j.igd.2024.100183

Jaiswal, K. K., Chowdhury, C. R., Yadav, D., Verma, R., Dutta, S., Jaiswal, K. S., & Karuppasamy, K. S. K. (2022). Renewable and sustainable clean energy development and impact on social, economic, and environmental health. *Energy Nexus*, *7*, 100118. DOI: 10.1016/j.nexus.2022.100118

Javaid, M., Haleem, A., Singh, R. P., & Suman, R. (2022). Enhancing smart farming through the applications of Agriculture 4.0 technologies. *International Journal of Intelligent Networks*, *3*, 150–164. DOI: 10.1016/j.ijin.2022.09.004

Johnson, B. B., & Becker, M. L. (2015). Social–ecological resilience and adaptive capacity in a transboundary ecosystem. *Society & Natural Resources*, *28*(7), 766–780. DOI: 10.1080/08941920.2015.1037035

Jones, P., Wynn, M., Hillier, D., & Comfort, D. (2017). The sustainable development goals and information and communication technologies. *Indonesian Journal of Sustainability Accounting and Management*, *1*(1), 1â-15.

Joseph, J., & Pandey, A. (2025). Democracy in the Age of Al: Ethical and Legal Considerations. *Democracy and Democratization in the Age of AI*, 19.

Kamalaldin, A., Sjödin, D., Hullova, D., & Parida, V. (2021). Configuring ecosystem strategies for digitally enabled process innovation: A framework for equipment suppliers in the process industries. *Technovation*, *105*, 102250. DOI: 10.1016/j.technovation.2021.102250

Kavitha, S., Banu, J. R., Arulazhagan, P., & Gunasekaran, M. (2020). Environmental impacts and sustainability assessment of food loss and waste valorization: Value chain analysis of food consumption. In *Food Waste to Valuable Resources* (pp. 359–388). Academic Press.

Kennedy, E., Fecheyr-Lippens, D., Hsiung, B. K., Niewiarowski, P. H., & Kolodziej, M. (2015). Biomimicry: A path to sustainable innovation. *Design Issues*, *31*(3), 66–73. DOI: 10.1162/DESI_a_00339

Kirchherr, J., Yang, N. H. N., Schulze-Spüntrup, F., Heerink, M. J., & Hartley, K. (2023). Conceptualizing the circular economy (revisited): An analysis of 221 definitions. *Resources, Conservation and Recycling*, *194*, 107001. DOI: 10.1016/j.resconrec.2023.107001

Kushwaha, M., Singh, S., Singh, V., & Dwivedi, S. (2024). Precision Farming: A Review of Methods, Technologies, and Future Prospects. *International Journal of Environment, Agriculture and Biotechnology*, *9*(2), 242–253. DOI: 10.22161/ijeab.92.27

Kuznets, S. (2019). Economic growth and income inequality. In *The gap between rich and poor* (pp. 25–37). Routledge. DOI: 10.4324/9780429311208-4

Laha, S. R., Pattanayak, B. K., Pattnaik, S., Mishra, D., Nayak, D. S. K., & Dash, B. B. (2023, September). An IOT-Based Soil Moisture Management System for Precision Agriculture: Real-Time Monitoring and Automated Irrigation Control. In *2023 4th International Conference on Smart Electronics and Communication (ICOSEC)* (pp. 451-455). IEEE.

Lurie-Luke, E. (2014). Product and technology innovation: What can biomimicry inspire? *Biotechnology Advances*, *32*(8), 1494–1505. DOI: 10.1016/j.biotechadv.2014.10.002 PMID: 25316672

Manyika, J., & Sneader, K. (2018). AI, automation, and the future of work: Ten things to solve for.

Marshall, K. P. (1999). Has technology introduced new ethical problems? *Journal of Business Ethics*, *19*(1), 81–90. DOI: 10.1023/A:1006154023743

McCarthy, A. M., Maor, D., McConney, A., & Cavanaugh, C. (2023). Digital transformation in education: Critical components for leaders of system change. *Social Sciences & Humanities Open*, *8*(1), 100479. DOI: 10.1016/j.ssaho.2023.100479

Mishra, D., Agarwal, N., Sharahiley, S., & Kandpal, V. (2024). Digital Financial Literacy and Its Impact on Financial Decision-Making of Women: Evidence from India. *Journal of Risk and Financial Management*, *17*(10), 468. DOI: 10.3390/jrfm17100468

Miyazaki, M., Moriya, H., & Miyauchi, A. (2019). Biomimetic design inspired sharkskin denticles for growth suppression of biofilm. *Journal of Photopolymer Science and Technology*, *32*(2), 295–301. DOI: 10.2494/photopolymer.32.295

Morseletto, P. (2020). Restorative and regenerative: Exploring the concepts in the circular economy. *Journal of Industrial Ecology*, *24*(4), 763–773. DOI: 10.1111/jiec.12987

Mosadeghrad, A. M. (2014). Factors influencing healthcare service quality. *International Journal of Health Policy and Management*, *3*(2), 77–89. DOI: 10.15171/ijhpm.2014.65 PMID: 25114946

Mühleisen, M. (2018). The impact of digital technology on society and economic growth. *Finance & Development*, •••, 6–8.

Nijkamp, P., Van den Bergh, C. J. M., & Soeteman, F. J. (1990). Regional sustainable development and natural resource use. *The World Bank Economic Review*, *4*(suppl_1), 153–188. DOI: 10.1093/wber/4.suppl_1.153

Ortiz-Villajos, J. M., & Sotoca, S. (2018). Innovation and business survival: A long-term approach. *Research Policy*, *47*(8), 1418–1436. DOI: 10.1016/j.respol.2018.04.019

Pan, A., Xu, S., & Zaidi, S. A. H. (2024). Environmental impact of energy imports: Natural resources income and natural gas production profitability in the Asia-Pacific Economic Cooperation Countries. *Geoscience Frontiers*, *15*(2), 101756. DOI: 10.1016/j.gsf.2023.101756

Pandey, A., & Joseph, J. (2025). Analyzing the Evolving Landscape of Digital Food Platforms and Technology: The Digital Plate. In *Food in the Metaverse and Web 3.0 Era: Intersecting Food, Technology, and Culture* (pp. 1-18). IGI Global Scientific Publishing.

Pandey, A., & Joseph, J. (2025). Emerging Trends in Blue Economy: A Roadmap Through the Lens of Sustainable Development. *Securing Sustainable Futures Through Blue and Green Economies*, 17-36.

Pandey, A., & Joseph, J. (2025). Leveraging Artificial Intelligence for Sustainable Development in Agriculture: An Exploratory Study. In *Artificial Intelligence and Data Science for Sustainability: Applications and Methods* (pp. 187-212). IGI Global Scientific Publishing.

Pandey, A., & Joseph, J. (2025). Cyber Physical Systems: Ethical and Legal Considerations for a Policy Design. In *Democracy and Democratization in the Age of AI* (pp. 285-302). IGI Global Scientific Publishing.

Parliament, E. (2017). *Circular economy: definition, importance and benefits.*

Patterson, N. (2022). *What is environmental sustainability? Goals with examples.* South. New Hampsh. Univ.

Purvis, B., Mao, Y., & Robinson, D. (2019). Three pillars of sustainability: In search of conceptual origins. *Sustainability Science*, *14*(3), 681–695. DOI: 10.1007/s11625-018-0627-5

Qadri, Y. A., Nauman, A., Zikria, Y. B., Vasilakos, A. V., & Kim, S. W. (2020). The future of healthcare internet of things: A survey of emerging technologies. *IEEE Communications Surveys and Tutorials*, *22*(2), 1121–1167. DOI: 10.1109/COMST.2020.2973314

Radicic, D., & Petković, S. (2023). Impact of digitalization on technological innovations in small and medium-sized enterprises (SMEs). *Technological Forecasting and Social Change*, *191*, 122474. DOI: 10.1016/j.techfore.2023.122474

Rejeb, A., Suhaiza, Z., Rejeb, K., Seuring, S., & Treiblmaier, H. (2022). The Internet of Things and the circular economy: A systematic literature review and research agenda. *Journal of Cleaner Production, 350*, 131439. DOI: 10.1016/j.jclepro.2022.131439

Rosa, W. (2017). Goal 4: Ensure inclusive and equitable quality education and promote lifelong learning opportunities for all. *A New Era in Global Health: Nursing and the United Nations 2030 Agenda for Sustainable Development, 283*.

Saarikko, T., Westergren, U. H., & Blomquist, T. (2020). Digital transformation: Five recommendations for the digitally conscious firm. *Business Horizons, 63*(6), 825–839. DOI: 10.1016/j.bushor.2020.07.005

Saini, M., Sengupta, E., Singh, M., Singh, H., & Singh, J. (2023). Sustainable Development Goal for Quality Education (SDG 4): A study on SDG 4 to extract the pattern of association among the indicators of SDG 4 employing a genetic algorithm. *Education and Information Technologies, 28*(2), 2031–2069. DOI: 10.1007/s10639-022-11265-4 PMID: 35975216

Saleh, H. M., & Hassan, A. I. (2022). Sustainability: A comprehensive approach to developing environmental technologies and conserving natural resources. In *Risk, Reliability and Sustainable Remediation in the Field of Civil and Environmental Engineering* (pp. 437-448). Elsevier.

Sanyaolu, M., & Sadowski, A. (2024). The role of Precision Agriculture Technologies in enhancing sustainable agriculture. *Sustainability (Basel), 16*(15), 6668. DOI: 10.3390/su16156668

Shafi, U., Mumtaz, R., García-Nieto, J., Hassan, S. A., Zaidi, S. A. R., & Iqbal, N. (2019). Precision agriculture techniques and practices: From considerations to applications. *Sensors (Basel), 19*(17), 3796. DOI: 10.3390/s19173796 PMID: 31480709

Shaw, D. R., & Allen, T. (2018). Studying innovation ecosystems using ecology theory. *Technological Forecasting and Social Change, 136*, 88–102. DOI: 10.1016/j.techfore.2016.11.030

Siriram, R. (2022). An innovative approach to overcoming technological challenges and improving firm performance in South Africa. *Technology in Society, 68*, 101865. DOI: 10.1016/j.techsoc.2022.101865

Tavanti, M. (2023). Technology Innovations for the SDGs. In *Developing Sustainability in Organizations: A Values-Based Approach* (pp. 389–404). Springer International Publishing. DOI: 10.1007/978-3-031-36907-0_13

Teh, D., & Rana, T. (2023). The use of Internet of Things, Big Data analytics and artificial intelligence for attaining UN's SDGs. In *Handbook of big data and analytics in accounting and auditing* (pp. 235–253). Springer Nature Singapore. DOI: 10.1007/978-981-19-4460-4_11

Tzoulas, K., Korpela, K., Venn, S., Yli-Pelkonen, V., Kaźmierczak, A., Niemela, J., & James, P. (2007). Promoting ecosystem and human health in urban areas using Green Infrastructure: A literature review. *Landscape and Urban Planning*, *81*(3), 167–178. DOI: 10.1016/j.landurbplan.2007.02.001

Van de Poel, I., & Kudina, O. (2022). Understanding technology-induced value change: A pragmatist proposal. *Philosophy & Technology*, *35*(2), 40. DOI: 10.1007/s13347-022-00520-8 PMID: 35441075

Velenturf, A. P., & Purnell, P. (2021). Principles for a sustainable circular economy. *Sustainable Production and Consumption*, *27*, 1437–1457. DOI: 10.1016/j.spc.2021.02.018

WCED (World Commission on Environment and Development). (1987). *Our Common Future*. UN.

Wezel, A., Casagrande, M., Celette, F., Vian, J. F., Ferrer, A., & Peigné, J. (2014). Agroecological practices for sustainable agriculture. A review. *Agronomy for Sustainable Development*, *34*(1), 1–20. DOI: 10.1007/s13593-013-0180-7

Wilhelm, A. G. (2002). *Democracy in the digital age: Challenges to political life in cyberspace*. Routledge. DOI: 10.4324/9780203902509

Yang, Y. (2000). Public Private Partnerships in the Social Sector. *Issues and Country Experiences in Asia and the Pacific. ABDI Policy Paper*, *1*, 353.

Zhang, Y., Mao, Y., Jiao, L., Shuai, C., & Zhang, H. (2021). Eco-efficiency, eco-technology innovation and eco-well-being performance to improve global sustainable development. *Environmental Impact Assessment Review*, *89*, 106580. DOI: 10.1016/j.eiar.2021.106580

Chapter 5
Predictive Analysis of Digital Payment Trends Using Deep Learning

Usharani Bhimavarapu
https://orcid.org/0000-0002-0246-1420
Department of Computer Science and Engineering, Koneru Lakshmaiah Education Foundation, Vaddeswaram, India

ABSTRACT

Digital transformation has significantly impacted the global financial landscape, particularly through the expansion of digital payment systems. This study investigates the trends and adoption patterns of digital payments from 2014 to 2024, leveraging advanced machine learning techniques for predictive analysis. Using an integrated deep learning model combining Bi-Stacked LSTM (Long Short-Term Memory) and Bi-Stacked GRU (Gated Recurrent Unit), we analyzed a comprehensive dataset derived from the Global Financial Inclusion Database and the Reserve Central Bank Consolidated Banking Database. The model effectively captures both long-term dependencies and short-term relationships in time-series data, providing valuable insights into the evolution of digital payment systems. Our approach offers an in-depth understanding of the factors influencing digital payment adoption, including demographic, regional, and policy-based variables, while also identifying challenges and growth opportunities in financial inclusion through digital platforms

DOI: 10.4018/979-8-3693-8477-0.ch005

INTRODUCTION

Digital transformation is transforming economies and businesses globally by adopting next-generation technologies into traditional operating models. From artificial intelligence (AI) to automation, digital solutions are enhancing business operations, driving innovation, and enabling more personalized customer experiences. For businesses, the transformation is not merely about keeping up with changing technologies but also about becoming data-driven, with better decision-making, customer engagement, and service delivery. Firms are increasingly leveraging the internet to construct improved supply chains, streamline processes, and offer differentiated products that can address evolving customer needs.

In addition to this corporate-level effect of digital transformation, its effect does not end at the corporate level. It is transforming entire economies by creating new avenues for growth, increasing access to basic services, and fostering financial inclusion. Foreign markets have been made accessible to small and medium enterprises (SMEs) and helped them to compete more with multinational corporations by digital technology. Online marketing, online banking, and e-commerce are just a few among the various means by which digital platforms are facilitating democratization of economic opportunity by allowing enterprises to go into markets they had not previously and enhance their potential to scale.

Perhaps the most important benefit of digital transformation is that it builds more inclusive economies and societies. By providing greater access to information, digital technologies are demolishing barriers to finance, education, and healthcare. Remote and disadvantaged communities, previously excluded from these services, can now gain from digital solutions that provide improved access to healthcare, e-learning, and financial services. This has a very profound impact on social mobility, enabling individuals and communities to get out of poverty and enhance their living standards.

Secondly, the adoption of online payment systems has also played a significant role in enhancing financial inclusion, especially in the case of emerging economies. Electronic payment systems are enabling millions of people who were previously outside formal financial systems to be included and engage in safe and efficient financial transactions. This has not only grown savings and investment for the individual but also enabled businesses to be more effective through the reduction of the cost of cash-based transactions. Mobile money platforms and digital money have enabled individuals to manage their finances, access loans, and participate in the broader economy.

But even with digital transformation having so much potential to bring about inclusivity, it also has its challenges. The digital divide continues to be a challenge, with unequal access to internet and technology infrastructure across regions, particularly rural and poor communities. To unlock the potential of digital transformation, governments, businesses, and other stakeholders must work together to bring the benefits of digital technologies to all while addressing challenges such as cyber-security, data protection, and digital literacy. Only through building a culture of mutual trust, cooperation, and equal access to technology can we ensure that digital transformation leads to long-term, inclusive growth for all.

Digital transformation matters for organizations and businesses as it makes them competitive in a fast-digitalizing economy. With rapidly changing technologies such as artificial intelligence, Internet of Things (IoT), and cloud computing, business companies have to change in line with them in order to drive operational efficiency, improve customers' experiences, and create new value propositions. Digital transformation enables companies to make their business processes rational, reduce costs, and offer innovative products and services for the changing customers' demands. It also allows organizations to base decisions on facts, resulting in more agile and adaptive models that can quickly respond to market fluctuations.

Outside of the corporate world, digitalization is the driving force behind inclusive growth in economies and societies. It expands access to education, health, financial services, and other basic services, particularly for rural and excluded populations. Digital platforms enable people to raise their capability levels, access healthcare remotely, and reach the global economy through digital payments and e-commerce. To businesses, digital transformation represents the creation of new industries and new opportunities, bringing the developed and developing world together. Digital transformation holds the secret to an improved, balanced, efficient, and sustainable future for governments, businesses, and citizens alike. There have been numerous models of digital transformation that have proven effective in many sectors, with each providing its own solution to the problem.

But they all impose limits on how valuable they are. The McKinsey 7S Framework (Ahmad et al., 2023), for example, is centrally concerned with internal organizational design and does not always account for outside market pressures and accelerating technological change. Deloitte's Digital Maturity Model (Ahmadi, 2024) is similarly based on maturity levels but glosses over the richness of the change and does not fully account for the work of outside disruption. Gartner's Digital Transformation Model (Ahmed., 2021) is technology-driven and doesn't consider organizational culture and people issues required in a successful one. Likewise, Forrester's 5-Step Digital Transformation Framework (Al-Hashedi, 2021) is adoption and strategy-oriented on technology but isn't transformational enterprise-wide. Prescriptive and dogmatic models like the Capability Maturity Model (CMM) (Ali, 2022) might struggle to cope with constantly changing contexts that continue to change rapidly, whereas the 3 Horizons of Growth (Alsenaani et al.,2022) looks at growth strategy in the long term and will thus not suit the demand for immediate change.

Lean Startup Model (Alzahrani et al, 2022) and fast iteration assumption might be less suitable for these kinds of industries that require concerted investments over a long term. Digital Transformation Pyramid (Berhane et al., 2023) pyramid is not able to show change complexity across the business units, whereas Business Process Reengineering (BPR) (Btoush, 2023) typically incorporates major changes resisted by employees and constituted by gigantic cost. Such other models like the Digital Acceleration Framework (Cao, 2019) are technology-driven and do not contain human and culture aspects, and the Open Innovation Model (Chatterjee, 2024) relies on the construction of cooperation culture, which in turn is not easy to build in traditional organisations.

Osterwalder's Business Model Canvas (Dai et al., 2022) does not deal with technology adoption towards digital transformation, but other business elements are covered. Technology-Organization-Environment (TOE) Framework (Gupta et al, 2022) also doesn't deal with relevant human elements and is focused more on outer and technical sides. The Innovation Diffusion Theory (Ileberi et al., 2021) focuses more on early adopters and overlooks slower adopters' needs, and the Enterprise Architecture Framework (Javaid et al., 2021) is hard to implement in agile contexts.

Customer-focused models, such as the Customer-Centric Model (Jemai, 2024), overemphasize customers' demands at the expense of the firm's skills. Agile strategies (Khando, 2022), being flexible, cannot flourish in rigorously controlled companies which are required to be planned. Total Quality Management (TQM) (Khedmati, 2020) emphasizes the management of quality at the expense of creativity and flexibility. Value Chain Analysis (Kumari et al, 2022) fails in its focus on digital management on a scale where it focuses too much in place of past business processes, and ITIL (Li et al., 2022) is service-management-focused at the expense of being more potent in transformational processes.

BCG Matrix (Mhlanga, 2023) is more appropriate for portfolio analysis than for intricate digital transformation. CRISP-DM (Piccarozzi, 2018) is aimed at more data mining and not customer experience and organizational change, while Six Sigma (Rtayli, 2020) is aimed at more process improvement rather than adaptability and innovation. Finally, linear models such as Accenture's Digital Transformation Roadmap (Sadgali et al., 2019) do not pay attention to the non-linear and iterative process of change, and the Strategy-Oriented Value-Based Healthcare Model (Sarno et al.,, 2020, Thudumu et .,2020, Vanini et al.,2023, Xu et al.,2017) is too specific in healthcare and lacking in cross-industry application.

Overall, the majority of these models are too technology-focused at the expense of human beings, culture, and organizational transformation. The majority of them are too prescriptive, too inflexible in the face of fast-evolving technologies, while others oversimplify to the point of being irrelevant or demand so much initial capital investment that they are only valuable to wealthy organizations. All this points towards more integrated and agile approaches to digital transformation.

The Bi-Stacked LSTM and Bi-Stacked GRU hybrid model is a solution to the shortcomings of previous digital transformation models by adopting new deep learning models that bring responsiveness, adaptability, and data-driven decision-making aspects. The model is distinct from previous models, which are constrained to prioritize strict structures or simplicity to offset complexity, as the hybrid model takes into account sequential and contextual dependency of data, making it highly influential in dynamic and evolving environments.

For starters, the model can utilize the capacity of GRUs and LSTMs to handle long-term dependencies and steer clear of vanishing gradients easily. This means it can deal with gigantic and intricate data and keep pace with fast-evolving technology without having to deal with rigid frameworks. As opposed to rigid frameworks such as McKinsey 7S Framework or Deloitte Digital Maturity Model, this method learns in real time from experience and can therefore react in real time to shifts in organizational requirements, customer actions, or technology trends.

Second, integration by Bi-Stacked architectures extends the capability to draw inferences on bidirectional relations between data in a way that includes consideration of both previous and subsequent contexts when analyzing. This rectifies the limitation of models such as the 3 Horizons of Growth and Digital Transformation Pyramid in neglecting interdependence between business units or strategic priorities.

Besides, the model balances technology solutions and people and culture drivers as a cohesive blend and produces actionable intelligence to leadership and employee engagement. This ability exceeds the capabilities of models like Gartner's Digital Transformation Model or PwC's Digital Acceleration Framework that are more likely to bias technology over people.

Lastly, the iterative and data-driven nature of this hybrid model enable it to adapt with new data, thus making it appropriate for business domains that require agility and innovation. Such flexibility is provided as a conscious opposite to the inflexibility of models such as the Capability Maturity Model or ITIL so that companies can respond to the nuance of digital change effectively while staying committed to their strategic objectives.

MATERIAL AND METHODOLOGY

The method is to gather data from Global Financial Inclusion Database and Reserve Central Bank Consolidated Banking Database from 2014-2024. Preprocessing the dataset involves missing value handling, normalization, and categorical data encoding. Dimensionality reduction is done without losing significant patterns using Principal Component Analysis (PCA) by feature extraction. An integrated Bi-Stacked LSTM and Bi-Stacked GRU model is utilized to examine temporal trend and to forecast digital payment adoption. Accuracy, precision, recall, and F1 score metrics are utilized to evaluate model performance. The method demonstrates drivers of digital payment expansion and financial inclusion.

Material

We harvested data sets from the Reserve Central Bank Consolidated Banking Database and the Global Financial Inclusion Database for the years 2014 to 2024. The data sets document extensive data regarding the growth of digital payments in the globe. Important attributes include the adoption level of digital payment channels, volume of digital payments, penetration of digital payment infrastructure, geographic and demographic trends, and policy impact on digital financial inclusion.

These figures give a true chronological division of how the electronic payment systems developed over the decade, to establish the move from traditional payment systems to electronic. The figures also enable us to analyze trends by country, measure the effect of government policy, and identify areas of challenge in achieving financial inclusion through electronic payments.

Preprocessing

Preprocessing of the dataset gathered involved several stages to clean, normalize, and prepare the data for analysis. We initially processed missing values either by filling them with corresponding statistical values (e.g., mean or median) or removing incomplete records based on context and the importance of missing values. We detected and eliminated duplicate records to eliminate redundancy and biased results. The data set was normalized to make the formats consistent, for example, by making sure that all date records were in a standard format and normalizing numerical values where appropriate.

Categorical variables such as mode of payment or demography type were encoded to be processed through techniques such as one-hot encoding or label encoding. Outliers were detected and addressed either by capping or removal depending on how they might affect results. Data fields were similarly normalized to a common unit for the sake of comparability, e.g., converting monetary values to a single currency or normalizing the volume of transactions for comparison. Lastly, the dataset was divided into train and test sets to facilitate model construction and testing. All the above preprocessing were performed to keep data organized and trustworthy for further analytical processes.

Feature Extraction

Feature extraction from the preprocessed data was obtained using Principal Component Analysis (PCA) to reduce dimensions and preserve the most important information. PCA discovered patterns and relations between the features and converted the original dataset into a new dataset of uncorrelated variables referred to as principal components. The principal components each captured a proportion of the dataset variance, and the initial components captured the majority of the information.

The data was standardized beforehand so that all the features would have the same contribution irrespective of the original scale. Then, PCA was conducted and the variance ratio explained was investigated to check how many components need to be retained. By choosing those factors that had explained a significant amount of variance (i.e., 95%), the data dimensionality was greatly reduced, and computational efficiency was enhanced without sacrificing accuracy. The parsimonious feature set was subsequently employed in downstream tasks like predictive modeling and clustering in an effort to keep the analysis efficient and interpretable.

Assessment of Digital Payment

The adoption and trends of digital payments were predicted based on an integrated deep learning model of Bi-Stacked LSTM and Bi-Stacked GRU models. The combined model utilizes the strengths of both the models in identifying sequential patterns and temporal relationships in the data. The Bi-Stacked LSTM layers are particularly efficient in handling long-term dependencies and the Bi-Stacked GRU layers are computationally effective with emphasis on short-term relations, hence their combination is highly effective in handling time-series data.

Data, in the form of electronic payment statistics between 2014 and 2024, was normalized and preprocessed prior to use for the first time to render it homogeneous. Transaction volume, user features, regional adoption rates, and policy effects were used as input features. The combined model was trained to forecast major trends, i.e., adoption rates and transaction increases, and at the same time classify regions or demographic segments into classes of their digital payment behavior.

For better performance, hyperparameters such as learning rate, batch size, and layer structure were optimized, and dropout layers were employed to avoid overfitting. Accuracy, precision, recall, and F1 score were utilized as the parameters of evaluation to compare the model performance. Bi-Stacked LSTM and Bi-Stacked GRU's application offered a robust framework, providing greater understanding of the factors influencing digital payment acceptance and difficulties encountered in various regions and time periods.

EXPERIMENTAL RESULTS

Experiment results show the capability of the hybrid Bi-Stacked LSTM and Bi-Stacked GRU model to predict and analyze digital payment acceptance trends. Having trained the model using the preprocessed data, it learned short-term trends and long-term trends from the time-series data. The performance of the model was evaluated based on performance measures such as precision, recall, accuracy, and F1 score, which all reflected high predictability. The findings provided insightful conclusions about the determinants of digital payments adoption, which include heterogeneity in population, heterogeneity in region, and policy intervention. The research provides additional insight into the changing dynamics of digital payments and provides realistic recommendations to the stakeholders who are interested in expanding financial inclusion.

Table 1 shows growth intensity of digital payments between 2014 and 2024 by region in terms of adoption rate, transaction volume, growth rate, and growth drivers. North America was the leader in 2014 with an adoption rate of 45% and a transaction volume of $120 billion driven by e-commerce and mobile commerce. Europe accelerated in 2015 to 50% adoption and $135 billion transaction thanks to government endorsement and use of mobile wallets. Smartphone penetration and mobile banking spread propelled Asia to 30% adoption and $90 billion transactions in 2016. Africa accelerated fast in 2017 through mobile money services such as M-Pesa to 20% adoption and $50 billion transactions. South America in 2018 was at 35% take-up and $110 billion in transactions via online shopping and supportive local policies. North America also recorded a 60% take-up and $200 billion in transactions in 2019 via increasing confidence levels of digital media. The 2020 COVID-19 pandemic drove Europe to the 75% take-up level, with $300 billion in transaction value due primarily to the move towards a contactless payment. Asia also kept expanding in 2021, with 55% take-up and $220 billion in transaction value, fueled by regulatory backing and digital wallets. South America and Africa also registered positive growth in 2022 and 2023, respectively, due to QR code adoption and fintech implementation. Digital payments reached an all-time high 70% penetration, $500 billion volume, and 25% growth rate in 2024, supported by universal acceptance and fintech collaborations.

Table 1. Intensity of digital payments

Year	Region	Adoption Rate (%)	Transaction Volume (Billion USD)	Growth Rate (%)
2014	North America	45	120	8
2015	Europe	50	135	12
2016	Asia	30	90	15
2017	Africa	20	50	10
2018	South America	35	110	14
2019	North America	60	200	15
2020	Europe	75	300	20
2021	Asia	55	220	18
2022	Africa	40	130	18
2023	South America	45	160	13
2024	Global	70	500	25

Table 2 presents the result of an Analysis of Variance (ANOVA) to compare digital payment trend differences by region and year. Source of variation "Between Groups (Region)" has Sum of Squares (SS) equal to 250.35 with 4 degrees of freedom (df) and Mean Square (MS) equal to 62.59 with an F-statistic value of 5.48 and a p-value of 0.002, indicating that regional difference is statistically significant. Similarly, "Between Groups (Year)" measures 540.80 for SS, 9 for df, and 60.09 for MS, with an F-statistic of 6.02 and a highly significant p-value of 0.0001, indicating differences by year as significant. The "Within Groups" variation, or explained by nothing, measures 290.72 with 45 df and an MS of 6.47. The Total variation is their sum, an overall SS of 1081.87 with 58 df. These findings point towards considerable payment variability both over geography and over time.

Table 2. ANOVA (analysis of variance) analysis

Source of Variation	Sum of Squares (SS)	Degrees of Freedom (df)	Mean Square (MS)	F-Statistic	p-Value
Between Groups (Region)	250.35	4	62.59	5.48	0.002
Between Groups (Year)	540.80	9	60.09	6.02	0.0001
Within Groups	290.72	45	6.47		
Total	1081.87	58			

Table 3 presents Pearson correlation statistics in order to analyze correlations between financial inclusion and digital payments. "Digital Payments Made" and "Financial Inclusion (Score)" present a positive Pearson correlation coefficient (r) of 0.85 (strong) which is statistically significant at p-value = 0.0002, and they present a strong relationship. Similarly, the correlation between "Digital Payments Received" and "Financial Inclusion (Score)" is 0.78 with a p-value of 0.001, indicating a very strong and significant positive correlation. Additionally, the correlation between "Digital Payments Made" and "Digital Payments Received" is very strong with an r of 0.92 and a p-value of 0.0001, indicating a very strong and statistically significant positive correlation. These findings indicate the direct relationship of digital payment habit and financial inclusion and received and paid payments connectivity.

Table 3. Pearson correlation statistics

Variable 1	Variable 2	Pearson Correlation (r)	p-Value
Digital Payments Made	Financial Inclusion (Score)	0.85	0.0002
Digital Payments Received	Financial Inclusion (Score)	0.78	0.001
Digital Payments Made	Digital Payments Received	0.92	0.0001

Table 4 illustrates the comparison of various models on accuracy, precision, recall, F1-score, and Area Under the Curve (AUC). The best performance was that of the Integrated Bi-Stacked LSTM & Bi-Stacked GRU model with a maximum accuracy of 92.5%, precision of 91.2%, recall of 93.0%, F1-score of 92.1%, and AUC of 94.2%, which shows its high prediction capability. GPT ranked in as the second best at 91.0% accuracy, 90.3% precision, 91.6% recall, 90.9% F1-score, and 92.7% AUC, showing how good a performer it was overall. Bi-LSTM and RNN were also good, with Bi-LSTM achieving 88.2% and RNN achieving 86.1%, proving themselves well-capable of handling sequential data tasks. The conventional Feedforward Neural Network (FNN) and GRU models also didn't lag behind with their accuracy levels being 84.3% and 84.7%, respectively. On the contrary, simple models such as Decision Tree and Support Vector Machine (SVM) had comparatively low accuracy levels of 70.9% and 77.3%, revealing their incapability to deal with complex data. Radial Basis Function Network (RBFN) and Convolutional Neural Network (CNN) also performed with accuracies of 79.8% and 80.5%, respectively, while Self-Organizing Map (SOM) performed at 75.4%, which proves to be poor performance on this task. Overall, the results prove the better performance of combined and deep learning models that are more sophisticated in predictive tasks.

Table 4. Performance comparison

Model	Accuracy (%)	Precision (%)	Recall (%)	F1-Score (%)	AUC (%)
Integrated Bi-Stacked LSTM & Bi-Stacked GRU	92.5	91.2	93.0	92.1	94.2
FNN (Feedforward Neural Network)	84.3	82.5	86.1	84.2	87.6
RBFN (Radial Basis Function Network)	79.8	77.3	80.5	78.9	83.4
SOM (Self-Organizing Map)	75.4	72.1	74.3	73.2	80.1
RNN (Recurrent Neural Network)	86.1	85.4	87.5	86.4	89.3
Bi-LSTM (Bidirectional LSTM)	88.2	87.5	89.0	88.2	91.0
GRU (Gated Recurrent Unit)	84.7	83.0	85.2	84.1	86.8
GPT (Generative Pre-trained Transformer)	91.0	90.3	91.6	90.9	92.7
CNN (Convolutional Neural Network)	80.5	78.9	81.2	80.0	82.5
SVM (Support Vector Machine)	77.3	75.0	78.0	76.4	81.2
Decision Tree	70.9	68.1	72.4	70.2	75.0

Table 5 presents the views of a total of ten interviewed financial sector stakeholders on digital payments, including their functions, regional outlook, awareness, adoption rate, challenges, benefits, and expectations. Awareness of digital payments is always extremely high between 84% (P8, Insurance Executive in Asia) and 95% (P2, Fintech Analyst in Europe), while their adoption rates are relatively lower between 65% (P8) and 90% (P6, Banking Executive in Europe). Key challenges differ by function and geography, i.e., security and infrastructure gaps in North America (P1), regulatory gaps in Europe (P2, P6), connectivity and digital literacy gaps in Asia (P3, P8), and low internet penetration in Africa (P4). Different benefits were listed, including quicker transactions and greater customer base (P1), cost reduction and financial inclusion (P3, P9), lower cost of operations (P2), and greater transparency (P5). Future potential is very high, with the interviewees looking forward to vast expansion, higher usage, and more innovation, although some referenced higher regulation (P5) and infrastructure investment (P10). Generally, the interviews document the potential for digital payments to revolutionize as well as challenges that still need to be solved.

Table 5. Interviewed financial sector participant regarding digital payments

Participant ID	Role/Position	Region	Awareness of Digital Payments (%)	Adoption of Digital Payments (%)
P1	Bank Manager	North America	90	85
P2	Fintech Analyst	Europe	95	80
P3	Government Official	Asia	88	75
P4	CEO, Payment Gateway	Africa	85	78
P5	Risk Manager	South America	92	83
P6	Banking Executive	Europe	89	90
P7	Financial Advisor	North America	87	70
P8	Insurance Executive	Asia	84	65
P9	Payment Solutions Expert	Middle East	91	88
P10	Regulatory Advisor	Global	93	76

CONCLUSION

This study is keen on the pivot role of digital transformation in deciding the direction of financial systems, and that is the application of digital payment systems globally. We are well placed to capture intricate temporal dynamics for a ten-year history of trends in digital payments using a hybrid Bi-Stacked LSTM and Bi-Stacked GRU model. The findings call for policy and technology implications in guiding the use of digital payment systems globally. The hybrid deep learning method was an economic way to predict and detect digital payment conduct, providing crucial insights for policymakers, banks, and tech firms. The findings can be supported by follow-up studies using other data sources and model updates to clarify digital financial inclusion matters.

REFERENCES

Ahmad, H., Kasasbeh, B., Aldabaybah, B., & Rawashdeh, E. (2023). Class balancing framework for credit card fraud detection based on clustering and similarity-based selection (SBS). *International Journal of Information Technology : an Official Journal of Bharati Vidyapeeth's Institute of Computer Applications and Management, 15*(1), 325–333. DOI: 10.1007/s41870-022-00987-w PMID: 35757149

Ahmadi, S. (2023). Open AI and its Impact on Fraud Detection in Financial Industry. *J. Knowl. Learn. Sci. Technol., 2*, 263–281.

Ahmed, M., Ansar, K., Muckley, C., Khan, A., Anjum, A., & Talha, M. (2021). A semantic rule based digital fraud detection. *PeerJ. Computer Science, 7*, e649. DOI: 10.7717/peerj-cs.649 PMID: 34435097

Al-Hashedi, K. G., & Magalingam, P. (2021). Financial fraud detection applying data mining techniques: A comprehensive review from 2009 to 2019. *Computer Science Review, 40*, 100402. DOI: 10.1016/j.cosrev.2021.100402

Ali, A., Razak, S. A., Othman, S. H., & Eisa, T. A. E. (2022). AI-Dhaqm, A.; Nasser, M.; Elhassan, T.; Elshafie, H.; Saif, A. Financial Fraud Detection Based on Machine Learning: A Systematic Literature Review. *Applied Sciences (Basel, Switzerland), 12*(19), 9637. DOI: 10.3390/app12199637

Alsenaani, K. Fraud Detection in Financial Services using Machine Learning. Master's Thesis, RIT 1 Lomb Memorial Dr, Rochester, NY, USA, 2022.

Alzahrani, R. A., & Aljabri, M. (2022). AI-based Techniques for Ad Click Fraud Detection and Prevention: Review and Research Directions. *J. Sens. Actuator Netw., 12*(1), 4. DOI: 10.3390/jsan12010004

Berhane, T., Walelign, T. M. A., & Seid, A. M. (2023). A Hybrid Convolutional Neural Network and Support Vector Machine-Based Credit Card Fraud Detection Model. *Mathematical Problems in Engineering, 2023*(1), 34627. DOI: 10.1155/2023/8134627

Btoush, E. A. L. M., Zhou, X., Gururajan, R., Chan, K. C., Genrich, R., & Sankaran, P. (2023). A systematic review of literature on credit card cyber fraud detection using machine and deep learning. *PeerJ. Computer Science, 9*, e1278.

Cao, W., Ming, Z., Xu, Z., Zhang, J., & Wang, Q. (2019). Online sequential extreme learning machine with dynamic forgetting factor. *IEEE Access : Practical Innovations, Open Solutions, 7*, 179746–179757.

Chatterjee, P., Das, D., & Rawat, D. B. (2024). Digital twin for credit card fraud detection: Opportunities, challenges, and fraud detection advancements. *Future Generation Computer Systems, 158*, 410–426. DOI: 10.1016/j.future.2024.04.057

Dai, S. Research on Detecting Credit Card Fraud Through Machine Learning Methods. In *Proceedings of the 2022 2nd International Conference on Business Administration and Data Science (BADS 2022)*, Kashgar, China, 28–30 October 2022; pp. 1030–1037.

Gupta, S., Varshney, T., Verma, A., Goel, L., Yadav, A. K., & Singh, A. (2022). A Hybrid Machine Learning Approach for Credit Card Fraud Detection. *International Journal of Information Technology Project Management, 13*(3), 1–13. DOI: 10.4018/IJITPM.313420

Ileberi, E., Sun, Y., & Wang, Z. (2021). Performance evaluation of machine learning methods for credit card fraud detection using SMOTE and AdaBoost. *IEEE Access : Practical Innovations, Open Solutions, 9*, 165286–165294.

Javaid, M., Haleem, A., Singh, R. P., Khan, S., & Suman, R. (2021). Blockchain technology applications for Industry 4.0: A literature-based review. *Blockchain Res. Appl., 2*(4), 100027. DOI: 10.1016/j.bcra.2021.100027

Jemai, J., Zarrad, A., & Daud, A. (2024). Identifying Fraudulent Credit Card Transactions Using Ensemble Learning. *IEEE Access : Practical Innovations, Open Solutions.*

Khando, K., Islam, M. S., & Gao, S. (2022). The Emerging Technologies of Digital Payments and Associated Challenges: A Systematic Literature Review. *Future Internet, 15*(1), 21. DOI: 10.3390/fi15010021

Khedmati, M., & Erfini, M. GhasemiGol, M. Applying support vector data description for fraud detection. arXiv 2020, arXiv:2006.00618.

Kumari, A., & Devi, N. C. (2022). The Impact of FinTech and Blockchain Technologies on Banking and Financial Services. *Technology Innovation Management Review, 12*(1/2), 12. DOI: 10.22215/timreview/1481

Li, A., Pandey, B., Hooi, C. F., & Pileggi, L. (2022). Dynamic Graph-Based Anomaly Detection in the Electrical Grid. *IEEE Transactions on Power Systems, 37*(5), 3408–3422. DOI: 10.1109/TPWRS.2021.3132852

Mhlanga, D. (2023). Block chain technology for digital financial inclusion in the industry 4.0, towards sustainable development? *Front. Blockchain, 6*, 1035405. DOI: 10.3389/fbloc.2023.1035405

Piccarozzi, M., Aquilani, B., & Gatti, C. (2018). Industry 4.0 in Management Studies: A Systematic Literature Review. *Sustainability (Basel), 10*(10), 3821. DOI: 10.3390/su10103821

Rtayli, N., & Enneya, N. (2020). Enhanced credit card fraud detection based on SVM-recursive feature elimination and hyper-parameters optimization. *Journal of Information Security and Applications, 55*, 102596. DOI: 10.1016/j.jisa.2020.102596

Sadgali, I., Sael, N., & Benabbou, F. (2019). Performance of machine learning techniques in the detection of financial frauds. *Procedia Computer Science, 148*, 45–54. DOI: 10.1016/j.procs.2019.01.007

Sarno, R., Sinaga, F., & Sungkono, K. R. (2020). Anomaly detection in business processes using process mining and fuzzy association rule learning. *Journal of Big Data, 7*(1), 5. DOI: 10.1186/s40537-019-0277-1

Thudumu, S., Branch, P., Jin, J., & Singh, J. (2020). A comprehensive survey of anomaly detection techniques for high dimensional big data. *Journal of Big Data, 7*(1), 1–30. DOI: 10.1186/s40537-020-00320-x

Vanini, P., Rossi, S., Zvizdic, E., & Domenig, T. (2023). Online payment fraud: From anomaly detection to risk management. *Financial Innovation, 9*(1), 66. DOI: 10.1186/s40854-023-00470-w

Xu, C., & Zhang, J. (2017). Collusive opinion fraud detection in online reviews: A probabilistic modeling approach. [TWEB]. *ACM Transactions on the Web, 11*(4), 1–28.

Chapter 6
Preferences and Usage of E-Banking Services Among Customers in Tripura, India

Supriya Dam
Netaji Subhash, India

ABSTRACT

The study evaluates the e-banking services of two prominent commercial banks in Northern Tripura through a customer survey, focusing on their usage and preferences. Field observations indicate a wide range of customer opinions regarding their preferences and usage of e-banking services. The results reveal significant similarities in client preferences for these services. However, the utilization of e-banking services exhibited a significant difference between ICICI and SBI clients. The informants demonstrated a clear preference for debit card transactions over credit cards and a tendency to favor savings options rather than loans. The data suggests that banks are experiencing growth in both urban and semi-urban areas. The survey indicates that respondents value hassle-free banking and stability, indicating mutual coexistence in their choices without any evidence of coopetition among bankers.

I. INTRODUCTION:

The banking sector is using technology to improve its service delivery system, aiming to lower costs and ensure smooth operations. This challenge goes beyond economic boundaries in today's digital age. E-banking, or online banking, is a self-service that offers 24/7 access to customers' accounts, enables electronic fund

DOI: 10.4018/979-8-3693-8477-0.ch006

transfers, and facilitates bill payments through an information technology platform. It replaces traditional banking practices with a more convenient and efficient banking experience. The new system aims to reduce customer waiting times, replace checkbook systems, and use electronic gadgets for more efficient operation. Ensuring transparency and accountability is crucial in this context. Ombati et al. (2010) define 'electronic banking' as the capacity of clients to conduct financial transactions online rather than visiting a physical branch. As a result, 'e-banking' is described as an online gateway that enables users to do various financial transactions, such as bill payments and investments (Pikkarainen et al., 2004). Accessing bank accounts, transferring money, and purchasing financial products or services via bank websites are all examples of electronic banking. Banks that do not accept transactions on their websites but just provide information are not deemed to provide electronic banking services under the terms of this study.

E-banking integrates various technologies, enabling customers to perform traditional banking services such as bill payments, balance inquiries, and fund transfers online without visiting a bank branch (Gopalakrishnan et al., 2003). Studies suggest that customers in third-world countries have embraced e-banking as a new banking method (Nyangosi et al., 2009) over traditional brick-and-mortar banking.

In the mid-1990s, India introduced 'anywhere banking' through private sector banks, which launched automated teller machines (ATMs) as the first step in this direction. ICICI Bank pioneered technological innovation in banking services by introducing online banking in 1996, revolutionizing its traditional delivery channel. In 1999, private banking operators like Citibank, IndusInd Bank, and HDFC Bank joined the banking expansion program through the proliferation of e-banking services (Sobia and Thangavel, 2017). Private banks are transforming e-banking into a necessity due to its low transaction costs and high-value offerings (Iyengar & Belvalkar, 2009). Again, e-banking features offer a competitive edge and an increased customer base, prompting public sector banks to adopt them for financial stability.

In recent years, breakthroughs in information technology (IT) have significantly transformed the banking landscape in India. It has become the primary driver of financial transactions, fundamentally changing how banks operate by offering improved delivery channels and more customer-friendly services. Technologies such as anywhere banking, telebanking, mobile banking, online banking, ATMs, credit/debit cards, smart cards, contact centers, customer relationship management (CRM), and data warehousing have all contributed to this transformation. Today, nearly all major banks in India, including ICICI Bank, UTI Bank, Citibank, Standard Chartered Bank, ABN Amro, SBI, and PNB, offer online services to their clients. ATMs have emerged as the most popular method for providing financial services globally. In India, customers can be categorized into two groups: those who use multiple banking channels and those who primarily rely on physical branch visits.

Venkatesh and Periasamy (2006) highlight the rapid shift from public-sector banks to multinational corporations and growing private-sector banks in the banking industry. The Indian banking industry is undergoing a significant transformation, with 'Concept Selling' at the forefront. The future potential lies in enhancing the range of new financial services through technology. The 21st century has seen substantial changes in foreign exchange banking resulting from economic liberalization, particularly in the past three years. Let us look at the tools and services of e-banking.

Figure 1. e-banking tools and services

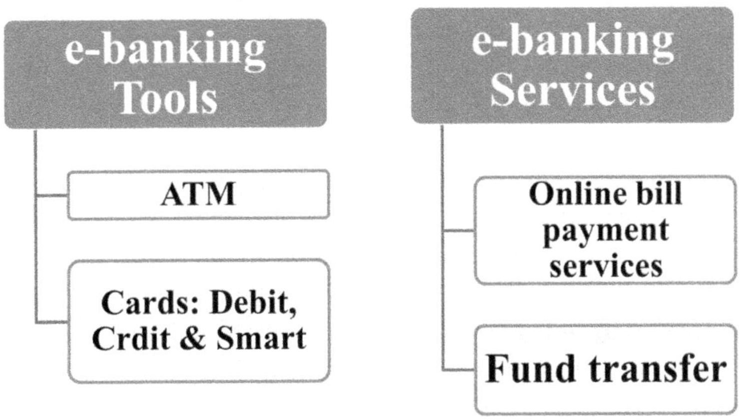

E-banking tools include ATM, debit, credit, and smart cards, providing services to clients. Automated Teller Machines (ATMs) are computerized devices that allow customers of financial institutions to conduct transactions in public spaces without the need for a human clerk or bank teller. They are designed for various functions, including balance inquiries, cash withdrawals, and other services depending on the bank's policies. To ensure security, users must enter a valid customer ID and password to log in. Debit Cards are advanced electronic banking technology that can be used in ATMs for balance inquiries, cash withdrawals, or for shopping at various counters. They ensure automatic deduction of funds by scratching them on the machine. Credit card systems are retail transaction settlements and credit systems, named after small plastic cards issued to users. Issuers lend money to consumers, and they gained popularity in India with foreign banks' introduction. A smart card is a plastic card, usually conform to the size of a credit card, that is used to store and retrieve personal information. It may have electronic memory and an embedded circuit.

E-banking services primarily involve online bill payments, including electric, telephone, and online funds transfers, among other services. Banks have partnerships with utility companies, service providers, and insurance companies nationwide, enabling easy payment of electricity, telephone, mobile phone, and insurance premium bills. Customers can register for one-time payments and set up automatic recurring payment instructions online. Banks typically do not charge customers for online bill payment. Customers in India have the ability to transfer money from one account to another, enabling them to send funds anywhere in the country. To initiate a transfer, clients must log in and provide the payee's account number, bank name, branch, and IFSC code. This process typically takes about one day, which is an improvement over the traditional three-day duration

Public and private sector banks have varying levels of automation, with private banks being able to utilize technology more effectively to improve operational efficiency in the face of uncertainty-related issues (Vyas, 2004). When technology-driven services were introduced in public sector banks, there was skepticism due to the reduced involvement of human resources in banking operations. The increase in private sector clients has led nationalized banks such as SBI, Canara Bank, Allahabad Bank, Punjab National Bank, Bank of Baroda, and Syndicate Bank to incorporate e-banking into their services. The State Bank of India (SBI), with over 65,000 branches, became the first nationalized bank in India to offer e-banking services in 2001, followed by other banks soon after.

This study addresses a research gap in service sector management, particularly in the banking industry. The survey, which was performed among clients in the public and commercial sectors in Tripura's North Tripura area, examines people's preferences and use of online banking services. Based on our analysis of current trends, the study delves into consumer preferences and usage of the two leading e-banking service providers, ICICI and SBI, in Northern Tripura. Our initial analysis suggests that both banks are equally competent in providing cost-efficient e-banking services to their clients. However, customer preferences vary greatly among different groups and locations. Both banks' e-banking practices suggest they can both complement and compete in their growth and development. The realization of the aforementioned situation prompted us to engage in the present study.

II. OBJECTIVES AND METHODOLOGY:

The study compares the e-banking services of State Bank of India (SBI) and Industrial Credit and Investment Corporation of India (ICICI) Bank in Northern Tripura, focusing on their online banking services. Both banks prioritize technological advancements for user-friendly services. The study aims to examine consumer perception and acceptance of e-banking services during the survey period. The study's primary goals are to evaluate the state of various e-banking services offered by both banks, as well as to perform comparative research on e-banking preferences and usage among commercial bank customers.

The study focused on the Dharmanagar and Kailasahar towns in Northern Tripura due to ICICI bank branches' urban-centric operations neglecting rural areas. This empirical study aimed to gather data from clients of two operating banks through field observation, considering internet banking usage and customer preferences. This exploration requires a pilot study of bank customers to ensure the accuracy of the information sought and any necessary adjustments for the final observation. The sample design is based on over 65,000 active account holders, representing 0.19 percent of the clients. The study utilized a convenience sample approach to select 120 bank customers as informants. In light of this, professional enumerators distributed a questionnaire to 120 bank customers, 100 of whom replied properly. In addition, consultation with bank management staff is crucial for achieving the objectives. The data is analyzed using standard statistical techniques such as mean, standard deviation, and ANOVA to obtain the resulting findings. The majority of the inferences will be derived from primary data, which may have limitations.

The study necessitates the use of secondary data. The study will utilize various secondary sources, including bank periodicals, State Level Bankers Committee (SLBC) reports, RBI bulletins, books, articles, and electronic reports, as per the study's requirements.

The study is divided into eight sections. The study commences with an introduction in Section I. Section II offers an overview of the objectives and methodology followed. This follows a detailed literature review. Section IV provides an outline of the study area. The next section will provide a detailed analysis of the national e-banking indicators of both banks. Section VI presents a detailed analysis of the study's findings, followed by a conclusion in the final section.

III. REVIEW OF LITERATURE:

Over the years, several studies have been conducted at both the industry and firm levels to examine the impact of e-banking on the productivity and profitability of commercial banks. It is important to briefly reference previous research related to this topic. These studies explore the effects of e-commerce on the banking industry, and there is a substantial amount of literature available on subjects such as e-banking, internet banking, and the intersection of IT and banking. Some studies have established statistical correlations between IT spending and performance measures like profitability. Others have investigated the impact of consumer satisfaction within the e-banking sector. Furthermore, some research has focused on the preferences and usage patterns of e-banking customers specifically in the Indian banking industry. Although each study presents different analyses, their ultimate aim is the same: to investigate the effects and implications of e-banking.

E-banking is a web-based system that facilitates online transactions, connecting banks, customers, and fund transfer parties through seamless interlinking. The initiative aimed to retain existing customers and introduce new ones to the banker base by enhancing the quality of services. E-banking, the use of electronic channels by banks, is revolutionizing the banking industry. Shaikh (2014) emphasizes the importance of electronic commerce in the global corporate landscape, with an increased emphasis on mobile computing, wireless Web, and mobile commerce. E-banking services have become an important distribution route, necessitating extensive investigation before acceptance. However, the main concern is whether customers are fully informed about the range of services offered by their banks, making it crucial to assess customer awareness of e-banking services (Priya, 2024). The promotion of e-banking services is primarily based on customer usage and satisfaction, among other factors. According to Delafrooz et al. (2013), the perceived usefulness, simplicity, effectiveness, and speed of e-banking operations have an impact on clients' usage. Boshkoska and Sotiroski (2018) highlight the importance of user-friendly interfaces, website design, safety, and security aspects in influencing the usage of online banking services.

Customer satisfaction is a subjective concept that encompasses various determinants and views, yet it also adheres to a core conceptual tenet. Customer satisfaction refers to how well a company's products or services meet or surpass its customers' expectations. It is an important part of marketing and is associated with post-purchase phenomena such as attitude change, repeat purchases, and brand loyalty. Negi and Kaur (2010) argued that client satisfaction is critical for long-term corporate performance, with the banking/finance and hospitality/sports businesses reporting better customer satisfaction than other industries. According to Bahri and Herawan (2020), satisfaction is proven when a product meets expectations, whereas dissatisfaction occurs when it fails to do so. Tse and Wilton (1988) define customer satisfaction as the consumer's response to the perceived difference between expectations and the final result after consumption. Post-purchase feedback provides valuable insights into the issue by comparing the expectations of the pre-purchase stage with the evaluation of certain services or products. Numerous factors influence customer satisfaction with e-banking, including convenience, cost-effectiveness of transactions, desired values, ease of use, and brand perception (Kumbhar, 2011). Factors including dependability, design, availability, convenience, and trustworthiness affect customer satisfaction (Addai et al., 2015).

Casaló et al. (2008) revealed that a website's perceived reputation and satisfaction had a direct and significant influence on consumer loyalty to a financial services website. Improving client requirements and business reputation may increase loyalty, retention rates, and revenue in the e-banking market. Oliver (2009) defines customer loyalty as a consistent commitment to repurchasing a preferred product or service, often resulting in repeat purchases of the same brand or set. Customer loyalty is essential in a competitive economic context, as evaluated by satisfaction, dependability, responsiveness, and empathy. According to Suleiman et al. (2012), responsiveness, contentment, and dependability are among the most important variables in client loyalty in e-banking.

Managing loyalty is critical for e-banking service quality, customer satisfaction, and e-loyalty from the customer's perspective. Customer loyalty research has generally focused on brand loyalty, with few studies exploring service loyalty notions (Sathiyavany & Shivany, 2018). This emphasizes the necessity of regulating behavior and state of mind in e-banking. Bankers' loyalty and patronage are directly linked to the quality of services provided, thereby enhancing client satisfaction (Boshkoska and Sotiroski, 2018). Redda's (2023) study found that e-banking quality indirectly promotes loyalty through customer satisfaction, and because the direct effect remains substantial even after satisfaction intervention, the mediation is deemed partial. A 5 percent increase in customer retention resulted in a 35 percent increase in return for the banking sector, 50 percent for insurance, and a significant 125 percent enhancement in the credit card segment (Chothani et al., 2004; Singh and Arora, 2011).

Online banking requires significant involvement from consumers, as it necessitates regular interaction with technology, such as computers and Internet connections (Mukherjee and Nath, 2003). A study by Kumbahar (2010) found that most customers are satisfied with the service and the attributes of online banking systems. Companies that offer a wide range of products and provide relevant website content, along with prompt and courteous responses, tend to enhance customer satisfaction. Similarly, Paul et al., (2016) study indicated that factors such as perceived risk, experience, benefits, ease of use, and uncertainty significantly impact customer perceptions of e-banking. According to Sayar et al. (2007), advancements in information technology and Internet banking have significantly transformed how banks operate and how consumers manage their banking activities. The study revealed that trust in the Internet plays a key role in shaping risk perception and consumer attitudes toward Internet banking. This indicates that trust is a vital factor in both interpersonal relationships and technological systems. Pandey et al., (2023) study on consumer awareness and usage of e-banking services revealed that while consumers are not frequently using these services, they have a strong desire to do so in the future. The study analyzed how banks are exploring the feasibility of using mobile phones as an alternative delivery channel for banking services.

Security variables for e-banking services are primarily based on reliability, safety, and privacy, as per the research by Politoglu and Ekin in 2001. E-banking is vulnerable to phishing, identity theft (Banu et al., 2019), and service provider information leakage, which can negatively impact users. The recent surge in cybercrimes has led to a significant increase in perceived use value, indicating a need for increased security measures (Masrek et al., 2018; Lu et al., 2006). Poder (2005) underscored the significance of a user-friendly interface, website reliability, transactional capabilities, and the promotion of consumer education about associated risks for successful e-banking. This ensures safe and secure online banking transactions for clients. Research indicates that computer literacy often hinders the adoption of e-banking, particularly in developing nations, according to Rajput (2015). Amene (2015) emphasizes the need for client education and awareness in the implementation of e-banking facilities.

Customer e-banking adoption is heavily influenced by demographic factors such as age, gender, marital status, ethnic origin, educational qualifications, employment, income, and residential location. According to Ameme's (2015) research, education level has a significant influence on customer acceptance and use of e-banking services, even when demographic indicators such as gender and employment are controlled for.

The convenience and user friendliness of online banking are significant factors that motivate customers to use it. The 24/7 accessibility of banking services, facilitated by user-friendly technology, is crucial for enhancing ease of use and thereby increasing customer satisfaction (Muiime & Biyaki, 2010; Asadullah & Yazdifar, 2016). A user-friendly website with a suitable webpage design, graphical user interface, and navigational tools ensures customers ease of use (Cooper, 1997).

The study examines the factors influencing the preferences and usage of e-banking services among two significant commercial banks in Northern Tripura. The study compares the current status of e-banking services in the area and investigates client preferences and usage variables through field observation.

IV. BRIEF ACCOUNT OF STUDY AREA:

The Government of Tripura has transitioned to digitalization since 2016, replacing manual transactions with a new digital system, marking a significant shift in the state's history. New technologies have facilitated the adoption of digital transactions by the urban educated middle class, making banking more accessible.

The inhabitants of Northern Tripura are composed of 19 distinct socio-religious groups, each with its own language and culture. The region is split into two districts: Unakoti and North, which have their headquarters at Kailasahar and Dharmanagar.

The region boasts a banking network of 51 commercial banks that cater to a diverse population with varying preferences and usages. People's primary motivation for banking preferences and usage is their innate desire to adopt technology solutions in transactions while maintaining the given level of transaction security. Customers prefer debit cards and mobile banking for e-banking due to their limited visits to bank branches during working hours. Social media significantly enhances e-banking transactions in Northern Tripura. SBI and ICICI Bank, the oldest banking institutions in both the public and private sectors, are adept at providing e-banking services to their customers.

Figure 2. Old map of Tripura

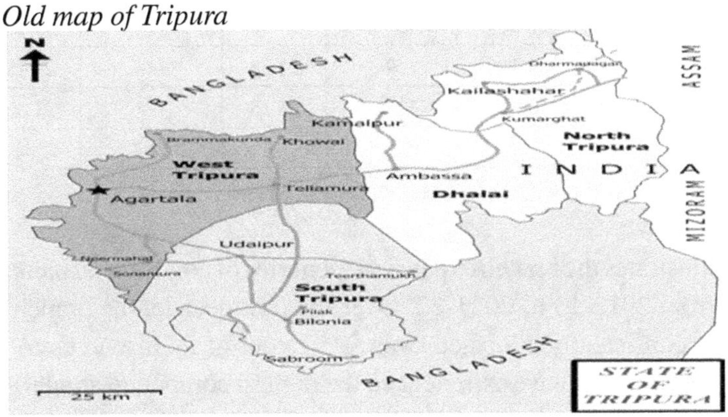

The above figure shows the four regions of Tripura: West Tripura, South Tripura, North Tripura, and Dhalai. West Tripura has been divided into three districts, while South and North Tripura have two districts each, and Dhalai is the only district. The study focuses on the former North Tripura region, covering an area of 2109.16 square kilometers, which includes the districts of Unakoti (686.97 square kilometers) and North Tripura (1422.19 square kilometers), with their respective headquarters located in Kailasahar and Dharmanagar. The next section will detail the growth of commercial banks' branches in Tripura between 2012–13 and 2021–22.

Table 1. Branch expansion of commercial banks in Tripura during 2012-13 to 2021-22

Year	Rural Areas		Semi-urban Areas		Urban Areas		Total
	Numbers	%age	Numbers	%age	Numbers	%age	
2012-13	217	57.11	84	22.11	79	20.79	380
2013-14	229	53.88	107	25.18	89	20.94	425
2014-15	248	53.80	117	25.38	96	20.82	461
2015-16	265	53.43	127	25.60	104	20.47	496
2016-17	269	52.95	131	25.79	108	21.09	508
2017-18	271	52.93	131	25.59	110	20.64	512
2018-19	273	51.22	148	27.77	112	20.66	533
2019-20	278	51.29	150	27.68	114	21.03	542
2020-21	279	50.73	157	28.55	114	20.73	550
2021-22	278	50.82	154	28.15	115	21.02	547
CAGR	2.51		6.25		3.83		3.71

Source: 112, 116, 120, 124, 128, 129, 131, 135 and 139 SLBC, Tripura

Table 1 illustrates the branch expansion scenarios of commercial banks operating in Tripura from 2012-13 to 2021-22. Over the past decade, the branch expansion program has consistently allocated over 50 percent of its resources to rural locations. Semi-urban areas have experienced the highest compound annual growth rate (CAGR) of 6.25 percent, attributed to the significant addition of branches between 2012-13 and 2021-22. In contrast, urban Tripura has seen the slowest growth, with only 36 branches added at a CAGR of 3.83 percent, which is slightly above the national CAGR of 3.71 percent. Currently, the state has 30 banks, including 16 private sector banks with 60 branches mostly located in urban areas. The remaining 14 public sector banks have the potential to expand their network to a total of 487 branches across the state.

Table 2. Status of ATM of SBI and ICICI banks operating in Tripura during 2014-21

Year	SBI				ICICI				State Total
	Rural	Semi-urban	Urban	Total (%)	Rural	Semi-urban	Urban	Total (%)	
2014	54	38	89	181 (51.42)	0	2	12	14 (3.98)	352
2015	54	39	96	189 (41.09)	0	2	12	14 (3.04)	460
2016	54	40	116	210 (43.57)	0	2	12	14 (2.91)	482
2017	55	40	117	212 (43.98)	0	2	12	14 (2.91)	482
2018	56	40	117	213 (42.52)	1	4	9	14 (2.79)	501

continued on following page

Table 2. Continued

Year	SBI				ICICI				State Total
	Rural	**Semi-urban**	**Urban**	**Total (%)**	**Rural**	**Semi-urban**	**Urban**	**Total (%)**	
2019	56	71	110	237 (44.89)	1	5	5	11 (2.08)	528
2020	56	71	110	237 (44.30)	1	5	5	11 (2.06)	535
2021	27	86	131	244 (43.65)	1	4	5	10 (1.79)	559
CAGR	-8.30	10.75	4.95	3.8	0	9.05	-10.37	-4.12	5.95

ATM: Automated Teller Machine, Source: 112, 120, 124, 128, 129, 131, 135 and 139 SLBC, Tripura.

Table 2 presents an overview of the status of automated teller machines (ATMs) in State Bank of India (SBI) and ICICI Bank in Tripura from 2014 to 2021. SBI has established a significant presence in Tripura's ATM service sector, consistently holding over 40 percent of the state's total ATM market share over the past eight years. The compound annual growth rate (CAGR) of SBI's ATMs has been positive across urban, semi-urban, and rural areas, with the highest growth rate of 10.75 percent observed in the semi-urban segment. Overall, SBI's CAGR for the period was 3.8 percent. In contrast, during the same eight-year period, SBI's number of ATMs in rural areas has decreased, while there has been a 2.26 times increase in semi-urban areas, indicating a policy shift towards prioritizing the semi-urban segment. On the other hand, ICICI Bank holds a smaller share of the ATM market in the state, achieving the highest CAGR of 9.05 percent in suburban areas. However, ICICI Bank's overall CAGR for the eight years was negative at -4.12 percent. Throughout the study period, both banks concentrated on suburban areas, where they experienced higher compound annual growth rates.

The State Bank of India (SBI) has consistently led the distribution of point-of-sale (POS) machines in the state. However, its market share has been gradually declining. In September 2018, SBI's market share was 57.47 percent. This decreased to 55.49 percent by December 2018, then further dropped to 54.88 percent in March 2019, and ultimately fell to 47.58 percent by December 2019. As of March 2022, SBI's share of the state's total POS machines stands at 39.5 percent, with the rural segment experiencing the most significant decline. In contrast, ICICI Bank's market share of the state's total POS machines was 4.52 percent in December 2019. This figure decreased further to 2.64 percent as of March 2022.

The State Bank of India (SBI) and ICICI Bank, two prominent banks in Northern Tripura, have been pioneers in implementing innovative technologies to promote "anywhere banking" across India while still maintaining their traditional banking methods. The availability of region-specific e-banking indicators is highly beneficial for evaluating the performance of selected banks within the same area. However, due to a lack of region-specific micro-indicators, this study examines the e-banking performance of these two national banks from 2016 to 2021. It analyzes three national-level e-banking indicators: mobile banking volumes and values, National Electronic Funds Transfer (NEFT) transactions, and debit and credit card transactions over the last six years.

V. INDICATORS OF E-BANKING OPERATIONS:

Table 3 examines the volume and value of mobile banking transactions conducted by ICICI Bank and SBI in India from 2016 to 2021. During this period, SBI experienced remarkable growth in mobile banking transactions, surpassing ICICI Bank in both volume and value. The analysis reveals that ICICI Bank also saw a significant increase in mobile banking transactions, with mean volume and value rising by 18.67 times and 7.28 times, respectively. In contrast, SBI's mobile banking transaction volume and value increased by 6.37 times from 2016 to 2021, ultimately reaching a total of 484.95 million transactions.

Table 3. Monthly volume and values of mobile banking transactions during 2016-2021

Year/ Months (Mean)	ICICI Bank			State Bank of India		
	Vol. (Nos)	Value (000)	Value Volume Ratio (VVR) (%)	Vol. (Nos)	Value (000)	Value Volume Ratio (VVR) (%)
2016	9831305	153961741	1557.98	18372348	392362050	2135.61
2017	17541293	382749808	2081.99	24024445	310754241	1293.49
2018	30557951	271400592	919.60	70349901	289303571	435.77
2019	71243752	4712638853	670.58	214648784	1177586072	582.07
2020	117592163	755322322	635.86	418789494	1344430558	321.24
2021	183581517	1120433059	610.32	8909655934	2498671472	28.00

Source: Reserve Bank of India Monthly Bulletins for 2016, 2917, 2018, 2019, 2020 and 2021.

Figure 2 depicts the Value-to-Volume Ratios (VVR) of two banks during the same time period. An analysis of mobile banking statistics from 2016 to 2021 reveals that State Bank of India (SBI) has a higher transaction volume compared to ICICI Bank, but ICICI has higher mean transaction values. The VVR of mobile banking transactions for both banks has underscored its importance over the past six years.

Figure 3. Comparison of VVR of ICICI bank and SBI during 2016-2021

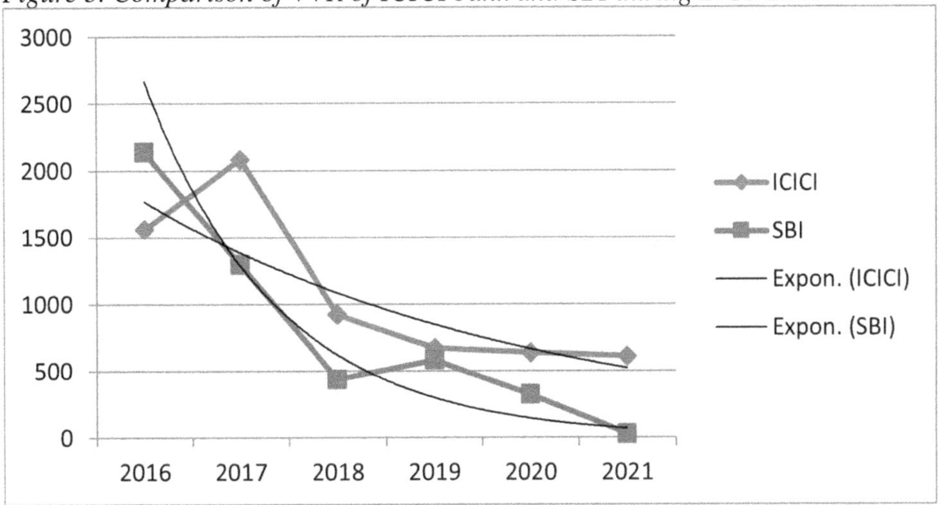

The chart in Figure 2 illustrates the value-to-volume ratio (VVR) of ICICI Bank and SBI over six years, starting from 2016. ICICI Bank's VVR has fluctuated from 1557.98 in 2016 to 2081.99 in 2017, before dropping to 610.32 in 2021. In contrast, SBI's VVR has ranged from 2135.61 in 2016 to 435.77 in 2018 and further declined to 28.00 in 2021. The exponential trend line suggests that ICICI Bank's VVR is likely to remain stronger than SBI's in the future. SBI's VVR shows a fluctuating pattern with a downward trend, whereas ICICI Bank's trend line remains relatively stable. This indicates that ICICI Bank's fund transfer policy during the reviewed period has been restrictive in terms of transaction value per transaction, resulting in clients in the ICICI segment favoring high-value transactions.

Table 4. National Electronic Fund Transfer (NEFT) of ICICI bank and SBI during 2016-2021

Year/ Months (Mean)	ICICI Bank			State Bank of India		
	Outward Payments (in Million)	Inward Receipts (in Million)	Net Receipts/ Payments	Outward Payments (in Million)	Inward Receipts (in Million)	Net Receipts/ Payments
2016	683531	698230	14699	1254160	1312393	58233
2017	896011	1032613	136602	1902257	2005022	102765
2018	1246210	1506676	260466	2719141	2896500	177359
2019	6429468	7347387	917919	11677356	14097150	2419795
2020	14654204	16840254	2186050	27665433	32179058	4513542

continued on following page

Table 4. Continued

Year/ Months (Mean)	ICICI Bank			State Bank of India		
	Outward Payments (in Million)	Inward Receipts (in Million)	Net Receipts/ Payments	Outward Payments (in Million)	Inward Receipts (in Million)	Net Receipts/ Payments
2021	20152667	21251479	1098812	26404249	35512412	9108164
CAGR (%)			**105.24**			**132.12**

Source: Reserve Bank of India Monthly Bulletins for 2016, 2017, 2018, 2019, 2020 & 2021.

Table 4 displays the NEFT transactions of two banks from 2016 to 2021. Both banks have demonstrated significant growth in electronic remittances during this period, including outward payments, inward receipts, and net transactions. ICICI Bank has seen substantial increases in all areas: outward payments have surged by a factor of 29.48, inward receipts by 30.44, and net receipts by an impressive 74.91 times. The compound annual growth rate (CAGR) for ICICI Bank's net receipts and payments stands at 105.24 percent. On the other hand, SBI's growth in NEFT transactions shows outward payments increasing by 21.05 times, inward receipts by 27.06 times, and net receipts by a remarkable 156.41 times, with a CAGR of 132.12 percent for net receipts. Notably, in 2017 and 2018, ICICI's net receipts increased by 1.33 times and 1.47 times compared to SBI's, respectively. However, SBI has consistently outperformed ICICI Bank in these categories since 2019, showing increases of 2.64 times, 2.06 times, and 8.29 times in 2019, 2020, and 2021, respectively. SBI's CAGR during this period was 136.12 percent, significantly higher than ICICI Bank's 105.24 percent. The net receipts and payments of both banks exhibit a strong positive correlation of 0.6485, indicating their competitive and complementary roles in mutual growth.

Table 5. Detail transactions of credit cards of ICICI and SBI during 2016-21

Months/ Year	ICICI				SBI			
	POS		ATM		POS		ATM	
	No of transactions	Amount (Rs Million)	No of transactions	Amount (Rs Million)	No of transactions	Amount (Rs Million)	No of transactions	Amount (Rs Million)
2016	**11121230**	**27323**	**26669**	**105**	**11737698**	**31317**	**83491**	**356**
2017	15463255	40019	27573	98	16191044	59171	106547	420
2018	18671150	52759	42384	147	21820069	78564	135100	517
2019	25341728	409123	51079	1033	29849304	577035	142587	2916
2020	23482060	705815	30063	1423	29114782	990852	92544	3612

continued on following page

Table 5. Continued

Months/ Year	ICICI				SBI			
	POS		ATM		POS		ATM	
	No of transactions	Amount (Rs Million)	No of transactions	Amount (Rs Million)	No of transactions	Amount (Rs Million)	No of transactions	Amount (Rs Million)
2021	32887843	1419005	34644	1608	35698602	1401343	83728	3082
CAGR (%)	19.81%	93.16%	4.46%	57.57%	20.37%	88.42%	0.05%	43.28%
Mean	21161211	422340.67	35402	735.67	24068583.17	523047.00	107332.83	1817.17
CV	33.41%	113.42%	24.76%	87.26%	34.48%	100.19%	22.04%	77.19%
ANOVA test result at 5% level of significance						F –ratio: 2.97683	P Value: 0.056076	Decision: Accepted

Source: Reserve Bank of India Monthly Bulletins for 2016, 2017, 2018, 2019, 2020 & 2021.

Table 5 presents a comprehensive analysis of credit card transactions conducted through Points of Sale (POS) and ATMs from 2016 to 2021. During this period, ICICI Bank witnessed a remarkable 2.96-fold increase in POS transactions, with the total number of transactions rising an astonishing 51.94 times. Transactions made through ATM credit cards also saw growth, increasing by 1.3 times, while the total transaction amount surged by 15.31 times. Similarly, State Bank of India (SBI) experienced significant growth in POS transactions, with the total amount increasing by 3.04 times and the number of transactions rising by 44.7 times during the same timeframe. SBI's ATM credit card transactions and the corresponding amounts saw an impressive growth rate of 8.65 times over the analysis period. Overall, ICICI Bank demonstrated a higher compound annual growth rate (CAGR) compared to SBI in all three categories, except for the number of POS transactions. SBI's CAGR for POS transactions was 20.37 percent, which was 0.56 percent higher than ICICI's 19.81 percent. However, ICICI Bank outperformed SBI in terms of total transaction amounts, achieving a CAGR of 93.16 percent compared to SBI's 83.42 percent. ICICI Bank also showed superior CAGR in ATM transactions at 4.46 percent and in total transactions at 57.57 percent, compared to SBI. In conclusion, the findings indicate that ICICI Bank is better positioned than SBI in the credit card segment for the period of 2016-2021.

It has been observed that SBI exhibits less variation from the mean in POS values, ATM transactions, and credit card values compared to ICICI. The only exception is POS transactions, where ICICI shows greater variation from the mean. In this context, we will test the following hypothesis by applying ANOVA at a 5 percent level of significance.

H_0: There is no difference between the means of SBI and ICICI banks in credit card transactions.

In Table 5, the F-ratio and p-value (2.97683 and 0.056076, respectively) indicate a difference in the means of credit card transactions between SBI and ICICI banks. Since the p-value (0.056076) is greater than 0.05, we accept the null hypothesis at the 5 percent level of significance. Therefore, the means of credit card transactions for SBI and ICICI banks are not significantly different.

Table 6. Detail transactions of debit cards of ICICI and SBI during 2016-21

Months/ Year	ICICI				SBI			
	POS		ATM		POS		ATM	
	No of transactions	Amount (Rs Million)	No of transactions	Amount (Rs Million)	No of transactions	Amount (Rs Million)	No of transactions	Amount (Rs Million)
2016	**21190722**	**30099**	**33228798**	**153354**	**41867685**	**49887**	**303399653**	**637244**
2017	32286352	46165	28842940	140038	76997362	110946	336017514	903750
2018	46598778	53594	32769710	164258	98618465	141265	376415687	1071765
2019	46598778	342343	33926237	943138	109617508	849554	329551385	5073601
2020	46598778	499958	24491213	1354838	103083156	1554878	169319683	8845783
2021	26476222	609422	23814081	1436648	98921328	1700674	183132189	9123733
CAGR (%)	**3.78%**	**65.09%**	**-5.40%**	**45.19%**	**15.41%**	**80.07%**	**-8.07%**	**55.83%**
Mean	**36624938.33**	**263596.83**	**29512163.17**	**698712.33**	**88184250.67**	**734534.00**	**282972685.17**	**4275979.33**
CV	**28.6%**	**88.64%**	**13.97%**	**81.17%**	**26.09%**	**93.49%**	**27.76%**	**85.34%**
ANOVA test result at 5% level of significance						F –ratio: 4.92437	P Value: 0.010113	Decision: Rejected

Source: Reserve Bank of India Monthly Bulletins for 2016, 2017, 2018, 2019, 2020 & 2021

Table 6 presents debit card transactions for ICICI Bank and SBI from point-of-sale (POS) and ATM sources during the period from 2016 to 2021. ICICI Bank has recorded a compound annual growth rate (CAGR) of 3.78 percent in POS transactions and a total growth of 65.09 percent over the past six years. SBI outperformed ICICI Bank, achieving a CAGR growth that exceeds ICICI's by 11.63 percent in POS transactions and 14.98 percent in total growth, indicating a clear advantage. In terms of ATM transactions, both banks saw significantly higher debit card usage compared to credit cards. However, there was a decline in ATM transactions for both banks during this period, with SBI experiencing a notable decrease of -8.07 percent, compared to ICICI Bank's decrease of -5.4 percent. Despite the downturn in ATM transactions, SBI's transaction value through ATMs rose to 55.83 percent, significantly higher than ICICI Bank's 45.19 percent. While ICICI Bank has the potential to outperform SBI in the credit card segment for both POS and ATM services, SBI has outperformed ICICI Bank in the debit card segment from 2016 to 2021.

ICICI Bank has consistently outperformed SBI in terms of variations from the mean in debit card ATM volumes, values, and POS values. However, SBI is gaining more POS volumes than ICICI Bank when considering the mean variation. To analyze this diverse dataset, it is essential to conduct an ANOVA at a 5% significance level.

H_0: There is no difference between the means of SBI and ICICI banks debit card transactions.

Table 6 presents an F ratio of 4.92437 and a p-value of 0.010113. At a 5% level of significance, the computed p-value is less than the alpha value (0.010113 < 0.05), which indicates that we reject the null hypothesis. This suggests that there is a significant difference between SBI and ICICI bank debit card transactions.

Table 7. Comparative mobile banking statistics of ICICI and SBI for 2023-24

Months	SBI		ICICI	
	Volume/Active customers	Value/Active customers	Volume/Active customers	Value /Active customers
January, 2023	19.19	41.80	27.38	144.58
February, 2023	17.74	41.94	26.91	144.23
March, 2023	20.45	48.36	29.95	172.28
April, 2023	20.61	45.52	30.44	158.66
May, 2023	22.16	47.56	30.81	164.93
June, 2023	23.01	46.17	30.12	160.30
July, 2023	22.79	46.82	33.80	168.89
August, 2023	23.41	46.69	32.25	166.41
September, 2023	23.74	46.73	31.34	163.54
October, 2023	24.13	48.49	33.40	174.92
November, 2023	23.82	49.51	32.38	167.75
December, 2023	25.37	51.03	34.38	173.32
January, 2024	25.52	51.53	33.06	166.78
CAGR	45.67%	1.62	1.46%	1.10%
Mean	22.46	47.09	31.25	163.58
CV	10.03%	5.98%	7.11%	5.71%
Kruskal-Wallis Test at 5 percent level			H statistic: 47.8302	P value: 0.00001

Source: RBI Monthly Bulletin.

Table 7 presents a comparison of mobile banking statistics between SBI and ICICI Bank for the 13-month period of 2023-2024. Overall, SBI demonstrates a stronger performance than ICICI Bank in aggregate. However, when it comes to the ratio of transaction volume to active consumers in mobile banking, ICICI Bank shows a greater impact than SBI. ICICI Bank surpassed SBI in the value-to-active customer ratio during this period, with its mean volume-to-active customer ratio being 8.79 higher than SBI's. Additionally, ICICI Bank exhibited lower variability from the mean (CV) compared to SBI. The difference in the value-to-active customer ratio was also in favor of ICICI Bank, with a mean difference of 116.49 and minimal variability from the mean. In terms of Compound Annual Growth Rate (CAGR), SBI is better positioned than ICICI Bank for both metrics. We will test the following hypothesis using the Kruskal-Wallis test at a 5 percent level of significance.

H_0: There is no difference between the means mobile banking statistics of both banks.

The results of the Kruskal-Wallis test indicate an H statistic of 47.8302 and a p-value of 0.00001. At the 5% significance level, the p-value is smaller than the alpha value, suggesting that there is no significant difference between the mobile banking statistics of the two banks.

Table 8. Comparative internet banking statistics of ICICI and SBI for 2023-24

Months	SBI		ICICI	
	Volume/Active customers	Value/Active customers	Volume/Active customers	Value /Active customers
January, 2023	3.38	411.24	18.84	8044.27
February, 2023	3.16	461.76	17.59	8507.88
March, 2023	3.54	517.26	21.45	9712.01
April, 2023	3.12	403.96	17.81	7490.91
May, 2023	3.17	486.97	20.30	8473.56
June, 2023	3.14	514.28	21.03	9751.63
July, 2023	3.27	463.95	25.72	9551.44
August, 2023	3.07	467.28	24.37	9735.77
September, 2023	2.93	514.56	24.04	9169.63
October, 2023	2.99	505.30	24.17	9675.35
November, 2023	2.99	496.28	23.31	9251.40

continued on following page

Table 8. Continued

Months	SBI		ICICI	
	Volume/Active customers	**Value/Active customers**	**Volume/Active customers**	**Value /Active customers**
December, 2023	3.10	583.25	24.81	10927.10
January, 2024	3.03	529.24	24.51	10522.91
CAGR	-0.84%	1.96%	2.04%	2.09%
Mean	3.15	488.87	22.15	9293.37
CV	5.17%	9.5%	12.21%	9.94%
X^2 test at 5 percent level			X^2 value: 16.79	P value: 0.99

Source: RBI Monthly Bulletin.

The table below compares the internet banking statistics of SBI and ICICI banks over a 13-month period from 2023 to 2024. According to RBI statistics, ICICI Bank surpasses SBI in terms of the volume of internet banking transactions per active customer. Furthermore, ICICI Bank consistently outperformed SBI regarding the value of internet banking transactions per customer throughout this period. In quantitative terms, ICICI's transaction volume per customer was 2.88% higher than that of SBI. However, SBI exhibited lower variability from the mean (CV) compared to ICICI. In terms of value per active customer for internet banking, the private bank demonstrated a significant advantage over the leading public sector bank, with a mean difference of 8,804.5 (9,293.37 - 488.87) per client. SBI's variability from the mean is slightly lower (9.94% compared to ICICI's 9.5%). Additionally, ICICI Bank has a better compound annual growth rate (CAGR) position in both metrics compared to SBI. The following hypothesis will be tested using a Chi-Squared (X^2) test at a 5% significance level.

H_0: Internet banking statistics of both banks are independent of each other.

Table 8 presents a chi-square (X^2) value of 16.79 and a p-value of 0.99 at the 5% significance level. Since the calculated p-value (0.99) is greater than the alpha value (0.05), the result is considered insignificant. Therefore, we reject the hypothesis that the Internet banking statistics of both banks are independent, concluding that the online banking metrics of the two banks are interdependent.

VI. RESULTS:

This section addresses data analysis and interpretation, utilizing a questionnaire distributed to 120 online respondents selected randomly through a convenience sampling technique. Surveyors collected 100 valid responses from a total of 120 clients visiting the SBI and ICICI bank branches located in Dharmanagar and Kailsahar, which are the headquarters of North Tripura and Unakoti districts. The remaining informants provided inadequate responses. The percentage representation of these findings is provided below.

Figure 4. Percentage of valid respondents' surveyed

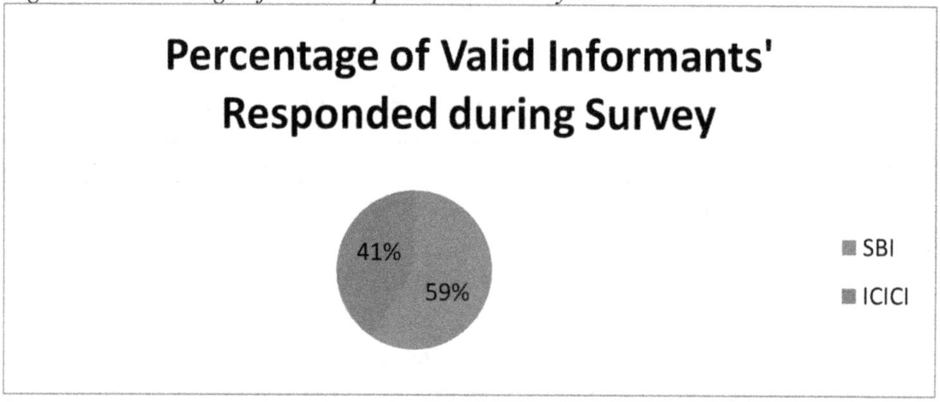

Figure 3 illustrates the distribution of valid responses, with men comprising 70 percent of it, while the rest are females. During the field survey, 41 respondents—ICICI account holders and 59 SBI customers—submitted valid responses.

Table 9. Qualitative services preferred by online customers' surveyed

Parameters of Enquiry	Descriptors			Rank
Preference for Hassle Free, Risk Free e-banking	**Response**	**Numbers**	**Percentage**	1
	Yes	95	95	
	No	05	05	
Preference for anytime/anywhere banking	**Response**	**Numbers**	**Percentage**	2
	Yes	65	65	
	No	35	35	
Preference for easy to operate	**Response**	**Numbers**	**Percentage**	4
	Yes	60	60	
	No	40	40	
Preference for time saving	**Response**	**Numbers**	**Percentage**	3
	Yes	62	62	
	No	38	38	

Source: Compiled during online survey

The survey revealed that clients from both banks expressed both qualitative and quantitative preferences. Qualitative preferences often align with customer expectations, although there may be some exceptions. These underlying preferences shown by customers can significantly influence their overall satisfaction with the banks. Table 9 provides detailed descriptions of these qualitative preferences. Notably, 91 percent of consumers believe that hassle-free, risk-free e-banking is essential, as it offers a convenient and secure banking experience. This finding aligns with the demand for anytime/anywhere banking, which was cited by 65 percent of respondents, and the importance of time savings, mentioned by 62 percent. Additionally, 60 percent of consumers prioritize transaction simplicity over other factors.

Figure 5 provides a summary of the frequency with which each customer has chosen to utilize e-banking services.

Figure 5. No. of times of e-banking transaction by customers'

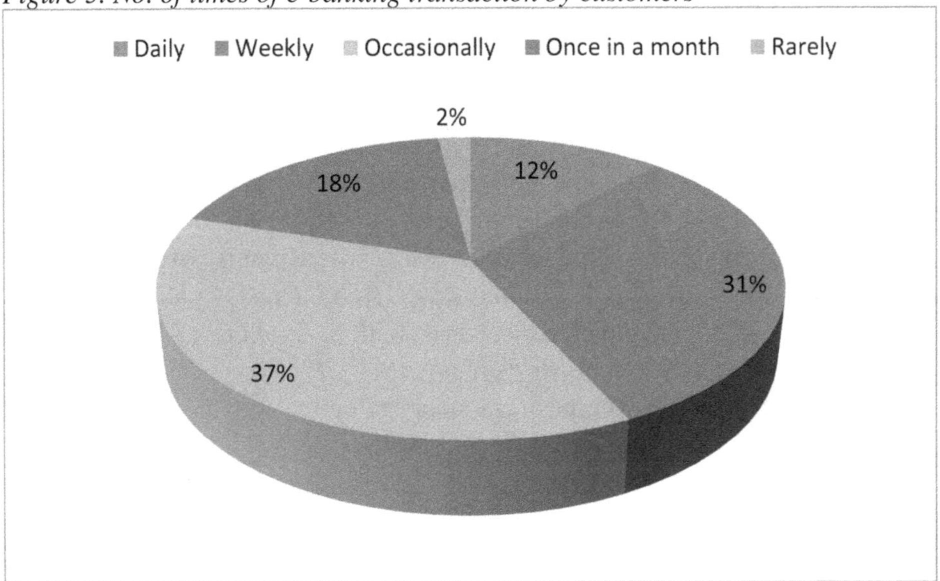

Figure 5 illustrates the frequency of e-banking transactions among the online clients surveyed. A significant portion of respondents, 37 percent, indicated that they prefer to conduct e-banking transactions occasionally. This is followed by 31 percent who engage in transactions on a weekly basis and 18 percent who use e-banking once or twice a month. Daily usage of e-banking services accounts for 12 percent of the respondents, primarily from the business community, while 2 percent report very rare usage. Next, we will test the following hypothesis at a 5 percent level of significance.

Ho: The preference for e-banking services among customers of ICICI and SBI is not significantly different.

Table 10. List of e-banking services preferred by ICICI bank and SBI customers surveyed

Parameters	ICICI Bank	SBI
ATM	41	59
Mobile Banking	37	35
Bill Payment	35	43
Debit Card/Credit Card	31	42
Electronic Fund Transfer	29	39
Check Book	28	46
Checking Balance	36	42
Stoppage of Payment	08	17

Source: Compiled during survey

Table 10 presents the results of a survey regarding preferred e-banking services. All respondents (100%) indicated a preference for ATM services, with 59% being employees of SBI and 41 percent being clients of ICICI Bank. During the survey, 78 percent of respondents favored services such as bill payments and balance checking. Additionally, 74 percent of customers expressed interest in online checkbook services, while 73 percent preferred debit and credit card facilities. Mobile banking and electronic fund transfer options were favored by 72 percent and 68 percent of respondents, respectively. The payment stoppage option was the least preferred, chosen by only 25 percent of the total respondents.

Table 11. Data summary

Groups	Mean	Std. Dev.
ICICI Bank I	30.625	10.1269
SBI II	40.375	11.7587

Source: Calculated through SPSS

Table 11 provides a summary of the hypothesis test data, highlighting a significant difference between the mean and standard deviation of two banks. ICICI Bank has a mean of 30.625 and a standard deviation of 10.1269, while State Bank of India (SBI) reports a mean of 40.375 and a standard deviation of 11.7587. The higher standard deviation for SBI indicates a greater spread of data compared to ICICI Bank.

Table 12. ANOVA summary

Source	Degree of Freedom	Sum of Squares	Mean Square	F-stat	P- value
	DF	SS	MS		
Between Group	1	380.25	380.25	3.15794	0.97282
Within Group	15	1685.75	120.4107		
Total	16	2066.00			

Source: Calculated through SPSS

The ANOVA summary (Table 12) indicates that the F-statistic and P-value were calculated at a 5 percent significance level, yielding values of 3.15794 and 0.97282, respectively. The calculated P-value is significantly higher than the tabulated value (i.e., 0.97282 > 0.05), which suggests that the null hypothesis (Ho) is significant. As a result, the null hypothesis (Ho) is accepted, showing that consumers at ICICI and SBI have identical preferences for e-banking services. Let us consider the following null hypothesis for further analysis.

Ho: There is no significant difference in the usages of e-banking services of customers of ICICI and SBI.

Table 13. Frequency of usages of e-banking services by customers of ICICI bank and SBI

Parameters	ICICI Bank	SBI
ATM	23	55
Mobile Banking	17	35
Bill Payment	16	39
Debit Card/ Credit Card	15	38
Electronic Fund Transfer	14	36
Cheque Book	13	45
Checking Balance	20	40
Stoppage of Payment	02	06

Source: Compiled during survey

Table 13 presents the frequency of e-banking service usage among surveyed bank customers. The usage patterns align closely with the preferences indicated in Table 8; however, the levels of usage varied significantly depending on the specific preferences expressed. In the survey, ATM usage was the most common, with 78 percent of respondents using this service. The next most frequent activities included checking account balances (60 percent), applying for a checkbook facility (58 percent), and making bill payments (55 percent). Additionally, 8 percent of respondents reported using the last-in-order stoppage of payments, which reflects their preferences as well. To analyze these findings, an analysis of variance (ANOVA) will be conducted at a 5 percent significance level.

Table 14. Data summary

Groups	N	Mean	Std. Dev.	Std. Error
ICICI Bank 1	8	15.000	6.1875	2.1876
SBI 2	8	36.75	13.977	4.9416

Source: Calculated through SPSS

Table 14 provides a statistical summary of the usage variables derived from the data analyzed using SPSS. The mean and standard deviation for usage at ICICI Bank are 15 and 6.1875, respectively. In contrast, for SBI, the mean and standard deviation are 36.75 and 13.977, respectively. The higher standard deviation for SBI indicates a significant variation in the usage variables compared to ICICI Bank.

Table 15. ANOVA summary

Source	SS	df	MS	
Between-treatments	1892.25	1	1892.25	F value= 16.1978
Within-treatments	1635.5	14	116.8214	P value= 0.001254
Total	3527.75	15		

Source: Calculated through SPSS

The F-statistics and P-values for the consumption variables are evaluated at a 5% significance level. The ANOVA summary (Table 13) reveals that the F-statistic is 16.1979, with a P-value of 0.001254. Since the estimated P-value (0.001254 < 0.05) is less than the significance level, we reject the null hypothesis (Ho). This indicates a significant difference in e-banking service utilization between ICICI and SBI clients, thereby supporting the acceptance of the alternative hypothesis.

VII. DISCUSSION AND CONCLUSION:

The Indian government's cashless economy and rising mobile phone usage have increased e-banking transactions. The COVID-19 epidemic and demonetization have only intensified this tendency. Banks are investing in new technology to improve their mobile banking apps, making them more convenient, safe, and easy to use. The Digital India initiative has boosted financial inclusion and enhanced digital infrastructure, hence making mobile banking more accessible. Mobile banking transactions offer vital data to banks, governments, and policymakers (Nikita & Bhatt, 2024).

Electronic Funds transfer (EFT) is a quick and easy means to move money between financial institutions or between banks utilizing computer-based technologies. This technology reduces the need for bank staff interaction and offers a variety of online solutions, making it more accessible to consumers. Banks provide a variety of EFT services, including National Electronic Funds Transfer (NEFT), Real Time Gross Settlement (RTGS), and Immediate Payment Service (IMPS), each tailored to specific client needs and preferences. Online banking services are becoming increasingly popular due to their simplicity of use. A variety of factors impact e-banking transactions, including transfer value, service availability, and settlement speed. Banks frequently provide their own digital wallets for extra online financial transactions. These elements, such as transaction limitations, costs, and settlement speed, influence e-banking transaction customs and usage.

Between 2016 and 2021, mobile banking transactions for both ICICI Bank and SBI experienced significant growth at the national level. ICICI Bank maintained a higher volume-value ratio (VVR) for mobile banking transactions compared to SBI, reflecting an increased value per transaction. Additionally, there was a strong positive correlation in the net receipts of NEFT transactions between the two banks, indicating both competitive and complementary roles in the market. Both banks also reported growth in debit and credit card transactions at POS and ATM locations. ICICI Bank had a higher value per ATM transaction for both debit and credit card segments compared to SBI. Furthermore, the debit card segment recorded more ATM transactions and higher transaction values than credit cards. This suggests that customers preferred using their debit cards for ATM transactions and that these transactions typically involved higher values, likely due to their reliance on savings accounts.

The increased use of ATMs and non-face-to-face banking activities has led to higher account balances and greater turnover. This trend could enhance bank profitability by providing access to low-cost financial resources. This conclusion is supported by the calculated equation's positive and significant coefficient, which indicates that the number of POS terminals positively impacts the volume of bank card transactions (Tari & Raeisi, 2021). As of December 2019, the State Bank of India (SBI) has established itself as a leading bank in Tripura. Tripura Gramin Bank (TGB) has the highest number of branches in the state, accounting for 12.55 percent of all bank branches. In contrast, ICICI Bank manages only 1.48 percent of the branches in the state. SBI excels over ICICI Bank in the distribution of ATMs and POS machines, with SBI operating more than 40 percent of the ATMs and 48 percent of the POS machines available in Tripura. During this period, ICICI Bank held a mere 2.08 percent of the ATMs and 4.52 percent of the POS machines in the state. Although ICICI Bank has focused its branch expansion program mainly on semi-urban areas, it has historically operated with an urban-centric approach.

ICICI Bank and SBI's e-banking facilities in Northern Tripura are comparable to national standards, showing no significant difference in customer usage, as confirmed by test results. The main question is whether these changes have led to a substantial increase in consumer volume. ICICI Bank, being urban-centric, primarily serves the financially stable middle-class clientele who possess better purchasing power. The bank's high minimum balance requirements for savings account holders allow for considerable funds to be allocated for profitable investments when compared to SBI. Over the years, ICICI has gained the trust of the community and attracted a growing number of loyal clients due to its focus on technology, e-banking services, and competitive interest rates. ICICI's personalized service, while at a higher cost, also saves investors time and effort, simplifying their financial transactions. In contrast, SBI, a well-established treasury bank, has consistently been the preferred choice for many customers, regardless of its lower but guaranteed returns on investment. Traditional customers tend to invest in SBI even when returns are less appealing. Following its recent merger in December 2019, SBI has emerged as the largest banking conglomerate in Tripura, emphasizing technology adoption to attract customers who favor private banks.

Dayal et al. (1999) suggest that retail banks can build strong customer relationships through trust-based collaboration. Aladwani (2001) emphasized the significance of client trust in online banking, arguing that trust-based collaboration may help retail banks build beneficial connections with their customers. The survey found that 28 percent of the participating consumers had actively maintained savings accounts with both ICICI and SBI for more than four consecutive years. This group preferred ICICI Bank for its hassle-free banking transactions, while they expressed strong support for SBI due to its stability. To prevent panic among similar client groups, the concept of mutual cohabitation in the market was evident among consumers. Jeremsky and Plastaras (2016) discussed the competitive environment of commercial banks and mutually beneficial relationships. Their study indicates that individual-level cohabitation is different from prior research on bank clients.

The bank's e-banking system includes a centralized database that is accessible over the internet. Its intranet functions as a network that connects the organization's central office to its many branches. The liberalization of the Indian economy began in the early 1990s and culminated in the passage of the Foreign Exchange Management Act (FEMA) in 1999, which superseded the Foreign Exchange Regulation Act (FERA) and drastically altered the legal framework controlling e-banking. However, several barriers to digital banking adoption exist, including low digital literacy, limited internet access, security concerns, regulatory compliance issues, customer service challenges, insufficient payment infrastructure, a lack of outreach to remote areas, and high technological infrastructure costs.

The survey results present conflicting statements from the consumers surveyed. The study reveals that consumers at ICICI and SBI have similar preferences for e-banking services. However, another finding highlights a significant difference in the utilization of e-banking services between clients of ICICI and SBI. These results are not absolute but rather part of a continuum, suggesting that further research in this area may be necessary. Customers are proactive in responding to e-banking transactions, demonstrating that no bank has an edge over others in terms of the e-banking services offered. This finding suggests that banks play a mutually beneficial role in meeting the growing demands of e-customers. Recent cyberattacks on e-banking services also underscore the need for continuous monitoring and enhancement of online financial transactions to maintain customer confidence.

REFERENCES

Addai, B., Ameyaw, B., Ashlley, E., & Quaya, I. (2015). Electronic Banking and Customer Satisfaction: Empirical Evidence from Ghana. *British Journal of Economics. Management and Trade*, *9*(3), 1–8.

Aladwani, A. M. (2001). Online banking: A field study of drivers, development challenges, and expectations. *International Journal of Information Management, 21*(4), 213–225. DOI: 10.1016/S0268-4012(01)00011-1

Amene, B. K. (2015). The Impact of Customer Demographic Variable on the Adoption and Use of Internet Banking in Developing Economies. *Journal of Internet Banking and Commerce*, *20*(2), 2–30.

Asdullah, M. A., & Yazdifar, H. (2016). Evaluation of Factors Influencing Youth towards Islamic Banking in Pakistan. *ICTAT Journal on Management Studies*, *2*(1), 217–223. DOI: 10.21917/ijms.2016.0030

Bahri, R. R., & Herawan, E. (2020). The Improving of Customer Satisfaction: Service Triangle Approach. *Advances in Social Science, Education and Humanities Research.* https://www.researchgate.net/publication/339232533_The_Improving_of_Customer_Satisfaction_Service_Triangle_Approach/fulltext/5e45404792851c7f7f345371/The-Improving-of-Customer-Satisfaction-Service-Triangle-Approach.pdf

Banu, A., Mohamed, N. S., & Parayitam, S. (2019). Online Banking and Customer Satisfaction: Evidence from India. *Asia-Pacific Journal of Management Research and Innovation*, *15*(1-2), 68–80. DOI: 10.1177/2319510X19849730

Boshkoska, M., & Sotirski, K. (2018). A Empirical Study of Customer Usage and Satisfaction with e-banking Services in the Republic of Macedonia. *Croatian Review of Economic* [CREBSS]. *Business and Social Statistics*, *4*(1), 1–13.

Casaló, L. V., Flavián, C., & Guinalíu, M. (2008). Towards loyalty development in the e-banking business. *Journal of Systems and Information Technology*, *10*(2), 120–134. DOI: 10.1108/13287260810897756

Cooper, R. G. (1997). Examining Some Myths about New Product Winners. In Katz, R. (Ed.), *The human side of managing technological innovation* (pp. 550–560). Oxford University Press.

Dayal, S., Landesbeg, H., & Zeisser, M. (1999). How to build trust online. *Marketing Management*, *8*(3), 64–69.

Delafrooz, N., Taleghani, M., Karami, R., & Moradi, A. (2013). Factors Affecting Adoption of Online Banking. *International Journal of Business and Behavioral Science*, *3*(2), 82–100.

Gan, C., Clemes, M., Limsombunchai, V., & Weng, A. (2006). *A Logit Analysis of Electronic Banking in New Zealand*, Discussion Paper No.108, Lincoln University, Canterbury, New Zealand. https://core.ac.uk/download/pdf/35458784.pdf

Gopalkrishnan, S., Wischnevsky, J. D., & Damanpour, F. (2003). A Multi-Level Analysis of Factors Influencing the Adoption of Internet Banking. *Engineering Management*, *50*(4), 413–426.

Jeremski, M., & Plastaras, B. (2016). The Competitive and Coexistence of Mutual and Commercial Banks in England, 1870-1914. *Cliometrica*, *10*(2), 151–179. DOI: 10.1007/s11698-015-0127-0

Kotler, P., & Keller, K. (2011). *Marketing Management* (14th ed.). Pearson.

Kumbahar, V. M. (2010). *Reliability and validity of 'eBankQual' Scale in ATM Service Settings: A Study. VINIMAYA, XXXI(4)*. National Institute of Bank Management.

Kumbahar, V. M. (2011). Factors Affecting the Customer Satisfaction in E-banking: Some Evidence from Indian Banks. *Management Research and Practice*, *3*(4), 1–14.

Lu, S. C., Lai, K. H., & Cheng, T. C. E. (2006). Adoption of Internet Service in Linier Shipping: An Empirical Study of Shippers' of Taiwan. *Transport Reviews*, *26*(2), 189–206. DOI: 10.1080/01441640500246713

Masrek, M. N., Syafiq, M., Halim, A., Khan, A., & Ramli, I. (2018). The Impact of Perceived Credibility and Perceived Quality on Trust and Satisfaction in Mobile Banking Context. *Asian Economic and Financial Review*, *8*(7), 1013–1025. DOI: 10.18488/journal.aefr.2018.87.1013.1025

Mukherjee, A., & Nath, P. (2003). A Model of Trust in Online Relationship Banking. *International Journal of Bank Marketing*, *21*(1), 5–15. DOI: 10.1108/02652320310457767

Musiime, A., & Biyaki, F. (2010). Bank Clients' Perception of Information Technology Usage, Service Delivery and Customer Satisfaction: Reflections on Uganda's Banking Sector. *Proceedings of the International Trade & Academic Research Conference (01-17)*. https://vdocuments.mx/documents/bank-clients-perception-of-information-technology-usage-service-delivery-and-customer-satisfaction-reflections-on-ugandas-banking-sector-fayth.html

Negi, M., & Kaur, D. P. (2010). A Study of Customer Satisfaction with Life Insurance In Candgarh Tricity. *Paradigm*, *14*(2), 29–44.

Nikita, T. A., & Bhatt, B. (2024). Growth Of Mobile Banking In India: Comprehensive Study. *Educational Administration: Theory and Practice*, *30*(1), 3403–3417.

Nyangosi, R., Arora, J. S., & Singh, S. (2009). The Evolution of e-banking: A Study of Indian and Kenyan Technology Awareness. *International Journal of Electronic Finance*, *3*(2), 149–155. DOI: 10.1504/IJEF.2009.026357

Oliver, R. L. (2009). Whence Customer Loyalty? *Journal of Marketing, Special Issue*, (63), 33–44.

Ombati, T. O., Magutu, P. O., Nyamwange, S. O., & Nyaoga, R. B. (2010). Technology and service quality in the banking industry: Importance and Performance of Various Factors Considered In the Electronic Banking Services. [AJBUMA]. *African Journal of Business Management*, *1*, 151–164.

Pandey, A., Patel, D. P., Sahu, S. K. & Gupta, P. (2023). Role of Digital Banking in Investors' Awareness and Investment Decision-Making. *International Journal of Multidisciplinary Research Transactions*, 5(9), 43.53.

Paul, J., Mittal, A., & Srivastav, G. (2016). Impact of Service Quality on Customer Satisfaction in Private and Public Sector Banks. *International Journal of Bank Marketing*, *35*(5), 606–622. https://www.researchgate.net/publication/283014318_Paul_J_Mittal_A_SrivastavaG_2016_Impact_of_Service_Quality_on_Customer_Satisfaction_in_Private_and_Public_Sector_Banks_35_5_Forthcoming. DOI: 10.1108/IJBM-03-2015-0030

Pikkarainen, T., Pikkarainen, K., Karjaluoto, H., & Pahnila, S. (2004). Consumer acceptance of online banking: An extension of the technology acceptance model. *Internet Research*, *14*(3), 224–235. DOI: 10.1108/10662240410542652

Poder, B. (2005). *Factors Influencing the Adoption and Usage of Internet Banking: A New Zealand Perspective*. Master Thesis, Auckland University of Technology.

Polatoglu, V. N., & Ekin, S. (2001). An Empirical Investigation of the Turkish Consumers' Acceptance of Internet Bank Services. *International Journal of Bank Marketing*, *19*(4), 156–165. DOI: 10.1108/02652320110392527

Priya, M. S. (2024). A Study on Customer Awareness, Preference on e-Banking Services. *Humanities and Social Science Studies*, *13*(1), 45–48.

Rajput, U. S. (2015). Customers' Perception of e-banking Service. *Pacific Business Review International*, *8*(4), 85–94.

Redda, E. H. (2023). E-banking quality and customer loyalty: The mediating role of customer satisfaction. *Banks and Bank Systems*, *18*(2), 177–188. DOI: 10.21511/bbs.18(2).2023.15

Sathiyavany, N., & Shivany, S. (2018). E-Banking Service Qualities, E-Customer Satisfaction, and e-Loyalty: A conceptual Model. *The International Journal of Social Sciences and Humanities Invention*, *5*(6), 4808–4819. DOI: 10.18535/ijsshi/v5i6.08

Sayar, C., & Wolfe, S. (2007). Internet banking market performance: UK. *International Journal of Bank Marketing*, *25*(3), 122–141. DOI: 10.1108/02652320710739841

Shaikh, M. A. (2014). Ethiopian bankers perception of electronic banking in ethiopia–a case of Adama City. *International Journal of Scientific and Research Publications*, *4*(9), 1–6.

Singh, S., & Arora, R. (2011). A Comparative Study of Banking Services and Customer Satisfaction in Public, Private and Foreign Banks. *Journal of Economics*, *2*(1), 45–56. DOI: 10.1080/09765239.2011.11884936

SLBC. (2016). 116th State Level Banker's Committee Meeting for Tripura, February, 2016, Quarterly Review, Agartala, Tripura, India.

SLBC. (2017). 121st State Level Banker's Committee Meeting for Tripura, March, 2017, Quarterly Review, Agartala, Tripura, India.

SLBC. (2018). 125th State Level Banker's Committee Meeting for Tripura, March, 2018, Quarterly Review, Agartala, Tripura, India.

SLBC. (2019). 129th State Level Banker's Committee Meeting for Tripura, March, 2019, Quarterly Review, Agartala, Tripura, India.

SLBC. (2020). 131st State Level Banker's Committee Meeting for Tripura, December, 2020, Quarterly Review, Agartala, Tripura, India.

SLBC. (2021). 135th State Level Banker's Committee Meeting for Tripura, March, 2021, Quarterly Review, Agartala, Tripura, India.

SLBC. (2022). 139th State Level Banker's Committee Meeting for Tripura, March, 2022, Quarterly Review, Agartala, Tripura, India.

SLBC. (2023). 142nd State Level Banker's Committee Meeting for Tripura, December, 2023, Quarterly Review, Agartala, Tripura, India.

Suleiman, G.P, Mat, N.K.M., Adesiyan, O.I, & Mohammed, A.S, & ALekam, J. (. (2012). Customer Loyalty in e-Banking: A Structural Equation Modelling (SEM) Approach. *American Journal of Economics*, (Special Issue), 55–59. DOI: 10.5923/j.economics.20120001.13

Tari, F., & Raeisi, H. (2021). The Role of Electronic Receipt and Payment Instruments in the Development of Banking Services. Iranian Journal of Accounting, Auditing & Finance. *Iranian Journal of Accounting. Auditing & Finance*, *4*(4), 83–96.

Tse, D. K., & Wilton, P. C. (1988). Models of Consumer Satisfaction Formation: An Extension. *JMR, Journal of Marketing Research*, *25*(2), 204–212. DOI: 10.1177/002224378802500209

Venkatesh, J. & Perisamy.P. (2007). Role of E-Banking in Emerging Scenario. *The Professional Banker*, 53-57

Chapter 7
Virtual Democracy: Exploring the Viability of Election Voting via Metaverse Technology

Nina Lestari
https://orcid.org/0009-0001-5007-2382
Universitas Muhammadiyah Makassar, Indonesia

Nur Azizah Wahyuni
Universitas Muhammadiyah Makassar, Indonesia

Muhammad Younus
https://orcid.org/0000-0001-9654-1546
Universitas Muhammadiyah Yogyakarta, Pakistan

Andi Luhur Prianto
Universitas Muhammadiyah Makassar, Indonesia

Aqmal Reza Amri
Universitas Muhammadiyah Makassar, Indonesia

Ahmad Harakan
Universitas Muhammadiyah Makassar, Indonesia

Achmad Nurmandi
Universitas Muhammadiyah Yogyakarta, Indonesia

Hajira Gul
https://orcid.org/0000-0001-9266-2412
Midwifery Association, Pakistan

Ibrahim Shah
Aga Khan University, Pakistan

Ihyani Malik
Universitas Muhammadiyah Makassar, Indonesia

ABSTRACT

The creation of the metaverse will change how we live, work, and play in a digital environment, one of which the metaverse opens up great opportunities for the development of virtual democracy. One of the implementations of virtual democracy is through digital election voting using the metaverse. A paradigm shift in democratic

DOI: 10.4018/979-8-3693-8477-0.ch007

participation is brought about by integrating the metaverse into election voting. In the metaverse, voters can participate in the election process through an immersive virtual environment; the digital platform also changes the voting experience. The objective of this study is to explore the feasibility of election voting through metaverse technology. The result of this research is that election voting using metaverse technology has been implemented in several countries, where the implementation uses a blockchain system that ensures every vote is recorded securely and cannot be manipulated, thereby reducing the risk of fraud. This research concludes that applying metaverse technology in election voting will significantly change virtual democratic activities.

1 INTRODUCTION

The "metaverse" concept refers to a collective virtual shared space formed by the fusion of physically persisting virtual reality and virtually enhanced physical reality. (Lee et al., 2021). In simpler terms, the metaverse is a virtual universe where humans can interact with the digital environment and each other directly (Nevelsteen, 2018). It is an interconnected universe between the internet, augmented reality experiences, and virtual reality spaces. It encompasses many things, including social interaction, work, commerce, education, and more (Scavarelli et al., 2021). The Metaverse opens the boundaries between the digital world and the physical world, providing engaging and interactive experiences beyond what is possible in the physical world alone. Big companies like Facebook (now known as Meta Platforms, Inc.), Epic Games (with Fortnite), and many others are spending much money to build the infrastructure and platforms of the metaverse, which is considered the next evolution of the internet (Jungherr & Schlarb, 2022).

Early examples of the metaverse concept can be found in science fiction literature, such as Neal Stephenson's novel "Snow Crash" (1992) and William Gibson's "Neuromancer" (1984)(Boehm, 2004). These novels depict the fascinating concept of virtual worlds where people interact with avatars. Virtual worlds such as Second Life (released in 2003) and online games such as World of Warcraft (released in 2004) provide an early glimpse into the proto-metaverse environment of the late 20th and early 21st centuries.(Heath, 2023). With the help of various platforms, people can create and inhabit virtual spaces, interact with each other, and engage in various activities.

In the early 2000s, the term "metaverse" became popular due to the book "Snow Crash" by Neal Stephenson, which referred to a virtual reality-based successor to the internet. (Dionisio et al., 2013). The metaverse concept has broadly expanded to encompass online social interaction, virtual experiences, and augmented reality.

Technological advancements, especially in virtual, augmented, artificial intelligence, and blockchain, have driven renewed interest in the metaverse in recent years. (Huynh-The et al., 2023). Major tech companies such as Facebook (now known as Meta Platforms, Inc.), Google, Microsoft, and others have spent money building platforms and technologies to create immersive, interconnected digital universes.

Today, the metaverse is considered the next frontier of the internet, with a wide range of applications that can be used, from social networking and entertainment to education, commerce, and more (Mystakidis, 2022). However, the metaverse is still in its infancy, and many companies, developers, and creators are excited to build a more interactive and engaging digital future. Implementing the metaverse faces several significant issues, from technological barriers to social and moral considerations. Building an interconnected and immersive virtual universe requires advanced technologies in various fields, including virtual reality (VR), augmented reality (AR), artificial intelligence (AI), networking, and more (Rane et al., 2023). Guaranteeing a seamless experience across different devices, platforms, and environments adds to the technical complexity.

To create a cohesive metaverse experience, it is crucial to ensure that virtual worlds, platforms, and ecosystems work well. This requires the development of protocols, standards, and technologies that allow systems to communicate and interact smoothly with each other. Scalability presents challenges due to the large and diverse user base in the metaverse, especially in terms of server infrastructure, bandwidth, and computing resources(Chang et al., 2022). A robust scalability solution is required to guarantee a smooth and responsive experience for millions or even billions of concurrent users.

Protecting user privacy and security on the metaverse is critical to preventing unauthorized access, data breaches, identity theft, and other cyber threats (Pakina & Solekhan, 2024). As the metaverse collects large amounts of user data, there are concerns about how companies and third parties store, manage, and use this data. Monitoring content and adhering to the metaverse rules to avoid harassment, hate speech, illegal acts, and other harmful behaviors is a big challenge. It is not easy to balance freedom of expression and creativity while implementing an effective content moderation mechanism.

It is extremely difficult to define and protect digital rights, intellectual property rights, and ownership rights of virtual assets in the metaverse. Legal and regulatory challenges include determining who owns the virtual property, goods, works, and experiences and how they can be bought, sold, traded, and protected. To foster diversity, equality, and inclusion, it is critical to ensure that the metaverse is accessible to people of different backgrounds, abilities, and socioeconomic status. To make the metaverse truly inclusive, it is imperative to address issues related to access to hardware, the internet, language, culture, and disability.

Challenges of implementing metaverse in voting: One of the most important things is maintaining the security and integrity of the voting process. Metaverse will require strong security measures to prevent hacking, tampering, or unauthorized access to voting systems and data (Y. Wang et al., 2023). In a virtual environment, it is not easy to verify the identity of voters. A reliable authentication and verification system is required to prevent fraudulent voting and ensure that every voter is eligible to participate. It is critical to ensure that the metaverse voting system is accessible to all voters, including those who cannot use technology or have disabilities. The user interface should be easy to understand and use for different user groups. The acceptance and legitimacy of Meta vision-based voting processes depend on building trust. To assure voters of the fairness and accuracy of the process, transparency in the system's operation, including how votes are cast, recorded, and counted, is essential.

New terms about technology are also growing in this sophisticated era. In addition to the multiverse, there is also the metaverse, which is being rumored to facilitate human activities, especially in the digital world, such as in business economics and marketing (Ali et al., 2023). The metaverse concept is considered a gateway to a virtual world in the future, which, of course, will be related to the digital world. Since the digital world is closely related to technology, especially the technology in our smartphones, everything in the future will be easy to achieve. Linguistically, the term "metaverse" consists of two words: "verse," which means "universe," and "meta," which means "beyond or beyond." These words are of Greek origin and mean "beyond the universe" or "beyond the universe." In the early 1990s, the term "metaverse" first appeared (Nestorović, 2023). At the time, the metaverse was seen as a way to connect humans (society) with the idea of avatars that relied heavily on technology. It is important to note that this virtual metaverse world consists of three main components: virtual reality (VR), artificial intelligence (AI), web 3.0 technology, and blockchain technology.

Nicely states, "The metaverse refers to a shared online virtual world, similar to video games like Second Life or Pokémon Go " (Sabtu, 2023). It (the metaverse) is a realistic three-dimensional environment where people can explore and interact with others in real-time." Stefanic states, "Metaverse is an online 3D world accessed through computers, smart devices, augmented reality, and virtual reality headsets " (Swami, 2024). Interaction and engagement are central to the principles of the metaverse, ensuring that users can be fully immersed in the online environment facilitated by metaverse technology." Metaverse was created to become a contemporary communication platform allowing everyone to carry out their daily activities, such as playing, working, socializing, and even performing virtual concerts.

A holistic and multifaceted approach is required to address the challenges associated with metaverse implementation. To improve performance, security, and interoperability, continue to develop technologies that support the metaverse, such as virtual reality, augmented reality, artificial intelligence, blockchain, and computer networks. Help technology companies, developers, and content creators work together to develop the protocols, technologies, and standards needed to build a connected and accessible metaverse. Create rules and regulations that support privacy, security, fairness, and inclusion in the metaverse while providing flexibility for progress and innovation. Through education, awareness campaigns, and open discussions on ethics, privacy, and security, society can better understand the potential and threats of the metaverse, create advanced security tools such as encryption, two-factor authentication, and threat detection to protect user data, and prevent cyber-attacks in the metaverse (Gulomov, 2024). Creating business opportunities, new markets, and creative revenue models for developers, content creators, and virtual asset owners to drive digital economic growth in the metaverse. Develop training courses and programs that help people and groups prepare for the metaverse and its potential, such as content development, community management, and digital security awareness. Ensuring that the metaverse is designed and operated with the various needs and perspectives of users in mind. This includes inclusion in decision-making, diverse cultural representation, and ease of access for people with disabilities.

This journal aims to conduct research on Virtual Democracy in Exploring the Viability of Election Voting through Metaverse Technology. Literature description of election voting through metaverse technology can be the main topic of discussion that contributes to understanding the use of metaverse technology. This research aims to advance our knowledge of technological advances, especially using metaverse technology for voting in elections through virtual democracy. This research aims to find relevant scientific publications and evaluate how much literature discusses using metaverse technology in election voting. The importance of this research lies in its emphasis on conducting election voting using metaverse technology. The study also comprehensively analyzes how metaverse technology plays a role in electoral voting in virtual democracies.

2 LITERATURE REVIEW

2.1 What is Metaverse

The metaverse is the further merging of the original and digital worlds by using programs and technology. (Zhao et al., 2022). The metaverse is a vast digital landscape that transcends the boundaries of physical reality. It encompasses interconnected virtual worlds where people can interact, socialize, create, and explore in real time (Iswanto et al., 2022). At its core, the metaverse represents the fusion of virtual and augmented reality technologies, artificial intelligence, and the internet, resulting in a dynamic and engaging digital universe that mirrors and often surpasses the composition of physical reality.(Dwivedi et al., 2022).

The Metaverse has great potential for social, educational, and economic advancement; it is not just a world of entertainment and recreation (Endarto & Martadi, 2022). The Metaverse enables new ways to cooperate, learn, and be productive. It includes virtual classrooms, remote workspaces, fun training simulations, and telemedicine applications. Metaverse also encourages cross-cultural discussion and cooperation on an unprecedented scale and serves as a platform for global connectivity and cultural exchange (Gaurav, 2023).

2.2 What is Election Voting

Voting is an important process in a democratic society in which eligible citizens participate in electing representatives or making decisions on public issues (Warren, 2009). Voting is a process known as an election (Dalton et al., 2003). This process involves voters casting ballots to express their policy preferences or candidates. Afterward, these votes are counted to determine the outcome of the election.

The voting process usually consists of several main steps, including voter registration, candidate nomination, campaigning, voting, and vote counting (Ranney, 1981). Eligible voters can vote through various methods, such as in person at a polling station, mail-in ballots, or electronic voting systems. Election authorities monitor the election process, enforce rules and regulations, and certify the results to maintain the legitimacy of the results (Maley, 2003). The principles of fairness, transparency, and accountability are essential to ensure the integrity of the election process (Norris & Nai, 2017).

2.3 Usage of Metaverse in Election Voting

A paradigm shift in democratic participation is brought about by integrating the metaverse into election voting. In the metaverse, voters can participate in election processes through immersive virtual environments using digital avatars and interfaces (Goldberg & Schär, 2023). VR, AR, and digital platforms also transform the voting experience. The potential benefits of this method include increased voter accessibility, especially for voters who have limited mobility or live in remote areas (Gimpel & Schuknecht, 2003). Additionally, this method enables innovative voting systems, such as blockchain-based secure voting systems, to increase transparency and trust in the electoral process (Farooq et al., 2022).

However, the application of metaverse technology in election voting raises ethical issues and major dilemmas (Benjamins et al., 2023). The most important thing is to ensure the security and integrity of the voting system, protect voters' privacy, and solve the problem of digital identity verification. In addition, to prevent certain voters from being marginalized, issues such as digital literacy, technology access, and inclusiveness must be addressed (Mossberger, 2008). Policymakers, technologists, and election authorities must work together to create a robust framework of rules, technical procedures, and security protocols that safeguard democracy and capitalize on the transformational possibilities of the metaverse (Prayitno et al., 2023).

Previous research on implementing direct democracy in a virtual world describes whether voting precedence will reflect voting precedence in the real world. The previous research presents a within-subject study in which participants are asked to allocate voting rights in two scenarios. The first scenario investigates participants' opinions about the distribution of voting rights. The second scenario presented participants with a case of unequal allocation of voting rights in a virtual world enforced by a smart contract. In both scenarios, participants allocated voting rights and assessed the fairness of their decisions. The results found that participants' voting preferences in the virtual world scenario did not reflect their preferences and beliefs in the real world (Oppenlaender, 2022). Therefore, voting systems in the metaverse need to be carefully designed to align with human values and ethics.

Figure 1. Authors connectivity

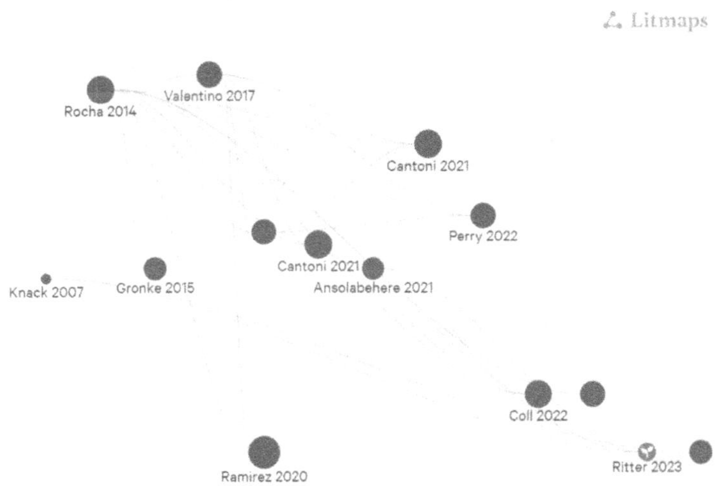

(LitMaps)

3 RESEARCH METHOD

3.1 Types of Research

This article explores the feasibility of implementing Metaverse Technology in Election Voting. Therefore, we believe that qualitative research methods are suitable for this research topic as they allow for thoroughly examining the theme, incorporating unbiased viewpoints and experiences.

Figure 2. Filters and keywords used for research

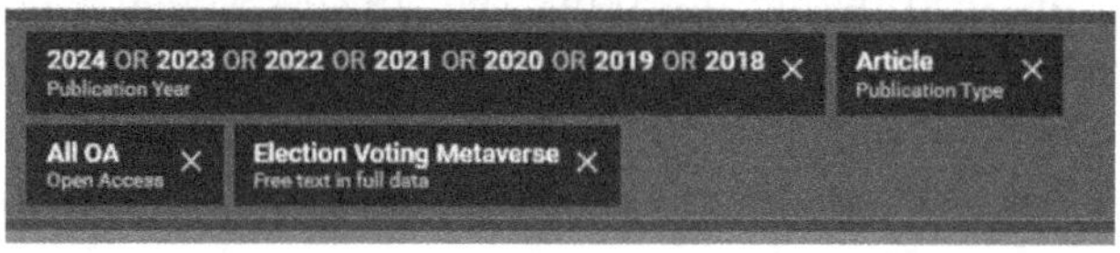

(Dimensions AI)

3.2 Research Source

Academic journals and the Dimension AI website were our sources for research for this article. However, our analysis shows that academic journals that offer in-depth analysis of experts' research have emerged as a reliable source of data and knowledge. We obtained data related to Academic Journals from various online database sources, including Emerald, Google Scholar, Cambridge Core, and others. The data has gone through a peer-review process, thus ensuring its reliability and accuracy.

Table 1. Data sources used to collect data

Source Name	Website Link
Dimension AI	https://app.dimensions.ai/discover/publication
Emerald	https://www.emerald.com/insight/
Cambridge Core	https://www.cambridge.org/core/
Google Scholar	https://scholar.google.com/

3.3 Data Collection Techniques

As researchers, we collect data by conducting literature reviews, which allows us to gather up-to-date knowledge. Our understanding of the data was successful because of the information that had been collected. We identified research gaps and important information for our brainstorming session. The first stage in conducting a literature review is to define the parameters of our investigation; in this case, this involved identifying the keywords we would use to search for information related to the article's subject matter, such as "election voting," metaverse," and others. Additionally, we limited our search to articles published within the last seven years. After conducting the initial review, we quickly perused the abstracts of the collected papers to ensure that they were relevant to our topic.

Figure 3. PRISMA diagram flow

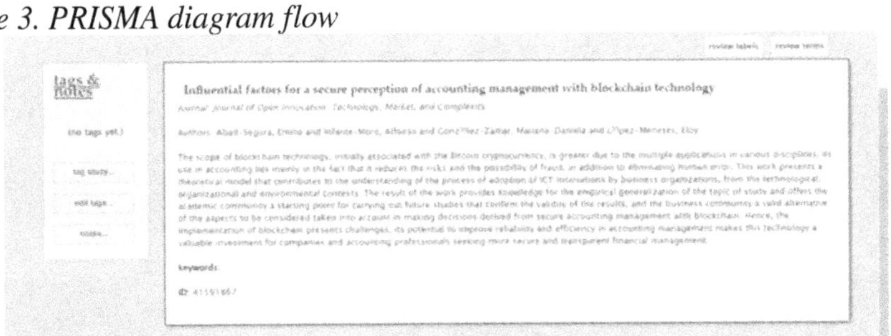

(Created by Author)

3.4 Data Analysis Techniques

Abstrackr is a no-cost web-based application designed to assist individuals in uploading and structuring findings from a comprehensive exploration of literature materials intended to formulate a systematic review. The integration of citations obtained through electronic inquiries conducted on databases containing scholarly articles was executed within the Abstrackr platform, where the subsequent evaluation of titles and abstracts ensued, determining their eligibility for inclusion or exclusion based on predetermined criteria for selection. This iterative procedure was further iterated until Abstrackr successfully anticipated and categorized the remaining unexamined citations into pertinent or inconsequential categories.

Figure 4. Abstrackr analysis flow process

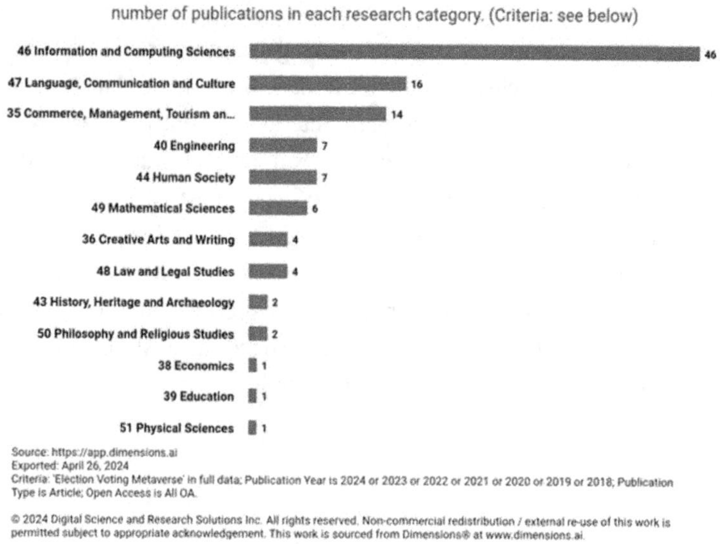

(Abstrackr)

4 RESULTS AND DISCUSSION

4.1 Results

4.1.1 Document by subject area

Figure 5. Publication by subject area

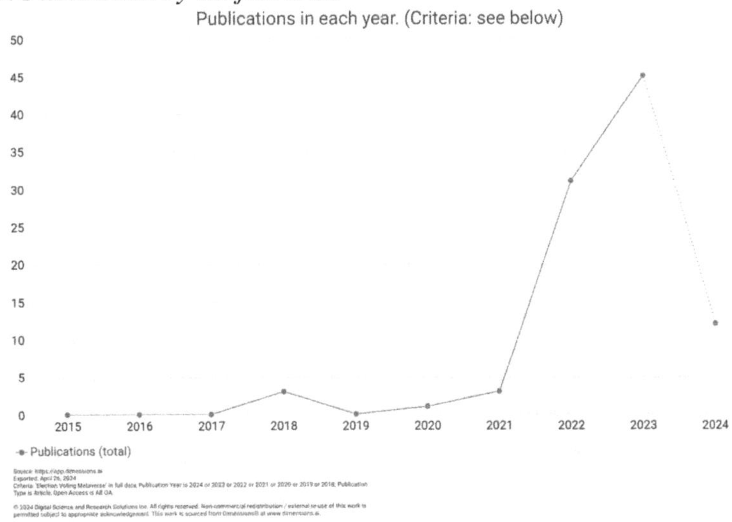

(Dimension AI)

Figure 5 above shows publication trends by subject generated by Dimensions for the keywords "metaverse" and "election voting." This data was retrieved on April 26, 2024, and includes publications from 2018 to 2024 that are both articles and open access. The "Information and Computing Sciences" category dominates with 46 publications, showing that research on the metaverse and election voting is strongly linked to computer science and information technology. This is not surprising given that the metaverse, as a rapidly evolving concept of virtual worlds, relies heavily on advanced computing technologies and digital infrastructure. Research in this category will likely include topics such as cybersecurity, blockchain, and artificial intelligence, all playing an important role in developing and securing voting platforms in the metaverse.

The second most numerous categories are "Language, Communication and Culture," with 16 publications. This shows that the social and cultural aspects of the metaverse are also receiving significant attention. Research in this category might focus on how communication and social interactions change in virtual environments and how culture and language adapt to new technologies such as the metaverse. It could also include the study of disinformation and propaganda in the context of elections taking place on digital platforms. The "Commerce, Management, Tourism and Services" category has 14 publications. This shows considerable interest in exploring how the metaverse can affect the business and management sectors. Research in this area might include the virtual economy, resource management in digital environments, and the legal implications of transactions in the metaverse. In addition, elections conducted in the metaverse also require good management to ensure the integrity and fairness of the process.

The "Engineering" and "Human Society" categories have seven publications each. For engineering, research might focus on developing hardware and software to support the metaverse and voting infrastructure. Whereas in the field of human society, research could include the social impact of using the metaverse in the election process, as well as how this technology can be used to increase voter participation and engagement. The "Mathematical Sciences" category has six publications demonstrating the importance of mathematical and statistical methods in analyzing election data and developing algorithms underlying metaverse technology. Studies in this area might include mathematical models for election outcome prediction, big data analysis of user activity in the metaverse, and development of encryption algorithms for voter data security.

The categories "Creative Arts and Writing" and "Law and Legal Studies" have four publications each. Research in creative arts might explore how the metaverse can be used as a new medium for artistic expression and writing and how voting can be interactive and engaging in a virtual environment. In legal studies, possible topics include the legal and regulatory framework needed to support voting in the metaverse, as well as privacy and human rights issues that may arise. The "History, Heritage and Archaeology" category had two publications, indicating that while there is interest in exploring how new technologies can be used to preserve and interpret history and cultural heritage, this is still a relatively new and under-explored area. Likewise, the "Philosophy and Religious Studies" category also has two publications, which may address the philosophical and ethical implications of using advanced technologies in the voting process and human interaction in the metaverse.

The categories "Economics," "Education," and "Physical Sciences" have one publication each. This shows that research in these areas is still very limited. However, there is interest in exploring the potential economic impact of the metaverse and voting and how these technologies can be used in education and physical sciences. Overall, this publication trend reflects the broad and diverse interest in various disciplines in the metaverse concept and its use in voting. This suggests that this new technology not only impacts the fields of technology and computer science but also has far-reaching implications on society's social, cultural, economic, legal, and ethical aspects.

4.1.2 Document by Years

Figure 6. Publication by years

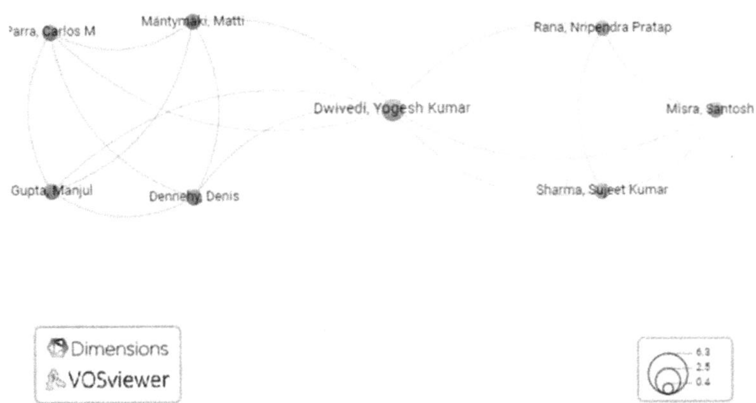

(Dimension AI)

Figure 6. shows the trend of yearly scientific publications related to the keywords “metaverse” and “election voting” based on data from Dimensions AI. The data covers the period from 2015 to 2024. The graph displays the total number of publications yearly, with a significant increase in recent years, especially from 2021 to 2023. From 2015 to 2016, the number of publications related to this topic was very low, almost zero. This reflects that in that period, scientific discussions and research on the metaverse and voting in the context of the metaverse had not received significant attention. It was only in 2017 that there was a slight increase, although still a very small number.

2018 showed a slight increase, with the number of publications reaching around 5. This may be due to the growing interest of academics in metaverse technology and its potential in various fields, including electronic voting. However, the number of publications is still relatively low, indicating that research in this area has not been a major focus. In 2019, the number of publications decreased again. This decrease could be due to several factors, including a possible focus on other topics or a lack of technological advancements that support further study of the metaverse and electronic voting.

Significant changes began to be seen in 2020 when the number of publications again increased slightly compared to the previous year. Then, in 2021, there was a significant spike, with the number of publications reaching more than 10. Further technological developments and increased awareness of the potential of the metaverse in various applications, including voting, may have influenced this surge. The year 2022 shows an even more dramatic increase, with the number of publications reaching more than 20. This increase reflects a significant increase in interest from the academic community toward studying the metaverse and how these technologies can be integrated into electronic voting systems. Factors such as the COVID-19 pandemic driving the use of digital technologies in various aspects of life may have also contributed to this increase.

The year 2023 is the peak of this trend, with the number of publications peaking at more than 40. This indicates a peak of interest and research on this topic, which may be driven by the growing maturity of metaverse technology and the growing number of experiments and practical implementations in voting. However, by 2024, there will be a sharp decline in the number of publications. This decline may be due to several factors. One could be that the topic has reached a saturation point in academic research, where many key aspects have been explored and documented in previous years. In addition, there may also be a shift in interest to other topics or technologies that are newer or more relevant to recent developments.

Overall, this trend shows the evolution of academic interest in the metaverse and electronic voting topic. From almost no publications at the beginning of the observed period to a significant peak in recent years, it illustrates how new technologies and concepts can attract widespread attention in the scientific community as they are developed and applied in real life. The decline seen in 2024 may also be cause for reflection for researchers and academics to re-evaluate future research directions. It may be necessary to examine how these technologies can be further integrated or combined with others to produce more relevant and beneficial innovations for society.

These trends also illustrate how technological changes and advancements can affect the focus of scientific research over time. As technology advances, new and innovative topics will continue to emerge and may replace those currently being researched. This demonstrates the fast-paced nature of research and the importance of academics staying up-to-date to remain relevant in their field. Overall, this graph provides an interesting insight into how research on the metaverse and electronic voting has evolved and changed in recent years and how these trends will likely continue to develop.

4.1.3 Document by Authors

Figure 7. Publication by author

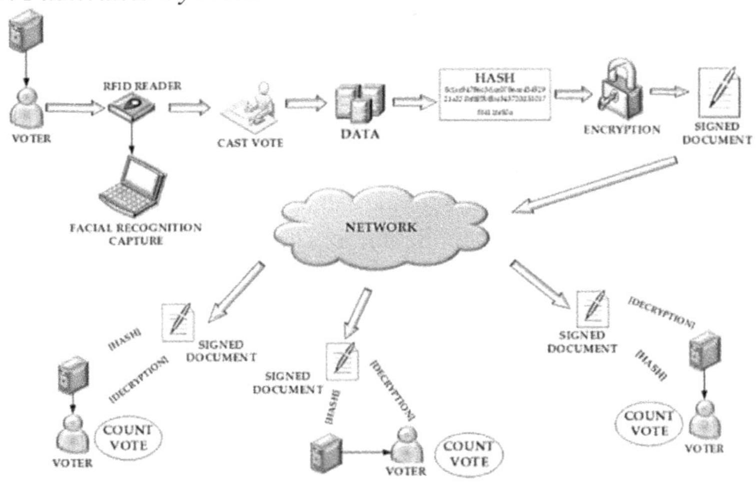

(Dimension AI)

Figure 7. shows a collaboration map of authors who published papers related to the keywords "metaverse" and "election voting." This graph was created using the visualization tool VOSviewer and data from Dimensions. This collaboration map shows the network of authors involved in research on these topics, with each author represented by a node connected by a line indicating their collaboration. In the center of this map, we can see Yogesh Kumar Dwivedi as the center of many collaborations. Dwivedi seems to be a very active author and has many collaborations with other authors in research on the metaverse and electronic voting. The collaboration network formed around Dwivedi includes several other authors, such as Nripendra Pratap Rana, Santosh Misra, and Sujeet Kumar Sharma, who are also actively involved in this research.

Nripendra Pratap Rana, who is seen as closely connected with Dwivedi, shows a strong collaboration between the two of them. Rana is also connected to other writers like Santosh Misra and Sujeet Kumar Sharma, creating a strong sub-network of collaboration around them. This suggests that Dwivedi, Rana, Misra, and Sharma are likely working together on some research projects or publications related to the metaverse and electronic voting. On the other hand, we also see another group of authors closely connected to each other but slightly separate from Dwivedi's group. This group includes authors such as Carlos M. Parra, Matti Mäntymäki, Manjul Gupta, and Denis Dennehy. This group also has quite intensive collaborations amongst themselves but does not seem to be very connected to the group led by Dwivedi.

Carlos M. Parra appears to be one of the lead authors in this group, with several lines of collaboration connecting him to other authors such as Mäntymäki, Gupta, and Dennehy. This suggests that Parra may be acting as a coordinator or leader in their collaboration network, similar to Dwivedi's role in his group. Interestingly, although there are two main collaboration groups on this map, they are still connected through Dwivedi, who links the two groups. This suggests that Dwivedi has an extensive collaboration network and may be important in bridging knowledge and ideas between the two research groups.

Overall, this collaboration map provides an overview of how key metaverse and electronic voting research authors collaborate. The collaborative groups formed indicate a strong synergy between these authors, which may contribute to developing and disseminating knowledge in this field. Looking at this trend of collaboration, it can be concluded that research on the metaverse and electronic voting is not being conducted by individuals working in isolation but rather by a network of interconnected researchers working together to produce more comprehensive and influential research. This collaboration allows authors to share resources, knowledge, and ideas, which in turn can accelerate research progress and innovation in this field.

This map also indicates the potential to expand collaboration in the future. With authors like Dwivedi having a wide network of collaborations, there is an opportunity to introduce and connect with other researchers who may not yet be involved in these networks. This could pave the way for broader, richer cross-disciplinary collaborations, ultimately leading to more significant findings and innovations. This collaboration trend also reflects the importance of networks and partnerships in academia. Authors with a wide and diverse network of collaborations are usually more likely to produce high-quality, high-impact research. They can access different perspectives and expertise, enriching and deepening their analysis and interpretations. Overall, this collaboration map shows publication trends by authors related to the metaverse and electronic voting and illustrates the dynamics and structure of collaboration among these researchers. By understanding how these authors interact and work together, we can better understand how knowledge in this field is evolving and how collaboration can continue to be encouraged and improved.

4.2 Discussion

4.2.1 Current State of Usage

The metaverse, a new class of Internet applications and social media platforms, incorporates many advanced technologies. The term "metaverse," first coined nearly two decades ago to describe a speculative virtual environment, now refers to a world where users of augmented reality technology only feel its psychological impact (Bojic,

2022). The use of metaverse technology is currently growing rapidly and is widely used in various sectors. The current state of use of metaverse technology can be seen from IT companies that continue to compete to create innovations, presenting real, authentic, cohesive, and interactive experiences (Mele et al., 2024). With the support of AI, metaverse can transform the workspace into a gamified virtual environment that can be accessed remotely (Németh et al., n.d.). The rapid advancement of metaverse technology is now being utilized in political activities (Bibri, 2022).

4.2.1.1 Usage of Metaverse Technology

The use of metaverse technology in political activities offers a range of innovative opportunities. Politicians can hold campaigns, debates, and rallies virtually, enabling wider participation without geographical restrictions (Kichanova, 2023). The metaverse can also be utilized for political training and citizen education on the democratic process through legislative simulations (Regina, 2022). Public participation can be enhanced through virtual forums and more interactive policy discussions (virtual diplomacy). Virtual diplomacy allows world leaders to meet and negotiate without needing physical travel. In addition to virtual diplomacy, there is also the concept of virtual democracy, where one form of implementation is election voting using metaverse technology.

Electoral voting using electronic devices is known as Electronic Voting (E-voting). The use of metaverse technology in the election voting process can increase government transparency and accountability by providing real-time data access (AL-Hawamleh et al., 2024). The application of blockchain technology-based e-voting to maintain security in the electronic-based voting process (Gopal et al., 2023). Blockchain enables the implementation of e-voting with consensus algorithms that reflect the principle of universal suffrage (one person, one vote) or implement other consensus mechanisms not currently used in national elections (e.g., weighted voting) (Kiayias & Lazos, 2022). With metaverse, the political process becomes more inclusive, allowing full participation of individuals in remote areas or with limited mobility.

4.2.1.2 Impact Metaverse Technology

The impact of metaverse technology on election voting includes various aspects that could revolutionize elections. Firstly, the metaverse has the potential to increase voter participation by removing geographical and physical barriers, allowing voters to cast a ballot from anywhere, provided they have internet access (Anim, 2022). Second, metaverse technology can increase the transparency and security of the electoral process through the use of blockchain, which ensures every vote is securely recorded and cannot be manipulated, thereby reducing the risk of fraud (Anim, 2022).

Implementing e-voting based on blockchain technology will greatly assist the conduct of elections. Blockchain technology can allow voters to be registered in a trusted and secure system. Through predetermined criteria in the blockchain system, the e-voting process will have validation capabilities to ensure the validity of the vote (Daramola & Thebus, 2020). The validation mechanism in blockchain covers the entire process, from the registration of potential voters to the audit of voting results (Jafar et al., 2021). Blockchain technology can provide features that support efficient, transparent, and secure elections through an end-to-end verification system (Panja & Roy, 2021).

4.2.1.3 User Experience Satisfaction

Several key factors, such as the quality of immersiveness, ease of use, and integration with daily activities, strongly influence user satisfaction with metaverse technology. Satisfaction is high when users interact in a realistic and engaging virtual environment, whether in gaming, working, shopping, studying, or political activities. Several countries, including the State of Thailand, have utilized metaverse technology in the election voting process; the Thai Democratic Party uses Zcoin Blockchain for direct e-voting (Gedar et al., 2023). Members can vote in two ways: first, through a polling station equipped with a Raspberry Pi-based voting system, and second, through a Blockchain-based application called D-Vote, which requires voters to submit a photo of their identity as proof. All voting information is then stored in a decentralized and distributed file system that can store large amounts of data, known as IPFS (Huang et al., 2020). This IPFS hash is then stored in Zcoin Blockchain technology (W. Wang et al., 2021). The success of Thailand in implementing metaverse technology in the election voting process shows opportunities for other countries to implement it.

Apart from Thailand, countries that have started adopting metaverse or blockchain technology in the election voting process include Estonia, Japan, and some states in the United States. Estonia successfully held an election where more than half of the votes were cast electronically. (Ehin et al., 2022). Japan has also conducted trials of blockchain-based voting systems in the context of social development proposals (Shirahada et al., 2020). Meanwhile, states such as West Virginia and Utah in the United States have tried blockchain voting applications for military voters (Healy Jr, 2023). Meanwhile, in Indonesia, election voting using Metaverse technology is still a discourse that will be discussed for implementation.

4.2.2 Challenges and Advantages of its Usage

Metaverse technology presents various challenges and benefits that must be considered for adoption. Metaverse can provide a more efficient and cost-effective logistics solution by reducing the need for physical polling stations and distribution of election materials (Murala & Panda, 2023). Secure digital identity verification can also ensure that only eligible voters can vote, thereby increasing the reliability of voter data. However, the implementation of these technologies also faces significant challenges, including the need for adequate technology infrastructure, digital access gaps, and concerns regarding data privacy and security (Habibzadeh et al., 2019). Strict regulations and public education will be key in overcoming these challenges and ensuring that the full benefits of metaverse technology can be optimized in the electoral process (Jagatheesaperumal et al., 2024).

4.2.2.1 Comparison with Traditional Service Delivery Methods

A comparison between traditional service delivery methods and metaverse technology in election voting shows significant differences in various aspects. Traditional methods require voters to be physically present at the polling station, which can be a barrier for those with limited mobility or who live in remote areas. The process is also prone to fraud, such as vote forgery and manipulation of results, and takes longer than manual vote counting. In the physical world, paper ballots provide a secure way to count votes in a democracy. Votes in a democracy. However, the success of traditional voting depends on the poll organizer, and centralized voting systems can suffer from security and efficiency limitations. Decentralized electronic voting based on blockchain technology offers an alternative to traditional voting.

In contrast, metaverse technology allows voters to cast ballots from anywhere with internet access, increasing accessibility and participation. The security and integrity of votes are further ensured by using blockchain, which ensures each vote is transparently recorded and cannot be altered or deleted once recorded. In addition, metaverse can reduce the costs and logistics associated with organizing physical polling stations and provide a publicly accessible audit trail to increase voter confidence in election results. However, challenges such as the need for adequate technological infrastructure, the digital divide, and privacy and data security issues remain to be overcome to optimize the adoption of this technology.

4.2.2.2 Advantages of Metaverse Technology over Traditional Methods

The advantages of metaverse technology over traditional methods of voting in elections are significant. Metaverse allows voters to vote from anywhere using internet access, overcoming the geographical and physical constraints that often hinder voter participation. This increases participation rates, especially among young voters and individuals with limited mobility. Votes are securely recorded and cannot be manipulated, reducing the risk of fraud and increasing public confidence in election results. Voters can also enjoy a more efficient and speedy voting process, with results that can be counted and verified in near real-time. With these features, metaverse provides a more modern, secure, and inclusive election solution than traditional methods.

4.2.2.3 Disadvantages or Limitations of Metaverse Technology

While offering an immersive and interactive virtual experience, Metaverse technology also has some drawbacks and limitations that are important to consider. One of these is the issue of user security and privacy, where personal data can be vulnerable to leakage or misuse. In addition, the infrastructure required to access the Metaverse, such as sophisticated hardware and stable internet connections, remains a challenge for some people and countries. There are concerns about the digital divide, where not all individuals or communities can easily access or utilize these technologies. In addition, the long-term psychological impact of intensive use of the Metaverse also requires further research to be fully understood.

4.2.3 Future Directions and Implications

Future directions and implications regarding electoral voting through metaverse technology show significant potential to revolutionize the democratic process. In the future, metaverse technology could provide a more inclusive and accessible platform for voters worldwide, removing the geographical and physical barriers that have hitherto been an obstacle.

4.2.3.1 Recommendations for Further Research

Recommendations for further research on election voting through metaverse technology include several important aspects. First, an in-depth study of data security and privacy is needed, specifically how blockchain technology can be optimized to ensure every vote is secure and voters' identities are protected. This research should also include the development of more sophisticated encryption protocols to prevent data manipulation. Second, there needs to be a study of the social and political impacts of adopting this technology, including how it may affect voter participation and public trust in the electoral system.

4.2.3.2 Suggestions for Policy and Practice

Several policy and practice suggestions need to be considered to ensure the successful implementation of election voting through metaverse technology. Governments and election bodies should adopt clear and comprehensive regulations, ensuring the security and privacy of voter data through sophisticated encryption protocols. In addition, investment in adequate digital infrastructure, including widespread internet access and supporting hardware, is required to make this technology accessible to all citizens. Education and training for voters on using metaverse technology is essential to increase participation. The government should work with technology and security experts to continuously develop and update systems to address potential cyber threats and ensure the integrity of the electoral process. Periodic evaluations and trials should be conducted to identify weaknesses and make improvements before full-scale implementation. With a holistic and sustainable policy approach, metaverse technology can be adopted safely and effectively, bringing the electoral process into a more inclusive and transparent digital era.

4.2.3.3 Anticipation of Technological Advancements

In anticipation of technological advances in election voting through the metaverse, several important steps must be taken. It is important to continue investing in cybersecurity research and development to deal with increasingly complex threats. Governments and election bodies should work with technology experts to develop systems that are resilient and accessible to all levels of society. Adaptive policies and regulations must be developed to accommodate technological changes and innovations. Voter training and education are essential so all voters understand how to use these new technologies and feel comfortable in the digital voting process.

4.2.3.4 Drawbacks and Practical Problems

The implementation of a metaverse election voting system presents several drawbacks and practical problems for election commissions. First, technological accessibility is a major concern, as not all voters have access to the high-end devices and stable internet required to participate in the metaverse. This creates a digital divide, potentially disenfranchising low-income or rural populations. Additionally, the complexity of virtual environments may alienate less tech-savvy voters, leading to lower participation rates. Security risks, such as hacking, voter impersonation, or data breaches, pose significant threats to the integrity of the election process. Moreover, ensuring the anonymity of votes while maintaining transparency in a virtual environment can be a challenge. Legal and regulatory frameworks are often not equipped to handle the nuances of metaverse technology, causing uncertainty in the enforcement of election laws. Lastly, high costs associated with developing and maintaining a metaverse platform could strain the resources of election commissions, especially in developing countries.

4.2.3.5 Security Improvements

The implementation of the metaverse election voting system enhances security after voting is completed through multiple advanced digital safeguards. Once voting concludes, blockchain technology ensures that votes remain immutable and tamper-proof, providing a transparent and decentralized ledger that cannot be altered or hacked. Additionally, integrating biometric verification during the voting process, such as facial recognition and other personal identifiers, guarantees the authenticity of voter participation, preventing post-election fraud or identity theft. Furthermore, real-time monitoring and artificial intelligence-driven analysis in the metaverse election environment can swiftly detect and flag any suspicious activity or potential cyber threats, ensuring the integrity of the final results. This layered security infrastructure increases trust in the election outcome and reduces vulnerabilities commonly associated with traditional voting systems.

4.3 Findings

4.3.1 Detailed Procedure of Metaverse Voting System

4.3.1.1 Voter Registration and Verification

Step 1.1: User Onboarding

- o Citizens enter the metaverse election platform via secure login using government-issued credentials or decentralized identity verification.
- o Blockchain technology verifies the identity of the voter using encrypted digital identities.

Step 1.2: Voter Validation

- o The system cross-references the voter's credentials with a national database (or blockchain ledger) to verify eligibility. This prevents double voting and non-eligible voters from accessing the election process.

4.3.1.2 Accessing the Voting Environment

Step 2.1: Entering the Virtual Polling Station

- After successful verification, voters enter a virtual polling station within the metaverse, which mirrors real-world voting environments. Each voter has a private, secure virtual voting booth.

Step 2.2: Election Dashboard

- Voters are presented with an intuitive election dashboard, where all candidates and policies are listed clearly. Information about candidates is available in various formats, such as text, videos, or interactive 3D holograms.

4.3.1.3 Casting the Vote

Step 3.1: Voting Mechanism

- Voters make their selections by interacting with the user-friendly VR interface. They can click, touch, or use voice commands to vote for their preferred candidate or option.

Step 3.2: Vote Encryption and Tokenization

- Once the voter confirms their choice, the vote is encrypted, ensuring privacy. A blockchain-based token is generated to represent the vote and prevent tampering.

4.3.1.4 Recording the Vote

Step 4.1: Blockchain Ledger

- The encrypted vote is immediately recorded on a secure, transparent blockchain ledger. Each vote is immutable, and any unauthorized changes are easily detectable.

Step 4.2: Confirmation to Voter

- A unique confirmation token is sent back to the voter, which can be used later to verify that their vote was counted without disclosing who they voted for.

4.3.1.5 Vote Auditing and Transparency

Step 5.1: Real-Time Monitoring

- o Election authorities and third-party observers can monitor real-time voting using blockchain nodes. All transactions are visible but anonymous, ensuring transparency and fraud detection.

Step 5.2: Post-Vote Audit

- o After the election, an automated audit of the blockchain-based voting ledger ensures that all votes are recorded correctly. This audit can be independently verified.

4.3.1.6 Tallying and Results Announcement

Step 6.1: Automated Tallying

- o Once the voting period ends, the blockchain system automatically tallies the votes, ensuring that all counted votes are legally cast.

Step 6.2: Result Declaration

- o Results are publicly announced in the metaverse, and voters can access a detailed report of the election process, including the audit results. Each voter can verify their vote's inclusion in the final tally using their confirmation token.

(https://doi.org/10.1007/978-3-030-89546-4_3)

4.3.2 Real World/Practical Examples of Metaverse Voting System

Several empirical studies and real-world examples of digital or metaverse voting systems have been piloted globally, offering insights into their viability, challenges, and potential solutions. Estonia, a notable example, implemented an Internet-based voting system (i-Voting) in 2005, allowing citizens to vote securely online in national elections. The system has been praised for its convenience and accessibility, especially for citizens living abroad, but concerns about cybersecurity and voter anonymity persist. More recently, blockchain technology has been explored in voting systems to enhance transparency and security, such as in Sierra Leone's 2018 elections, where blockchain was used to verify results. However, challenges related to scalability and technological literacy remain. South Korea has been at the forefront of the metaverse, with Seoul planning to integrate blockchain for decentralized voting in the metaverse as part of its "Metaverse Seoul" initiative. However, technical hurdles like ensuring voter identity, preventing fraud, and establishing a regulatory framework pose significant challenges. These examples underscore the potential of digital and metaverse voting systems to revolutionize electoral processes but highlight the need for robust cybersecurity measures, public trust-building, and legal frameworks.

4.3.3 Voters Perspective

While largely experimental, the metaverse election voting method has gained attention, especially in countries like South Korea. Their "Metaverse Seoul" initiative offers insights into how such systems might work. Voters can engage in a fully immersive virtual environment, interacting with election processes and casting votes using decentralized blockchain technology. Early pilot programs provide a glimpse into the experiences of voters and election commissions alike. The metaverse method presents unique opportunities and challenges from a voter's perspective. Voters appreciate the convenience of voting from anywhere, reducing physical barriers to participation, especially for those with mobility issues or those living abroad. The immersive nature of the metaverse offers a more engaging experience than traditional online voting, allowing voters to visualize candidates, election materials, and debates more effectively. However, voters have expressed concerns about the learning curve in navigating the virtual environment and privacy and security issues that are crucial in ensuring voter trust.

Election commissions have also faced several hurdles. Managing elections in a metaverse environment demands significant technological infrastructure, advanced cybersecurity protocols, and a level of technological literacy among voters. Furthermore, commissions must deal with the potential for hacking, fraud, and digital manipulation and ensure equal access to technology for all citizens. Feedback from these pilots often stresses the need for comprehensive digital literacy campaigns, thorough testing of blockchain systems, and tighter legal frameworks to safeguard the integrity of such elections. These experiences suggest that while metaverse voting offers the potential for more inclusive and engaging elections, it also requires significant investment in security, education, and infrastructure to be viable.

5 CONCLUSION

The rapid development of technology makes humans compete to create the latest technology that can be used in everyday life, one of which is metaverse technology. Metaverse is a new class of Internet applications and social media platforms that combine many advanced technologies in the metaverse, where humans can interact with the digital environment. Each other is directly or commonly referred to as the virtual universe, with various applications that can be used, ranging from social networking and entertainment to education, commerce, and democratic activities, which can also be carried out with metaverse technology. There has been much talk about implementing virtual democracy; one form of implementation is electronic voting (e-voting) in elections using metaverse technology. Using metaverse technology in the election voting process can increase government transparency and accountability by providing real-time data access using blockchain-based metaverse technology. Blockchain technology can provide features that support efficient, transparent, and secure elections through an end-to-end verification system.

Several countries have applied metaverse technology in election voting, including Thailand, the Thai Democratic Party using Zcoin Blockchain for direct e-voting, Estonia, Japan, and several states in the United States. It is very different when compared between implementing traditional and election voting using metaverse technology. Traditionally, ballots provide a secure way to count votes in a democracy. However, the success of traditional voting depends on the organizers of the vote, and centralized voting systems can suffer from security and efficiency limitations. Decentralized electronic voting based on blockchain technology offers an alternative to traditional voting. Metaverse technology allows voters to cast a ballot from anywhere with internet access, increasing accessibility and participation. Metaverse has the potential to increase voter participation by removing geographical and physical barriers, thus allowing voters to vote from anywhere as long as they have internet access.

However, adequate infrastructure and privacy concerns must be addressed through appropriate regulation. In-depth voter education and close collaboration between governments, technologists, and citizens will be key to implementing these technologies inclusively in the democratic process. The publication trends by subject generated by Dimensions related to the keywords metaverse and election voting show that metaverse technologies not only impact the fields of technology and computer science but also have far-reaching implications on social, cultural, economic, legal, and ethical aspects of society. Meanwhile, the annual scholarly publications related to the keywords metaverse and election voting based on data from Dimensions AI provide interesting insights into how research on the metaverse and electronic voting has evolved and changed in recent years, as well as how this trend is likely to continue to develop in the future. Furthermore, the collaboration of authors who publish scholarly works related to the keywords metaverse and election voting shows that research on the metaverse and electronic voting is not conducted by individuals working in isolation but by a network of interconnected researchers working together to produce more comprehensive and influential research.

6 ACKNOWLEDGMENT

The research work of this article was supported by the Department of Public Administration of Universitas Muhammadiyah Makassar. The researcher would like to express his immense gratitude to his supporters, who have provided all the necessary insight and expertise to assist in this research.

REFERENCES

Adams, S. O., & Paul, C. (2023). E-government development indices and attaining United Nations sustainable development goals in Africa: A cross-sectional data analysis. *European Journal of Sustainable Development Research, 7*(4), em0234. Advance online publication. DOI: 10.29333/ejosdr/13576

AL-Hawamleh, A., Altarawneh, M., Hikal, H., & Elfedawy, A.AL-Hawamleh. (2024). Blockchain technology and virtual asset accounting in the metaverse: A comprehensive review of future directions. *International Journal of Computing and Digital Systems, 15*(1), 1595–1614. DOI: 10.12785/ijcds/1501113

Ali, M., Naeem, F., Kaddoum, G., & Hossain, E. (2023). Metaverse communications, networking, security, and applications: Research issues, state-of-the-art, and future directions. *IEEE Communications Surveys and Tutorials*.

Anim, P. (2022). *Exploring the citizen engagement metaverse: Testing virtual reality for citizen feedback on public space design options*. The University of Regina.

Benjamins, R., Rubio Viñuela, Y., & Alonso, C. (2023). Social and ethical challenges of the metaverse: Opening the debate. *AI and Ethics, 3*(3), 689–697. DOI: 10.1007/s43681-023-00278-5

Bibri, S. E. (2022). The social shaping of the metaverse as an alternative to the imaginaries of data-driven smart Cities: A study in science, technology, and society. *Smart Cities, 5*(3), 832–874. DOI: 10.3390/smartcities5030043

Boehm, C. (2004). Hiro" of the Platonic: Neal Stephenson's" Snow Crash. *Journal of the Fantastic in the Arts, 14*(4 (56), 394–408.

Bojic, L. (2022). Metaverse through the prism of power and addiction: What will happen when the virtual world becomes more attractive than reality? *European Journal of Futures Research, 10*(1), 22. DOI: 10.1186/s40309-022-00208-4

Chang, L., Zhang, Z., Li, P., Xi, S., Guo, W., Shen, Y., Xiong, Z., Kang, J., Niyato, D., Qiao, X., & Wu, Y. (2022). 6G-Enabled Edge AI for Metaverse: Challenges, Methods, and Future Research Directions. *Journal of Communications and Information Networks*, *7*(2), 107–121. DOI: 10.23919/JCIN.2022.9815195

Dalton, R. J., Cain, B. E., & Scarrow, S. E. (2003). *Democratic publics and democratic institutions. Democracy Transformed?* Expanding Political Opportunities in Advanced Industrial Democracies.

Daramola, O., & Thebus, D. (2020). Architecture-centric evaluation of blockchain-based smart contract e-voting for national elections. *Informatics (MDPI)*, *7*(2), 16. DOI: 10.3390/informatics7020016

Dionisio, J. D. N., Iii, W. G. B., & Gilbert, R. (2013). 3D virtual worlds and the metaverse: Current status and future possibilities. *ACM Computing Surveys*, *45*(3), 1–38. DOI: 10.1145/2480741.2480751

Dwivedi, Y. K., Hughes, L., Baabdullah, A. M., Ribeiro-Navarrete, S., Giannakis, M., Al-Debei, M. M., Dennehy, D., Metri, B., Buhalis, D., Cheung, C. M. K., Conboy, K., Doyle, R., Dubey, R., Dutot, V., Felix, R., Goyal, D. P., Gustafsson, A., Hinsch, C., Jebabli, I., & Wamba, S. F. (2022). Metaverse beyond the hype: Multidisciplinary perspectives on emerging challenges, opportunities, and agenda for research, practice, and policy. *International Journal of Information Management*, *66*, 102542. DOI: 10.1016/j.ijinfomgt.2022.102542

Ehin, P., Solvak, M., Willemson, J., & Vinkel, P. (2022). Internet voting in Estonia 2005–2019: Evidence from eleven elections. *Government Information Quarterly*, *39*(4), 101718. DOI: 10.1016/j.giq.2022.101718

Endarto, I. A., & Martadi, M. (2022). Analysis of the potential implementation of the metaverse in interactive educational media. *BARIK-Journal of S1 Visual Communication Design, 4*(1), 37–51.

Farooq, M. S., Iftikhar, U., & Khelifi, A. (2022). *A framework to make the voting system transparent using blockchain technology*. IEEE Access. DOI: 10.1109/ACCESS.2022.3180168

Gaurav, A. (2023). Metaverse and Globalization: Cultural Exchange and Digital Diplomacy. *Data Science Insights Magazine, Insights2Techinfo.*

Gedar, M. B. L., Sharma, M. C., & Lodha, S. (2023). Use Cases of Blockchain Technology in Voting System and Healthcare Sector. *Principal Investigator*, 131.

Gimpel, J. G., & Schuknecht, J. E. (2003). Political participation and the accessibility of the ballot box. *Political Geography, 22*(5), 471–488. DOI: 10.1016/S0962-6298(03)00029-5

Goldberg, M., & Schär, F. (2023). Metaverse governance: An empirical analysis of voting within Decentralized Autonomous Organizations. *Journal of Business Research, 160,* 113764. DOI: 10.1016/j.jbusres.2023.113764

Gopal, S. B., Jayaprasath, M., Poongodi, C., Johnson, S., Nanthiya, D., & Mithunkumar, R. T. (2023). Blockchain-based e-voting application–a survey. *2023 International Conference on Sustainable Computing and Data Communication Systems (ICSCDS),* 1340–1347. DOI: 10.1109/ICSCDS56580.2023.10104596

Gulomov, S. (2024). Regulatory Frameworks for Metaverse Platforms: Challenges and Opportunities. *International Conference on Legal Sciences, 2*(1), 144–151. https://science-zone.org/index.php/conference/article/view/91

Habibzadeh, H., Nussbaum, B. H., Anjomshoa, F., Kantarci, B., & Soyata, T. (2019). A survey on cybersecurity, data privacy, and policy issues in cyber-physical system deployments in smart cities. *Sustainable Cities and Society, 50,* 101660. DOI: 10.1016/j.scs.2019.101660

Healy, J. J.Jr. (2023). Veto the Black-Box Politics: How Implementing Blockchain Technology into the United States Voting System Will Give Our World the Transparency We Deserve. *Hofstra Law Review, 52,* 131.

Heath, D. R. (2023). The Metaverse and how it will revolutionize everything. In *Journal of Information Technology Case and Application Research* (Vol. 25, Issue 1). Liveright Publishing. DOI: 10.1080/15228053.2022.2136927

Huang, H., Lin, J., Zheng, B., Zheng, Z., & Bian, J. (2020). *When blockchain meets distributed file systems: An overview, challenges, and open issues.* IEEE Access.

Huynh-The, T., Pham, Q.-V., Pham, X.-Q., Nguyen, T. T., Han, Z., & Kim, D.-S. (2023). Artificial intelligence for the metaverse: A survey. *Engineering Applications of Artificial Intelligence, 117,* 105581. DOI: 10.1016/j.engappai.2022.105581

Iswanto, N. I. P., Widhiantoro, D., Munawar, Z., & Komalasari, R. (2022). Pemanfaatan Metaverse Di Bidang Pendidikan Utilization Of Metaverse In Education. *Jurnal Teknologi Informasi Komunikasi (e-Journal), 9*(1), 44–52.

Jafar, U., Aziz, M. J. A., & Shukur, Z. (2021). Blockchain for electronic voting system—Review and open research challenges. *Sensors (Basel), 21*(17), 5874. DOI: 10.3390/s21175874 PMID: 34502764

Jagatheesaperumal, S. K., Ahmad, K., Al-Fuqaha, A., & Qadir, J. (2024). Advancing Education Through Extended Reality and Internet of Everything Enabled Metaverses: Applications, Challenges, and Open Issues. *IEEE Transactions on Learning Technologies, 17*, 1120–1139. DOI: 10.1109/TLT.2024.3358859

Jungherr, A., & Schlarb, D. B. (2022). The extended reach of game engine companies: How Epic games and Unity technologies provide platforms for extended reality applications and the metaverse. *Social Media + Society, 8*(2), 20563051221107640. DOI: 10.1177/20563051221107641

Kiayias, A., & Lazos, P. (2022). SoK: blockchain governance. *Proceedings of the 4th ACM Conference on Advances in Financial Technologies*, 61–73. DOI: 10.1145/3558535.3559794

Kichanova, V. (2023). Private Cities, the Metaverse and the Future of Non-Territorial Governance. *Journal of Special Jurisdictions, 4*(1).

Lee, L.-H., Braud, T., Zhou, P., Wang, L., Xu, D., Lin, Z., Kumar, A., Bermejo, C., & Hui, P. (2021). All One Needs to Know about Metaverse: A Complete Survey on Technological Singularity, Virtual Ecosystem, and Research Agenda. *ArXiv Preprint ArXiv:2110.05352*. http://arxiv.org/abs/2110.05352

Maley, M. (2003). Transplanting election regulation. *Election Law Journal, 2*(4), 479–497. DOI: 10.1089/153312903322483191

Mele, C., Russo Spena, T., & Russo, S. P. (2024). Experimenting on the metaverse to foster innovation. *Spanish Journal of Marketing - ESIC*. Advance online publication. DOI: 10.1108/SJME-05-2023-0117

Mossberger, K. (2008). Toward digital citizenship: Addressing inequality in the information age. In *Routledge Handbook of Internet Politics* (pp. 173–185). Routledge.

Murala, D. K., & Panda, S. K. (2023). Metaverse: A study on immersive technologies. *Metaverse and Immersive Technologies: An Introduction to Industrial, Business and Social Applications*, 1–41. DOI: 10.1002/9781394177165.ch1

Mystakidis, S. (2022). Metaverse. *Encyclopedia, 2*(1), 486–497. DOI: 10.3390/encyclopedia2010031

NATIONAL. (n.d.). *R. I. B. P. H.* THE RESULTS OF THE ALIGNMENT OF THE ACADEMIC TEXT OF THE DRAFT LAW ON THE NATIONAL LONG-TERM DEVELOPMENT PLAN FOR.

Németh, R., Firuza, B., & Erdős, F. (n.d.). *Virtual Teamwork in Gamified 3D Environment*.

Nestorović, Č. (2023). Critical Geopolitics. In *Contributions to International Relations: Vol. Part F1828* (pp. 85–150). Springer. DOI: 10.1007/978-3-031-45325-0_3

Nevelsteen, K. J. L. (2018). The virtual world is defined from a technological perspective and is applied to video games, mixed reality, and the Metaverse. *Computer Animation and Virtual Worlds*, *29*(1), e1752. DOI: 10.1002/cav.1752

Norris, P., & Nai, A. (2017). *Election watchdogs: transparency, accountability and integrity*. Oxford University Press. DOI: 10.1093/acprof:oso/9780190677800.001.0001

Oppenlaender, J. (2022). The perception of smart contracts for the governance of the metaverse. *Proceedings of the 25th International Academic Mindtrek Conference*, 1–8. DOI: 10.1145/3569219.3569300

Pakina, R., & Solekhan, M. (2024). The Influence of Information Technology on Privacy and Surveillance Law in Indonesia: The Balance Between Security and Human Rights.... *Journal of Scientech Research and Development*, *6*(1), 273–286. https://www.idm.or.id/JSCR/index.php/JSCR/article/view/376%0Ahttps://www.idm.or.id/JSCR/index.php/JSCR/article/download/376/285

Panja, S., & Roy, B. (2021). A secure end-to-end verifiable e-voting system using blockchain and cloud server. *Journal of Information Security and Applications*, *59*, 102815. DOI: 10.1016/j.jisa.2021.102815

Prayitno, W., Tumangkar, T., & Mulyani, S. (2023). *The metaverse symbol of civilization transfer in the middle of digital economic hegemony: synthesis of progressive law of the post-modern era*. Seven Editora.

Rane, N., Choudhary, S., & Rane, J. (2023). Enhanced product design and development using Artificial Intelligence (AI), Virtual Reality (VR), Augmented Reality (AR), 4D/5D/6D Printing, Internet of Things (IoT), and blockchain: A review. SSRN *Electronic Journal, 4*. DOI: 10.2139/ssrn.4644059

Ranney, A. (1981). *Candidate selection*. Democracy at the Polls.

Regina, P. A. (2022). *Exploring the Citizen Engagement Metaverse: Testing Virtual Reality for Citizen Feedback on Public Space Design Options*. The University of Regina.

Sabtu, M. A. S. (2023). Metaverse and Soft Skills Development Through Video Games. In *Metaverse applications for new business models and disruptive innovation* (pp. 120–132). IGI Global., DOI: 10.4018/978-1-6684-6097-9.ch008

Scavarelli, A., Arya, A., & Teather, R. J. (2021). Virtual reality and augmented reality in social learning spaces: A literature review. *Virtual Reality (Waltham Cross), 25*(1), 257–277. DOI: 10.1007/s10055-020-00444-8

Shirahada, K., Oyama, H., & Ohsaki, T. (2020). Local Social Innovation by Blockchain Technology: A Trial in a Provincial City in Japan. *Business Innovation with New ICT in the Asia-Pacific: Case Studies*, 349–365. DOI: 10.1007/978-981-15-7658-4_16

Swami, P. (2024). *Metaverse: Transforming the User Experience in the Gaming and Entertainment Industry*. IGI Global., https://www.igi-global.com/chapter/metaverse/349151%0Awww.igi-global.com/chapter/metaverse/349151

Wang, W., Wang, L., Xu, S., Wang, J., & Fu, K. (2021). Sharingchain : A privacy protection scheme based on blockchain in the supply chain. *IMCEC 2021 - IEEE 4th Advanced Information Management, Communicates, Electronic and Automation Control Conference, 4*, 995–999. DOI: 10.1109/IMCEC51613.2021.9482088

Wang, Y., Su, Z., Zhang, N., Xing, R., Liu, D., Luan, T. H., & Shen, X. (2023). A Survey on Metaverse: Fundamentals, Security, and Privacy. *IEEE Communications Surveys and Tutorials, 25*(1), 319–352. DOI: 10.1109/COMST.2022.3202047

Warren, M. E. (2009). Citizen participation and democratic deficits: Considerations from the perspective of democratic theory. In *Activating the Citizen: Dilemmas of Participation in Europe and Canada* (pp. 17–40). Springer. DOI: 10.1057/9780230240902_2

Zhao, Y., Jiang, J., Chen, Y., Liu, R., Yang, Y., Xue, X., & Chen, S. (2022). Metaverse: Perspectives from graphics, interactions, and visualization. *Visual Informatics, 6*(1), 56–67. DOI: 10.1016/j.visinf.2022.03.002

Chapter 8

Employee Perception Towards Customer Satisfaction, Digital Transformation, Financial Security, and Risk in the Indian Banking Sector

Ajay Kumar Singh
https://orcid.org/0000-0003-0429-0925
Department of Humanities and Social Sciences, Graphic Era University, Dehradun, India

S. Srinivasan
https://orcid.org/0009-0002-0179-9849
Department of Humanities and Social Sciences, Graphic Era University, Dehradun, India

ABSTRACT

Digital transformation (DT) helps to increase the performance, productivity, profits, and product quality in the banking sector. DT is also eager to increase online banking and customer's satisfaction at a greater level. However, employees are facing multiple challenges to adjust with the current DT in the banking sector of developing countries. This chapter, therefore, explores the perception of employees towards DT of the banking sector in India using primary information. Necessary information is collected from 176 employees of public and private banks in Dehradun and Delhi. The descriptive statistical method is used to analyse the primary data with regards

DOI: 10.4018/979-8-3693-8477-0.ch008

to perception of employees on 30 different items or questions. These are divided into four constructs i.e., DT, financial security (FS), financial risk (FR) and customer' satisfaction (CS). The correlation coefficients and linear regression models are also considered to examine the association among these constructs.

1. INTRODUCTION

The application of information and communication technology (I&CT) are serving as a best mediator to solve multi-dimensional issues of humanity in multiple dimensions. I&CT is supportive of easy processes for increasing the communication among the large number of economic agents in production, marketing, business, financial and banking sectors. It is a crucial driver to increase DT. I&CT is also significant to increase the usability of available information in the social, economic, technological, financial and political domain. I&CT has multiple usages in almost all sectors. For instance, I&CT is playing a vital role to reduce the climate change impact in the agricultural sector. I&CT is also working as a key barrier to reduce environmental degradation. I&CT is also working as a catalyst to increase the dissemination of scientific output across research communities and manufacturing firms. I&CT is helpful to increase financial stability and inclusion in the financial sector (Alshubiri et al., 2019). I&CT is also a creator of new business and entrepreneurship (Singh & Jyoti, 2023).

I&CT helps to develop a digital platform for resource distribution among the users to attain their desired goals (Al-Naimi et al., 2024). I&CT is helping to improve the progressiveness of the health sector. In the environmental sector, I&CT is a fruit of technological advancement. I&CT is supportive to increase the efficiency of marketing, advertisement and publicity of new products in the business sector. Most specifically, I&CT enables digital communication across economic agents in diverse fields (Binuyo & Aregbeshola, 2014). Technological advancement and I&CT help to increase the transition of the banking sector towards DT. It helps to ensure the secure lifestyle of common people (Rahman et al., 2024). Therefore, technology has become an essential component of society and the financial sector (Osei et al., 2023). DT is crucial to increase financial literacy of youth (Chufal et al., 2025). Consequently, it is significantly associated with human development and technological development (Gupta, 2023). Technological advancement is an originator for creating innovation, I&CT tools, digital devices, mobile apps, and digital ecosystem which are facilitating multiple ways to increase the performance, productivity, and efficiency and profits of financial and non-financial organizations including banking sector (Islam et al., 2019).

Technological advancement, thus, also promotes DT and digitalization of the banking industry. Digitalization and its tools like artificial intelligence, and blockchain are helping the financial sector (Rahman et al., 2024). Digitalization, therefore, is a revolution in the banking sector for improving its delivery channels and information process (Carbo-Valverde, 2017). It could be a significant determinant to increase the technical skills of employees in the financial sector (Carbo-Valverde, 2017). Information technology (IT) is essential to increase skills of employees (Saeed & Ahmed, 2023). Hence, banking is among the sectors that have high dependency on technological progress (Akshisar et al., 2015). DT is a digital platform to increase the extensive use of the internet in different sectors. Therefore, the number of internet users has significantly increased globally (Changchit et al., 2017). However, it creates a challenge for the banking industry to increase the attention of customers to adopt online banking services (Changchit et al., 2017).

DT is providing multiple benefits in the banking sector (Sehgal & Garg, 2020; Vignesh, 2022; Bueno et al., 2024). For example, mobile technologies are helping the banking sector (Alzaidi, 2022). DT helps to increase the customer's participation in e-commerce, and online transaction of financial services in the banking industry (Kitsios et al., 2021; Vignesh, 2022). It is also supportive to save time, minimize operating cost, increase monitoring and offer multiple products in the banking industry (Kitsios et al., 2021). DT promotes digital banking through laptop, computer and smartphone (Vignesh, 2022). Further digital banking is supportive to meet diverse needs like online cash transfer, getting online statements, paying online bills, and making online investment for the customers (Vignesh, 2022). Internet banking is transforming the traditional banking system to an innovative, informative and modern banking system. Internet banking is also fruitful to increase development of competition and performance of the banking industry (Akshisar et al., 2015).

Internet banking is supportive to increase cost advantage, profitability, and reduce risk in the banking industry (Tunay et al., 2015). Thus, internet banking is changing the landscape of the banking sector across countries (Roy et al., 2017). Digital banking system is crucial for enhancing the operation, efficiency, cost minimization and profit optimization of the banking industry. Hence, extensive investment in digital channels and internet security also enhance the progress of the banking sector (Theiri & Hadoussa, 2024). Financial security in online banking is also a substantial driver to increase customer's intention to adopt DT in the banking industry (Aliyu et al., 2014). DT brings growth opportunities and challenges in the banking industry and financial sector (Vignesh, 2022). However, it is also reported a diverse impact of DT on banking and financial sector across countries.

Banking and financial sector has a significant contribution to increase social and economic development of all communities in India (Gupta, 2023). Banking industry enhances the financial capacity and strength of a country (Islam et al.,

2019). The Indian banking industry has a crucial share in terms of number of customers and employees in the world. India is the fourth largest economy in its GDP size in the world. Thus, the Indian banking sector has a dominant position in the world's banking sector. The Indian banking industry provides loan facilities to common people, farmers, businessmen and industrialists for the short-term and long-term. Banking sector, therefore, boosts the entire Indian economy. In the last two decades, the government of India took several initiatives to boost the Indian banking sector. "Digital India" is an important policy initiative that is implemented by the Government of India (GoI) to promote digitalization in all sectors of the Indian economy. Nowadays, the Indian banking industry and non-financial sector are moving towards digitalization. These are also adopting various digital technologies to attain competitive advantages and economic profits.

The Indian banking industry is also using digital tools, technology and other scientific mechanisms to enhance its growth and performance. The banking industry is also targeted to increase customers satisfaction and quality improvement through digitalization and DT. The Indian banking system is also adopting various advanced technologies like Robotic Process Automation, cloud computing, Artificial Intelligence (AI), blockchain, etc. for reducing operating expenditure and to increase efficiency (Gupta, 2023). It is a significant impact of DT and digitization on the banking sector of India (Gupta, 2023). However, the impact of DT on the banking sector is not found uniform across banks in India. The banking industry has high diversity in digital infrastructure, digital devices, and digital instruments across public, private and foreign banks in India. Accordingly, the banking industry has a high variation in technical efficiency (TE) of banks in India (Bhatia & Mahendru, 2015; Kumar & Gulati, 2018). TE of the banking sector may be improved as digitalization and DT of it.

As earlier researchers could not examine the perception of employees towards DT of the banking sector in India. Therefore, the main aim of this chapter is to explain the progress of DT of the banking sector in India using a time trend analysis. Thereupon, it explores the perception of employees towards DT, customer's satisfaction (CS), financial security (FS) and financial risk (FR) in the banking sector of India using primary information. It identified 30 items or questions to explore the perception of employees in the banking industry. These 30 items are divided into four constructs i.e., DT, financial security (FS), financial risk (FR) and customer' satisfaction (CS). Accordingly, it uses correlation coefficient analysis to examine the association among five constructs. It also develops linear regression models for assessing the interconnection among DT, FS and FR. It also explains the policy suggestions to increase DT and FS, and reduce FR in the Indian banking sector. Finally, it suggests scope of further research in the domain of digitalization and its implications on banking industry and financial organization in India and other countries.

2. REVIEW OF LITERATURE

2.1. DT and Problems of Employees and Customers in Banking Sector

DT and digitalization are working as revolutionary gears for increasing performance, profits, growth, volume and quality of services in the banking and financial sectors. DT is also creating numerous problems and obstacles for customers and employees in the banking industry. For instance, the workload of the employees is significantly increased in the banking industry due to DT. Therefore, it increases the mental stress for employees. DT also appeared to reduce performance of employees due to their low technological skills. DT also shows a negative implication on cooperation of employees. DT is also found unsuccessful due to low and inappropriate technological knowledge of employees. Regulatory compliance and cybersecurity risk are serious matters due to DT of banking industry (Bueno et al., 2024). Financial security risk is a significant challenge in DT of the banking sector (Alnemer, 2022).

Further, financial security risk is also caused to reduce intentions of customers to adopt internet banking (Chauhan et al., 2019). For example, it is reported an INR 700 billion worth of cyber fraud cases were reported in India during 2008 – 2017 (Gupta, 2023). Islam et al. (2019) also claimed a security risk in online transactions in Bangladesh. Ahmadi (2024) also reported security related concerns in cloud computing. Legacy systems and low infrastructure are primary challenges for the banking sector in its DT (Bueno et al., 2024). Thus, the banking sector should reduce cyber security risk to increase the trust of customers in DT. Trust is a significant driver to increase adoption of digital technology in the banking sector (Alnemer, 2022). The Indian banking system has also adopted the digitalization transformation of this sector (Gupta, 2023). Although, the banking system is facing problems due to data security and low cyber security in India (Gupta, 2023). DT of the Indian banking sector is also facing challenges due to low digital literacy, low financial inclusion, low internet speed and inappropriate digital infrastructure (Gupta, 2023).

2.2. Implications of DT in Banking Sector

DT is highly useful to enhance the production and efficiency of banking and financial sectors. Further, DT also determines the business models and process of the business sector (Kitsios et al., 2021). DT shows a significant impact on the outcome and performance of the banking industry (Porfírio et al., 2024). DT is also a driving factor that suggests viable solutions to address the existing problems in the banking sector (Diener & Špaček, 2021). Digital banking sector is also favourable for increasing economic stability and financial inclusivity (Bueno et al., 2024). Digital banking is also promoted to increase the relationship of customers with banks without their physical presence. Existing researchers, and banking and financial experts examined the role of digitalization, digital technologies and DT in banking sectors across countries using diverse indicators (Gaudio et al., 2021). There are many technologies like I&CT, artificial intelligence (AI), cloud computing, financial technology (FinTech), and electronic-based banking services are using by banking sector to achieve their diverse purposes (Aliyu et al., 2014; Akshisar et al., 2015; Asadi et al., 2017; Cheng et al., 2022; Baker et al., 2023).

Cloud computing is helping to transform the use of the internet in business and organizations (Asadi et al., 2017). Cloud computing is also helping the banking sector to improve processing capacity and financial services (Yan, 2017). Cloud computing provides high internet speed with low cost in e-learning, healthcare and e-commerce sectors (Vinoth et al., 2022). E-commerce is essential to increase mobile banking, internet marketing, online transaction processing and automated data gathering systems (Vinoth et al., 2022). I&CT is helping the banking sector to increase the electronic banking system in India (Aliyu et al., 2014). Use of I&CT shows a positive impact on performance of the banking sector in MENA countries (Al-Naimi et al., 2024). Thus, information technology (IT) is necessary for the banking system for increasing the connection of customers with their bank accounts regularly through the internet (Shu & Strassmann, 2005; Dangolani, 2011; Li et al., 2021).

Information technology (IT) is also supportive to increase the movement of the banking industry towards e-banking (Lasmini et al., 2019). E-banking helps to provide uniform accessibility of banking services to customers through online platforms and avoid their physical presence (Li et al., 2021). A businessman cannot take effective decisions and get success in business without IT (Dangolani, 2011). Moreover, IT is beneficial for the banking industry for improving their services for increasing customer's satisfaction (Akshisar et al., 2015). IT is developing multiple channels for increasing use of ATMs and mobile banking (Dangolani, 2011). Technology could be useful to create new markets, new products, and efficient ways for increasing service delivery in the banking industry (Dangolani, 2011). I&CT is supportive to increase financial inclusion as it promotes digital payment systems effectively (Alshubiri et al., 2019). I&CT investment and its cost efficiency also determine performance of the banking sector (Binuyo & Aregbeshola, 2014). I&CT is also a significant determinant to increase financial inclusion. Accordingly, financial inclusion also shows significant impact on total deposits and financial services (Baker et al., 2023).

The performance of banking sector can also be measured in terms of return on assets, return on equity, return on capital, profit per employee, return on investment, net profit, growth in profits, productivity of employees and total deposits (Binuyo & Aregbeshola, 2014; Akshisar et al., 2015; Tunay et al., 2015; Islam et al., 2019; Baker et al., 2023; Theiri & Hadoussa, 2024). Digitalization is also supportive to increase transparency in the banking sector (Theiri & Hadoussa, 2024). Tunay et al. (2015) examined the role of internet banking for increasing banking performance in 30 European countries. Internet banking is also providing multiple services to the customers at minimum cost (Roy et al., 2017). Lasmini et al. (2019) reported a positive change in financial performance due to adoption of e-banking (i.e., internet banking and mobile banking) in public banks of Indonesia. Mobile banking is helping to increase the financial accessibility for customers easily (Baptista & Oliveira, 2015). Islam et al. (2019) examined the implication of online banking on various indicators like return on assets and return of equity of the banking sector in Bangladesh. It claimed that ROA and ROE were low after implementation of internet banking. However, ROA and ROE are higher in those banks which are providing online banking facilities in Bangladesh. The trend in profitability of the banking sector is also reported positive after adopting digital banking in Bangladesh.

Akshisar et al. (2015) observed the implications of the electronic-based banking system on profitability of the banking industry across developed and developing countries. Electronic banking systems (EBS) could be effective to increase profitability of the banking industry (Akshisar et al., 2015). EBS is also significant for increasing customer's satisfaction (Aliyu et al., 2014). However, the banking sector in developing countries could not improve their profitability due to low technology infrastructure, and ATMs networks (Akshisar et al., 2015). Credit cards, debit cards and ATMs also determine the profits of the banking sector (Akshisar et al., 2015). ATMs facilitate customers to withdraw money at any time. Gaudio et al. (2021) found that profits and financial stability of the banking industry could be improved due to application of I&CT in 28 European countries. I&CT is a crucial determinant to increase accessibility of financial products and services for the customers in the financial sector (Wellalage et al., 2021). Carbo-Valverde (2017) examined the impact of digitalization on financial stability in the banking sector. Theiri and Hadoussa (2024) also perceived a positive relationship between financial stability and DT in Tunisia.

Gupta (2023) conducted a review study for assessing the role of industrialization in the banking industry as giving more emphasis on industry 4.0 revolution in India. Baker et al. (2023) also examined the contribution of financial technology (FinTech) to improve financial performance of the banking industry in Jordan and UAE using multiple regression analysis. It noticed the total deposits and net profits are improved due to application of FinTech in the banking sector. Financial sector can reduce marginal cost and increase productivity as using FinTech and digitalization in it (Carbo-Valverde, 2017). Theiri and Hadoussa (2024) also observed the role of digitization for increasing the financial performance of banking industry in Africa. This study used return of assets and equity as best indicators of banking performance. The conclusion of this study claims a positive association of performance of the banking sector with DT. Digitalization also could improve digital services, profitability and financial stability (Theiri & Hadoussa, 2024). Singh et al. (2025) observe the problems of customers due to application of digital technologies in Indian banking sector.

2.3. Perception of Customers towards DT in Banking Sector

Manzano et al. (2009) also analyze the role of consumers' innovativeness to adopt internet banking in Spain. It noticed a crucial impact of consumer innovativeness to e-banking and it also reduced risk perception of customers. Using the survey of customers and employees, Dangolani (2011) investigated the role of information technology (IT) in the banking system of Iran. It noted that IT could be beneficial to increase network transactions and visibly of employees, and reduce time of customers. Malhotra and Singh (2010) investigated factors increasing internet banking services in India. Conclusion of this study indicates that private and foreign banks are providing better internet banking to the customers. While size, experience, financing pattern and ownership of banks have significant impact on extension of internet banking services. Aliyu et al. (2014) identified indicators for promoting online banking and customer service delivery in Malaysia. Online banking is the best promoter to increase customer service delivery as it increases convenience and security, and reduces cost in the banking industry. Online banking also creates an internet communication for customers to avail banking facilities (Islam et al., 2019). Martins et al. (2014) examined the perceived risk and behaviour intention to use internet banking in Portugal. Internet banking is significantly determined by performance and effort expectancy of the customers. Baptista and Oliveira (2015) examined the determinants of mobile banking acceptance in Africa.

Tam and Oliveira (2016) examine the performance of individuals who use m-banking using the TTF model. It suggested that system, information and service qualities enhance the intention of individuals to adopt m-banking. Roy et al. (2017) observed the perception of customers towards internet banking and its acceptance rate in the Indian banking sector. It indicates that external and internal risk show an impact on customers' belief and use of internet banking. Online banking also provides faster and consistent services to customers (Li et al., 2021). Online banking is also supportive to reduce the cost of the banking sector (Islam et al., 2019). In India, Chauhan et al. (2019) claimed the security risk is denied for customers to use internet banking. While domain-specific innovativeness would be useful to reduce financial risk in the banking sector. Cloud computing is highly supportive in the IT sector and it provides multiple benefits to financial organizations (Ahmadi, 2024). Asadi et al. (2017) observed the factors enhancing the intention of customers to adopt cloud computing adoption in the Malaysian banking industry. It found that trust, cost, security and privacy are significant to increase the contribution of customers to adopt cloud computing.

Cloud computing is also beneficial to save money for users in financial activities (Vinoth et al., 2022). Cloud computing is also supportive to increase commercial online banking (Vinoth et al., 2022). Cloud computing is also increasing flexibility, scalability and cost-efficiency of financial institutions (Ahmadi, 2024). Changchit et al. (2017) investigated the factors enhancing the customer's perception for using mobile banking (m-banking). M-banking is also useful for users to access account balance, pay bills and transfer funds as per their convenience, and at any time (Tam & Oliveira, 2016). Kitsios et al. (2021) observe the acceptance rate of DT in the banking industry of Greece using surveys of customers. Diener and Špaček (2021) identified the obstacles of the banking sector due to DT in Germany. It concluded that market knowledge and product and participation of employees and customers are crucial barriers in DT of the banking industry.

Li et al. (2021) observed the impact of cloud services, banking system security, quality of services, and e-learning on satisfaction level of customers. It noticed that customer satisfaction is determined by cloud services, security, e-learning and service quality in the banking sector. Vignesh (2022) perceived the perception of employees in the Indian banking industry using descriptive analysis. Alzaidi (2022) observed factors affecting the intention for customers to adopt mobile banking in Saudi Arabia. It argued that relative advantage and ease of use help to increase the intention of users to adopt mobile banking. Mobile banking is working as a crucial tool to increase accessibility of financial services (Rahman et al., 2024). Service quality, system quality and information quality are also determining the intention of people to adopt mobile apps for making digital payments (Ali et al., 2023). Moreover, anxiety also increased the intention of people to use mobile apps for online payment during COVID-19 in Pakistan.

Deepthi et al. (2022) observed the perception of employees and factors increasing the intentions of the banking sector to adopt AI in India. Rahman et al. (2023) investigated challenges and importance to adopt AI in the banking sector of Malaysia. It found that AI is useful to detect fraud and reduce risk in the banking sector. However, it also reported that data security and privacy, and regulatory requirements are challenges for the banking sector to adopt AI. Porfírio et al. (2024) investigated the perceived implication of the DT process on performance of the banking sector in Portugal. It concluded that DT is useful to increase business volume and performance of the banking sector. Rahman et al. (2024) investigated the behavioral intentions of individuals for using mobile banking in Malaysia during COVID-19. It concluded that trust and personal innovation helps to increase the pursuit of individuals to adopt mobile banking.

2.4. Perception of Employees towards DT in Banking Sector

Banking sector is adopting different digital technologies to attain certain goals. Cloud computing technology is significant for the banking sector. However, the adoption of a specific technology by the banking sector depends on multiple indicators. Cheng et al. (2022) examined cloud computing on performance and risk-taking capacity of the banking sector in China. It noticed that the banking sector desired to adopt cloud computing to reduce cost and risk, and increase profit efficiency. Muduli and Choudhury (2024) observed the significance of technology acceptance and workforce agility in digital technology adoption in the banking sector of India. It claimed that acceptance of digital technology led to increased performance of the banking sector. Banking industry should increase the mindset of employees using digital technologies.

2.5. Conclusion of Review of Literature

The above-mentioned literature concluded that banking sectors are using different technologies across countries (Table 1). Most scholars have identified various benefits that motivate to increase DT in the banking sector. For instance, DT is significant for increasing banking performance in multi-dimensional aspects like profits, quality of their services, new products, efficiency and productivity. Also, banking and financial institutions are facing security risk and regulatory issues in DT. Existing studies also observed the behavioural intentions of customers and employees in banking and financial sectors across countries. However, limited studies could examine the perception of employees towards DT and other actions that help to increase customer' satisfaction in India.

Table 1. Brief summary of theoretical and empirical review

Main objective	Study Area	Methods	Main DVs	Major IVs	Main Findings	Author(s)
Impact of information technology (IT) on banking industry	Iran	Descriptive analysis			IT is helpful to save time for customers, and reduce expenses and increase network transactions.	Dangolani (2011)
Association between e-banking and profitability of banking sector	Asian countries	Cross-sectional and time series data investigation	ROA and ROE	GDP, average lending rate total deposits, e-banking	Internet banking makes significant changes in the retail banking sector and it is helpful for increasing distribution channels.	Hosein (2013)
Effect of I&CT cost efficiency on performance of banking industry	South Africa	Dynamic panel model	Return on capital and return on equity	I&CT	Return on capital and return on equity could be improved as implementation of I&CT.	Binuyo and Aregbeshola (2014)
Effect of electronic banking in profitability	Across developed and developing countries	Dynamic panel analysis	Return on assets and return on equity	ATMs, number of branches	Electronic banking services show a significant impact on profitability of the banking sector.	Akshisar et al. (2015)
Observe the association of internet banking with bank performance	30 European countries	Panel causality model	Return on assets and return on equity	Internet banking	Internet banking is positively associated with bank performance	Tunay et al. (2015)
Factors enhancing the intention of customers to adopt cloud computing in banking industry	Malaysia	Diffusion theory			Trust, cost, security and privacy enhance the intention of customers to adopt cloud computing.	Asadi et al. (2017)

continued on following page

Table 1. Continued

Main objective	Study Area	Methods	Main DVs	Major IVs	Main Findings	Author(s)
Impact of I&CT on FD	GCC countries	Fixed effect model	FD	Fixed broadband, internet users, broad money supply	I&CT shows a significant impact on FD. Technological development is supportive to increase FD.	Alshubiri et al. (2019)
Association of e-banking with financial performance of public bank	Indonesia	Partial correlation analysis	Return on equity	Internet banking and mobile banking, risk, bank size and business cycles	E-banking is favourable for increasing financial performance.	Lasmini et al. (2019)
Observed the perception of customer to adopt internet banking	India	TAM model and SEM approach			Adoption of internet banking is determined by usefulness, ease of use and attitude of the customers.	Chauhan et al. (2019)
Impact of online banking on bank's performance	Bangladesh	Descriptive analysis	ROA and ROE	Internet users	Internet banking has more impact on ROA and ROE.	Islam et al. (2019)
Perception of employees from the role of HR in BPR	India	Parametric and non-parametric test			HR plays a key role in PBR programs.	Sehgal and Garg (2020)
Acceptance rate of DT in banking sector	Greece	Multivariate analysis		Perceived usefulness, perceived ease, perceived self-efficacy, intention to use, usage behaviour	Targeted education programmes must be executed to increase DT.	Kitsios et al. (2021)
Impact of I&CT on profits and risk of financial distress	28 EU countries	Panel data analysis	Profits and risk of financial distress	I&CT diffusion, ATM penetration	I&CT exercises help to increase profits. I&CT also could assist to increase financial stability.	Gaudio et al. (2021)

continued on following page

Table 1. Continued

Main objective	Study Area	Methods	Main DVs	Major IVs	Main Findings	Author(s)
Examine the importance of I&CT in FI of entrepreneurs	Africa	Regression analysis	FI	I&CT	FI of entrepreneurs is positively associated with I&CT.	Wellalage et al. (2021)
Perceived the problems of banking sector due to DT	German	Inductive content analysis			Customers and employees have high attention towards DT.	Diener and Špaček (2021)
Factors increasing the intentions of customers for using internet banking	Vietnam	Simple descriptive analysis			Perceived usefulness, attitude, innate innovativeness, and internet experience are helpful to increase the intention of customers to use internet banking.	Nguyen-Viet et al. (2021)
Identified the indicators that increase the intention of banking sector to adopt AI	India	Logistic regression mode	Customers of services	AI adoption	AI is useful to decrease cost and satisfaction of customers.	Deepthi et al. (2022)
Examine the determinants of digital banking adoption	Saudi Arabia	TAM model and logistic regression model			Ease of use and usefulness shows a vital impact on adoption of digital banking.	Alnemer (2022)
Examine the employee's perspective on digital banking	India	Descriptive analysis	Adoption of technology	Age, education, profession, usage	Untrained employees show a negative impact on overall success.	Vignesh (2022)
Examine the challenge for adopting AI in banking sector and consumers intentions on it	Malaysia	Descriptive analysis			AI is useful to detect fraud and increase risk prevention.	Rahman et al. (2023)

continued on following page

Table 1. Continued

Main objective	Study Area	Methods	Main DVs	Major IVs	Main Findings	Author(s)
Implication of IT on banking performance	Iran	ARDL model	Performance of banks	IT	IT has a noteworthy impact on the performance of banks.	Saeed & Ahmed (2023)
Impact of financial technologies on financial performance of banking sector	Jordan and United Arab Emirates	Regression analysis	Total deposits and net profits	Financial technology	Total deposits and net profits are positively related to financial technology.	Baker et al. (2023)
Impact of DT in banking sector	Portugal	Ground theory		Gender, age, education, tenure of bank, DT process,	DT is significant for improving employees' skills and stakeholders' digital experience.	Porfírio et al. (2024)
Technology acceptance and performance of banking sector	India	Descriptive analysis			Technology acceptance is helpful to increase the performance of the banking sector.	Muduli and Choudhury (2024)
Effect of digitization on financial performance of banking sector	Africa	GLSE model	Financial performance	DT	Financial performance of banking sector is positively associated with DT.	Theiri and Hadoussa (2024)
Impact of I&CT on performance of banking sector	MENA countries	GMM model	Banking performance	I&CT	I&CT has a positive impact on bank's performance.	Al-Naimi et al. (2024)

3. RESEARCH METHOD AND MATERIALS

3.1. Study Area

The study area of this research is Dehradun and Delhi. Both the cities are finalized as per the convenient, financial limitation, feasibility of travel plan and availability of time for the research team. While the employees (bankers) of public and private banks are used as respondents in this research.

3.2. Source of Secondary and Primary Data

Necessary secondary data for certain activities are also taken from Reserve Bank of India (RBI) (Government of India), world development indicator (The world bank) and international monetary fund (IMF). As this chapter is primarily based on primary data. The required data pertinent to this study is taken from randomly selected 167 employees of public and private banks in Dehradun and Delhi.

3.3. Data Collection Method

This chapter used survey method to collect the require information from the respondents. The personal interview of individual respondent is conducted using a well-structured questionnaire. The personal interview of respondents is completed during January 2023 to April 2024.

3.4. Format of Questionnaire

It includes 30 items or questions that are divided in five different constructs. These constructs are prescribed according to existing literature. While these items (questions) are based on a 7-point Likert scale. Although, previous studies are also adopted 5-point Likert scale to observe the perceptions of respondents on various subjects in banking industry and financial organization, and other sectors (Aliyu et al., 2014; Kitsios et al., 2021; Vignesh, 2022; Rahman et al., 2024).

3.5. Application of Simple Descriptive Analysis (SDA)

Aliyu et al. (2014) applied SEM to explore the association between online banking and customer delivery. Baptista and Oliveira (2015) applied the SEM model to examine the determinant for accepting mobile banking in Africa. Tam and Oliveira (2016) developed SEM to explore the importance of M-banking for individuals.

Asadi et al. (2017) used diffusion theory for analysing the intention of customers to adopt cloud computing in the banking sector.

Li et al. (2021) adopted structural equation modelling to examine the customer satisfaction affecting indicators in the banking industry. Alnemer (2022) developed the TAM model to analyze the factors encouraging adoption of digital banking in Saudi Arabia. It found that digital banking adoption also depends on demographic profile, occupation and income of the customers. Rahman et al. (2024) applied sequential least square model and SEM to examine the intentions of individuals to adopt mobile banking. SEM is highly useful to explain the large number of statistical models (Baptista & Oliveira, 2015). SEM is a statistical method for examining the causal association among the indicators or items (Martins et al., 2014). The researcher of this chapter collects qualitative data in a 7-point Likert scale to examine the perception of employees towards DT in the banking sector of India. Thus, SDA is used for analysing the data in this chapter.

3.6. Validity and Reliability Tests for Items and Constructs

The actual properties of all items or questions are based on 7-point Likert scale (i.e., 1= Strongly Disagree; 2= Disagree; 3 = Somewhat Disagree; 4 = Neither Agree nor Disagree; 5 = Somewhat Agree; 6 = Agree; 7 = Strongly Agree) in this chapter. Hence, it is mandatory to check the validity of all items in each construct. Thus, Cronbach's alpha (α) test is instigated to check the validity of each item (Rahman et al., 2024). This test also measured the scale reliability and internal consistency of each indicator (Aliyu et al., 2014).

3.7. Formulation of Regression Analysis

The existing scholars applied diverse empirical models to explore the impact of digital technology, I&CT, financial technology (FinTech), internet banking, cloud computing etc. on different indicators of the banking sector. Malhotra and Singh (2010) employed multiple regression models to examine the factors leading to internet banking services in India. Binuyo and Aregbeshola (2014) considered the OLS model to explore the impact of I&CT cost efficiency on performance on the banking sector in South Africa. Akshisar et al. (2015) examined the contribution of electronic banking systems for increasing their profitability using dynamic panel data models. Tunay et al. (2015) developed a panel causality model to examine the implications of internet banking on profitability of the banking industry in 30 EU countries. Logistic regression model is also used to examine the factors enhancing digital banking (Alnemer, 2022). Baker et al. (2023) developed multiple regression models to examine the impact of FinTech on total deposits and net profits of the banking sector in Jordan and UAE. Linear regression models are executed to examine the interconnection among the CS, DT, FS and FR in this chapter. Following regression equations are adopted:

$$(CS)_e = \alpha_0 + \alpha_1 (DT)_e + \alpha_2 (FS)_e + \alpha_3 (FR)_e + \mu_e \quad (1)$$

$$(DT)_e = \beta_0 + \beta_1 (CS)_e + \beta_2 (FS)_e + \beta_3 (FR)_e + \varphi_e \quad (2)$$

$$(FS)_e = \xi_0 + \xi_1 (DT)_e + \xi_2 (CS)_e + \xi_3 (FR)_e + \delta_e \quad (3)$$

$$(FR)_e = \theta_0 + \theta_1 (DT)_e + \theta_2 (CS)_e + \theta_3 (FS)_e + \lambda_e \quad (4)$$

Here, *CS* is customer's satisfaction; *DT* is DT; *FS* is financial security; *FR* is financial risk; α_0, β_0, ξ_0 and θ_0 are constant coefficients; α_s, β_s, ξ_s and θ_s are regression coefficients of corresponding independent variables; *e* is respondents (i.e., $e = 1, 2, ..., 167$); $\mu_e, \varphi_e, \delta_e$ and λ_e are the error-terms in the mentioned equations. Cameron & Trivedi's decomposition of IM-test also applied to recognize the presence of heteroskedasticity in the cross-sectional data. Variance inflation factor (VIF) is also estimated to examine the existence of linear correlation among the constructs. SPSS and STATA statistical software are used for descriptive and regression analysis.

4. RESULTS AND DISCUSSION

4.1. Execution of DT in Indian Banking Sector

The initiation of digitalization in the banking sector in India and other countries began in the 1980s (Carbo-Valverde, 2017; Gupta, 2023). That time the prime objective of digitalization is to improve customer satisfaction and maintain accounts and ledger in the Indian banking industry (Gupta, 2023). Thereafter, RBI introduced a committee for implementation of digitalization and use of digital technologies in the Indian banking sector in 1988 under Dr. C. Rangarajan (Gupta, 2023). Subsequently, India also adopted the core banking system (CBS). CBS is proposed to increase customers' comforts across the banking system in India (Gupta, 2023). At present the Indian banking industry is using diverse tools and scientific mechanisms to increase its DT. DT depends on digital technologies, digital infrastructure, digital resources, digital skills, digital literacy and digital accessibility of individuals in organizations. Digital technology is helping to make significant changes in the financial landscape across countries (Alnemer, 2022). At present, the main focus of the banking sector is to provide best, fast, accurate and better banking facilities to their customers (Gupta, 2023). Thus, the prime agenda of the banking sector is to be digitized in India (Gupta, 2023).

The Indian banking system passed through four different phases i.e., mechanization (1980s), automation (1990s), internet and mobile (2000s) and internet of everything (present) (Gupta, 2023). In the 1980s, the mechanization used MICR, Encoder, manual checks and transactions in the banking sector. In the 1990s, automation systems used ATMs, electronic fund transfer, branch connectivity and computerization in India. Automation is a process to control a system automatically in the banking industry (Baker et al., 2023). In the 2000s, the internet and mobile are applying IMPS, RGTS, NEFT, online banking, biometrics, mobile banking and cheque transactions. Nowadays, the internet of everything is using artificial intelligence, I&CT, cloud computing and blockchain in the Indian banking system. AI could be helpful to decrease cost and increase the customers experience of services in India (Deepthi et al., 2022).

4.2. Growth of DT in Indian Banking Sector

The trend in the number of employees in different categories of the Indian banking sector is presented in Figure 1. Figure 1 implies that the number of employees in public sector banks has declined. While the number of employees in private sector banks increased after 2007 - 08. Foreign and regional rural banks could not increase the number of employees in India. It means that customers have lower dependency on regional rural and foreign banks in India. Therefore, foreign and regional rural banks could not increase the number of employees.

Figure 1. Trend in bank group-wise distribution of employees (in numbers) in scheduled commercial banks in India

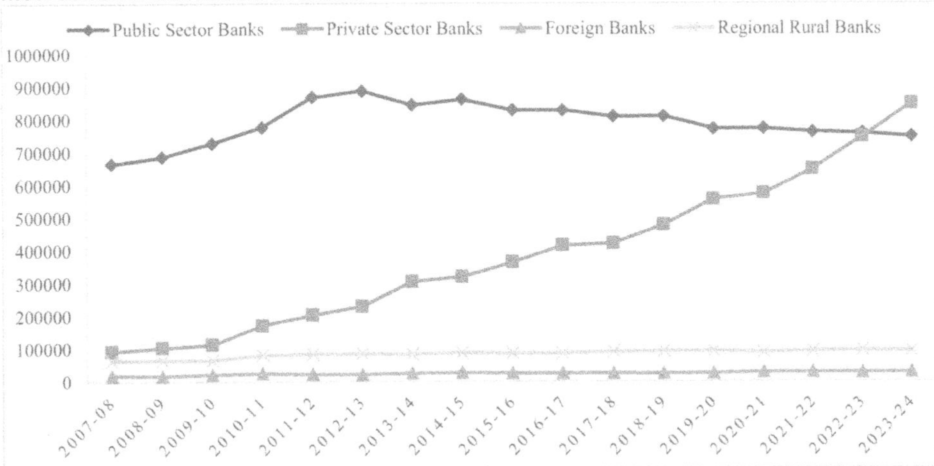

(RBI, GoI)

The progress of the number of branches of commercial banks in rural, urban, semi-urban and metropolitan areas is given in Figure 2. Figure 2 indicates that the number of branches of commercial banks show an increasing trend in India. Urban and metropolitan areas have more population size, job opportunities, businessmen, economically active people and infrastructure. Therefore, urban and metropolitan areas have more branches as compared to rural and semi-urban areas.

Figure 2. Trend in population group-wise number of branches of scheduled commercial banks in India

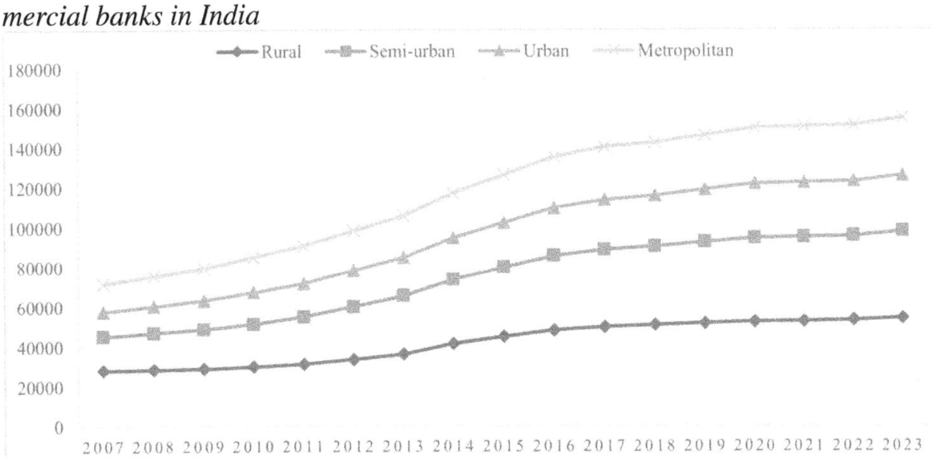

(RBI, GoI)

Figure 3 shows India's progress in various mediums of credit transfer during 2019-20 to 2023-24. Figure 3 indicates that India achieved remarkable progress to increase the intention of people to make digital payments through UPI app. The Indian banking sector, therefore, is significantly moving towards DT.

Figure 3. Progress in volume (in Lakh) of credit transfers in India

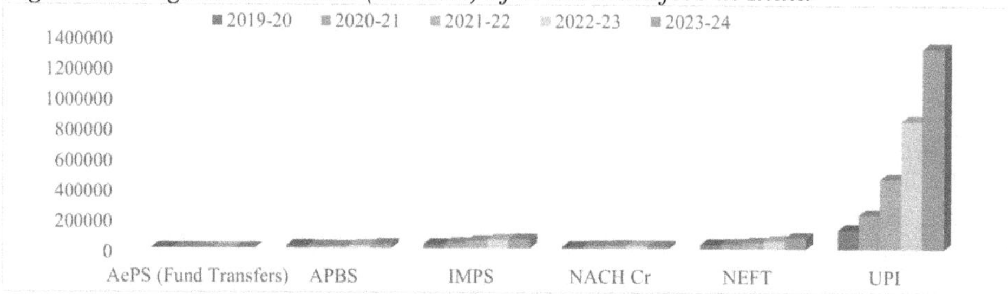

(RBI, GoI)

Figure 4 presents India's progress in debit transfers and direct debits during 2019-20 to 2023-24. Figure 4 claims that volume of NACH for debits transfer and direct debits is continuously increasing in India during the mentioned time periods. The figure provides a clarity that the Indian banking industry is effectively moving towards DT.

Figure 4. Progress in volume (in Lakh) of debit transfers and direct debits in India

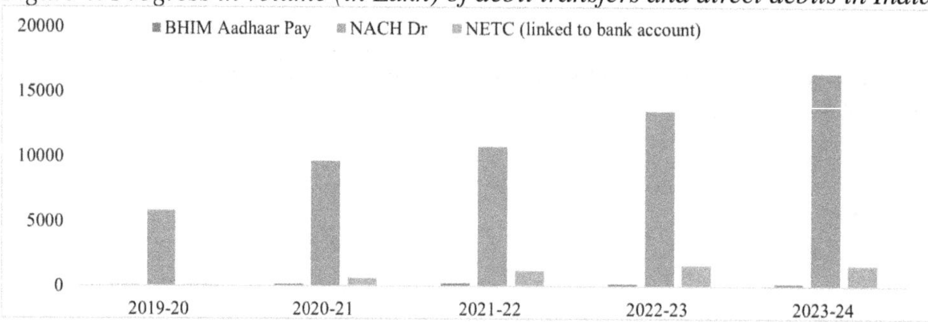

(RBI, GoI)

Figure 5 shows the progress in volume of payments through credit and debits cards in India during 2019-20 to 2023-24. Figure 5 implies that payments through credit cards will continuously increase after 2019-2020. While payments through debit cards decreased after the mentioned financial year. Hence, it indicates that trust of customers on online banking is increasing continuously.

Figure 5. Progress in volume (in Lakh) of card payment in India

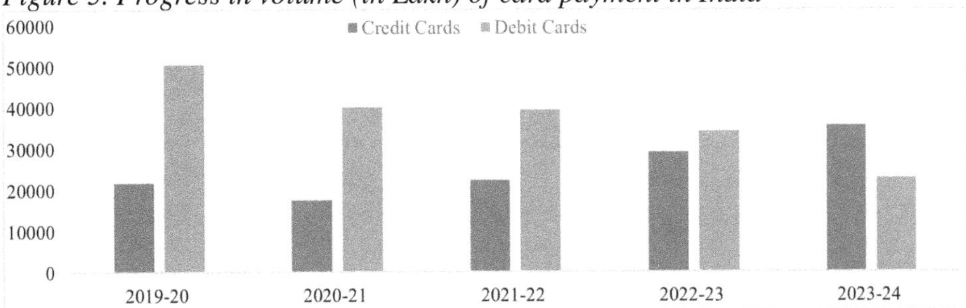

(RBI, GoI)

Figure 6 presents India's progress in DT promoting indicators in India during 2005 – 2022. Figure 6 infer that the number of fixed broad subscriptions, mobile cellular subscriptions and internet users are significantly improved in India. These are the effective and conducive indicators for improving the progress of digitalization. The data also reflect that India has positive progress in DT.

Figure 6. Progress in DT enhancing indicators in India

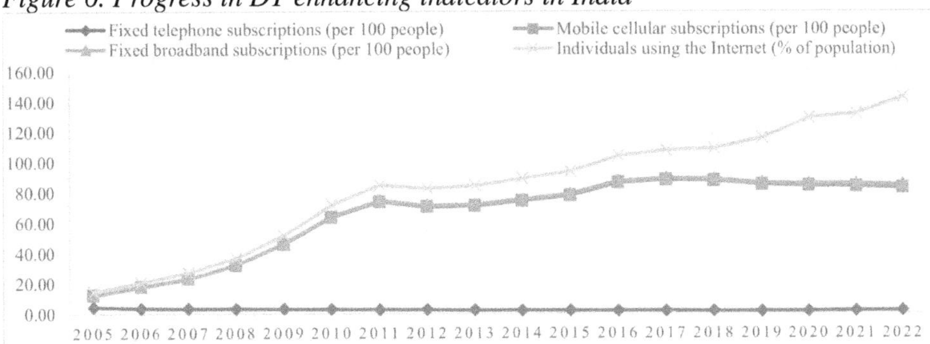

(WDI The World Bank)

Figure 7 indicates India's progress in the number of ATMs users and commercial bank branches per million adults in India during 2005-2021. Figure 7 infers that the number of ATMs users has consistently increased after 2005. Number ATMs users also reflects the progress of DT in the banking sector.

Figure 7. Progress in number of ATMs users and commercial bank branches in India

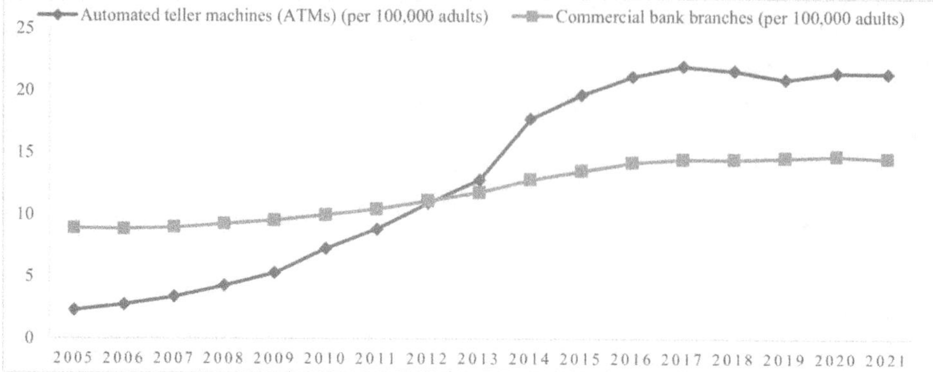

(WDI The World Bank)

4.3. Descriptive Analysis of Employee's Responses on CS, DT, FR and FS Related Items

The statistical summary and scale reliability of all items is presented in Table 2. As the actual data of these items are in Likert scale. Hence, it is obvious that most items appear in abnormal forms as per the statistical values of standard deviation (SD) and skewness (Table 2). Thereupon, the statistical properties of Cronbach's α -value for all items are more than 0.65. Hence, all items have appropriate scale reliability.

Table 2. Statistical summary and scale reliability of items

Constructs	Symbol	Mean	SD	Skewness	Cronbach's α -value
Customer's Satisfaction (*CS*)	*CS1*	5.9401	1.2208	-2.1171	0.6913
	CS2	5.9581	1.1426	-2.1540	0.6864
	CS3	6.1317	1.1748	-2.6270	0.6622
	CS4	5.6228	1.2055	-1.5004	0.7409
	CS5	5.5689	1.0948	-1.2676	0.7146
	CS6	5.3533	1.5757	-1.3826	0.7770
	CS7	5.8144	1.1597	-1.8659	0.6831

continued on following page

Table 2. Continued

Constructs	Symbol	Mean	SD	Skewness	Cronbach's α -value
DT	*DT*1	5.5928	1.0819	-1.6286	0.6562
	*DT*2	5.2455	1.5541	-1.2150	0.7054
	*DT*3	5.8263	1.1615	-1.4861	0.6895
	*DT*4	5.8563	1.2187	-2.0870	0.6250
	*DT*5	5.7485	1.2645	-1.5989	0.6734
	*DT*6	5.6228	1.2005	-1.3805	0.6096
	*DT*7	5.6228	1.1802	-1.4860	0.6036
Financial Risk (FR)	*FR*1	5.8204	1.2336	-1.8182	0.8127
	*FR*2	5.7246	1.1805	-2.2528	0.8230
	*FR*3	5.8144	1.0037	-1.9884	0.8253
	*FR*4	5.9521	1.1606	-1.9471	0.8317
	*FR*5	5.5749	1.2194	-1.4443	0.8085
	*FR*6	5.5868	1.1885	-1.7511	0.8016
	*FR*7	5.7665	1.2121	-1.8864	0.8077
	*FR*8	5.8563	1.1316	-1.9928	0.8243
	*FR*9	5.7844	1.1623	-1.7446	0.8098
Financial Security (FS)	*FS*1	5.4910	1.3660	-1.5457	0.6508
	*FS*2	5.7784	1.1481	-1.8597	0.6558
	*FS*3	5.7844	1.2806	-1.8190	0.6805
	*FS*4	5.9042	1.0712	-1.8146	0.6503
	*FS*5	5.8084	1.0351	-1.4740	0.7329
	*FS*6	5.7725	1.1907	-1.7014	0.6940
	*FS*7	6.0120	1.1353	-2.2034	0.6821

Source: Author's estimation based on primary data.

The frequency and percentage for all items/questions are given in Table 3. 7 items/questions are designed to know the perception of employees to increase the customer's satisfaction. As per the view of employees, the banking sector is taking several steps to increase the customer's satisfaction. Banks are providing information about technology and security to customers on a regular basis. Banks are also giving quick responses on customer's delayed payments. Bank is also organizing training programmes for the rural and urban customers to increase their understanding towards the latest technology. The bank is strictly following the guidelines to solve the registered complaints of the customers. Banks are also providing proper solutions to the customers through mobile calls. Duplicate SIM cards are also provided to the customers by the banks. Despite that, customers are facing problems to take loans from banks due to the detailed and inclusive process of security, privacy and verification.

Table 3. Frequency and percentage of items in each construct

Constructs	Items/Questions	Scale	1	2	3	4	5	6	7
Customer's Satisfaction (*CS*)	Technology and security timely updates by the banks for customers (*CS*1)	Frequency	3	4	2	4	20	79	55
		Percentage	1.80	2.40	1.20	2.40	11.98	47.31	32.93
	Money debited from the account but delayed in crediting to the beneficiary's account in RTGS, NEFT and ATM transactions is settled quickly by banks (*CS*2)	Frequency	3	1	4	6	15	87	51
		Percentage	1.8	0.6	2.4	3.6	9.0	52.1	30.5
	Banks provide technology awareness programs for both rural and urban customers in their regional languages (*CS*3).	Frequency	3	4	1	2	8	81	68
		Percentage	1.80	2.40	0.60	1.20	4.79	48.50	40.72
	Turnaround time for the complaints registered by the customers to the banks is strictly followed (*CS*4).	Frequency	4	1	3	7	55	58	39
		Percentage	2.40	0.60	1.80	4.19	32.93	34.73	23.35
	Banks provide solutions for imposter calls to customers (*CS*5).	Frequency	1	2	6	15	35	84	24
		Percentage	0.60	1.20	3.59	8.98	20.96	50.30	14.37
	Bank solution for duplicate SIM (SIM cloning) to get their bank account (*CS*6).	Frequency	10	3	6	18	25	72	33
		Percentage	5.99	1.80	3.59	10.78	14.97	43.11	19.76
	Security, privacy, detailed verifications of user input, and	Frequency	2	3	4	10	16	93	39
		Percentage	1.20	1.80	2.40	5.99	9.58	55.69	23.35
DT	Clustering ATMs based on transaction patterns and cash demand similarities can be used to estimate cash demand (*DT*1).	Frequency	2	2	4	11	38	88	22
		Percentage	1.20	1.20	2.40	6.59	22.75	52.69	13.17
	Uploading the bank's cheque image on the app can be used instead of depositing it physically (*DT*2).	Frequency	9	3	10	18	32	66	29
		Percentage	5.39	1.80	5.99	10.78	19.16	39.52	17.37
	Lack of guidance for interacting with internet banking/mobile banking/ digital wallets (*DT*3).	Frequency	1	2	7	11	19	81	46
		Percentage	0.60	1.20	4.19	6.59	11.38	48.50	27.54
	Banks initiatives for technology updating for dummy keypads and pinhole cameras in ATMs (*DT*4).	Frequency	3	4	2	10	10	95	43
		Percentage	1.80	2.40	1.20	5.99	5.99	56.89	25.75
	Lack of trained workforce create barriers in banking activities (*DT*5).	Frequency	3	2	7	8	28	73	46
		Percentage	1.80	1.20	4.19	4.79	16.77	43.71	27.54
	AI-driven automation could result in the obsolescence of some skills in banks (*DT*6)	Frequency	2	3	4	16	31	77	34
		Percentage	1.20	1.80	2.40	9.58	18.56	46.11	20.36
	The compatibility of the RPA banking system with the existing infrastructure poses the biggest challenge (*DT*7).	Frequency	2	3	4	16	27	85	30
		Percentage	1.20	1.80	2.40	9.58	16.17	50.90	17.96

continued on following page

Table 3. Continued

Constructs	Items/Questions	Scale	1	2	3	4	5	6	7
	Frauds increases due to the use of unknown/unverified apps (*FR*1).	Frequency	3	4	1	8	29	73	49
		Percentage	1.80	2.40	0.60	4.79	17.37	43.71	29.34
	Hackers can access customers' sensitive information by compromising credentials on search engines (*FR*2).	Frequency	4	3	3	5	22	103	27
		Percentage	2.40	1.80	1.80	2.99	13.17	61.68	16.17
	Disruption in banking operations due to server breakdown (*FR*3).	Frequency	2	1	2	8	26	97	31
		Percentage	1.20	0.60	1.20	4.79	15.57	58.08	18.56
	RTGS/NEFT system does not accept future value dated transactions (*FR*4).	Frequency	1	4	6	4	13	87	52
		Percentage	0.60	2.40	3.59	2.40	7.78	52.10	31.14
Financial Risk (*FR*)	Check on technology fraud on social media accounts by the banks for customers (*FR*5).	Frequency	3	3	1	21	30	78	31
		Percentage	1.80	1.80	0.60	12.58	17.964	46.71	18.56
	Network crashes, and the threat of cybercrime challenges faced by banks due to cloud computing (*FR*6).	Frequency	3	4	2	12	33	88	25
		Percentage	1.80	2.40	1.20	7.19	19.76	52.69	14.97
	Data theft, data leaks, Malware attacks & hacking are the major risk associated with Digital wallet (*FR*7).	Frequency	3	4	2	7	28	83	40
		Percentage	1.80	2.40	1.20	4.19	16.77	49.70	23.95
	Low infrastructure, risk perception, illiteracy, low compliances and financial unawareness, and services create barriers for financial development (*FR*8).	Frequency	2	3	4	5	21	91	41
		Percentage	1.20	1.80	2.40	2.99	12.57	54.49	24.55
	In branchless banks we can't be sure that the person on the other end of	Frequency	2	3	4	8	26	84	40
		Percentage	1.20	1.80	2.40	4.79	15.57	50.30	23.95

continued on following page

Table 3. Continued

Constructs	Items/Questions	Scale	1	2	3	4	5	6	7
Financial Security (*FS*)	Face, and voice recognition can enhance the security of digital banking transactions (*FS*1).	Frequency	7	1	6	3	59	54	37
		Percentage							
	Using a mobile application can make cardless ATM transactions handy, and secure and can also ease out the process of logging in again and again (*FS*2).	Frequency	3	1	5	6	29	85	38
		Percentage	1.80	0.60	2.99	3.59	17.37	50.90	22.75
	The security of internet banking can be enhanced using biometrics (*FS*3).	Frequency	5	1	2	11	28	71	49
		Percentage	2.99	0.60	1.20	6.59	16.77	42.51	29.34
	Using a mobile application can make cardless ATM transactions handy and more awareness is needed from the security aspect concerned (*FS*4).	Frequency	2	2	1	4	36	73	49
		Percentage	1.20	1.20	0.60	2.40	21.56	43.71	29.34
	Risk of a security breach, online fraud, and leakage of confidential information (*FS*5).	Frequency	1	2	3	5	40	76	40
		Percentage	0.60	1.20	1.80	2.99	23.95	45.51	23.95
	Hackers can access sensitive data by creating a third-party phishing website (*FS*6).	Frequency	2	4	3	8	29	79	42
		Percentage	1.20	2.40	1.80	4.79	17.37	47.31	25.15
	The security of internet banking can be enhanced using biometrics and followed by the current process of OTP (*FS*7).	Frequency	3	2	1	4	23	75	59
		Percentage	1.80	1.20	0.60	2.40	13.77	44.91	35.33

Source: Author's estimation based on primary data.

continued on following page

Employees provide different perceptions of DT in the banking sector (Table 3). It is suggested by the employees that clustering ATMs based on transaction patterns and cash demand similarities can be used to estimate cash demand. Banks should take the initiative to upload the bank's cheque image on the app instead of depositing it physically to increase DT. Lack of guidelines for interacting with internet banking is creating challenges for DT. Also, bank initiative for technology updating for dummy keypads and phone cameras in ATMs is also positive in DT. Thereafter, lack of trained workforce is creating barriers in banking activities. AI-driven automation is also increasing the undesirability of employees. The compatibility of the RPA banking system with the existing infrastructure poses the biggest challenge in DT of the banking sector.

The chapter finalizes the 9 questions related to financial risk in the banking sector due to its transformation towards digitalization (Table 3). Financial fraud increases due to adoption of unverified apps by the customers. Hackers can also access customers' sensitive information by compromising credentials on search engines. Server breakdown may also increase disruption in banking activities. Employees also accept that the RTGS/NEFT system does not have future value. Financial risk also

Table 3. Continued

increases due to network crashes and the threat of cybercrime in the banking sector. Data theft, data leaks, Malware attacks & hacking are also increasing financial risk. Also, low infrastructure, risk perception, illiteracy, low compliances and financial unawareness, and services create barriers for financial development.

Financial security would be improved as adoption of face and voice recognition of digital banking (Table 3). Biometric may be another action to increase financial security. There is also a requirement to increase more awareness among the customers towards security aspects concerned. Customers should not share the confidential information among the unauthorized person to increase financial security. The banking sector should not use third-party websites to avoid the financial risk. Biometrics process in internet banking would be favourable to increase financial security.

It is also found a positive correlation among CS, DT, FS and FR (Table 4). DT is positively correlated with customer's satisfaction, financial security and financial risk. Financial security is also positively associated with financial risk, customer's satisfaction and DT. Hence, DT, FS, FR and CS have a complex and significant association with each other. The regression coefficients of IVs with respective DVs are observed positive (Table 5). The results claim that DT and financial security are helpful to increase customer's satisfaction. Financial risk, financial security and customer's satisfaction are supportive to increase the DT of the banking industry. Further, DT is found significant for increasing financial risk and financial security. Financial security to be improved as DT and customer's satisfaction increase. Thus, it is noticed a positive and significant interconnection among DT, CS, FS and FR in the Indian banking industry.

Table 4. Correlation coefficients among the constructs

Constructs	*CS*	*DT*	*FR*	*FS*
CS	1	0.677**	0.800**	0.707**
DT	0.677**	1	0.741**	0.607**
FR	0.800**	0.741**	1	0.652**
FS	0.707**	0.607**	0.652**	1

Source: Author's estimation based on primary data.

Table 5. Interconnection among the constructs

Dependent Variables (*DVs*)	*CS*			*DT*			*FR*			*FS*		
Number of obs.	167			167			167			167		
F - Value	129.35			75.61			137.14			62.6		
Prob > F	0.000			0.000			0.000			0.000		
R-squared	0.7042			0.5819			0.7162			0.5353		
Adj. R-squared	0.6987			0.5742			0.711			0.5268		
Mean VIF	2.26			2.77			2.19			2.9		
Cameron & Trivedi's decomposition of IM-test [Chi2]	14.05			23.98			29.29			35.24		
Independent Variables (*IVs*)	Coef.	Std. Err.	P>|t|	Coef.	Std. Err.	P>|t|	Coef.	Std. Err.	P>|t|	Coef.	Std. Err.	P>|t|
DT	0.1098	0.0680	0.108	-	-	-	0.3677	0.0619	0.000	0.1844	0.0805	0.023
CS	-	-	-	0.1434	0.0888	0.108	0.5137	0.0669	0.000	0.4478	0.0866	0.000
FR	0.5176	0.0674	0.000	0.4838	0.0815	0.000	-	-	-	0.1291	0.0933	0.168
FS	0.3146	0.0608	0.000	0.1691	0.0738	0.023	0.0900	0.0650	0.168	-	-	-
Constant Coefficients	0.3441	0.2883	0.234	1.0489	0.3205	0.001	0.2034	0.2880	0.481	1.4241	0.3269	0.000

Source: Author's estimation based on primary data.

5. CONCLUSION AND POLICY GUIDELINES

This chapter observed multiple benefits and problems of the banking sector due to adoption of DT in India and other countries as per existing theoretical literature. The bankers are also facing diverse problems due to their low technical skills, low understanding towards new technology, and additional burden on work. It also observed that India's progress in digital banking and number of branches have significantly increased. For instance, the number of branches of commercial branches increased after 2007 in urban and metropolitan areas of India. The volume of credit transfer through UPI apps is also exponentially increased in India. Accordingly, the volume of debit transfers through online banking will also improve in India after 2019-20. Thereupon, the number of credit card users will also increase in India after 2019-20. Most importantly, the percentage share of fixed telephone subscriptions, individuals using the internet and mobile cellular subscription are also shown an increasing trend in India. Accordingly, the number of ATMs users is also showing a progressive trend in India. Hence, it is reported that the banking sector is moving towards digitalization and DT.

The perception of employees produces different opinions on CS, DT, FR and FS in the banking sector. The banking sector is taking several steps to increase customer's satisfaction. For instance, banking is providing technology and security related information to the customers. Bank is also organizing awareness progress for the customers. Despite that customer's satisfaction decreases due to lack of security, low privacy and detailed verifications in the banking sector. DT is providing multiple benefits to banks and customers. DT is also creating different challenges in the banking sector. For example, lack of guidelines, lack of trained workers, AI-driven automation and compatibility of the RPA are creating barriers in DT of the banking sector. Financial risk increases due to applications unverified by the customers, attack of hackers on servers, server breakdown, technology fraud, network crashes, threat of cybercrime, data theft, data leaks, Malware attacks in banking industry of India. Therefore, financial security may be improved by implementing biometrics and face and voice recognition.

The appropriate implementation of DT in the banking sector requires appropriate training and skills in India (Vignesh, 2022). Banking sector should also provide regular training to the employees to increase their digital skills and knowledge towards emerging technologies. Appropriate digital infrastructure would also increase the DT of the banking sector. Banking industry should increase huge investment in I&CT sector for promoting digital channels and internet security to increase DT (Theiri & Hadoussa, 2024). Investment in I&CT would be imperative to increase DT of the banking sector. Banking industry should ensure the cybersecurity to increase the trust of customers in DT. Banking sector should reduce financial fraud in online banking.

6. SIGNIFICANCE AND INNOVATION OF THE CHAPTER

The chapter explores India's progress in DT of the banking sector using time trend analysis of different indicators. Thereupon, the statistical and empirical analysis of this chapter is primarily based on actual information that is collected through personal interviews of employees. Hence, this is the originality and novelty of this chapter. Thereupon, it also makes crucial contributions to the theoretical literature in numerous aspects. Theoretical literature of this chapter explains the current problems of employees and customers in the banking sector, implications of DT in banking sector, and perception of customers and employees towards DT in banking sector. It also divides 30 items in four crucial constructs. Descriptive statistical technique is used for analyzing the primary data. The correlation coefficient analytical technique is also applied to examine the association among these constructs. Simple linear regression equations are also adopted to examine the interconnection among these constructs. Thereupon, it proposes multiple practical policy implications for increasing the DT of India banking sector. Finally, it recommended scope of further research in the area of digitalization and its implications in the banking sector.

7. LIMITATIONS AND SCOPE OF FURTHER RESEARCH

This chapter has several limitations. The sample size of this chapter is very small. The respondents are taken from Dehradun and Uttarakhand. Hence, the results of this chapter cannot be generalized across the banking system of India. Hence, further study can be conducted to increase more sample size from different states of India. Social, economic, educational qualification, geographical location, gender, age of employment also plays a significant role to be familiar with DT. Also, this could not run CFA, structural equation modelling and other robust statistical and empirical models for data analysis. Further, this chapter could also not use mentioned indicators in CFA and regression analysis. This chapter also could not examine the implications on financial risk and fraud on performance of the banking sector. It also recognized the implication of financial risk and fraud on DT of the banking sector. Business cycles are also caused to increase financial risk and reduce financial investment. Although, this chapter could not explain how business cycles are harmful for increasing the performance of the banking sector? Hence, abovementioned issues can be considered in further research.

REFERENCES

Ahmadi, S. (2024). systematic literature review on cloud computing security: Threats and mitigation strategies. *Journal of Information Security*, *15*(1), 148–167. DOI: 10.4236/jis.2024.152010

Akshisar, I., Tunay, K. B., & Tunay, N. (2015). The effects of innovations on bank performance: The case of electronic banking services. *Procedia: Social and Behavioral Sciences*, *195*(1), 369–375. DOI: 10.1016/j.sbspro.2015.06.336

Al-Naimi, A. A., Yaseen, A., Alnaimat, M. A., Abed, S. A., & Farooq, U. (2024). The impact of information and communication technology on commercial banks' performance: Evidence from MENA. *Uncertain Supply Chain Management*, *12*(3), 1997–2004. DOI: 10.5267/j.uscm.2024.2.006

Aldás-Manzano, J., Lassala-Navarré, C., Ruiz-Mafé, C., & Sanz-Blas, S. (2009). The role of consumer innovativeness and perceived risk in online banking usage. *International Journal of Bank Marketing*, *27*(1), 53–75. DOI: 10.1108/02652320910928245

Ali, A., Hameed, A., Moin, M. F., & Khan, N. A. (2023). Exploring factors affecting mobile-banking app adoption: A perspective from adaptive structuration theory. *Aslib Journal of Information Management*, *75*(4), 773–795. DOI: 10.1108/AJIM-08-2021-0216

Aliyu, A. A., Rosmain, T., & Takala, J. (2014). Online banking and customer service delivery in Malaysia: Data screening and preliminary findings. *Procedia: Social and Behavioral Sciences*, *129*(1), 562–570. DOI: 10.1016/j.sbspro.2014.03.714

Alnemer, H. A. (2022). Determinants of digital banking adoption in Kingdom of Saudi Arabia: A technology acceptance model approach. *Digital Business*, *2*(1), 1–8. DOI: 10.1016/j.digbus.2022.100037

Alshubiri, F., Jamil, S. A., & Elheddad, M. (2019). The impact of ICT on financial development: Empirical evidence from the Gulf Cooperation Council countries. *International Journal of Engineering Business Management*, *11*(1), 1–12. DOI: 10.1177/1847979019870670

Alzaidi, M. S. (2022). Exploring the determinants of mobile banking adoption in the context of Saudi Arabia. *International Journal of Customer Relationship Marketing and Management*, *13*(1), 1–16. DOI: 10.4018/IJCRMM.289206

Asadi, S., Nilashi, M., Husin, A. R. C., & Yadegaridehkordi, E. (2017). Customers perspectives on adoption of cloud computing in banking sector. *Information Technology and Management*, *18*(4), 305–330. DOI: 10.1007/s10799-016-0270-8

Baker, H., Kaddumi, T. A., Nassar, M. D., & Muqattash, R. S. (2023). Impact of financial technology on improvement of banks' financial performance. *Journal of Risk and Financial Management*, *16*(4), 1–21. DOI: 10.3390/jrfm16040230

Baptista, G., & Oliveira, T. (2015). Understanding mobile banking: The unified theory of acceptance and use of technology combined with cultural moderators. *Computers in Human Behavior*, *50*(1), 418–430. DOI: 10.1016/j.chb.2015.04.024

Bhatia, A., & Mahendru, M. (2015). Assessment of technical efficiency of public sector banks in India using data envelopment analysis. *Eurasian Journal of Business and Economics*, *8*(15), 115–140.

Binuyo, A. O., & Aregbeshola, R. A. (2014). The impact of information and communication technology (ICT) on commercial bank performance: Evidence from South Africa. *Problems and Perspectives in Management*, *12*(3), 59–68.

Bueno, L. A., Sigahi, T. F. A. C., Rampasso, I. S., Filho, W. L., & Anholon, R. (2024). Impact of digitization on operational efficiency in the banking sector: Thematic analysis and research agenda proposal. *International Journal of Information Management Data Insights*, *4*(1), 1–12. DOI: 10.1016/j.jjimei.2024.100230

Carbo-Valverde, S. (2017). The impact of digitalization of banking and financial stability. *Journal of Financial Management. Markets and Institutions*, *5*(1), 133–140.

Changchit, C., Lonkani, R., & Sampet, J. (2017). Mobile banking: Exploring determinants of its adoption. *Journal of Organizational Computing and Electronic Commerce*, *27*(3), 239–261. DOI: 10.1080/10919392.2017.1332145

Chauhan, V., Yadav, R., & Choudhary, V. (2019). Analyzing the impact of consumer innovativeness and perceived risk in internet banking adoption. *International Journal of Bank Marketing*, *37*(1), 323–339. DOI: 10.1108/IJBM-02-2018-0028

Cheng, M., Qu, Y., Jiang, C., & Zhao, C. (2022). Is cloud computing the digital solution to the future of banking. *Journal of Financial Stability*, *63*(1), 1–20. DOI: 10.1016/j.jfs.2022.101073

Chufal, H. S., Singh, R., Danai, L., & Singh, A. K. (2025). Financial behaviours, literacy, and well-being among youth in India. In Reddy, K. J. (Ed.), *Behavioral Economics and Neuroeconomics of Health and Healthcare* (pp. 95–126). IGI Global., DOI: 10.4018/979-8-3693-6055-2.ch006

Dangolani, S. K. (2011). The impact of information technology in banking system (a case study in bank Keshavarzi IRAN). *Procedia: Social and Behavioral Sciences*, *30*(1), 13–16. DOI: 10.1016/j.sbspro.2011.10.003

Deepthi, B., Gupta, P., Rai, P., & Arora, H. (2022). Assessing the Dynamics of AI Driven Technologies in Indian Banking and Financial Sector. *Vision (Basel), 0*(0), 1–14. DOI: 10.1177/09722629221087371

Diener, F., & Špaček, M. (2021). DT in banking: A managerial perspective on barriers to change. *Sustainability, 13*(4), 1–21. DOI: 10.3390/su13042032

Gaudio, B. L. D., Porzio, C., Sampagnaro, G., & Verdoliva, V. (2021). How do mobile, internet and ICT diffusion affect the banking industry? an empirical analysis. *European Management Journal, 39*(3), 327–332. DOI: 10.1016/j.emj.2020.07.003

Gupta, R. (2023). Industry 4.0 Adaption in Indian banking sector—A review and agenda for future research. *Vision (Basel), 27*(1), 24–32. DOI: 10.1177/0972262921996829 PMID: 36977304

Hosein, S. S. M. (2013). Consideration the effect of e-banking on bank profitability; Case study selected Asian countries. *Journal of Economics & Sustainable Development, 4*(11), 112–117. https://www.iiste.org/Journals/index.php/JEDS/article/view/6851

Islam, S., Kabir, M. R., Dovash, R. H., Nafee, S. E., & Saha, S. (2019). Impact of online banking adoption on bank's profitability: Evidence from Bangladesh. *European Journal of Business and Management Research, 4*(3), 1–10. https://www.ejbmr.org/index.php/ejbmr/article/view/38. DOI: 10.24018/ejbmr.2019.4.3.38

Kitsios, F., Giatsidis, I., & Kamariotou, M. (2021). DT and strategy in the banking sector: Evaluating the acceptance rate of e-services. *Journal of Open Innovation, 7*(204), 1–14. DOI: 10.3390/joitmc7030204

Kumar, S. K., & Gulati, R. (2018). Evaluation of technical efficiency and ranking of public sector banks in India: An analysis from cross-sectional perspective. *International Journal of Productivity and Performance, 57*(7), 40–568.

Lasmini, R. S., Busiarti, A. P., Tasman, A., & Susant, F. A. (2019). The relationship between e-banking and financial performance of Go public bank in Indonesia. *Advances in Economics. Business and Management Research, 124*(1), 903–909.

Li, F., Lu, H., Hou, H., Cui, K., & Darbandi, M. (2021). Customer satisfaction with bank services: The role of cloud services, security, e-learning and service quality. *Technology in Society, 64*(1), 120–123. DOI: 10.1016/j.techsoc.2020.101487

Malhotra, P., & Singh, P. (2010). An analysis of Internet banking offerings and its determinants in India. *Internet Research, 20*(1), 87–106. DOI: 10.1108/10662241011020851

Martins, C., Oliveira, T., & Popovič, A. (2014). Understanding the internet banking adoption: A unified theory of acceptance and use of technology and perceived risk application. *International Journal of Information Management*, *34*(1), 1–13. DOI: 10.1016/j.ijinfomgt.2013.06.002

Muduli, A., & Choudhury, A. (2024). Digital technology adoption, workforce agility and digital technology outcomes in the context of the banking industry of India. *Journal of Science and Technology Policy Management*, DOI: 10.1108/JSTPM-01-2024-0018

Nguyen-Viet, B., Ngoc Huynh, K., & McMillan, D. (2021). Empirical analysis of internet banking adoption in Vietnam. *Cogent Economics & Finance*, *9*(1), 1–14. DOI: 10.1080/23322039.2021.1992876

Osei, L. K., Cherkasova, Y., & Oware, K. M. (2023). Unlocking the full potential of DT in banking: A bibliometric review and emerging trend. *Future Business Research*, *9*(30), 1–10. DOI: 10.1186/s43093-023-00207-2

Porfírio, J. A., Felício, J. A., & Carrilho, T. (2024). Factors affecting DT in banking. *Journal of Business Research*, *171*(1), 1–9. DOI: 10.1016/j.jbusres.2023.114393

Rahman, M., Ming, T. H., Baigh, T. A., & Sarker, M. (2023). Adoption of artificial intelligence in banking services: An empirical analysis. *International Journal of Emerging Markets*, *18*(10), 4270–4300. DOI: 10.1108/IJOEM-06-2020-0724

Rahman, M., Yee, H. P., & Masud, Md. A., K., & Uzir, Md. U. H. (2024). Examining the dynamic of mobile banking app. adoption during the COVI-19 pandemic: A digital shift in the crisis. *Digital Business*, *5*(1), 1–15.

Roy, S. K., Balaji, M. S., Kesharwani, A., & Sekhon, H. (2017). Predicting internet banking adoption in India: A perceived risk perspective. *Journal of Strategic Marketing*, *25*(5-6), 418–438. DOI: 10.1080/0965254X.2016.1148771

Saeed, Y. A. H., & Ahmed, R. A. (2023). The impact of information technology on the performance of commercial banks through the faithful representation of accounting information system. *International Journal of Professional Business Review*, *8*(9), 1–11. DOI: 10.26668/businessreview/2023.v8i9.1758

Sehgal, S., & Garg, P. (2020). The human challenges of the digital world: the paradigm of employee expectations in the banking sector. *e-journal - First Pan IIT International Management Conference – 2018*. DOI: 10.2139/ssrn.3743389

Shu, W., & Strassmann, P. A. (2005). Does information technology provide banks with profit? *Information & Management*, *42*(5), 781–787. DOI: 10.1016/j.im.2003.06.007

Singh, A. K., Ashraf, S. N., & Gupta, M. (2025). Digital transformation and customer's problems in banking industry of India. In Tunio, M. (Ed.), *Applications of Career Transitions and Entrepreneurship* (pp. 1–34). IGI Global Scientific Publishing., DOI: 10.4018/979-8-3693-4163-6.ch001

Singh, A. K., & Jyoti, B. (2023). Does digitalization have a bi-directional causal relationship with the entrepreneurship ecosystem? Evidence from a country-wise panel data analysis. In Yanamandra, R., & Indiran, L. (Eds.), *Handbook of Research on Designing Sustainable Strategies to Develop Entrepreneurial Intention* (pp. 178–172). IGI Global., DOI: 10.4018/978-1-6684-8781-5.ch007

Tam, C., & Oliveira, T. (2016). Understanding the impact of m-banking in individual performance: Delone & McLean and TTF perspective. *Computers in Human Behavior*, *61*(1), 233–244. DOI: 10.1016/j.chb.2016.03.016

Theiri, S., & Hadoussa, S. (2024). Digitization effects on banks' financial performance: The case of an African country. *Competitiveness Review*, *34*(1), 144–162. DOI: 10.1108/CR-10-2022-0147

Tunay, K. B., Tunay, N., & Akshisar, I. (2015). Interaction between internet banking and bank performance: The case of Europe. *Procedia: Social and Behavioral Sciences*, *195*(1), 363–358. DOI: 10.1016/j.sbspro.2015.06.335

Vignesh, A. (2022). Employees perspective on digital banking. *Asian Journal of Management*, *13*(3), 223–226. DOI: 10.52711/2321-5763.2022.00039

Vinoth, S., Vemula, H. L., Harapayya, B., Mamgain, P., Hasan, M. F., & Naved, M. (2022). Application of cloud computing in banking and e-commerce and related security threats. *Materials Today: Proceedings*, *51*(8), 2172–2175. DOI: 10.1016/j.matpr.2021.11.121

Wellalage, N. H., Hunjra, A. I., & Manita, R. (2021). Information communication technology and financial inclusion of innovative entrepreneurs. *Technological Forecasting and Social Change*, *163*(1), 1–10. DOI: 10.1016/j.techfore.2020.120416

Yan, G. (2017). Application of cloud computing in banking: Advantages and challenges. *Advances in Economics. Business and Management Research*, *33*(1), 29–33.

KEY TERMS AND DEFINITIONS

Banking Industry: It is a financial organization that accepts deposits from the public, businessmen and individuals. Also, it provides them return on their deposits. It also provides loan facilities to the economic agents for various purposes. Banking industry maintains the money liquidity in the financial market.

Customer's Satisfaction: It meets desirability and requirement of customers in all aspects like quality service, quality products, appropriate information, privacy, financial and legal security, immediate response and resolve customer's concerns, etc.

Digital Banking: It reduces the paper work in physical forms and increases the dependency of customers and employees on digital platforms in the banking sector.

DT: It is a process that increases the involvement of employees and customers in digital banking, online banking, e-banking, mobile banking, e-transaction as using different I&CT tools and mechanical devices.

E-commerce: E-commerce refers to the dependency of customers and producers for buying and selling of products through the internet.

Financial Security (FS): It ensures and provides the legal security of network, data, software, personal identity and privacy of customers from any financial attacks and avoids financial fraud.

Financial Inclusion: It provides the accessibility and usability of financial services, products, financial investment and financial knowledge and financial security to individuals.

Financial Risk (FR): It reduces the perception and behaviours of customers to decrease investment in financial institutions.

Financial Technology (FinTech): It is the combination of finance and technology to meet the diverse needs of customers and service providers in the financial sector.

Mobile Banking (M-banking): It provides the financial and products services to customers through mobile phone, smartphone and other devices.

Chapter 9

Leveraging Bi-Stacked ANN for Organizational Values in the Context of Digital Transformation

Usharani Bhimavarapu
https://orcid.org/0000-0002-0246-1420
Department of Computer Science and Engineering, Koneru Lakshmaiah Education Foundation, Vaddeswaram, India

ABSTRACT

The digital age has brought unprecedented opportunities for organizations to innovate and transform their operations, emphasizing the importance of measuring digital maturity and organizational values. This study leverages a bi-stacked Artificial Neural Network (ANN) architecture to measure a comprehensive digital index, integrating insights from people management values. The dataset, collected from 132 companies, was preprocessed and refined through feature extraction, including parameters such as the Relative Importance Value (RIV) for future business impact and the Rate of Satisfaction Value (RSV) with people management practices, quantified using a Likert scale. The bi-stacked ANN, designed with multiple layers and dropout mechanisms, processed these features to generate an accurate and reliable digital index. By combining advanced machine learning techniques and organizational value assessments, the proposed approach provides a scalable framework for understanding digital readiness while emphasizing the critical role of people management in driving business transformation

DOI: 10.4018/979-8-3693-8477-0.ch009

INTRODUCTION

With the information age, convergence of business and information technologies has become a potent engine for industry revolution globally. Information technologies (IT) provide the hardware, software, and platforms through which companies can simplify processes, facilitate communication, and make more informed decisions. The emergence of digital platforms, cloud computing, artificial intelligence (AI), and big data analytics has provided companies with unprecedented opportunities to innovate and respond to changes in the market at a quicker rate. The technologies allow companies to operate more effectively, reduce costs, and deliver better customer experiences, thereby achieving a competitive edge.

The age of the digital has also brought new business models that are technology-based to create value. Enterprises now operate in highly networked environments, with digital ecosystems and collaborations replacing value chains. To cite an example, firms like Uber, Airbnb, and Amazon have disrupted traditional industries by connecting buyers and sellers directly through digital platforms. These new business models are scalable, global, and flexible, all of which were things that could not be achieved under traditional business arrangements.

Besides, there has been a powerful effect that digital technologies have on the interaction of companies with customers. Online sites, mobile apps, and social networking platforms have come to be essential information resources for constructing a company's relationship with customers, and in obtaining vital information from customers regarding what they desire or require. With the help of data analysis, businesses possess the ability to provide personalized products and services, forecast customer demand, and market better. It has led to a shift in attitude from product-based conventional techniques to customer-based strategies, with one of the primary drivers being customer experience to ensure business success.

Operationally, the digital age has enabled businesses to automate the majority of their processes, rendering them more efficient and precise. RPA and AI analytics are technologies that are currently being used to monitor repetitive processes, while cloud applications provide the staging for scalable processes. This enables human resources to be directed to higher-level work, encouraging innovation and enhancing workers' productivity. Moreover, the fact that it is possible to track business performance in real-time based on data insights has facilitated companies to make better decisions, enhancing business operation efficiency further.

However, business and information technologies converging is not problem-free, particularly data security, confidentiality, and ever-changing adapting requirements. As more data accumulation by companies and increased use of computer systems, companies are faced with higher vulnerability to cyberattack as well as issues on keeping sensitive information away from unauthorized parties. Besides, ever-evolving technologies imply that businesses need to be agile and constantly update their systems and processes to survive in the marketplace. Despite such challenges, the digital age brings enormous opportunities to businesses willing to change and leverage technology to drive growth and innovation.

Digital transformation is the alignment of digital technologies in a business's all its functions, reshaping it at its core and the manner in which it generates value for customers. It is not merely the adoption of new technologies but even the reorganization of business models, processes, and organizations. With digital transformation, businesses can be more efficient, innovate faster, and deliver more targeted experiences to its customers. Technologies such as cloud computing, artificial intelligence (AI), big data analytics, and the Internet of Things (IoT) are fueling this change, allowing businesses to make data-driven decisions, automate processes, and remain competitive in an increasingly digitalised world.

In addition to technology, digital transformation frequently also involves changing organizational culture and attitude. It calls for a change towards increased collaboration, flexibility, and responsiveness of the labor force. Every employee at all levels needs to adopt digital tools and methods in order to catalyze the change, which could involve learning new skills, re-designing the workflow, and ongoing learning. When businesses adopt digital transformation, they are agile and hence capable of quickly reacting to market needs, customer demands, and industry disruption. Although the journey can be complex, those who make digital transformation a reality can gain an incredible competitive advantage in a constantly evolving market.

Porter's Five Forces Model (Porter et al., 2023) Does not take into account the dynamic nature of digital markets and competition through innovation. Value Chain Analysis (Porter et al., 2023) Is based on physical operations and, in most cases, does not consider digital capabilities and virtual value chain complexity. Business Model Canvas (Osterwalder & Pigneur, 2023) Is oversimplified in terms of business dynamics and does not take into account the complex interactions in digital ecosystems. Digital Maturity Model (Westerman et al., 2023) Subjective and does not always include industry-specific issues or the rate of tech change. McKinsey 7S Framework (Waterman et al., 2023) Does not assign digital transformation center stage, with a tendency to miss technology-centric components such as cloud computing or AI. SWOT Analysis (Humphrey, 2023) Does not assign center stage to rapidly changing technology threats or digital environment-based opportunities. Customer Journey Mapping (Shaw & Ivens, 2023) Tends to concentrate on the customer experience in a snapshot of time and fail to consider real-time alterations in digital interactions. The Balanced Scorecard (Kaplan & Norton, 2023) Classical models tend to disregard technology-driven innovation effects and customer-focused metrics in the new digital age. Lean Startup Methodology (Ries, 2023) Is best applied to startups and would less be applicable for larger, established companies that are in the process of digital transformation. B2B Sales Funnel (Aaron & Schilling, 2023) Does not consider the richness of multichannel digital marketing programs and customer touchpoints. Technology Acceptance Model (TAM) (Davis, 2023) It fails to provide understanding of how the external environment drivers, e.g., industry norms or technology innovation acceleration, influence adoption.Diffusion of Innovations Theory (Rogers, 2023) It makes an assumption that technology adoption is a linear process, while adoption patterns in the online setting may be more dynamic and complicated. The Resource-Based View (RBV) (Barney, 2023) Focuses more on tangible assets and overlooks the intangible assets that are at the center of digital transformation, including data and intellectual capital. Blue Ocean Strategy (Kim & Mauborgne, 2023) Underestimates the disruptive power of emerging technologies and digital competition, and it is challenging to find new blue oceans. Disruptive Innovation Theory (Christensen, 2023) Is concerned with a fundamental understanding of technological disruption and does not account for incremental or platform-based innovation models prevalent in digital technologies. The Technology-Organization-Environment (TOE) Framework (Tornatzky & Fleischer, 2023) Could be too overarching, not accounting for specific challenges and opportunities of digital transformation in specific industries. Porter's Value Discipline Model (Porter et al., 2023) Is unsuitable for the speed demanded by digital business environments, where innovation must be a constant process. Customer Relationship Management (CRM) Models (Payne & Frow, 2023) Most CRM models are prehistoric and cannot accommodate fully contemporary digital engagement approaches, including AI-powered customer understanding and automation. The DeLone and McLean IS Success Model (DeLone & McLean, 2023) Is centered on information systems success but does not have a focus on new technologies such as AI, blockchain, and how they are being integrated into current systems. Enterprise Architecture (EA) Models (Zachman, 2023) Are generally inflexible and insensitive to the pace of technology change or changing needs of digital businesses. Open Innovation Model (Chesbrough, 2023) Coupled with the hyper-digitization of a worldwide business world. This can result in intellectual property liabilities or inefficiency, if cooperation in due time is succeeded by complexity. The Innovation Value Chain (Hansen & Birkinshaw, 2023) This doesn't always capture in its embeds the rhythm of agile and iterative processes inherent in digital product R&D and tech innovation. Digital Divide Model (Norris, 2023) While it addresses gaps in digital access, it does not address digital literacy, which is a growing concern in most organizations undergoing transformation. The Capability Maturity Model (CMM) (CMMI Institute, 2023) It has the tendency to focus on software and software processes to the detriment of the whole business and digital transformation strategy. The Business Ecosystem Model (Iansiti & Levien, 2023) Can be unaware of the speedy innovation and disruption that occur in digital ecosystems, and it can make adaptation challenging for firms.

As such, Bi-Stacked Artificial Neural Network (Bi-Stacked ANN) offers a viable solution to overcome most of the bottlenecks that occur in current models used in business and information technologies, especially during the digital technology era. One of the greatest advantages of Bi-Stacked ANN is that it can cope with intricate and dynamic environments, overcoming the shortcomings of such conventional models as Porter's Five Forces or the SWOT Analysis that do not take into account the pace with which digital markets change and the disruptive power of technological change. Bi-Stacked ANN, by virtue of its deep learning structure, can perceive nonlinear correlations and patterns in the data that might otherwise go unnoticed by more surface-level models like the Business Model Canvas or Value Chain Analysis, which are more prone to oversimplification.

Moreover, Bi-Stacked ANN is more capable of incorporating real-time feedback and adjustment loops, thereby being more sensitive to the dynamic nature of the virtual world than other models like Customer Journey Mapping or the Balanced Scorecard, which are more likely to overlook dynamic, time-sensitive customer interactions. Its capacity to consolidate huge amounts of information across various touchpoints guarantees that it can keep pace with rapidly evolving technology threats and opportunities, a shortcoming of earlier models like the Resource-Based View (RBV) or Technology Acceptance Model (TAM), which tend to neglect intangible digital resources and outside environmental variables.

Additionally, Bi-Stacked ANN can overcome the strategy-to-action gap through offering more precise, actionable intelligence from sophisticated data sources and thereby avoiding the inflexibility of models such as Enterprise Architecture or the Capability Maturity Model (CMM), which are behind the pace of technological change. Its deep learning architecture also avoids the confines of the Disruptive Innovation Theory that has a tendency to highlight narrow technological disruption. In its processing of immense amounts of business and operational data, the Bi-Stacked ANN is able to detect incremental or platform-type innovations driving sustained business growth during the digital age.

Essentially, Bi-Stacked ANN offers a more forward-looking, data-centric, and adaptive solution than existing models, addressing the imperative for companies to keep pace with the constant presence of digital evolution. It allows companies to surf the storm of the digital era, find new business opportunities, and lead the pack in a technology-driven emerging world.

MATERIALS AND METHODOLOGY

The approach uses a bi-stacked Artificial Neural Network (ANN) to predict the digital index from data for values of people management. The primary parameters of Relative Importance Value (RIV) and the Rate of Satisfaction Value (RSV) were computed based on a Likert scale following preprocessing and feature extraction. These two variables were used as input features in the ANN, a two-stacked network that was meant to identify subtle relationships. The first stack reformed and sanitized the features to generate intermediate representations that were then analyzed by the second stack. The last layer generated the digital index, which was optimized with the Adam optimizer to reduce error. This method assures precise and comparable digital index measurement while emphasizing the organizational values' contribution.

Material

The study employed a questionnaire survey approach in data collection, which was assisted by human resource experts from different firms. The experts worked diligently to ensure the completeness and accuracy of the gathered data. Complete datasets were collected from 132 firms, which were deemed adequate for statistical analysis. Of significance is that the response rate of the questionnaires sent out was an extremely high 84.6%, reflecting high levels of participation and interest in research.

The sample population in the research was constructed in such a way that it comprised companies of all sizes without placing any cap on the number of workers. The openness in this respect guaranteed a wide coverage of the subject among a wide organizational context. The participation of companies of different sizes—small or micro-businesses as well as larger companies—allowed the research to capture the multi-faceted reactions of companies to the challenges and opportunities of the digital age.

Special focus was laid on micro and small enterprises since they are likely to be start-up driven, i.e., responsive and innovative. These firms are generally more sensitive to new trends, and hence their coverage was important in an attempt to find the overall importance of digital transformation. The information collected through these varied institutions was informative regarding the way businesses of every size view and grow with the swiftly changing virtual landscape. This rich data source assisted in answering the research queries and trends that could potentially direct future attempts to strategically leverage digitalization across industries.

Preprocessing

The collected dataset was subjected to intense preprocessing phase for it to become statistically prepared to be analyzed as well as get meaningful inferences. The beginning was with summarizing data in the completed questionnaires and making it digitalized, compiling answers of 132 firms into formatted form. Transferring the information into an organized dataset so that variables as well as characteristics can have homogeneity was undertaken.

Next, the dataset was searched for errors such as missing values, duplicate records, or inapplicable answers. Missing values were addressed according to standard procedures by filling values through statistical operations or by discarding incomplete records based on the nature and extent of missing values. Duplicate records, if present, were identified and removed to make the dataset pure in nature. Inappropriate answers, such as outliers or meaningless values, were flagged and corrected wherever possible.

Categorical variables such as company size and industry type were coded to make analysis possible, while numerical variables such as the number of employees were normalized in a bid to get all variables onto an equal footing. Normalization was particularly necessary for ensuring that no variable dominated the result unfairly.

In addition, exploratory data analysis (EDA) was carried out to uncover patterns, trends, and associations among variables. This included developing summary statistics and visualizations in order to get a better idea of the dataset and guide subsequent analyses.

By effective cleaning and preprocessing of the dataset, it was made certain that the data was free from errors, well-structured, and ready for strong statistical analysis, laying a strong foundation for answering the research questions effectively.

Feature Extraction

Principal Component Analysis (PCA) was also implemented as a feature extraction algorithm that minimizes the dataset's dimension while retaining most of its variance. The technique started with the process of standardization, by which each of the features had its mean forced to zero and standard deviation normalized to one. This was in order to enable all the variables, irrespective of their initial scale, to participate equally in the analysis. Then, a covariance matrix was calculated in the hope of acquiring some insight into feature relationships and correlation patterns.

Based on the covariance matrix, the eigenvalues and eigenvectors were computed. The eigenvectors were the directions of the new feature space, or principal components, and the eigenvalues were the proportion of variance explained by the component. The principal components were ordered by their eigenvalues, and a subset of components was chosen to keep most of the variance in the dataset, usually keeping a threshold such as 95% of the total variance.

After identifying the principal components, the initial dataset was changed by projecting it onto them. This provided a lower dimension of features that were linear combinations of the original variables but not correlated with each other. Not only did the transformation reduce complexity from the dataset, but also eliminated redundancy and noise, hence rendering the dataset amenable for additional analysis such as classification or clustering.

Through feature extraction with PCA, the information was successfully compressed into a more compact and richer representation of information. Not only improved computation efficiency but also corrected multicollinearity and noise in the original features such that the features retained most of the important information for the analysis.

Digital Index Measurement

After feature selection and preprocessing, the bi-stacked Artificial Neural Network (ANN) model was used to forecast the digital index with the addition of people management values insights in the firms. Bi-stacked ANN is a two-stacked neural network learning model for identifying intricate relationships between the data. Both stacks contain some fully connected layers, and ReLU activation functions have been employed to introduce non-linearity so that the network can learn sophisticated patterns in the right way. Dropout layers were introduced to prevent overfitting and enable generalization.

In order to quantify the values of people management within the companies, there were two significant parameters taken into consideration: Relative Importance Value (RIV) for the company's future and the Rate of Satisfaction Value (RSV) for their adoption within people management. Measurements of these parameters were on a Likert scale of 1 to 6. RIV assessed the relevance of management values in relation to people (1—entirely irrelevant to 6—entirely relevant) and RSV assessed satisfaction with their application (1—extremely dissatisfied to 6—entirely satisfied). These measured values were included in the feature set that was provided as input to the bi-stacked ANN.

The initial stack of the ANN was employed to process the extracted features in order to capture higher-level representations of people management values' relative importance and satisfaction relationships in relation to how they influence the digital index. The output feature set of significant patterns that were built at the mid-stream level by the first stack were then heavily processed by the second stack. By using the sequence learning approach, more in-depth examination of the internal organization of the data was preserved.

The final output layer of the bi-stacked ANN combined the fine-grained representations of the two stacks to generate the digital index. Based on whether the output is continuous scores or classification, the layer used a suitable activation function, e.g., sigmoid for continuous scores or softmax for classification. Model training utilized the Adam optimizer, optimizing a loss function such as Mean Squared Error (MSE) or Cross-Entropy in an effort to achieve high accuracy.

This approach enabled the measurement of the digital index with accuracy based on the levels of significance and satisfaction of the people management values in the companies. Through the utilization of the capacity and depth of the bi-stacked ANN, the approach provided a robust and comprehensive model for the analysis of complex data in digital transformation and organizational values.

Experimental Results

Results of the experiment support the validity of the bi-stacked Artificial Neural Network (ANN) in accurately measuring the digital index with relevant parameters of people's management values. The model was validated through data gathered from 132 companies towards the measurement of Relative Importance Value (RIV) and the Rate of Satisfaction Value (RSV) on the Likert scale. The bi-stacked ANN model was able to effectively identify the intricate inter-relationship among features with a remarkable performance in predicting the digital index compared to traditional methods. The results indicate that the model considers both technology-driven and people-oriented variables while assessing digital maturity. Table1 presents a comparison of two types: Digitalization in Customer-Related Solutions and Employee-Focused Measures based on various performance indicators.

For Relative Importance Value (RIV), Digitalization of Customer-Related Solutions has a higher score of 5.2 compared to Employee-Focused Measures with a score of 4.8, indicating a slightly higher priority for digitalization for customer-related solutions. The Rate of Satisfaction Table 2 presents the factor analysis result with focus on two main statistical tests: Kaiser-Meyer-Olkin (KMO) Measure and Bartlett's Test of Sphericity. Kaiser-Meyer-Olkin (KMO) Measure = 0.832, which is in the range "meritorious" (0.8–0.89), and this measure tells us that sample size is good enough for factor analysis needs and variables are well enough intercorrelated that the same analysis will prove to be useful. Bartlett's Test of Sphericity provides a chi-square value of 352.67 with $p < 0.001$, which shows the correlation matrix is not an identity matrix and factor analysis can therefore be conducted on the data. The test also confirms the validity of the obtained factor structure from the analysis since it guarantees there are patterns in the data of interest.

(RSV) is also higher for Digitalization in Customer-Related Solutions (4.6) than for Employee-Focused Measures (4.4), since there is higher satisfaction with attempts at digitalization in customer-related solutions.

Based on model performance metrics, Mean Squared Error (MSE) is lower for Digitalization in Customer-Related Solutions (0.023) compared to Employee-Focused Measures (0.030), which means that the customer-related solutions model is performing better.

Based on the measurement criteria, Accuracy for Digitalization in Customer-Related Solutions is higher at 89% compared to Employee-Focused Measures at 85%, indicating better overall performance in customer-related solutions. Precision and Recall for Digitalization in Customer-Related Solutions are higher with precision being 0.91 and recall being 0.88 compared to 0.87 and 0.85 for Employee-Focused Measures, respectively. The F1-Score that balances precision and recall is greater for Digitalization in Customer-Related Solutions at 0.89 compared to Employee-Focused Measures at 0.86. According to the Principal Component Analysis (PCA) results, the Variance Explained is higher for Digitalization in Customer-Related Solutions (95%) compared to Employee-Focused Measures (92%), indicating a better correlation of data in the customer-related solutions model.

The Model Convergence measure shows that both the models converge at the same locations, with Digitalization in Customer-Related Solutions converging at 150 epochs and Employee-Focused Measures converging at 140 epochs. Lastly, the Overfitting (Dropout Rate) is higher in the Digitalization in Customer-Related Solutions model at 20%, compared to 15% in the Employee-Focused Measures model, which shows slightly higher need for regularization against overfitting in the customer-related solutions model.

Table 1. Digitalization in customer-related solutions and employee-focused measures

Category	Digitalization in Customer-Related Solutions	Employee-Focused Measures
Relative Importance Value (RIV)	5.2	4.8
Rate of Satisfaction Value (RSV)	4.6	4.4
Mean Squared Error (MSE)	0.023	0.030
Accuracy	89%	85%
Precision	0.91	0.87
Recall	0.88	0.85
F1-Score	0.89	0.86

continued on following page

Table 1. Continued

Category	Digitalization in Customer-Related Solutions	Employee-Focused Measures
Variance Explained (PCA)	95%	92%
Model Convergence (Epochs)	150	140
Overfitting (Dropout Rate)	20%	15%

Table 2 reveals factor analysis output, and two most significant statistical tests: Kaiser-Meyer-Olkin (KMO) Measure and Bartlett's Test of Sphericity. Kaiser-Meyer-Olkin (KMO) Measure is 0.832, between "meritorious" (0.8–0.89), and implies that the sample size is appropriate enough to undertake factor analysis and that variables are strongly correlated in a way that this analysis will be significant. Bartlett's Test of Sphericity is 352.67 with a p-value of less than 0.001, and it is statistically significant. It shows that the correlation matrix is not an identity matrix and that factor analysis is appropriate for the data set. The statistical significance of this test further verifies the factor structure derived from the analysis as being significant, and it proves that the data contains patterns worth exploring.

Table 2. Factor analysis

Test	Value	Interpretation
Kaiser-Meyer-Olkin (KMO) Measure	0.832	Meritorious (0.8–0.89)
Bartlett's Test of Sphericity	$\chi^2 = 352.67$	$p < 0.001$ (Significant)

Table 3 shows the outcome of the analysis of variance (ANOVA), which investigates the difference in group means. The Source of Variation has two parts: Between Groups and Within Groups. The Sum of Squares Between Groups is 123.45, and the Within Groups is 542.56, and the Total Sum of Squares is 666.01.

The degrees of freedom (df) for Between Groups is 3 and for Within Groups is 128. The Mean Square values, which are the sum of squares divided by the degrees of freedom, are 41.15 for Between Groups and 4.24 for Within Groups. The F-statistic is 5.32, a ratio of the Between Groups mean square to the Within Groups mean square. This F-value of 0.002, $p < 0.05$, is significant statistically, meaning that there are statistically significant differences among the group means. Lastly, the Partial η^2 value of 0.15 represents a medium effect size, or the fact that about 15% of the variance in the dependent measure is explained by group differences.

Table 3. Analysis of variance (ANOVA)

Source of Variation	Sum of Squares	df	Mean Square	F	p-value	Partial η^2
Between Groups	123.45	3	41.15	5.32	0.002	0.15
Within Groups	542.56	128	4.24			
Total	666.01	131				

Table 4 gives the degree of importance and satisfaction level of different corporate values on the Likert scale with information for Relative Importance Value (RIV), Rate of Satisfaction Value (RSV), Mean, Standard Deviation (SD), and percentage of companies with rating 5-6 (Important/Satisfied) for each value.

Company value Customer Focus is at a mean of 5.15 with an RSV of 4.8 and an RIV of 5.5, and a standard deviation of 0.67. Around 82% of the companies have an opinion that this value is important or satisfying. Innovation and Creativity follows at an RIV of 5.2 and an RSV of 4.5, a mean of 4.85, and a standard deviation of 0.71, and it is thought about by 78% of companies as important or fulfilling.

Employee Well-being is rated 5.3 on RIV and 4.7 on RSV, has a mean of 5.00 and standard deviation of 0.65, and is highly rated by 80% of firms.

The term Sustainability has an RIV of 4.9 and an RSV of 4.2, with a mean of 4.55 and a higher standard deviation of 0.80, indicating that 75% of firms rate it as important or satisfying. Integrity and Ethics is the leader with a highest RIV of 5.8 and an RSV of 5.0, mean of 5.40, and lowest standard deviation of 0.56, and 88% rated it as important or satisfactory. Lastly, Collaboration and Teamwork has an RIV of 5.4, an RSV of 4.6, a mean of 5.00, and a standard deviation of 0.60, and 81% of the companies considered it as high. These numbers show a general tendency to be very important to all corporate values, but with different degrees of satisfaction.

Table 4. Importance and satisfaction levels based on a Likert scale

Corporate Value	Relative Importance Value (RIV)	Rate of Satisfaction Value (RSV)	Mean	Standard Deviation (SD)	% of Companies Rating 5-6 (Important/ Satisfied)
Customer Focus	5.5	4.8	5.15	0.67	82%
Innovation and Creativity	5.2	4.5	4.85	0.71	78%
Employee Well-being	5.3	4.7	5.00	0.65	80%
Sustainability	4.9	4.2	4.55	0.80	75%
Integrity and Ethics	5.8	5.0	5.40	0.56	88%
Collaboration and Teamwork	5.4	4.6	5.00	0.60	81%

CONCLUSION

The research validates the accuracy of a bi-stacked Artificial Neural Network (ANN) in assessing the digital index of companies based on vital parameters like the importance of people management values and levels of satisfaction. Application of RIV and RSV as measurable indicators validates organizational values' contribution to determining digital transformation programs. The findings validate the ability of the bi-stacked ANN to identify advanced patterns in the data, along with a legitimate and scalable approach to measuring digital maturity. Likert scale measurement also enables standard measurement of organizational processes to yield actionable feedback to businesses of any size. This framework not only encourages thought on digital readiness but also focuses on the interplay among technology acceptance and human value-oriented determinants, building a viable paradigm for future research and utilitarian practice of digital transformation.

REFERENCES

Aaron, D., & Schilling, M. A. (2023). *The B2B sales funnel: Understanding the new buyer journey*. Salesforce.com.

Barney, J. B. (2023). Firm resources and sustained competitive advantage. *Journal of Management*, *17*(1), 99–120. DOI: 10.1177/014920639101700108

Chesbrough, H. W. (2023). *Open innovation: The new imperative for creating and profiting from technology*. Harvard Business School Press.

Christensen, C. M. (2023). *The innovator's dilemma: When new technologies cause great firms to fail*. Harvard Business Review Press.

CMMI Institute. (2023). *CMMI for development, version 1.3*. Carnegie Mellon University.

Davis, F. D. (2023). Perceived usefulness, perceived ease of use, and user acceptance of information technology. *Management Information Systems Quarterly*.

DeLone, W. H., & McLean, E. R. (2023). Information systems success: The quest for the dependent variable. *Information Systems Research*, *3*(1), 60–95. DOI: 10.1287/isre.3.1.60

Hansen, M. T., & Birkinshaw, J. (2023). The innovation value chain. *Harvard Business Review*, *85*(6), 121–130. PMID: 17580654

Humphrey, A. S. (2023). *SWOT analysis for management consulting*. SRI Alumni Association.

Iansiti, M., & Levien, R. (2023). The new competitive advantage: The evolution of business ecosystems. *Harvard Business Review*, *82*(10), 92–103.

Kaplan, R. S., & Norton, D. P. (2023). *The balanced scorecard: Measures that drive performance*. Harvard Business Review Press.

Kim, W. C., & Mauborgne, R. (2023). *Blue ocean strategy: How to create uncontested market space and make the competition irrelevant*. Harvard Business School Press.

Norris, P. (2023). *Digital divide: Civic engagement, information poverty, and the internet worldwide*. Cambridge University Press.

Osterwalder, A., & Pigneur, Y. (2023). *Business model generation: A handbook for visionaries, game changers, and challengers* (2nd ed.). Wiley.

Payne, A., & Frow, P. (2023). A strategic framework for customer relationship management. *Journal of Marketing*, *69*(4), 167–176. DOI: 10.1509/jmkg.2005.69.4.167

Porter, M. E. (2023). *Competitive advantage: Creating and sustaining superior performance*. Free Press.

Porter, M. E. (2023). *Competitive strategy: Techniques for analyzing industries and competitors*. Free Press.

Ries, E. (2023). *The lean startup: How today's entrepreneurs use continuous innovation to create radically successful businesses*. Crown Business.

Rogers, E. M. (2023). *Diffusion of innovations* (5th ed.). Free Press.

Shaw, C., & Ivens, J. (2023). *Building great customer experiences*. Palgrave Macmillan.

Tornatzky, L. G., & Fleischer, M. (2023). *The processes of technological innovation*. Lexington Books.

Treacy, M., & Wiersema, F. (2023). *The discipline of market leaders: Choose your customers, narrow your focus, dominate your market*. Addison-Wesley.

Waterman, R. H., Peters, T. J., & Phillips, J. R. (2023). Structure is not organization. *Business Horizons*.

Westerman, G., Calméjane, C., Ferraris, P., & Bonnet, D. (2023). *Digital transformation: A roadmap for billion-dollar organizations*. MIT Center for Digital Business.

Zachman, J. A. (2023). A framework for information systems architecture. *IBM Systems Journal*, *26*(3), 276–292. DOI: 10.1147/sj.263.0276

Compilation of References

Aagaard, A. (2019). The concept and frameworks of digital business models. Digital business models: Driving transformation and innovation, 1-26.

Aaron, D., & Schilling, M. A. (2023). *The B2B sales funnel: Understanding the new buyer journey*. Salesforce.com.

Abdullahi, A. S., Haron, H., & Taib, C. M. (2018). The use of information technology in the internal audit process: An exploratory study in the Nigerian public sector. *Journal of Accounting. Finance and Auditing Studies*, *4*(1), 51–68.

Abdullahi, M. H., Abdul, R. M., & Arif, A. (2018). Factors influencing the adoption of information technology in public sector auditing: Evidence from Nigeria. *Journal of Information Systems and Technology Management*, *15*(1), 3–20.

Adams, S. O., & Paul, C. (2023). E-government development indices and attaining United Nations sustainable development goals in Africa: A cross-sectional data analysis. *European Journal of Sustainable Development Research*, *7*(4), em0234. Advance online publication. DOI: 10.29333/ejosdr/13576

Addai, B., Ameyaw, B., Ashlley, E., & Quaya, I. (2015). Electronic Banking and Customer Satisfaction: Empirical Evidence from Ghana. *British Journal of Economics. Management and Trade*, *9*(3), 1–8.

Addo, H., & Boateng, R. (2016). Internal audit effectiveness, IT infrastructure capability, and financial reporting quality. *Journal of Accounting in Emerging Economies*, *6*(1), 4–25.

Adenle, A. A., De Steur, H., Mwongera, C., Rola-Rubzen, F., de Barcellos, M. D., Vivanco, D. F., Timilsina, G. R., Possas, C., Alders, R., Chertow, M., Poons, S., & Scholes, B. (2023). Global UN 2030 agenda: How can science, technology and innovation accelerate the achievement of sustainable development goals for all? *PLOS Sustainability and Transformation*, *2*(10), e0000085. DOI: 10.1371/journal.pstr.0000085

Aerts, A., & Bogdan-Martin, D. (2021). Leveraging data and AI to deliver on the promise of digital health. *International Journal of Medical Informatics*, *150*, 104456. DOI: 10.1016/j.ijmedinf.2021.104456 PMID: 33866232

Ahmad, H., Kasasbeh, B., Aldabaybah, B., & Rawashdeh, E. (2023). Class balancing framework for credit card fraud detection based on clustering and similarity-based selection (SBS). *International Journal of Information Technology : an Official Journal of Bharati Vidyapeeth's Institute of Computer Applications and Management*, *15*(1), 325–333. DOI: 10.1007/s41870-022-00987-w PMID: 35757149

Ahmadi, S. (2023). Open AI and its Impact on Fraud Detection in Financial Industry. *J. Knowl. Learn. Sci. Technol.*, *2*, 263–281.

Ahmadi, S. (2024). systematic literature review on cloud computing security: Threats and mitigation strategies. *Journal of Information Security*, *15*(1), 148–167. DOI: 10.4236/jis.2024.152010

Ahmed, M., Ansar, K., Muckley, C., Khan, A., Anjum, A., & Talha, M. (2021). A semantic rule based digital fraud detection. *PeerJ. Computer Science*, *7*, e649. DOI: 10.7717/peerj-cs.649 PMID: 34435097

Akhigbe, R., Amos, K., & Adeoti-Adekeye, B. (2018). The impact of information technology on internal auditing: A comparative analysis of banks in Nigeria. *Journal of Internet Banking and Commerce*, *23*(2), 1–22.

Akshisar, I., Tunay, K. B., & Tunay, N. (2015). The effects of innovations on bank performance: The case of electronic banking services. *Procedia: Social and Behavioral Sciences*, *195*(1), 369–375. DOI: 10.1016/j.sbspro.2015.06.336

Aladwani, A. M. (2001). Online banking: A field study of drivers, development challenges, and expectations. *International Journal of Information Management*, *21*(4), 213–225. DOI: 10.1016/S0268-4012(01)00011-1

Aldás-Manzano, J., Lassala-Navarré, C., Ruiz-Mafé, C., & Sanz-Blas, S. (2009). The role of consumer innovativeness and perceived risk in online banking usage. *International Journal of Bank Marketing*, *27*(1), 53–75. DOI: 10.1108/02652320910928245

Alemayehu, M., & Molla, A. (2017). Understanding the determinants of mobile health acceptance and its impact on health information systems' success: A structural equation modeling approach. *Government Information Quarterly*, *34*(1), 93–104.

Al-Hashedi, K. G., & Magalingam, P. (2021). Financial fraud detection applying data mining techniques: A comprehensive review from 2009 to 2019. *Computer Science Review*, *40*, 100402. DOI: 10.1016/j.cosrev.2021.100402

Alhassan, M. D., & Adam, I. O. (2021). The effects of digital inclusion and ICT access on the quality of life: A global perspective. *Technology in Society*, *64*, 101511. DOI: 10.1016/j.techsoc.2020.101511

AL-Hawamleh, A., Altarawneh, M., Hikal, H., & Elfedawy, A.AL-Hawamleh. (2024). Blockchain technology and virtual asset accounting in the metaverse: A comprehensive review of future directions. *International Journal of Computing and Digital Systems*, *15*(1), 1595–1614. DOI: 10.12785/ijcds/1501113

Ali, A., Hameed, A., Moin, M. F., & Khan, N. A. (2023). Exploring factors affecting mobile-banking app adoption: A perspective from adaptive structuration theory. *Aslib Journal of Information Management*, *75*(4), 773–795. DOI: 10.1108/AJIM-08-2021-0216

Ali, A., Razak, S. A., Othman, S. H., & Eisa, T. A. E. (2022). AI-Dhaqm, A.; Nasser, M.; Elhassan, T.; Elshafie, H.; Saif, A. Financial Fraud Detection Based on Machine Learning: A Systematic Literature Review. *Applied Sciences (Basel, Switzerland)*, *12*(19), 9637. DOI: 10.3390/app12199637

Ali, M., Naeem, F., Kaddoum, G., & Hossain, E. (2023). Metaverse communications, networking, security, and applications: Research issues, state-of-the-art, and future directions. *IEEE Communications Surveys and Tutorials*.

Aliyu, A. A., Rosmain, T., & Takala, J. (2014). Online banking and customer service delivery in Malaysia: Data screening and preliminary findings. *Procedia: Social and Behavioral Sciences*, *129*(1), 562–570. DOI: 10.1016/j.sbspro.2014.03.714

Alles, M. G., & Brennan, G. (2016). The promise of big data and analytics in the accounting, auditing, and finance professions: Opportunities and challenges. *Journal of Accounting Research*, *54*(4), 1085–1091.

Alles, M. G., & Kogan, A. (2020). Robotic Process Automation (RPA) in auditing: A field study. *Journal of Emerging Technologies in Accounting*, *17*(2), 45–55.

Alles, M., & Brennan, G. (2016). The impact of robotic process automation on the internal audit function. *Journal of Information Systems*, *30*(3), 21–44.

Alles, M., & Brennan, N. (2016). The use of data analytics in the internal audit setting: An extended discussion. *Journal of Information Systems*, *30*(2), 111–124.

Alles, M., & Kogan, A. (2020). *Transforming the Internal Audit Function: The Journey to Continuous Assurance*. ISACA.

Almarabeh, T., Abuhashesh, M., & Alsmadi, I. (2017). Investigating e-Government Services Adoption from Citizens' Perspective: A Structural Equation Modeling Approach. *Information Development, 33*(5), 452–468.

Al-Matar, N. (2023). Optimizing supply chain coordination through cross-functional integration: A dynamic model using optimal control theory. *International Journal for Applied Information Management, 3*(2), 70–81. DOI: 10.47738/ijaim.v3i2.52

Al-Naimi, A. A., Yaseen, A., Alnaimat, M. A., Abed, S. A., & Farooq, U. (2024). The impact of information and communication technology on commercial banks' performance: Evidence from MENA. *Uncertain Supply Chain Management, 12*(3), 1997–2004. DOI: 10.5267/j.uscm.2024.2.006

Alnemer, H. A. (2022). Determinants of digital banking adoption in Kingdom of Saudi Arabia: A technology acceptance model approach. *Digital Business, 2*(1), 1–8. DOI: 10.1016/j.digbus.2022.100037

Alsenaani, K. Fraud Detection in Financial Services using Machine Learning. Master's Thesis, RIT 1 Lomb Memorial Dr, Rochester, NY, USA, 2022.

Al-Shorbaji, N., & Al-Shorbaji, N. (2021). Improving healthcare access through digital health: the use of information and communication technologies. *Healthcare Access, 10*.

Alshubiri, F., Jamil, S. A., & Elheddad, M. (2019). The impact of ICT on financial development: Empirical evidence from the Gulf Cooperation Council countries. *International Journal of Engineering Business Management, 11*(1), 1–12. DOI: 10.1177/1847979019870670

Alzahrani, R. A., & Aljabri, M. (2022). AI-based Techniques for Ad Click Fraud Detection and Prevention: Review and Research Directions. *J. Sens. Actuator Netw., 12*(1), 4. DOI: 10.3390/jsan12010004

Alzaidi, M. S. (2022). Exploring the determinants of mobile banking adoption in the context of Saudi Arabia. *International Journal of Customer Relationship Marketing and Management, 13*(1), 1–16. DOI: 10.4018/IJCRMM.289206

Amene, B. K. (2015). The Impact of Customer Demographic Variable on the Adoption and Use of Internet Banking in Developing Economies. *Journal of Internet Banking and Commerce, 20*(2), 2–30.

Anderson, J., & Rainie, L. (2018). Improvements ahead: How humans and AI might evolve together in the next decade. *Pew Research Centers: Artificial Intelligence and the future of humans, 4*.

Anderson, S. (2022). Financial Sustainability and IT Investment: A Guide for Internal Audit. *Financial Strategy Journal, 40*(1), 45–61.

Anim, P. (2022). *Exploring the citizen engagement metaverse: Testing virtual reality for citizen feedback on public space design options.* The University of Regina.

Ardra, S., & Barua, M. K. (2022). Halving food waste generation by 2030: The challenges and strategies of monitoring UN sustainable development goal target 12.3. *Journal of Cleaner Production, 380*, 135042. DOI: 10.1016/j.jclepro.2022.135042

Arens, A. A., Elder, R. J., Beasley, M. S., & Hogan, C. E. (2019). *Auditing and assurance services: An integrated approach* (17th ed.). Pearson.

Aristizabal-Alzate, C. E., & González-Manosalva, J. (2021). Revisión de las medidas en pro de la eficiencia energética Y la sostenibilidad de la industria del cemento a nivel mundial. *Revista UIS Ingenierías, 20*(3). Advance online publication. DOI: 10.18273/revuin.v20n3-2021006

Asadi, S., Nilashi, M., Husin, A. R. C., & Yadegaridehkordi, E. (2017). Customers perspectives on adoption of cloud computing in banking sector. *Information Technology and Management, 18*(4), 305–330. DOI: 10.1007/s10799-016-0270-8

Asdullah, M. A., & Yazdifar, H. (2016). Evaluation of Factors Influencing Youth towards Islamic Banking in Pakistan. *ICTAT Journal on Management Studies, 2*(1), 217–223. DOI: 10.21917/ijms.2016.0030

Auditor-General of Namibia. (2017). *Annual Report 2016/2017.*

Autio, E., & Thomas, L. (2014). *Innovation ecosystems* (pp. 204-288). The Oxford handbook of innovation management.

Avraamidou, M., & Karacapilidis, N. (2016). A constructivist evaluation framework for ICT-based design for sustainability. *Sustainable Production and Consumption, 8*, 161–176.

Babbie, E. R. (2016). *The Basics of Social Research.* Cengage Learning.

Babu, G. C. N., Gupta, S., Bhambri, P., Leo, L. M., Rao, B. H., & Kumar, S. (2021). A semantic health observation system development based on the IoT sensors. *Turkish Journal of Physiotherapy and Rehabilitation, 32*(3), 1721–1729.

Bahri, R. R., & Herawan, E. (2020). The Improving of Customer Satisfaction: Service Triangle Approach. *Advances in Social Science, Education and Humanities Research.* https://www.researchgate.net/publication/339232533_The_Improving_of_Customer_Satisfaction_Service_Triangle_Approach/fulltext/5e45404792851c7f7f345371/The-Improving-of-Customer-Satisfaction-Service-Triangle-Approach.pdf

Baker, H., Kaddumi, T. A., Nassar, M. D., & Muqattash, R. S. (2023). Impact of financial technology on improvement of banks' financial performance. *Journal of Risk and Financial Management, 16*(4), 1–21. DOI: 10.3390/jrfm16040230

Banu, A., Mohamed, N. S., & Parayitam, S. (2019). Online Banking and Customer Satisfaction: Evidence from India. *Asia-Pacific Journal of Management Research and Innovation, 15*(1-2), 68–80. DOI: 10.1177/2319510X19849730

Baptista, G., & Oliveira, T. (2015). Understanding mobile banking: The unified theory of acceptance and use of technology combined with cultural moderators. *Computers in Human Behavior, 50*(1), 418–430. DOI: 10.1016/j.chb.2015.04.024

Barnett, J., Lambert, S., & Fry, I. (2019). The Hazards of Indicators: Insights from the Environmental Vulnerability Index. *Annals of the Association of American Geographers, 109*(3), 713–728.

Barney, J. (1991). Firm resources and sustained competitive advantage. *Journal of Management, 17*(1), 99–120. DOI: 10.1177/014920639101700108

Benjamins, R., Rubio Viñuela, Y., & Alonso, C. (2023). Social and ethical challenges of the metaverse: Opening the debate. *AI and Ethics, 3*(3), 689–697. DOI: 10.1007/s43681-023-00278-5

Berhane, T., Walelign, T. M. A., & Seid, A. M. (2023). A Hybrid Convolutional Neural Network and Support Vector Machine-Based Credit Card Fraud Detection Model. *Mathematical Problems in Engineering, 2023*(1), 34627. DOI: 10.1155/2023/8134627

Bhambri, P., & Bhandari, A. (2005, March). Different protocols for wireless security. In National Conference on Advancements in Modeling and Simulation (Vol. 8). LLRIET.

Bhambri, P., & Gupta, O. P. (2012, December). Development of phylogenetic tree based on Kimura's Method. In 2012 2nd IEEE International Conference on Parallel, Distributed and Grid Computing (pp. 721-723). IEEE. DOI: 10.1109/PDGC.2012.6449910

Bhambri, P., & Singh, I. (2005, March). Electrical actuation systems. In National Conference on Application of Mathematics in Engg. & Tech (pp. 58-60).

Bhambri, P., Gupta, S., & Bhandari, A. (2005). Soft computing techniques. In UGC Sponsored National Conference (Abstract Book) (p. 100).

Bhambri, P., Aggarwal, M., Singh, H., Singh, A. P., & Rani, S. (2022). Uprising of EVs: Charging the future with demystified analytics and sustainable development. In *Decision Analytics for Sustainable Development in Smart Society 5.0: Issues, Challenges and Opportunities* (pp. 37–53). Springer Nature Singapore. DOI: 10.1007/978-981-19-1689-2_3

Bhambri, P., & Gupta, S. (2005, March). A survey & comparison of permutation possibility of fault tolerant multistage interconnection networks. In *National Conference on Application of Mathematics in Engineering & Technology* (Vol. 13). MIMIT.

Bhambri, P., & Kautish, S. (2024). Technological advancements in promoting ecosystem health. In Leal Filho, W., Kautish, S., Wall, T., Rewhorn, S., & Paul, S. K. (Eds.), *Digital technologies to implement the UN Sustainable Development Goals* (pp. 413–432). Springer., DOI: 10.1007/978-3-031-68427-2_21

Bhambri, P., & Singh, M. (2024). Emotional sentiment analysis by machine learning from EEG of brainwave data. In Bhambri, P., Soni, R., & Tran, T. A. (Eds.), *Smart healthcare systems: AI and IoT perspectives* (pp. 171–186). CRC Press., DOI: 10.1201/9781032698519-13

Bhambri, P., Singh, M., Dhanoa, I. S., & Kumar, M. (2022). Deployment of ROBOT for HVAC duct and disaster management. *Oriental Journal of Computer Science and Technology, 15*(10203), 1–8. DOI: 10.13005/ojcst15.010203.01

Bhambri, P., Singh, S., Sangwan, S., Devi, J., & Jain, S. (2023). Plants recognition using leaf image pattern analysis. *Journal of Survey in Fisheries Sciences, 10*(2S), 3863–3871.

Bhambri, P., & Tripathy, B. (2024). Internet of Medical Things for Abnormality Detection in Infants using Mobile Phone App with Cry Signal Analysis. In *Smart Healthcare Systems* (pp. 236–248). CRC Press.

Bhatia, A., & Mahendru, M. (2015). Assessment of technical efficiency of public sector banks in India using data envelopment analysis. *Eurasian Journal of Business and Economics, 8*(15), 115–140.

Bibri, S. E. (2022). The social shaping of the metaverse as an alternative to the imaginaries of data-driven smart Cities: A study in science, technology, and society. *Smart Cities, 5*(3), 832–874. DOI: 10.3390/smartcities5030043

Bigliardi, B., Ferraro, G., Filippelli, S., & Galati, F. (2020). The influence of open innovation on firm performance. *International Journal of Engineering Business Management, 12*, 1847979020969545. DOI: 10.1177/1847979020969545

Binuyo, A. O., & Aregbeshola, R. A. (2014). The impact of information and communication technology (ICT) on commercial bank performance: Evidence from South Africa. *Problems and Perspectives in Management, 12*(3), 59–68.

Black, R., & Green, E. (2019). Data Anonymization Techniques in Modern Internal Audit. *Privacy and Security Journal, 27*(4), 89–104.

Boehm, C. (2004). Hiro" of the Platonic: Neal Stephenson's" Snow Crash. *Journal of the Fantastic in the Arts, 14*(4 (56), 394–408.

Bogue, R. (2019). Robots in recycling and disassembly. *The Industrial Robot, 46*(4), 461–466. DOI: 10.1108/IR-03-2019-0053

Bojic, L. (2022). Metaverse through the prism of power and addiction: What will happen when the virtual world becomes more attractive than reality? *European Journal of Futures Research, 10*(1), 22. DOI: 10.1186/s40309-022-00208-4

Boshkoska, M., & Sotirski, K. (2018). A Empirical Study of Customer Usage and Satisfaction with e-banking Services in the Republic of Macedonia. *Croatian Review of Economic* [CREBSS]. *Business and Social Statistics, 4*(1), 1–13.

Braungart, M., McDonough, W., & Bollinger, A. (2007). Cradle-to-cradle design: Creating healthy emissions–a strategy for eco-effective product and system design. *Journal of Cleaner Production, 15*(13-14), 1337–1348. DOI: 10.1016/j.jclepro.2006.08.003

Brown, A., & Davis, C. (2018). *Strategic Management: A Competitive Advantage Approach, Concepts and Cases*. Pearson.

Brown, A., & Lee, K. (2023). Ontologies in e-governance: Streamlining public services for inclusive development. *Government Information Quarterly, 40*(2), 101–115.

Brown, A., & Lee, K. (2023). Semantic interoperability in digital transformation: Challenges and solutions. *Journal of Knowledge Management, 27*(4), 112–130.

Brown, A., & Miller, J. (2018). Maximizing Audit Efficiency through IT Integration. *Journal of Information Systems, 25*(2), 45–62.

Brown, C., & Miller, D. (2020). The role of Information Technology in enhancing internal audit in the public sector. *Public Administration Review, 75*(2), 210–228.

Brown, S., & Smith, P. (2020). Fostering an Innovative Organizational Culture for IT Adoption in Internal Audit. *Journal of Audit Innovation, 15*(2), 89–105.

Btoush, E. A. L. M., Zhou, X., Gururajan, R., Chan, K. C., Genrich, R., & Sankaran, P. (2023). A systematic review of literature on credit card cyber fraud detection using machine and deep learning. *PeerJ. Computer Science*, *9*, e1278.

Bueno, L. A., Sigahi, T. F. A. C., Rampasso, I. S., Filho, W. L., & Anholon, R. (2024). Impact of digitization on operational efficiency in the banking sector: Thematic analysis and research agenda proposal. *International Journal of Information Management Data Insights*, *4*(1), 1–12. DOI: 10.1016/j.jjimei.2024.100230

Bwalya, K. J., Akande, T. O., & Lubinda, J. B. (2020). Impact of information technology in the internal audit of public institutions in Zambia: A case of selected government ministries. *Journal of Economics and Behavioral Studies*, *12*(1), 82–97.

Bwalya, K. J., Chileshe, N., & Lubinda, C. K. (2020). IT Adoption in Public Sector Internal Auditing: Evidence from African Countries. *Journal of Finance and Management in Public Services*, *1*(2), 25–42.

Bwalya, K. J., Kalungu-Banda, A., & Samujh, H. (2020). Factors influencing the adoption of information technology in public sector internal audit in Africa: Evidence from Zambia. *Journal of Information Systems*, *34*(1), 27–49.

Caiado, R. G. G., de Freitas Dias, R., Mattos, L. V., Quelhas, O. L. G., & Leal Filho, W. (2017). Towards sustainable development through the perspective of eco-efficiency-A systematic literature review. *Journal of Cleaner Production*, *165*, 890–904. DOI: 10.1016/j.jclepro.2017.07.166

Cao, Q., Beden, S., & Beckmann, A. (2022). A core reference ontology for steelmaking process knowledge modelling and information management. *Computers in Industry*, *135*, 103574. DOI: 10.1016/j.compind.2021.103574

Cao, W., Ming, Z., Xu, Z., Zhang, J., & Wang, Q. (2019). Online sequential extreme learning machine with dynamic forgetting factor. *IEEE Access : Practical Innovations, Open Solutions*, *7*, 179746–179757.

Carbo-Valverde, S. (2017). The impact of digitalization of banking and financial stability. *Journal of Financial Management. Markets and Institutions*, *5*(1), 133–140.

Casaló, L. V., Flavián, C., & Guinalíu, M. (2008). Towards loyalty development in the e-banking business. *Journal of Systems and Information Technology*, *10*(2), 120–134. DOI: 10.1108/13287260810897756

Cerchione, R., Centobelli, P., Zerbino, P., & Anand, A. (2020). Back to the future of knowledge management systems off the beaten paths. *Management Decision*, *58*(9), 1953–1984. DOI: 10.1108/MD-11-2019-1601

Chan, D. Y., Hancock, J., & Rice, S. (2018). *A 21st Century Imperative: The Use of Data Analytics in Internal Auditing*. ISACA Journal.

Chang, A. (2018). Cultural Adaptation and IT Integration in Internal Audit: A Case Study Approach. *Journal of Information Systems, 22*(4), 176–195.

Changchit, C., Lonkani, R., & Sampet, J. (2017). Mobile banking: Exploring determinants of its adoption. *Journal of Organizational Computing and Electronic Commerce, 27*(3), 239–261. DOI: 10.1080/10919392.2017.1332145

Chang, L., Zhang, Z., Li, P., Xi, S., Guo, W., Shen, Y., Xiong, Z., Kang, J., Niyato, D., Qiao, X., & Wu, Y. (2022). 6G-Enabled Edge AI for Metaverse: Challenges, Methods, and Future Research Directions. *Journal of Communications and Information Networks, 7*(2), 107–121. DOI: 10.23919/JCIN.2022.9815195

Chan, Y. E., & Reich, B. H. (2018). IT alignment in public sector organizations: A literature review. *Journal of Information Technology, 33*(4), 287–311.

Chatterjee, P., Das, D., & Rawat, D. B. (2024). Digital twin for credit card fraud detection: Opportunities, challenges, and fraud detection advancements. *Future Generation Computer Systems, 158*, 410–426. DOI: 10.1016/j.future.2024.04.057

Chauhan, V., Yadav, R., & Choudhary, V. (2019). Analyzing the impact of consumer innovativeness and perceived risk in internet banking adoption. *International Journal of Bank Marketing, 37*(1), 323–339. DOI: 10.1108/IJBM-02-2018-0028

Cheng, M., Qu, Y., Jiang, C., & Zhao, C. (2022). Is cloud computing the digital solution to the future of banking. *Journal of Financial Stability, 63*(1), 1–20. DOI: 10.1016/j.jfs.2022.101073

Cheng, Y., Awan, U., Ahmad, S., & Tan, Z. (2021). How do technological innovation and fiscal decentralization affect the environment? A story of the fourth industrial revolution and sustainable growth. *Technological Forecasting and Social Change, 162*, 120398. DOI: 10.1016/j.techfore.2020.120398

Chen, S. (2021). Technological Integration in Internal Audit: Best Practices and Strategies. *IT and Management Journal, 15*(4), 78–93.

Chen, S. (2022). Challenges and strategies in implementing IT in public sector auditing: A case study analysis. *Public Finance Management, 25*(1), 78–94.

Chen, X., Lu, Y., & Wang, B. (2019). A social constructivist perspective on organizational environmental sustainability practices. *Organization & Environment, 32*(1), 57–76.

Cherp, A., George, C., & Kirkpatrick, C. (2004). A methodology for assessing national sustainable development strategies. *Environment and Planning. C, Government & Policy*, *22*(6), 913–926. DOI: 10.1068/c0310j

Chesbrough, H. W. (2023). *Open innovation: The new imperative for creating and profiting from technology*. Harvard Business School Press.

Chinyamurindi, W., & Shale, K. (2017). Challenges of information technology adoption in internal audit in South Africa. *Southern African Journal of Accountability and Auditing Research*, *19*(1), 1–16.

Chinyamurindi, W., & Shale, S. (2017). Internal Audit Function in the Public Sector: A South African Perspective. *African Journal of Economic and Management Studies*, *8*(2), 250–266.

Christensen, C. M. (2015). *The innovator's dilemma: when new technologies cause great firms to fail*. Harvard Business Review Press.

Christensen, C. M. (2023). *The innovator's dilemma: When new technologies cause great firms to fail*. Harvard Business Review Press.

Chufal, H. S., Singh, R., Danai, L., & Singh, A. K. (2025). Financial behaviours, literacy, and well-being among youth in India. In Reddy, K. J. (Ed.), *Behavioral Economics and Neuroeconomics of Health and Healthcare* (pp. 95–126). IGI Global., DOI: 10.4018/979-8-3693-6055-2.ch006

Ciborra, C. U. (2002). *The labyrinths of information: Challenging the wisdom of systems*. Oxford University Press.

Clark, R., & Turner, H. (2021). Remote Work and Collaborative Practices in Auditing: A Post-Pandemic Perspective. *Journal of Remote Collaboration*, *28*(2), 89–105.

CMMI Institute. (2023). *CMMI for development, version 1.3*. Carnegie Mellon University.

Cooper, R. G. (1997). Examining Some Myths about New Product Winners. In Katz, R. (Ed.), *The human side of managing technological innovation* (pp. 550–560). Oxford University Press.

Cullen, R. (2001). Addressing the digital divide. *Online Information Review*, *25*(5), 311–320. DOI: 10.1108/14684520110410517

Dai, S. Research on Detecting Credit Card Fraud Through Machine Learning Methods. In *Proceedings of the 2022 2nd International Conference on Business Administration and Data Science (BADS 2022)*, Kashgar, China, 28–30 October 2022; pp. 1030–1037.

Dalton, R. J., Cain, B. E., & Scarrow, S. E. (2003). *Democratic publics and democratic institutions. Democracy Transformed?* Expanding Political Opportunities in Advanced Industrial Democracies.

Dangolani, S. K. (2011). The impact of information technology in banking system (a case study in bank Keshavarzi IRAN*).Procedia: Social and Behavioral Sciences*, *30*(1), 13–16. DOI: 10.1016/j.sbspro.2011.10.003

Daramola, O., & Thebus, D. (2020). Architecture-centric evaluation of blockchain-based smart contract e-voting for national elections. *Informatics (MDPI)*, *7*(2), 16. DOI: 10.3390/informatics7020016

Davis, F. D. (2023). Perceived usefulness, perceived ease of use, and user acceptance of information technology. *Management Information Systems Quarterly*.

Dayal, S., Landesbeg, H., & Zeisser, M. (1999). How to build trust online. *Marketing Management*, *8*(3), 64–69.

Deepthi, B., Gupta, P., Rai, P., & Arora, H. (2022). Assessing the Dynamics of AI Driven Technologies in Indian Banking and Financial Sector. *Vision (Basel)*, *0*(0), 1–14. DOI: 10.1177/09722629221087371

Delafrooz, N., Taleghani, M., Karami, R., & Moradi, A. (2013). Factors Affecting Adoption of Online Banking. *International Journal of Business and Behavioral Science*, *3*(2), 82–100.

Deloitte. (2021). *2021 Global Internal Audit Survey*. Deloitte Development LLC.

DeLone, W. H., & McLean, E. R. (2023). Information systems success: The quest for the dependent variable. *Information Systems Research*, *3*(1), 60–95. DOI: 10.1287/isre.3.1.60

Denner, M. S., Püschel, L. C., & Röglinger, M. (2018). How to exploit the digitalization potential of business processes. *Business & Information Systems Engineering*, *60*(4), 331–349. DOI: 10.1007/s12599-017-0509-x

Dey, S., Veerendra, G. T. N., Padavala, S. S. A. B., & Manoj, A. P. (2023). Recycling of e-waste materials for controlling the environmental and human health degradation in India. *Green Analytical Chemistry*, *7*, 100085. DOI: 10.1016/j.greeac.2023.100085

Dhirani, L. L., Mukhtiar, N., Chowdhry, B. S., & Newe, T. (2023). Ethical dilemmas and privacy issues in emerging technologies: A review. *Sensors (Basel)*, *23*(3), 1151. DOI: 10.3390/s23031151 PMID: 36772190

Diener, F., & Špaček, M. (2021). DT in banking: A managerial perspective on barriers to change. *Sustainability*, *13*(4), 1–21. DOI: 10.3390/su13042032

Dionisio, J. D. N., Iii, W. G. B., & Gilbert, R. (2013). 3D virtual worlds and the metaverse: Current status and future possibilities. *ACM Computing Surveys*, *45*(3), 1–38. DOI: 10.1145/2480741.2480751

Dixon, R., & Woodhead, A. (2017). Continuous auditing: A literature review. *Journal of Accounting Literature*, *39*, 18–48.

Dogan, E. (2017). A strategic approach to innovation. *Journal of Management Marketing and Logistics*, *4*(3), 290–300.

Du, Y., Wang, X., & Liu, L. (2017). Big data in auditing research: Current status and future trends. *Journal of Accounting and Economics*, *64*(2-3), 478–505.

Dwivedi, Y. K., Hughes, L., Baabdullah, A. M., Ribeiro-Navarrete, S., Giannakis, M., Al-Debei, M. M., Dennehy, D., Metri, B., Buhalis, D., Cheung, C. M. K., Conboy, K., Doyle, R., Dubey, R., Dutot, V., Felix, R., Goyal, D. P., Gustafsson, A., Hinsch, C., Jebabli, I., & Wamba, S. F. (2022). Metaverse beyond the hype: Multidisciplinary perspectives on emerging challenges, opportunities, and agenda for research, practice, and policy. *International Journal of Information Management*, *66*, 102542. DOI: 10.1016/j.ijinfomgt.2022.102542

Dwivedi, Y. K., Hughes, L., Kar, A. K., Baabdullah, A. M., Grover, P., Abbas, R., Andreini, D., Abumoghli, I., Barlette, Y., Bunker, D., Chandra Kruse, L., Constantiou, I., Davison, R. M., De', R., Dubey, R., Fenby-Taylor, H., Gupta, B., He, W., Kodama, M., & Wade, M. (2022). Climate change and COP26: Are digital technologies and information management part of the problem or the solution? An editorial reflection and call to action. *International Journal of Information Management*, *63*, 102456. DOI: 10.1016/j.ijinfomgt.2021.102456

Edenhofer, O., Pichs-Madruga, R., Sokona, Y., Seyboth, K., Kadner, S., Zwickel, T., & Matschoss, P. (Eds.). (2011). *Renewable energy sources and climate change mitigation: Special report of the intergovernmental panel on climate change*. Cambridge University Press. DOI: 10.1017/CBO9781139151153

Ehin, P., Solvak, M., Willemson, J., & Vinkel, P. (2022). Internet voting in Estonia 2005–2019: Evidence from eleven elections. *Government Information Quarterly*, *39*(4), 101718. DOI: 10.1016/j.giq.2022.101718

Ehrenfeld, J. R. (2005). Eco-efficiency. *Journal of Industrial Ecology*, *9*(4), 6–8. DOI: 10.1162/108819805775248070

El Haggar, S. (2010). *Sustainable industrial design and waste management: cradle-to-cradle for sustainable development*. Academic Press.

Elassy, M., Al-Hattab, M., Takruri, M., & Badawi, S. (2024). Intelligent transportation systems for sustainable smart cities. *Transportation Engineering*, 100252.

Endarto, I. A., & Martadi, M. (2022). Analysis of the potential implementation of the metaverse in interactive educational media. *BARIK-Journal of S1 Visual Communication Design, 4*(1), 37–51.

Eom, S. J., Lee, H. N., & Rho, J. J. (2016). Factors affecting smartphone adoption for accessing government services in South Korea. *Government Information Quarterly, 33*(4), 667–680.

EY. (2021). *Reimagining internal audit in financial services*. EY Global Services Limited.

Fallah Shayan, N., Mohabbati-Kalejahi, N., Alavi, S., & Zahed, M. A. (2022). Sustainable development goals (SDGs) as a framework for corporate social responsibility (CSR). *Sustainability (Basel), 14*(3), 1222. DOI: 10.3390/su14031222

Farooq, M. S., Iftikhar, U., & Khelifi, A. (2022). *A framework to make the voting system transparent using blockchain technology*. IEEE Access. DOI: 10.1109/ACCESS.2022.3180168

Foth, M., Brynskov, M., & Ojala, T. (2016). *Citizen's Right to the Digital City: Urban Interfaces, Activism, and Placemaking*. Springer.

Francis, R., & Bekera, B. (2014). A metric and frameworks for resilience analysis of engineered and infrastructure systems. *Reliability Engineering & System Safety, 121*, 90–103. DOI: 10.1016/j.ress.2013.07.004

Gadhi, S. (2020). How digital infrastructure can help us through the COVID-19 crisis. *Erişim Tarihi*, *11*, 2020.

Gan, C., Clemes, M., Limsombunchai, V., & Weng, A. (2006). *A Logit Analysis of Electronic Banking in New Zealand*, Discussion Paper No.108, Lincoln University, Canterbury, New Zealand. https://core.ac.uk/download/pdf/35458784.pdf

Garcia, A., & Chen, R. (2018). Transformative impact of IT on internal audit processes. *Journal of Organizational Technology*, *25*(3), 123–145.

Garcia, A., & Chen, R. (2019). Overcoming Technical Barriers: Enhancing IT Knowledge among Internal Auditors. *International Journal of Auditing Technology, 18*(3), 112–130.

Garcia, E., Martin, T., Johnson, L., & Williams, R. (2021). Information Technology adoption in the public sector: A comprehensive review. *Government Information Quarterly*, *38*(4), 101052.

Garcia, M., & Patel, R. (2024). Advancements in ontology engineering for smart cities: A case study on inclusive urban development. *Semantic Web Journal, 15*(2), 89–105.

Garson, D. (2006). *Public information technology and e-governance: Managing the virtual state*. Jones & Bartlett Learning.

Gaudio, B. L. D., Porzio, C., Sampagnaro, G., & Verdoliva, V. (2021). How do mobile, internet and ICT diffusion affect the banking industry? an empirical analysis. *European Management Journal, 39*(3), 327–332. DOI: 10.1016/j.emj.2020.07.003

Gaurav, A. (2023). Metaverse and Globalization: Cultural Exchange and Digital Diplomacy. *Data Science Insights Magazine, Insights2Techinfo*.

Gedar, M. B. L., Sharma, M. C., & Lodha, S. (2023). Use Cases of Blockchain Technology in Voting System and Healthcare Sector. *Principal Investigator*, 131.

Gimpel, J. G., & Schuknecht, J. E. (2003). Political participation and the accessibility of the ballot box. *Political Geography*, *22*(5), 471–488. DOI: 10.1016/S0962-6298(03)00029-5

Goldberg, M., & Schär, F. (2023). Metaverse governance: An empirical analysis of voting within Decentralized Autonomous Organizations. *Journal of Business Research*, *160*, 113764. DOI: 10.1016/j.jbusres.2023.113764

Gopalkrishnan, S., Wischnevsky, J. D., & Damanpour, F. (2003). A Multi-Level Analysis of Factors Influencing the Adoption of Internet Banking. *Engineering Management*, *50*(4), 413–426.

Gopal, S. B., Jayaprasath, M., Poongodi, C., Johnson, S., Nanthiya, D., & Mithunkumar, R. T. (2023). Blockchain-based e-voting application–a survey. *2023 International Conference on Sustainable Computing and Data Communication Systems (ICSCDS)*, 1340–1347. DOI: 10.1109/ICSCDS56580.2023.10104596

Gordijn, J., & Akkermans, H. (2001). Designing and evaluating e-business models. *IEEE Intelligent Systems*, *16*(04), 11–17. DOI: 10.1109/5254.941353

Granstrand, O., & Holgersson, M. (2020). Innovation ecosystems: A conceptual review and a new definition. *Technovation*, *90*, 102098. DOI: 10.1016/j.technovation.2019.102098

Gruber, T. R. (1993). A translation approach to portable ontology specifications. *Knowledge Acquisition*, *5*(2), 199–220. DOI: 10.1006/knac.1993.1008

Guarino, N. (1998). Formal ontology in information systems. In *Proceedings of the First International Conference on Formal Ontology in Information Systems (FOIS '98)* (pp. 3–15). IOS Press.

Guldbrandsson, K., Hall, H., & Lindhult, E. (2019). Smart City in Progress: A Study of Smart City Development in the Making. *Journal of Urban Technology*, *26*(4), 1–22.

Gulomov, S. (2024). Regulatory Frameworks for Metaverse Platforms: Challenges and Opportunities. *International Conference on Legal Sciences, 2*(1), 144–151. https://science-zone.org/index.php/conference/article/view/91

Gupta, P., Schermann, M., & Mohan, R. (2016). Internal Audit in the 21st Century: Challenges and Opportunities. *Journal of Accounting, Auditing & Finance*, *31*(3), 343–349.

Gupta, R. (2023). Industry 4.0 Adaption in Indian banking sector—A review and agenda for future research. *Vision (Basel)*, *27*(1), 24–32. DOI: 10.1177/0972262921996829 PMID: 36977304

Gupta, R., & Sharma, V. (2017). Machine Learning in Internal Audit: A Comprehensive Review. *Journal of Intelligent Auditing*, *30*(3), 101–118.

Gupta, S., Varshney, T., Verma, A., Goel, L., Yadav, A. K., & Singh, A. (2022). A Hybrid Machine Learning Approach for Credit Card Fraud Detection. *International Journal of Information Technology Project Management*, *13*(3), 1–13. DOI: 10.4018/IJITPM.313420

Habibzadeh, H., Nussbaum, B. H., Anjomshoa, F., Kantarci, B., & Soyata, T. (2019). A survey on cybersecurity, data privacy, and policy issues in cyber-physical system deployments in smart cities. *Sustainable Cities and Society*, *50*, 101660. DOI: 10.1016/j.scs.2019.101660

Haleem, A., Javaid, M., Qadri, M. A., & Suman, R. (2022). Understanding the role of digital technologies in education: A review. *Sustainable operations and computers, 3*, 275-285.

Hanna, K. T. (2022). What is the Digital Divide and How is it being Bridged? TechTarget., Retrieved March 15, 2023, from.

Hansen, M. T., & Birkinshaw, J. (2023). The innovation value chain. *Harvard Business Review*, *85*(6), 121–130. PMID: 17580654

Harleen, B. (2016). A prediction technique in data mining for diabetes mellitus. *Journal of Management Sciences and Technology*, *4*(1), 1–12.

Healy, J. J.Jr. (2023). Veto the Black-Box Politics: How Implementing Blockchain Technology into the United States Voting System Will Give Our World the Transparency We Deserve. *Hofstra Law Review*, *52*, 131.

Heath, D. R. (2023). The Metaverse and how it will revolutionize everything. In *Journal of Information Technology Case and Application Research* (Vol. 25, Issue 1). Liveright Publishing. DOI: 10.1080/15228053.2022.2136927

Heeks, R. (2017). Information and Communication Technology (ICT) and the Sustainable Development Goals (SDGs): A Fast Track Roadmap. *Institute for Development Policy and Management Working Paper*, 1-31.

Hosein, S. S. M. (2013). Consideration the effect of e-banking on bank profitability; Case study selected Asian countries. *Journal of Economics & Sustainable Development*, *4*(11), 112–117. https://www.iiste.org/Journals/index.php/JEDS/article/view/6851

Huang, C. L. (2017). An empirical investigation of factors influencing the effectiveness of internal audit in Taiwanese firms. *International Journal of Auditing*, *21*(1), 36–47.

Huang, H., Lin, J., Zheng, B., Zheng, Z., & Bian, J. (2020). *When blockchain meets distributed file systems: An overview, challenges, and open issues*. IEEE Access.

Hui, C. X., Dan, G., Alamri, S., & Toghraie, D. (2023). Greening smart cities: An investigation of the integration of urban natural resources and smart city technologies for promoting environmental sustainability. *Sustainable Cities and Society*, *99*, 104985. DOI: 10.1016/j.scs.2023.104985

Humphrey, A. S. (2023). *SWOT analysis for management consulting*. SRI Alumni Association.

Huynh-The, T., Pham, Q.-V., Pham, X.-Q., Nguyen, T. T., Han, Z., & Kim, D.-S. (2023). Artificial intelligence for the metaverse: A survey. *Engineering Applications of Artificial Intelligence*, *117*, 105581. DOI: 10.1016/j.engappai.2022.105581

Iansiti, M., & Levien, R. (2023). The new competitive advantage: The evolution of business ecosystems. *Harvard Business Review*, *82*(10), 92–103.

IFAC. (2021). *ISA 315 (Revised), Identifying and Assessing the Risks of Material Misstatement Through Understanding the Entity and Its Environment*. International Auditing and Assurance Standards Board.

Ileberi, E., Sun, Y., & Wang, Z. (2021). Performance evaluation of machine learning methods for credit card fraud detection using SMOTE and AdaBoost. *IEEE Access : Practical Innovations, Open Solutions*, *9*, 165286–165294.

Imgrund, F., Fischer, M., Janiesch, C., & Winkelmann, A. (2018). Approaching digitalization with business process management. *Proceedings of the MKWI*, 1725-1736.

Institute of Internal Auditors (IIA). (2020). [*Internal Audit Emerging Stronger Post-Crisis*. IIA Global.]. *COVID*, •••, 19.

Institute of Internal Auditors (IIA). (2021). *Global Technology Audit Guide (GTAG) series*. https://na.theiia.org/standards-guidance/Public%20Documents/GTAG%20 Document.pdf

Institute of Internal Auditors (IIA). (2021). *Insights on Building Trust Through Internal Audit*. IIA Global.

ISACA. (2021). *State of Cybersecurity 2021: Part 3: Cybersecurity Culture*. ISACA.

Islam, H. (2025). Nexus of economic, social, and environmental factors on sustainable development goals: The moderating role of technological advancement and green innovation. *Innovation and Green Development*, *4*(1), 100183. DOI: 10.1016/j.igd.2024.100183

Islam, S., Kabir, M. R., Dovash, R. H., Nafee, S. E., & Saha, S. (2019). Impact of online banking adoption on bank's profitability: Evidence from Bangladesh. *European Journal of Business and Management Research*, *4*(3), 1–10. https://www.ejbmr.org/index.php/ejbmr/article/view/38. DOI: 10.24018/ejbmr.2019.4.3.38

Issa, H., Sun, T., & Vasarhelyi, M. A. (2016). Research ideas for artificial intelligence in auditing: The formalization of audit and workforce supplementation. *Journal of Emerging Technologies in Accounting*, *13*(2), 1–20. DOI: 10.2308/jeta-10511

Iswanto, N. I. P., Widhiantoro, D., Munawar, Z., & Komalasari, R. (2022). Pemanfaatan Metaverse Di Bidang Pendidikan Utilization Of Metaverse In Education. *Jurnal Teknologi Informasi Komunikasi (e-Journal)*, *9*(1), 44–52.

Jabeen, A., Pallathadka, H., Pallathadka, L. K., & Bhambri, P. (2021). E-CRM successful factors for business enterprises case studies. *Journal of Maharaja Sayajirao University of Baroda*, *55*(01), 1332–1342.

Jafar, U., Aziz, M. J. A., & Shukur, Z. (2021). Blockchain for electronic voting system—Review and open research challenges. *Sensors (Basel)*, *21*(17), 5874. DOI: 10.3390/s21175874 PMID: 34502764

Jagatheesaperumal, S. K., Ahmad, K., Al-Fuqaha, A., & Qadir, J. (2024). Advancing Education Through Extended Reality and Internet of Everything Enabled Metaverses: Applications, Challenges, and Open Issues. *IEEE Transactions on Learning Technologies*, *17*, 1120–1139. DOI: 10.1109/TLT.2024.3358859

Jain, A., Singh, M., & Bhambri, P. (2021, August). Performance evaluation of IPv4-IPv6 tunneling procedure using IoT. [). IOP Publishing.]. *Journal of Physics: Conference Series*, *1950*(1), 012010. DOI: 10.1088/1742-6596/1950/1/012010

Jaiswal, K. K., Chowdhury, C. R., Yadav, D., Verma, R., Dutta, S., Jaiswal, K. S., & Karuppasamy, K. S. K. (2022). Renewable and sustainable clean energy development and impact on social, economic, and environmental health. *Energy Nexus*, *7*, 100118. DOI: 10.1016/j.nexus.2022.100118

Javaid, M., Haleem, A., Singh, R. P., Khan, S., & Suman, R. (2021). Blockchain technology applications for Industry 4.0: A literature-based review. *Blockchain Res. Appl.*, *2*(4), 100027. DOI: 10.1016/j.bcra.2021.100027

Javaid, M., Haleem, A., Singh, R. P., & Suman, R. (2022). Enhancing smart farming through the applications of Agriculture 4.0 technologies. *International Journal of Intelligent Networks*, *3*, 150–164. DOI: 10.1016/j.ijin.2022.09.004

Jemai, J., Zarrad, A., & Daud, A. (2024). Identifying Fraudulent Credit Card Transactions Using Ensemble Learning. *IEEE Access : Practical Innovations, Open Solutions*.

Jeremski, M., & Plastaras, B. (2016). The Competitive and Coexistence of Mutual and Commercial Banks in England, 1870-1914. *Cliometrica*, *10*(2), 151–179. DOI: 10.1007/s11698-015-0127-0

Johnson, B. B., & Becker, M. L. (2015). Social–ecological resilience and adaptive capacity in a transboundary ecosystem. *Society & Natural Resources*, *28*(7), 766–780. DOI: 10.1080/08941920.2015.1037035

Johnson, L., & Smith, J. (2024). Ontology-driven healthcare systems: Enabling personalized medicine through semantic integration. *Healthcare Informatics Research*, *30*(1), 78–95.

Johnson, L., & Smith, P. (2021). Employee perception and engagement with sustainability-driven information technology initiatives in the public sector. *Public Administration Review*, *81*(3), 380–391.

Johnson, M. (2019). Leadership Support and IT Adoption: A Comprehensive Study in Internal Audit. *Journal of Organizational Technology*, *26*(1), 45–63.

Johnson, M., & Brown, S. (2019). Adaptability of Microsoft Office applications in Namibian internal audit. *International Journal of Auditing Technology, 18*(2), 67–84.

Johnson, R., & White, L. (2018). Integrating IT and internal audit for enhanced public sector performance. *International Journal of Public Administration, 41*(7), 561–578.

Jones, P., Wynn, M., Hillier, D., & Comfort, D. (2017). The sustainable development goals and information and communication technologies. *Indonesian Journal of Sustainability Accounting and Management, 1*(1), 1â-15.

Jones, L., & Smith, P. (2022). Contemporary communication needs within audit teams. *Communication in Organizational Environments, 30*(4), 321–340.

Jones, M. (2020). Strategic Alignment of IT in Internal Audit: A Contemporary Perspective. *Journal of IT Governance, 18*(1), 34–50.

Jones, P., & Johnson, P. (2020). *Strategic Management: An Integrated Approach.* Routledge.

Joseph, J., & Pandey, A. (2025). Democracy in the Age of Al: Ethical and Legal Considerations. *Democracy and Democratization in the Age of AI*, 19.

Jungherr, A., & Schlarb, D. B. (2022). The extended reach of game engine companies: How Epic games and Unity technologies provide platforms for extended reality applications and the metaverse. *Social Media + Society*, *8*(2), 20563051221107640. DOI: 10.1177/20563051221107641

Kakabadse, A., Kakabadse, N. K., & McGowan, C. (2019). E-procurement Systems Adoption in Developing Countries: The Case of Ghana. *Electronic Government, an International Journal, 16*(4), 318-333.

Kamalaldin, A., Sjödin, D., Hullova, D., & Parida, V. (2021). Configuring ecosystem strategies for digitally enabled process innovation: A framework for equipment suppliers in the process industries. *Technovation, 105*, 102250. DOI: 10.1016/j.technovation.2021.102250

Kaplan, R. S., & Norton, D. P. (2023). *The balanced scorecard: Measures that drive performance*. Harvard Business Review Press.

Kashona, S. (2019). The effectiveness of internal control and internal audit in fraud detection and prevention: A case study of Ministry of Finance-Namibia (*Doctoral dissertation, University of Namibia).*

Kaur, A., Bhambri, P., & Singla, S. K. (2024). Sentimental analysis using RNN, CNN, and LSTM: A comparative study of accuracy and computational efficiency. *Library Progress International*, *44*(3), 4424–4431.

Kaur, J., Bhambri, P., & Gupta, O. P. (2013). Distance based phylogenetic trees with bootstrapping. *International Journal of Computer Applications*, *47*(24), 6–10. DOI: 10.5120/7502-0364

Kaur, P., & Bhambri, P. (2015). To design an algorithm for text watermarking. [The SIJ]. *The Standard International Journals*, *3*(5), 62–67. DOI: 10.9756/SIJCSEA/V3I3/03050150101

Kavitha, S., Banu, J. R., Arulazhagan, P., & Gunasekaran, M. (2020). Environmental impacts and sustainability assessment of food loss and waste valorization: Value chain analysis of food consumption. In *Food Waste to Valuable Resources* (pp. 359–388). Academic Press.

Kennedy, E., Fecheyr-Lippens, D., Hsiung, B. K., Niewiarowski, P. H., & Kolodziej, M. (2015). Biomimicry: A path to sustainable innovation. *Design Issues*, *31*(3), 66–73. DOI: 10.1162/DESI_a_00339

Khando, K., Islam, M. S., & Gao, S. (2022). The Emerging Technologies of Digital Payments and Associated Challenges: A Systematic Literature Review. *Future Internet*, *15*(1), 21. DOI: 10.3390/fi15010021

Khedmati, M., & Erfini, M. GhasemiGol, M. Applying support vector data description for fraud detection. arXiv 2020, arXiv:2006.00618.

Kiayias, A., & Lazos, P. (2022). SoK: blockchain governance. *Proceedings of the 4th ACM Conference on Advances in Financial Technologies*, 61–73. DOI: 10.1145/3558535.3559794

Kichanova, V. (2023). Private Cities, the Metaverse and the Future of Non-Territorial Governance. *Journal of Special Jurisdictions*, *4*(1).

Kim, W. C., & Mauborgne, R. (2023). *Blue ocean strategy: How to create uncontested market space and make the competition irrelevant*. Harvard Business School Press.

Kinene, M. J. (2017). Influence of information and communication technology on performance of financial audits in government ministries in Kenya. (*Master's Thesis, Kenyatta University*).

Kirchherr, J., Yang, N. H. N., Schulze-Spüntrup, F., Heerink, M. J., & Hartley, K. (2023). Conceptualizing the circular economy (revisited): An analysis of 221 definitions. *Resources, Conservation and Recycling*, *194*, 107001. DOI: 10.1016/j.resconrec.2023.107001

Kitsios, F., Giatsidis, I., & Kamariotou, M. (2021). DT and strategy in the banking sector: Evaluating the acceptance rate of e-services. *Journal of Open Innovation*, *7*(204), 1–14. DOI: 10.3390/joitmc7030204

Kotler, P., & Keller, K. (2011). *Marketing Management* (14th ed.). Pearson.

KPMG. (2020). *The Future of Audit. KPMG International Cooperative*. KPMG International Cooperative.

KPMG. (2021). *Evolving Internal Audit: A Data & Analytics Perspective*. KPMG International Cooperative.

Kraus, S., Durst, S., Ferreira, J. J., Veiga, P., Kailer, N., & Weinmann, A. (2022). Digital transformation in business and management research: An overview of the current status quo. *International Journal of Information Management*, *63*, 102466. DOI: 10.1016/j.ijinfomgt.2021.102466

Kraus, S., Jones, P., Kailer, N., Weinmann, A., Chaparro-Banegas, N., & Roig-Tierno, N. (2021). Digital transformation: An overview of the current state of the art of research. *SAGE Open*, *11*(3), 21582440211047576. DOI: 10.1177/21582440211047576

Kshirsagar, P. R., Jagannadham, D. B. V., Ananth, M. B., Mohan, A., Kumar, G., & Bhambri, P. (2022, May). Machine learning algorithm for leaf disease detection. In AIP Conference Proceedings (Vol. 2393, No. 1). AIP Publishing. DOI: 10.1063/5.0074122

Kumari, A., & Devi, N. C. (2022). The Impact of FinTech and Blockchain Technologies on Banking and Financial Services. *Technology Innovation Management Review*, *12*(1/2), 12. DOI: 10.22215/timreview/1481

Kumar, S. K., & Gulati, R. (2018). Evaluation of technical efficiency and ranking of public sector banks in India: An analysis from cross-sectional perspective. *International Journal of Productivity and Performance*, *57*(7), 40–568.

Kumbahar, V. M. (2010). *Reliability and validity of 'eBankQual' Scale in ATM Service Settings: A Study. VINIMAYA, XXXI(4)*. National Institute of Bank Management.

Kumbahar, V. M. (2011). Factors Affecting the Customer Satisfaction in E-banking: Some Evidence from Indian Banks. *Management Research and Practice*, *3*(4), 1–14.

Kushwaha, M., Singh, S., Singh, V., & Dwivedi, S. (2024). Precision Farming: A Review of Methods, Technologies, and Future Prospects. *International Journal of Environment, Agriculture and Biotechnology*, *9*(2), 242–253. DOI: 10.22161/ijeab.92.27

Kuznets, S. (2019). Economic growth and income inequality. In *The gap between rich and poor* (pp. 25–37). Routledge. DOI: 10.4324/9780429311208-4

Laha, S. R., Pattanayak, B. K., Pattnaik, S., Mishra, D., Nayak, D. S. K., & Dash, B. B. (2023, September). An IOT-Based Soil Moisture Management System for Precision Agriculture: Real-Time Monitoring and Automated Irrigation Control. In *2023 4th International Conference on Smart Electronics and Communication (ICOSEC)* (pp. 451-455). IEEE.

Lasmini, R. S., Busiarti, A. P., Tasman, A., & Susant, F. A. (2019). The relationship between e-banking and financial performance of Go public bank in Indonesia. *Advances in Economics. Business and Management Research, 124*(1), 903–909.

Lee, L.-H., Braud, T., Zhou, P., Wang, L., Xu, D., Lin, Z., Kumar, A., Bermejo, C., & Hui, P. (2021). All One Needs to Know about Metaverse: A Complete Survey on Technological Singularity, Virtual Ecosystem, and Research Agenda. *ArXiv Preprint ArXiv:2110.05352*. http://arxiv.org/abs/2110.05352

Lee, K. (2020). Driving Successful IT Adoption: The Role of Leadership in Internal Audit. *Journal of Information Technology Integration, 25*(2), 78–95.

Lee, K., & Brown, A. (2023). Semantic blockchain: Enabling interoperability through ontology engineering. *Blockchain Research, 12*(3), 67–82.

Lee, K., & Wang, Q. (2018). Efficiency gains associated with IT tools in internal audit. *Journal of Information Systems, 15*(1), 56–78.

Li, A., Pandey, B., Hooi, C. F., & Pileggi, L. (2022). Dynamic Graph-Based Anomaly Detection in the Electrical Grid. *IEEE Transactions on Power Systems, 37*(5), 3408–3422. DOI: 10.1109/TPWRS.2021.3132852

Li, F., Lu, H., Hou, H., Cui, K., & Darbandi, M. (2021). Customer satisfaction with bank services: The role of cloud services, security, e-learning and service quality. *Technology in Society, 64*(1), 120–123. DOI: 10.1016/j.techsoc.2020.101487

Lu, J., & Yang, Y. (2020). Government social media, public participation, and environmental sustainability: Evidence from China. *Government Information Quarterly, 37*(3), 101479.

Lurie-Luke, E. (2014). Product and technology innovation: What can biomimicry inspire? *Biotechnology Advances, 32*(8), 1494–1505. DOI: 10.1016/j.biotechadv.2014.10.002 PMID: 25316672

Lu, S. C., Lai, K. H., & Cheng, T. C. E. (2006). Adoption of Internet Service in Linier Shipping: An Empirical Study of Shippers' of Taiwan. *Transport Reviews*, *26*(2), 189–206. DOI: 10.1080/01441640500246713

Maley, M. (2003). Transplanting election regulation. *Election Law Journal*, *2*(4), 479–497. DOI: 10.1089/153312903322483191

Malhotra, P., & Singh, P. (2010). An analysis of Internet banking offerings and its determinants in India. *Internet Research*, *20*(1), 87–106. DOI: 10.1108/10662241011020851

Manyika, J., & Sneader, K. (2018). AI, automation, and the future of work: Ten things to solve for.

Marshall, C., & Rossman, G. B. (2016). *Designing qualitative research*. Sage publications.

Marshall, K. P. (1999). Has technology introduced new ethical problems? *Journal of Business Ethics*, *19*(1), 81–90. DOI: 10.1023/A:1006154023743

Martins, C., Oliveira, T., & Popovič, A. (2014). Understanding the internet banking adoption: A unified theory of acceptance and use of technology and perceived risk application. *International Journal of Information Management*, *34*(1), 1–13. DOI: 10.1016/j.ijinfomgt.2013.06.002

Masrek, M. N., Syafiq, M., Halim, A., Khan, A., & Ramli, I. (2018). The Impact of Perceived Credibility and Perceived Quality on Trust and Satisfaction in Mobile Banking Context. *Asian Economic and Financial Review*, *8*(7), 1013–1025. DOI: 10.18488/journal.aefr.2018.87.1013.1025

Maxwell, J. A., & Miller, B. A. (2018). Categorizing and connecting strategies in qualitative data analysis. In *Handbook of qualitative research* (pp. 743–760). Sage publications.

McCarthy, A. M., Maor, D., McConney, A., & Cavanaugh, C. (2023). Digital transformation in education: Critical components for leaders of system change. *Social Sciences & Humanities Open*, *8*(1), 100479. DOI: 10.1016/j.ssaho.2023.100479

McKinsey & Company. (2023). The role of ontologies in digital transformation: Insights from industry leaders. https://www.mckinsey.com/reports

Mele, C., Russo Spena, T., & Russo, S. P. (2024). Experimenting on the metaverse to foster innovation. *Spanish Journal of Marketing - ESIC*. Advance online publication. DOI: 10.1108/SJME-05-2023-0117

Mhlanga, D. (2023). Block chain technology for digital financial inclusion in the industry 4.0, towards sustainable development? *Front. Blockchain*, *6*, 1035405. DOI: 10.3389/fbloc.2023.1035405

Mihret, D. G., & Yismaw, A. W. (2017). The role of organizational support in the adoption of information technology in the public sector. *International Journal of Accounting & Information Management*, *25*(2), 217–235.

Miller, B., & White, L. (2017). Challenges in IT Adoption and Usage in Internal Audit: A Survey Analysis. *Technology and Audit Practice*, *14*(4), 210–230.

Miller, P., & Johnson, L. (2016). Ensuring Reliability in Internal Audit Systems: The Role of Regular Software Updates. *Journal of Reliability Engineering*, *21*(2), 56–72.

Mishra, D., Agarwal, N., Sharahiley, S., & Kandpal, V. (2024). Digital Financial Literacy and Its Impact on Financial Decision-Making of Women: Evidence from India. *Journal of Risk and Financial Management*, *17*(10), 468. DOI: 10.3390/jrfm17100468

Miyazaki, M., Moriya, H., & Miyauchi, A. (2019). Biomimetic design inspired sharkskin denticles for growth suppression of biofilm. *Journal of Photopolymer Science and Technology*, *32*(2), 295–301. DOI: 10.2494/photopolymer.32.295

Mohanta, H. C., Geetha, B. T., Alzaidi, M. S., Dhanoa, I. S., Bhambri, P., Mamodiya, U., & Akwafo, R. (2022). An Optimized PI Controller-Based SEPIC Converter for Microgrid-Interactive Hybrid Renewable Power Sources. *Wireless Communications and Mobile Computing*, *2022*(1), 6574825. DOI: 10.1155/2022/6574825

Morseletto, P. (2020). Restorative and regenerative: Exploring the concepts in the circular economy. *Journal of Industrial Ecology*, *24*(4), 763–773. DOI: 10.1111/jiec.12987

Mosadeghrad, A. M. (2014). Factors influencing healthcare service quality. *International Journal of Health Policy and Management*, *3*(2), 77–89. DOI: 10.15171/ijhpm.2014.65 PMID: 25114946

Mossberger, K. (2008). Toward digital citizenship: Addressing inequality in the information age. In *Routledge Handbook of Internet Politics* (pp. 173–185). Routledge.

Muduli, A., & Choudhury, A. (2024). Digital technology adoption, workforce agility and digital technology outcomes in the context of the banking industry of India. *Journal of Science and Technology Policy Management*, DOI: 10.1108/JSTPM-01-2024-0018

Mühleisen, M. (2018). The impact of digital technology on society and economic growth. *Finance & Development*, •••, 6–8.

Mukherjee, A., & Nath, P. (2003). A Model of Trust in Online Relationship Banking. *International Journal of Bank Marketing*, *21*(1), 5–15. DOI: 10.1108/02652320310457767

Murala, D. K., & Panda, S. K. (2023). Metaverse: A study on immersive technologies. *Metaverse and Immersive Technologies: An Introduction to Industrial, Business and Social Applications*, 1–41. DOI: 10.1002/9781394177165.ch1

Musiime, A., & Biyaki, F. (2010). Bank Clients' Perception of Information Technology Usage, Service Delivery and Customer Satisfaction: Reflections on Uganda's Banking Sector. *Proceedings of the International Trade & Academic Research Conference (01-17)*. https://vdocuments.mx/documents/bank-clients-perception-of-information-technology-usage-service-delivery-and-customer-satisfaction-reflections-on-ugandas-banking-sector-fayth.html

Mystakidis, S. (2022). Metaverse. *Encyclopedia*, *2*(1), 486–497. DOI: 10.3390/encyclopedia2010031

NATIONAL. (n.d.). *R. I. B. P. H.* THE RESULTS OF THE ALIGNMENT OF THE ACADEMIC TEXT OF THE DRAFT LAW ON THE NATIONAL LONG-TERM DEVELOPMENT PLAN FOR.

Naysary, B. (2022). Big data analytics application in multi-criteria decision making: The case of eWallet adoption. SSRN *Electronic Journal*. DOI: 10.2139/ssrn.4076471

Negi, M., & Kaur, D. P. (2010). A Study of Customer Satisfaction with Life Insurance In Candgarh Tricity. *Paradigm*, *14*(2), 29–44.

Németh, R., Firuza, B., & Erdős, F. (n.d.). *Virtual Teamwork in Gamified 3D Environment.*

Nestorović, Č. (2023). Critical Geopolitics. In *Contributions to International Relations: Vol. Part F1828* (pp. 85–150). Springer. DOI: 10.1007/978-3-031-45325-0_3

Nevelsteen, K. J. L. (2018). The virtual world is defined from a technological perspective and is applied to video games, mixed reality, and the Metaverse. *Computer Animation and Virtual Worlds*, *29*(1), e1752. DOI: 10.1002/cav.1752

Nguyen-Viet, B., Ngoc Huynh, K., & McMillan, D. (2021). Empirical analysis of internet banking adoption in Vietnam. *Cogent Economics & Finance*, *9*(1), 1–14. DOI: 10.1080/23322039.2021.1992876

Nijkamp, P., Van den Bergh, C. J. M., & Soeteman, F. J. (1990). Regional sustainable development and natural resource use. *The World Bank Economic Review*, *4*(suppl_1), 153–188. DOI: 10.1093/wber/4.suppl_1.153

Nikita, T. A., & Bhatt, B. (2024). Growth Of Mobile Banking In India: Comprehensive Study. *Educational Administration: Theory and Practice*, *30*(1), 3403–3417.

Norris, P. (2023). *Digital divide: Civic engagement, information poverty, and the internet worldwide*. Cambridge University Press.

Norris, P., & Nai, A. (2017). *Election watchdogs: transparency, accountability and integrity*. Oxford University Press. DOI: 10.1093/acprof:oso/9780190677800.001.0001

North, K., Aramburu, N., & Lorenzo, O. J. (2020). Promoting digitally enabled growth in SMEs: A framework proposal. *Journal of Enterprise Information Management*, *33*(1), 238–262. DOI: 10.1108/JEIM-04-2019-0103

Nyangosi, R., Arora, J. S., & Singh, S. (2009). The Evolution of e-banking: A Study of Indian and Kenyan Technology Awareness. *International Journal of Electronic Finance*, *3*(2), 149–155. DOI: 10.1504/IJEF.2009.026357

Oliver, R. L. (2009). Whence Customer Loyalty? *Journal of Marketing, Special Issue*, (63), 33–44.

Ombati, T. O., Magutu, P. O., Nyamwange, S. O., & Nyaoga, R. B. (2010). Technology and service quality in the banking industry: Importance and Performance of Various Factors Considered In the Electronic Banking Services. [AJBUMA]. *African Journal of Business Management*, *1*, 151–164.

Oppenlaender, J. (2022). The perception of smart contracts for the governance of the metaverse. *Proceedings of the 25th International Academic Mindtrek Conference*, 1–8. DOI: 10.1145/3569219.3569300

Ortiz-Villajos, J. M., & Sotoca, S. (2018). Innovation and business survival: A long-term approach. *Research Policy*, *47*(8), 1418–1436. DOI: 10.1016/j.respol.2018.04.019

Osei, L. K., Cherkasova, Y., & Oware, K. M. (2023). Unlocking the full potential of DT in banking: A bibliometric review and emerging trend. *Future Business Research*, *9*(30), 1–10. DOI: 10.1186/s43093-023-00207-2

Osterwalder, A., & Pigneur, Y. (2023). *Business model generation: A handbook for visionaries, game changers, and challengers* (2nd ed.). Wiley.

Paika, E. V., & Bhambri, E. P. (2013). Edge detection-fuzzy inference system. *International Journal of Management and Information Technology*, *4*(1), 148–155. DOI: 10.24297/ijmit.v4i1.811

Pakina, R., & Solekhan, M. (2024). The Influence of Information Technology on Privacy and Surveillance Law in Indonesia: The Balance Between Security and Human Rights.... *Journal of Scientech Research and Development*, *6*(1), 273–286. https://www.idm.or.id/JSCR/index.php/JSCR/article/view/376%0Ahttps://www.idm.or.id/JSCR/index.php/JSCR/article/download/376/285

Pal, K. (2022). Supply chain resilience management using a semantically-enhanced web service Portal. *Advances in Logistics, Operations, and Management Science*, •••, 264–285. DOI: 10.4018/978-1-6684-5882-2.ch017

Pan, A., Xu, S., & Zaidi, S. A. H. (2024). Environmental impact of energy imports: Natural resources income and natural gas production profitability in the Asia-Pacific Economic Cooperation Countries. *Geoscience Frontiers*, *15*(2), 101756. DOI: 10.1016/j.gsf.2023.101756

Pandey, A., & Joseph, J. (2025). Analyzing the Evolving Landscape of Digital Food Platforms and Technology: The Digital Plate. In *Food in the Metaverse and Web 3.0 Era: Intersecting Food, Technology, and Culture* (pp. 1-18). IGI Global Scientific Publishing.

Pandey, A., & Joseph, J. (2025). Cyber Physical Systems: Ethical and Legal Considerations for a Policy Design. In *Democracy and Democratization in the Age of AI* (pp. 285-302). IGI Global Scientific Publishing.

Pandey, A., & Joseph, J. (2025). Emerging Trends in Blue Economy: A Roadmap Through the Lens of Sustainable Development. *Securing Sustainable Futures Through Blue and Green Economies*, 17-36.

Pandey, A., & Joseph, J. (2025). Leveraging Artificial Intelligence for Sustainable Development in Agriculture: An Exploratory Study. In *Artificial Intelligence and Data Science for Sustainability: Applications and Methods* (pp. 187-212). IGI Global Scientific Publishing.

Pandey, A., Patel, D. P., Sahu, S. K. & Gupta, P. (2023). Role of Digital Banking in Investors' Awareness and Investment Decision-Making. *International Journal of Multidisciplinary Research Transactions*, 5(9), 43.53.

Panja, S., & Roy, B. (2021). A secure end-to-end verifiable e-voting system using blockchain and cloud server. *Journal of Information Security and Applications*, *59*, 102815. DOI: 10.1016/j.jisa.2021.102815

Pardo, T. A., & Tayi, G. K. (2017). Introducing Blockchain Technology for the Information Management Profession. *Proceedings of the Association for Information Science and Technology, 54*(1), 24–32.

Parliament, E. (2017). *Circular economy: definition, importance and benefits.*

Patel, A. (2021). Navigating Technical Challenges: A Study of IT Adoption in Internal Audit *Processes.Journal of Information Systems, 19*(2), 89–107.

Patel, A. (2021). Pivotal role of Microsoft Visio and Project in internal audit. *Journal of Information Technology Integration, 22*(4), 189–207.

Patel, R., & Garcia, M. (2024). Ontology engineering for inclusive digital transformation. *Journal of Inclusive Development, 9*(2), 34–50.

Patterson, N. (2022). *What is environmental sustainability? Goals with examples.* South. New Hampsh. Univ.

Paul, J., Mittal, A., & Srivastav, G. (2016). Impact of Service Quality on Customer Satisfaction in Private and Public Sector Banks. *International Journal of Bank Marketing, 35*(5), 606–622. https://www.researchgate.net/publication/283014318_Paul_J_Mittal_A_SrivastavaG_2016_Impact_of_Service_Quality_on_Customer_Satisfaction_in_Private_and_Public_Sector_Banks_35_5_Forthcoming. DOI: 10.1108/IJBM-03-2015-0030

Payne, A., & Frow, P. (2023). A strategic framework for customer relationship management. *Journal of Marketing, 69*(4), 167–176. DOI: 10.1509/jmkg.2005.69.4.167

Piccarozzi, M., Aquilani, B., & Gatti, C. (2018). Industry 4.0 in Management Studies: A Systematic Literature Review. *Sustainability (Basel), 10*(10), 3821. DOI: 10.3390/su10103821

Pikkarainen, T., Pikkarainen, K., Karjaluoto, H., & Pahnila, S. (2004). Consumer acceptance of online banking: An extension of the technology acceptance model. *Internet Research, 14*(3), 224–235. DOI: 10.1108/10662240410542652

Poder, B. (2005). *Factors Influencing the Adoption and Usage of Internet Banking: A New Zealand Perspective.* Master Thesis, Auckland University of Technology.

Polatoglu, V. N., & Ekin, S. (2001). An Empirical Investigation of the Turkish Consumers' Acceptance of Internet Bank Services. *International Journal of Bank Marketing, 19*(4), 156–165. DOI: 10.1108/02652320110392527

Porfírio, J. A., Felício, J. A., & Carrilho, T. (2024). Factors affecting DT in banking. *Journal of Business Research, 171*(1), 1–9. DOI: 10.1016/j.jbusres.2023.114393

Porter, M. E. (2023). *Competitive advantage: Creating and sustaining superior performance*. Free Press.

Porter, M. E. (2023). *Competitive strategy: Techniques for analyzing industries and competitors*. Free Press.

Prayitno, W., Tumangkar, T., & Mulyani, S. (2023). *The metaverse symbol of civilization transfer in the middle of digital economic hegemony: synthesis of progressive law of the post-modern era*. Seven Editora.

Priya, M. S. (2024). A Study on Customer Awareness, Preference on e-Banking Services. *Humanities and Social Science Studies*, *13*(1), 45–48.

Purvis, B., Mao, Y., & Robinson, D. (2019). Three pillars of sustainability: In search of conceptual origins. *Sustainability Science*, *14*(3), 681–695. DOI: 10.1007/s11625-018-0627-5

Putra, A. C. (2022). Pengaruh pertumbuhan pdrb usaha mikro kecil menengah (Umkm) terhadap pertumbuhan ekonomi Surabaya. *Jurnal Lemhannas RI*, *10*(2), 65–78. DOI: 10.55960/jlri.v10i2.278

PwC. (2020). *Internal Audit in 2020 and Beyond*. PricewaterhouseCoopers LLP.

PwC. (2021). *Technology Trends 2021: Internal Audit*. PricewaterhouseCoopers LLP.

Qadri, Y. A., Nauman, A., Zikria, Y. B., Vasilakos, A. V., & Kim, S. W. (2020). The future of healthcare internet of things: A survey of emerging technologies. *IEEE Communications Surveys and Tutorials*, *22*(2), 1121–1167. DOI: 10.1109/COMST.2020.2973314

Radicic, D., & Petković, S. (2023). Impact of digitalization on technological innovations in small and medium-sized enterprises (SMEs). *Technological Forecasting and Social Change*, *191*, 122474. DOI: 10.1016/j.techfore.2023.122474

Rahman, M., Ming, T. H., Baigh, T. A., & Sarker, M. (2023). Adoption of artificial intelligence in banking services: An empirical analysis. *International Journal of Emerging Markets*, *18*(10), 4270–4300. DOI: 10.1108/IJOEM-06-2020-0724

Rahman, M., Yee, H. P., & Masud, Md. A., K., & Uzir, Md. U. H. (2024). Examining the dynamic of mobile banking app. adoption during the COVI-19 pandemic: A digital shift in the crisis. *Digital Business*, *5*(1), 1–15.

Rajput, U. S. (2015). Customers' Perception of e-banking Service. *Pacific Business Review International*, *8*(4), 85–94.

Rane, N., Choudhary, S., & Rane, J. (2023). Enhanced product design and development using Artificial Intelligence (AI), Virtual Reality (VR), Augmented Reality (AR), 4D/5D/6D Printing, Internet of Things (IoT), and blockchain: A review. SSRN *Electronic Journal, 4*. DOI: 10.2139/ssrn.4644059

Ranney, A. (1981). *Candidate selection*. Democracy at the Polls.

Rattan, M., Bhambri, P., & Shaifali, M. (2005, February). Information retrieval using soft computing techniques. In *National Conference on Bio-informatics Computing* (Vol. 7). TIET.

Redda, E. H. (2023). E-banking quality and customer loyalty: The mediating role of customer satisfaction. *Banks and Bank Systems*, *18*(2), 177–188. DOI: 10.21511/bbs.18(2).2023.15

Regina, P. A. (2022). *Exploring the Citizen Engagement Metaverse: Testing Virtual Reality for Citizen Feedback on Public Space Design Options*. The University of Regina.

Rejeb, A., Suhaiza, Z., Rejeb, K., Seuring, S., & Treiblmaier, H. (2022). The Internet of Things and the circular economy: A systematic literature review and research agenda. *Journal of Cleaner Production*, *350*, 131439. DOI: 10.1016/j.jclepro.2022.131439

Rensmann, T. (Ed.). (2017). *Small and Medium-sized enterprises in international economic law*. Oxford University Press.

Research, I. B. M. (2024). Ontology-driven AI: Transforming industries through semantic technologies. https://www.ibm.com/research/whitepapers

Ries, E. (2023). *The lean startup: How today's entrepreneurs use continuous innovation to create radically successful businesses*. Crown Business.

Rogers, E. M. (2023). *Diffusion of innovations* (5th ed.). Free Press.

Rosa, W. (2017). Goal 4: Ensure inclusive and equitable quality education and promote lifelong learning opportunities for all. *A New Era in Global Health: Nursing and the United Nations 2030 Agenda for Sustainable Development, 283*.

Roy, S. K., Balaji, M. S., Kesharwani, A., & Sekhon, H. (2017). Predicting internet banking adoption in India: A perceived risk perspective. *Journal of Strategic Marketing*, *25*(5-6), 418–438. DOI: 10.1080/0965254X.2016.1148771

Rozo-García, F. (2020). Revisión de las tecnologías presentes en la industria 4.0. *Revista UIS Ingenierías*, *19*(2), 177–191. DOI: 10.18273/revuin.v19n2-2020019

Rtayli, N., & Enneya, N. (2020). Enhanced credit card fraud detection based on SVM-recursive feature elimination and hyper-parameters optimization. *Journal of Information Security and Applications*, *55*, 102596. DOI: 10.1016/j.jisa.2020.102596

Saarikko, T., Westergren, U. H., & Blomquist, T. (2020). Digital transformation: Five recommendations for the digitally conscious firm. *Business Horizons*, *63*(6), 825–839. DOI: 10.1016/j.bushor.2020.07.005

Sabtu, M. A. S. (2023). Metaverse and Soft Skills Development Through Video Games. In *Metaverse applications for new business models and disruptive innovation* (pp. 120–132). IGI Global., DOI: 10.4018/978-1-6684-6097-9.ch008

Sachs, J. D., Schmidt-Traub, G., Kroll, C., Lafortune, G., & Fuller, G. (2019). *Sustainable development report 2019*. Bertelsmann Stiftung and Sustainable Development Solutions Network.

Sadgali, I., Sael, N., & Benabbou, F. (2019). Performance of machine learning techniques in the detection of financial frauds. *Procedia Computer Science*, *148*, 45–54. DOI: 10.1016/j.procs.2019.01.007

Saeed, Y. A. H., & Ahmed, R. A. (2023). The impact of information technology on the performance of commercial banks through the faithful representation of accounting information system. *International Journal of Professional Business Review*, *8*(9), 1–11. DOI: 10.26668/businessreview/2023.v8i9.1758

Saini, M., Sengupta, E., Singh, M., Singh, H., & Singh, J. (2023). Sustainable Development Goal for Quality Education (SDG 4): A study on SDG 4 to extract the pattern of association among the indicators of SDG 4 employing a genetic algorithm. *Education and Information Technologies*, *28*(2), 2031–2069. DOI: 10.1007/s10639-022-11265-4 PMID: 35975216

Saldana, J. (2016). The coding manual for qualitative researchers. *Sage (Atlanta, Ga.)*.

Saleh, H. M., & Hassan, A. I. (2022). Sustainability: A comprehensive approach to developing environmental technologies and conserving natural resources. In *Risk, Reliability and Sustainable Remediation in the Field of Civil and Environmental Engineering* (pp. 437-448). Elsevier.

Sanyaolu, M., & Sadowski, A. (2024). The role of Precision Agriculture Technologies in enhancing sustainable agriculture. *Sustainability (Basel)*, *16*(15), 6668. DOI: 10.3390/su16156668

Sarno, R., Sinaga, F., & Sungkono, K. R. (2020). Anomaly detection in business processes using process mining and fuzzy association rule learning. *Journal of Big Data*, *7*(1), 5. DOI: 10.1186/s40537-019-0277-1

Sathiyavany, N., & Shivany, S. (2018). E-Banking Service Qualities, E-Customer Satisfaction, and e-Loyalty: A conceptual Model. *The International Journal of Social Sciences and Humanities Invention*, *5*(6), 4808–4819. DOI: 10.18535/ijsshi/v5i6.08

Saunders, M., Lewis, P., & Thornhill, A. (2018). *Research methods for business students*.

Sayar, C., & Wolfe, S. (2007). Internet banking market performance: UK. *International Journal of Bank Marketing*, *25*(3), 122–141. DOI: 10.1108/02652320710739841

Scavarelli, A., Arya, A., & Teather, R. J. (2021). Virtual reality and augmented reality in social learning spaces: A literature review. *Virtual Reality (Waltham Cross)*, *25*(1), 257–277. DOI: 10.1007/s10055-020-00444-8

Scholl, H. J. (2013). E-government success factors: Mapping practical tools to theoretical foundations. *Government Information Quarterly*, *30*(2), 142–151.

Schuppan, T. (2019). Factors influencing the diffusion of electronic procurement in German local governments. *Government Information Quarterly*, *36*(1), 120–127.

Sehgal, S., & Garg, P. (2020). The human challenges of the digital world: the paradigm of employee expectations in the banking sector. *e-journal - First Pan IIT International Management Conference – 2018*. DOI: 10.2139/ssrn.3743389

Shafi, U., Mumtaz, R., García-Nieto, J., Hassan, S. A., Zaidi, S. A. R., & Iqbal, N. (2019). Precision agriculture techniques and practices: From considerations to applications. *Sensors (Basel)*, *19*(17), 3796. DOI: 10.3390/s19173796 PMID: 31480709

Shaikh, M. A. (2014). Ethiopian bankers perception of electronic banking in ethiopia–a case of Adama City. *International Journal of Scientific and Research Publications*, *4*(9), 1–6.

Shareef, M. A., Dwivedi, Y. K., Kumar, V., & Kumar, U. (2020). Digital government maturity model for measuring and managing digital transformation. *Government Information Quarterly*, *37*(3), 101496.

Sharma, R., Bhambri, P., & Sohal, A. K. (2020). Energy bio-inspired for MANET. *International Journal of Recent Technology and Engineering*, *8*(6), 5580–5585.

Shaw, C., & Ivens, J. (2023). *Building great customer experiences*. Palgrave Macmillan.

Shaw, D. R., & Allen, T. (2018). Studying innovation ecosystems using ecology theory. *Technological Forecasting and Social Change*, *136*, 88–102. DOI: 10.1016/j.techfore.2016.11.030

Shirahada, K., Oyama, H., & Ohsaki, T. (2020). Local Social Innovation by Blockchain Technology: A Trial in a Provincial City in Japan. *Business Innovation with New ICT in the Asia-Pacific: Case Studies*, 349–365. DOI: 10.1007/978-981-15-7658-4_16

Shu, W., & Strassmann, P. A. (2005). Does information technology provide banks with profit? *Information & Management*, *42*(5), 781–787. DOI: 10.1016/j.im.2003.06.007

Sikopo, L., & Dube, T. (2018). The impact of information technology integration on public sector service delivery: A case study of Namibia. *The Southern African Journal of Accountability and Auditing Research*, *19*(1), 37–56.

Singh, A. P., Aggarwal, M., Singh, H., & Bhambri, P. (2021). Sketching of EV network: A complete roadmap. In Sustainable Development Through Engineering Innovations: Select Proceedings of SDEI 2020 (pp. 431-442). Springer Singapore.

Singh, A. P., Aggarwal, M., Singh, H., & Bhambri, P. (2021). Sketching of EV network: A complete roadmap. In Sustainable Development Through Engineering Innovations: Select Proceedings of SDEI 2020 (pp. 431-442). Springer Singapore. DOI: 10.1007/978-981-15-9554-7_37

Singh, A. K., Ashraf, S. N., & Gupta, M. (2025). Digital transformation and customer's problems in banking industry of India. In Tunio, M. (Ed.), *Applications of Career Transitions and Entrepreneurship* (pp. 1–34). IGI Global Scientific Publishing., DOI: 10.4018/979-8-3693-4163-6.ch001

Singh, A. K., & Jyoti, B. (2023). Does digitalization have a bi-directional causal relationship with the entrepreneurship ecosystem? Evidence from a country-wise panel data analysis. In Yanamandra, R., & Indiran, L. (Eds.), *Handbook of Research on Designing Sustainable Strategies to Develop Entrepreneurial Intention* (pp. 178–172). IGI Global., DOI: 10.4018/978-1-6684-8781-5.ch007

Singh, M., Bhambri, P., Lal, S., Singh, Y., Kaur, M., & Singh, J. (2021). Design of the effective technique to improve memory and time constraints for sequence alignment. *International Journal of Applied Engineering Research (Netherlands)*, *6*(02), 127–142.

Singh, P., Singh, M., & Bhambri, P. (2004, November). Interoperability: A problem of component reusability. In *International Conference on Emerging Technologies in IT Industry* (Vol. 60). PCTE.

Singh, S., & Arora, R. (2011). A Comparative Study of Banking Services and Customer Satisfaction in Public, Private and Foreign Banks. *Journal of Economics*, *2*(1), 45–56. DOI: 10.1080/09765239.2011.11884936

Siriram, R. (2022). An innovative approach to overcoming technological challenges and improving firm performance in South Africa. *Technology in Society*, *68*, 101865. DOI: 10.1016/j.techsoc.2022.101865

SLBC. (2016). 116th State Level Banker's Committee Meeting for Tripura, February, 2016, Quarterly Review, Agartala, Tripura, India.

SLBC. (2017). 121st State Level Banker's Committee Meeting for Tripura, March, 2017, Quarterly Review, Agartala, Tripura, India.

SLBC. (2018). 125th State Level Banker's Committee Meeting for Tripura, March, 2018, Quarterly Review, Agartala, Tripura, India.

SLBC. (2019). 129th State Level Banker's Committee Meeting for Tripura, March, 2019, Quarterly Review, Agartala, Tripura, India.

SLBC. (2020). 131st State Level Banker's Committee Meeting for Tripura, December, 2020, Quarterly Review, Agartala, Tripura, India.

SLBC. (2021). 135th State Level Banker's Committee Meeting for Tripura, March, 2021, Quarterly Review, Agartala, Tripura, India.

SLBC. (2022). 139th State Level Banker's Committee Meeting for Tripura, March, 2022, Quarterly Review, Agartala, Tripura, India.

SLBC. (2023). 142nd State Level Banker's Committee Meeting for Tripura, December, 2023, Quarterly Review, Agartala, Tripura, India.

Smith, A., & Johnson, B. (2019). Public sector sustainability: Emerging trends and challenges. *Journal of Public Policy*, *45*(3), 301–318.

Smith, A., Johnson, B., Williams, C., Davis, D., Wilson, E., Anderson, F., & Taylor, Z. (2021). The impact of Information Technology on public sector sustainability: A systematic review. *Sustainability*, *13*(7), 3659.

Smith, A., Jones, B., & Brown, C. (2020). Constructivist research philosophy in the context of IT adoption for sustainability in government organizations. *Journal of Public Administration: Research and Theory*, *30*(3), 455–470.

Smith, J. (2019). *Financial Management: Principles and Applications*. Pearson.

Smith, J., & Johnson, A. (2022). Recognizing the Pivotal Role of Internal Audit: A Leadership Perspective on IT Adoption. *International Journal of Auditing Technology*, *21*(1), 56–74.

Smith, J., & Johnson, L. (2024). Ontology-based AI: A new paradigm for intelligent systems. *Artificial Intelligence Review*, *57*(1), 123–140.

Smith, J., & Johnson, L. (2024). Ontology-based knowledge management systems: A review of recent trends and applications. *Journal of Knowledge Management, 28*(3), 45–60.

Smith, J., & Taylor, D. (2020). Foundational role of Microsoft Excel and Word in internal auditing systems. *Journal of Audit Innovation, 12*(3), 112–130.

Smith, K. (2017). Environmental Sustainability through IT Adoption: Lessons from Internal Audit Practices. *Sustainability Management Review, 12*(4), 67–84.

Smith, R., & Johnson, A. (2021). Strategic application of technology in enhancing audit accuracy. *Technology and Audit Practice, 8*(2), 45–67.

Suleiman, G.P, Mat, N.K.M., Adesiyan, O.I, & Mohammed, A.S, & ALekam, J. (. (2012). Customer Loyalty in e-Banking: A Structural Equation Modelling (SEM) Approach. *American Journal of Economics*, (Special Issue), 55–59. DOI: 10.5923/j.economics.20120001.13

Sullivan, G. M. (2017). A primer on the validity of assessment instruments. *Journal of Graduate Medical Education, 9*(2), 145–147. PMID: 22655129

Swami, P. (2024). *Metaverse: Transforming the User Experience in the Gaming and Entertainment Industry*. IGI Global., https://www.igi-global.com/chapter/metaverse/349151%0Awww.igi-global.com/chapter/metaverse/349151

Tam, C., & Oliveira, T. (2016). Understanding the impact of m-banking in individual performance: Delone & McLean and TTF perspective. *Computers in Human Behavior, 61*(1), 233–244. DOI: 10.1016/j.chb.2016.03.016

Tari, F., & Raeisi, H. (2021). The Role of Electronic Receipt and Payment Instruments in the Development of Banking Services. Iranian Journal of Accounting, Auditing & Finance. *Iranian Journal of Accounting. Auditing & Finance, 4*(4), 83–96.

Tavanti, M. (2023). Technology Innovations for the SDGs. In *Developing Sustainability in Organizations: A Values-Based Approach* (pp. 389–404). Springer International Publishing. DOI: 10.1007/978-3-031-36907-0_13

Teece, D. J. (2010). Business models, business strategy and innovation. *Long Range Planning, 43*(2-3), 172–194. DOI: 10.1016/j.lrp.2009.07.003

Teh, D., & Rana, T. (2023). The use of Internet of Things, Big Data analytics and artificial intelligence for attaining UN's SDGs. In *Handbook of big data and analytics in accounting and auditing* (pp. 235–253). Springer Nature Singapore. DOI: 10.1007/978-981-19-4460-4_11

The Auditor-General of Namibia. (2017). *Report of the Auditor-General on the performance audit of information technology governance in selected government ministries for the period ended 31 March 2017.* Office of the Auditor-General, Republic of Namibia.

Theiri, S., & Hadoussa, S. (2024). Digitization effects on banks' financial performance: The case of an African country. *Competitiveness Review, 34*(1), 144–162. DOI: 10.1108/CR-10-2022-0147

Thudumu, S., Branch, P., Jin, J., & Singh, J. (2020). A comprehensive survey of anomaly detection techniques for high dimensional big data. *Journal of Big Data, 7*(1), 1–30. DOI: 10.1186/s40537-020-00320-x

Tornatzky, L. G., & Fleischer, M. (2023). *The processes of technological innovation.* Lexington Books.

Treacy, M., & Wiersema, F. (2023). *The discipline of market leaders: Choose your customers, narrow your focus, dominate your market.* Addison-Wesley.

Tse, D. K., & Wilton, P. C. (1988). Models of Consumer Satisfaction Formation: An Extension. *JMR, Journal of Marketing Research, 25*(2), 204–212. DOI: 10.1177/002224378802500209

Tunay, K. B., Tunay, N., & Akshisar, I. (2015). Interaction between internet banking and bank performance: The case of Europe. *Procedia: Social and Behavioral Sciences, 195*(1), 363–358. DOI: 10.1016/j.sbspro.2015.06.335

Tzoulas, K., Korpela, K., Venn, S., Yli-Pelkonen, V., Kaźmierczak, A., Niemela, J., & James, P. (2007). Promoting ecosystem and human health in urban areas using Green Infrastructure: A literature review. *Landscape and Urban Planning, 81*(3), 167–178. DOI: 10.1016/j.landurbplan.2007.02.001

UN DESA. (2018). *Public Administration Innovation and Sustainable Development.* UN.

UN DESA. (2018). *Public Administration Innovation and Sustainable Development.* United Nations.

United Nations. (2018). The Impact of Digital Transformation on Sustainable Development. *United Nations Department of Economic and Social Affairs*, 1-51.

United Nations. (2020). *E-Government Survey 2020: Digital Government in the Decade of Action for Sustainable Development.* United Nations Department of Economic and Social Affairs.

Van de Poel, I., & Kudina, O. (2022). Understanding technology-induced value change: A pragmatist proposal. *Philosophy & Technology, 35*(2), 40. DOI: 10.1007/s13347-022-00520-8 PMID: 35441075

Vanini, P., Rossi, S., Zvizdic, E., & Domenig, T. (2023). Online payment fraud: From anomaly detection to risk management. *Financial Innovation, 9*(1), 66. DOI: 10.1186/s40854-023-00470-w

Velenturf, A. P., & Purnell, P. (2021). Principles for a sustainable circular economy. *Sustainable Production and Consumption, 27*, 1437–1457. DOI: 10.1016/j.spc.2021.02.018

Venkatesh, J. & Perisamy.P. (2007). Role of E-Banking in Emerging Scenario. *The Professional Banker*, 53-57

Venkatesh, V., & Davis, F. D. (2000). A theoretical extension of the Technology Acceptance Model: Four longitudinal field studies. *Management Science, 46*(2), 186–204. DOI: 10.1287/mnsc.46.2.186.11926

Vignesh, A. (2022). Employees perspective on digital banking. *Asian Journal of Management, 13*(3), 223–226. DOI: 10.52711/2321-5763.2022.00039

Vinoth, S., Vemula, H. L., Harapayya, B., Mamgain, P., Hasan, M. F., & Naved, M. (2022). Application of cloud computing in banking and e-commerce and related security threats. *Materials Today: Proceedings, 51*(8), 2172–2175. DOI: 10.1016/j.matpr.2021.11.121

Wang, J. (2020). User-Centric Design in Internal Audit Systems. *Human-Computer Interaction Journal, 35*(1), 120–136.

Wang, W., Wang, L., Xu, S., Wang, J., & Fu, K. (2021). Sharingchain : A privacy protection scheme based on blockchain in the supply chain. *IMCEC 2021 - IEEE 4th Advanced Information Management, Communicates, Electronic and Automation Control Conference, 4*, 995–999. DOI: 10.1109/IMCEC51613.2021.9482088

Wang, Y., Su, Z., Zhang, N., Xing, R., Liu, D., Luan, T. H., & Shen, X. (2023). A Survey on Metaverse: Fundamentals, Security, and Privacy. *IEEE Communications Surveys and Tutorials, 25*(1), 319–352. DOI: 10.1109/COMST.2022.3202047

Wang, Y., Wang, Q., Xu, L., Zhang, Y., & Fan, S. (2022). Intelligent virtual wardrobe system based on Android. *2022 Global Conference on Robotics, Artificial Intelligence and Information Technology (GCRAIT), 14*, 434-438. DOI: 10.1109/GCRAIT55928.2022.00098

Warren, M. E. (2009). Citizen participation and democratic deficits: Considerations from the perspective of democratic theory. In *Activating the Citizen: Dilemmas of Participation in Europe and Canada* (pp. 17–40). Springer. DOI: 10.1057/9780230240902_2

Waterman, R. H., Peters, T. J., & Phillips, J. R. (2023). Structure is not organization. *Business Horizons.*

WCED (World Commission on Environment and Development). (1987). *Our Common Future*. UN.

Wellalage, N. H., Hunjra, A. I., & Manita, R. (2021). Information communication technology and financial inclusion of innovative entrepreneurs. *Technological Forecasting and Social Change, 163*(1), 1–10. DOI: 10.1016/j.techfore.2020.120416

West, D. M. (2019). Blockchain for government: Benefits and implications of distributed ledger technology for information sharing. *Government Information Quarterly, 36*(3), 434–440.

Westerman, G., Calméjane, C., Ferraris, P., & Bonnet, D. (2023). *Digital transformation: A roadmap for billion-dollar organizations.* MIT Center for Digital Business.

Wezel, A., Casagrande, M., Celette, F., Vian, J. F., Ferrer, A., & Peigné, J. (2014). Agroecological practices for sustainable agriculture. A review. *Agronomy for Sustainable Development, 34*(1), 1–20. DOI: 10.1007/s13593-013-0180-7

White, L. (2018). Cybersecurity Measures for Ensuring Data Protection in Internal Audit. *Cybersecurity Review, 22*(3), 112–129.

Wilhelm, A. G. (2002). *Democracy in the digital age: Challenges to political life in cyberspace.* Routledge. DOI: 10.4324/9780203902509

Williams, C. A., Schallmo, D., & Scornavacca, E. (2022). How applicable are digital maturity models to SMEs?: A conceptual framework and empirical validation approach. *International Journal of Innovation Management, 26*(03), 2240010. DOI: 10.1142/S1363919622400102

World Economic Forum. (2023). Digital transformation and inclusive growth: A framework for developing economies. https://www.weforum.org/reports

Xu, C., & Zhang, J. (2017). Collusive opinion fraud detection in online reviews: A probabilistic modeling approach. [TWEB]. *ACM Transactions on the Web, 11*(4), 1–28.

Yan, G. (2017). Application of cloud computing in banking: Advantages and challenges. *Advances in Economics. Business and Management Research, 33*(1), 29–33.

Yang, J., Liao, M., Wang, Y., Chen, L., He, L., Ji, Y., Xiao, Y., Lu, Y., Fan, W., Nie, Z., Wang, R., Qi, B., & Yang, F. (2022). Opportunistic osteoporosis screening using chest CT with artificial intelligence. *Osteoporosis International, 33*(12), 2547–2561. DOI: 10.1007/s00198-022-06491-y PMID: 35931902

Yang, Y. (2000). Public Private Partnerships in the Social Sector. *Issues and Country Experiences in Asia and the Pacific. ABDI Policy Paper, 1*, 353.

Yuanda, L., & Shinta, T. (2023). Pengaruh Pertumbuhan Jumlah Usaha Mikro Kecil Dan Menengah Terhadap Pertumbuhan Ekonomi Kabupaten Pelalawan Dalam Perspektif Ekonomi Islam. *Jurnal Ekonomi Islam, 1*(2), 60–68.

Zachman, J. A. (2023). A framework for information systems architecture. *IBM Systems Journal, 26*(3), 276–292. DOI: 10.1147/sj.263.0276

Zhang, J. J., Lichtenstein, Y., & Gander, J. (2015). Designing scalable digital business models. In Business models and modelling (pp. 241-277). Emerald Group Publishing Limited.

Zhang, Y., Mao, Y., Jiao, L., Shuai, C., & Zhang, H. (2021). Eco-efficiency, eco-technology innovation and eco-well-being performance to improve global sustainable development. *Environmental Impact Assessment Review, 89*, 106580. DOI: 10.1016/j.eiar.2021.106580

Zhao, Y., Jiang, J., Chen, Y., Liu, R., Yang, Y., Xue, X., & Chen, S. (2022). Metaverse: Perspectives from graphics, interactions, and visualization. *Visual Informatics, 6*(1), 56–67. DOI: 10.1016/j.visinf.2022.03.002

About the Contributors

Patricia Ordóñez de Pablos is a professor in the Department of Business Administration in the Faculty of Business and Economics at The University of Oviedo, Spain. She completed her education in The London School of Economics, UK. Her teaching and research interests focus on the areas of strategic management, knowledge management, organizational learning, intellectual capital and information technologies, with special interest in Asia (Bhutan, China, Laos, Myanmar). She is Editor-in-Chief of the International Journal of Learning and Intellectual Capital (IJLIC) and International Journal of Asian Business and Information Management (IJABIM), respectively. She has edited books for IGI Global, Elsevier, Routledge, and Springer. In 2021, 2022 and 2023, she earned placement on Stanford University's "Ranking of the World Scientists: World's Top 2% Scientists" list. Additionally she is listed in World Top Scientists of Research.com in the Areas of Social Science and Humanities in Spain.

Jose Emilio Labra Gayo. Full Professor at the Department of Computer Science, University of Oviedo, Spain. He founded WESO (Web Semantics Oviedo) research group in 2004 and collaborates with different companies and institutions around the world applying semantic technologies. The development of RDF data portals led to his interest in RDF validation. Member of the W3C Data Shapes working group which developed SHACL, co-editor of the ShEx specification and current member of RDF Star Working Group. He implemented the SHACL and ShEx library, maintains the online RDF validator services RDFShape and WikiShape, and is currently writing the Shapes-rs validation libraries in Rust. He is co-author of the Knowledge Graphs and the Validating RDF Data books and has published more than 100 papers in these areas.

***

Neeta Baporikar is an independent researcher and prior to this, she was Professor/Director(Business Management) at Harold Pupkewitz Graduate School of Business, Namibia University of Science and Technology, Namibia. Head-Scientific Research, with the Ministry of Higher Education CAS-Salalah, Sultanate of Oman, Professor (Strategy and Entrepreneurship) at IIIT Pune and BITS India. With a decade-plus of experience in the industry, consultancy, and training, she made a lateral switch to research and academics in 2000. Prof Baporikar holds D.Sc. (Management Studies) USA, Ph.D. (Management), SP Pune University, INDIA with MBA (Distinction) and Law (Hons.) degrees. Apart from this, she is an external reviewer, Oman Academic Accreditation Authority, an Accredited Management Teacher, a Qualified Trainer, an FDP from EDII, a Doctoral Guide, and a Board Member of the Academic Advisory Committee in accredited B-Schools. She has to her credit many conferred doctorates, 350+ scientific publications, and authored 30+ books in the areas of Strategy, Entrepreneurship, Management, and Higher Education. She is also a member of the international and editorial advisory board, an reviewer for Emerald, IGI, Inderscience, Wiley, etc.

Pankaj Bhambri is affiliated with the Department of Information Technology at Guru Nanak Dev Engineering College in Ludhiana. Additionally, he fulfills the role of the Convener for his Departmental Board of Studies. He possesses nearly two decades of teaching experience. His research work has been published in esteemed worldwide and national journals, as well as conference proceedings. Dr. Bhambri has garnered extensive experience in the realm of academic publishing, having served as an editor for a multitude of books in collaboration with esteemed publishing houses such as CRC Press, Elsevier, Scrivener, and Bentham Science. In addition to his editorial roles, he has demonstrated his scholarly prowess by authoring numerous books and contributing chapters to distinguished publishers within the academic community. Dr. Bhambri has been honored with several prestigious accolades, including the ISTE Best Teacher Award in 2023 and 2022, the I2OR National Award in 2020, the Green ThinkerZ Top 100 International Distinguished Educators award in 2020, the I2OR Outstanding Educator Award in 2019, the SAA Distinguished Alumni Award in 2012, the CIPS Rashtriya Rattan Award in 2008, the LCHC Best Teacher Award in 2007, and numerous other commendations from various government and non-profit organizations. He has provided guidance and oversight for numerous research projects and dissertations at the postgraduate and Ph.D. levels. He successfully organized a diverse range of educational programmes, securing financial backing from esteemed institutions such as the AICTE, the TEQIP, among others. Dr. Bhambri's areas of interest encompass machine learning, bioinformatics, wireless sensor networks, and network security.

Manshu Goyal is a dedicated law graduate and a practicing advocate at the District Court of Modinagar, Ghaziabad. With a strong academic foundation in legal studies, he graduated with a degree in law from Swami Vivekanand Subharti University, Meerut, where he excelled in subjects such as criminal law, civil litigation, and legal drafting. Since entering the legal profession, Manshu has gained valuable experience representing clients in a wide range of cases, including family disputes, property matters, and criminal defenses.

Jipson Joseph has a PhD in Ethics from DVK Bangalore. Currently, he is a Research Scholar in the School of Law at Christ University, Bangalore. His research interests are in the fields of ethics, gender studies, constitutional law, human rights, human security, food security, environmental justice, developmental policies and global poverty.

Achmad Nurmandi is a Professor at the Department of Government Affairs and Administration, Jusuf Kalla School of Government, Universitas Muhammadiyah Yogyakarta, Indonesia. His research interests are on e-government, urban governance and strategic management in the public sector and published in many international journal and Book Chapter, such as International Journal of Public Sector Management, Transforming Government: People, Policy and Process, Jamba Journal of Disaster Studies, Asian Review of Political Science, Journal of Human Behavior in the Social Environment, Public Policy and Administration, Global Encyclopedia of Public Administration, Public Policy, and Governance, Springer. He is currently the Secretary of the Asia Pacific Society for Public Affairs (APSPA). He is also the Editor-in-Chief of Jurnal Studi Pemerintahan (Journal of Government and Politics) and a Guest Editor of International Journal of Public Sector Performance Management and International Journal of Sustainable Society.

Ananya Pandey is a Research Scholar in School of Law at Christ University, Bangalore. She has her research interests in the field of Constitutional Law, Environment Law, Human Rights, Food Security, Intellectual Property Law and Jurisprudence.

Rachna Rana is working as Associate Professor in the Department of Computer Science & Engineering at Ludhiana Group of Colleges in Ludhiana. She possesses nearly two decades of teaching experience. Her areas of interest includes machine learning, wireless sensor networks, and network security.

|Rachna Rana - Contributing Author|Rachna Rana is working as Associate Professor in the Department of Computer Science & Engineering at Ludhiana Group of Colleges in Ludhiana. She possesses nearly two decades of teaching experience.

Her areas of interest includes machine learning, wireless sensor networks, and network security.

Ajay K. Singh is working as an Associate Professor (Research) in the Department of Humanities and Social Science, Graphic Era (Deemed to be University) Dehradun. He has worked as Assistant Professor (Economics) in the School of Liberal Arts & Management, DIT University Dehradun for 6 years. He did Post-Doctorate Research with EDI of India, Ahmedabad, Gujarat (India). He received MPhil (Economics) from DAVV Indore (India), and PhD (Economics) from IIT Indore (India. He has published several research papers in the diversified area such as climate change, agricultural productivity, assessment of food security; estimation of GFSI, development of environmental sustainability index (ESI) and its association with socio-economic indicators; measurement and determinants of entrepreneurship ecosystem, and dimension of sustainable development and its interlinkages with economic development.

Srinivasan Vasan has been working in the Department of Humanities and Social Sciences at Graphic Era (Deemed to be University) as an Assistant Professor. With a wealth of experience, Mr. Srinivasan has accumulated 14 years of extensive teaching and field-level expertise. Prior to his current role, he served in the Ministry of Health and Family Welfare, Government of India, and gained valuable experience. He also contributed as a Guest Faculty at the university level and served for nearly 2 years in the State Government Public Works Department as a Mobilization Training Specialist. In the past year, Mr. S. Srinivasan has enriched his experience by actively participating in a tuberculosis project funded by GFATM and USAID, providing a platform for further exploration of his research and practical field-based knowledge. His scholarly contributions include publishing 65 papers, with 18 more under peer review in various UGC-CARE, SCOPUS, and peer-reviewed journals.

Muhammad Younus I graduated in 2019 from the Karachi Institute of Economics and Technology University in Karachi, Pakistan, and got a Bachelor's degree in Computer Science. The four-year undergraduate program in Computer Science formed the basis of my perseverance towards achieving an in-depth knowledge in the field. After graduation, I worked for the past few years as a business IT analyst in the product and research development of a logistics startup in Pakistan called TPL Logistics. We aim to Digitize Logistics Operations in Pakistan from the First Mile to the Last Mile. After this, I graduated in 2024 from the Universitas Muhammadiyah Yogyakarta in Yogyakarta, Indonesia, and got a Master's Degree in Government Science. My research interest is transforming governance and the public sector through technology. This Experience has given me the confidence and also kindled a desire to do research. The interdisciplinary nature has convinced me in taking this decision as it is the ideal choice for an exciting research career. At the same time, I am confident of contributing originally to the ongoing work. By working under the guidance of distinguished Team, I shall certainly be able to exploit my pote

Index

A

AI 2, 4, 7, 8, 9, 11, 16, 17, 18, 19, 21, 22, 25, 27, 32, 35, 50, 51, 53, 63, 71, 72, 75, 81, 120, 126, 127, 128, 130, 133, 134, 135, 140, 151, 189, 190, 194, 199, 203, 212, 213, 214, 217, 222, 224, 227, 231, 236, 242, 244, 247, 252, 258, 259, 260
Auditing 75, 76, 77, 79, 86, 87, 99, 107, 108, 109, 110, 111, 113, 137, 186, 209

B

Banking industry 40, 157, 158, 159, 160, 184, 221, 222, 223, 224, 225, 226, 227, 228, 229, 233, 234, 235, 236, 238, 245, 247, 252, 253, 254, 255
Barriers to Technology Adoption 8
Bi-stacked ANN 257, 261, 264, 265, 269
Bi-Stacked GRU 139, 143, 144, 145, 146, 148, 149, 150
Bi-Stacked LSTM 139, 143, 144, 145, 146, 148, 149, 150
Blockchain 11, 16, 22, 28, 32, 47, 71, 81, 104, 112, 114, 120, 128, 152, 188, 189, 190, 191, 192, 197, 203, 204, 205, 206, 208, 209, 210, 211, 212, 213, 214, 215, 216, 217, 218, 221, 222, 236, 260

C

Circular Economy 118, 121, 133, 134, 135, 136, 137
Customer's satisfaction 219, 222, 224, 225, 235, 240, 241, 242, 245, 247, 255
Customer Survey 155

D

Deep Learning 139, 143, 145, 148, 150, 151, 261
Democratizing Technology Developments 31, 45
Digital banking 180, 184, 221, 224, 225, 231, 234, 244, 245, 246, 250, 254, 255
Digital index 257, 262, 264, 265, 269
Digital Payments 139, 141, 144, 145, 146, 147, 148, 149, 150, 152, 227, 238
Digital technology 32, 40, 120, 129, 134, 140, 223, 228, 234, 235, 253, 261
Digital Transformation 2, 3, 4, 5, 6, 7, 8, 9, 11, 15, 16, 22, 23, 25, 26, 27, 28, 31, 32, 35, 39, 42, 43, 52, 53, 55, 65, 66, 67, 69, 70, 71, 72, 113, 114, 115, 120, 134, 136, 139, 140, 141, 142, 143, 150, 219, 254, 257, 259, 260, 262, 265, 269, 271

E

e-Banking Services 155, 156, 158, 159, 160, 161, 162, 163, 175, 176, 177, 180, 181, 182, 184
Economic Growth 1, 2, 31, 45, 50, 51, 52, 53, 54, 55, 62, 63, 67, 115, 116, 117, 118, 125, 126, 133, 134, 191
Election Voting 187, 188, 191, 192, 194, 195, 197, 199, 201, 203, 204, 205, 206, 207, 208, 211, 212

F

Feature extraction 144, 145, 257, 262, 263, 264
Financial Inclusion 139, 140, 143, 144, 146, 147, 148, 149, 152, 179, 223, 224, 254, 255
Financial risk 220, 222, 227, 235, 241, 243, 244, 245, 247, 248, 255
Financial security 219, 220, 221, 222, 223, 235, 241, 244, 245, 247, 255
Food Security 122

I

Information Technology 1, 26, 27, 28, 70, 71, 73, 74, 75, 76, 77, 78, 79, 80, 86, 87, 89, 90, 92, 94, 96, 98, 103, 104,

105, 107, 108, 109, 110, 111, 112, 113, 114, 116, 127, 151, 152, 156, 161, 182, 183, 197, 215, 217, 221, 224, 226, 229, 250, 251, 253, 270
Internal Audit 73, 74, 75, 76, 77, 78, 79, 86, 87, 88, 89, 90, 91, 92, 93, 94, 95, 96, 97, 98, 99, 100, 101, 102, 103, 104, 105, 106, 107, 108, 109, 110, 111, 112, 113, 114

L

Likert scale 233, 234, 240, 257, 262, 264, 265, 268, 269

M

Machine Learning 11, 25, 26, 32, 63, 71, 79, 81, 98, 104, 105, 110, 139, 151, 152, 153, 257
Metaverse 135, 187, 188, 189, 190, 191, 192, 193, 194, 195, 197, 198, 199, 200, 201, 202, 203, 204, 205, 206, 207, 208, 209, 210, 211, 212, 213, 214, 215, 216, 217, 218

N

North Tripura 158, 163, 174

O

Objectives of Social Equality and Economic Inclusion 31, 48
Ontology Engineering 31, 32, 33, 43, 45, 46, 47, 48, 49, 50, 51, 52, 53, 54, 55, 65, 66, 67, 70, 71
Organizational values 78, 257, 262, 265, 269

P

People management 257, 262, 264, 265, 269
Preferences 4, 17, 19, 22, 54, 123, 155, 158, 159, 160, 162, 163, 175, 177, 178, 179, 181, 192, 193
Preprocessing 143, 144, 262, 263, 264
Promotion of Socio-Economic Development 43
Public Sector Sustainability 73, 74, 76, 79, 80, 81, 82, 102, 113, 114

S

SMEs 1, 2, 3, 4, 5, 6, 7, 8, 9, 10, 11, 12, 14, 15, 16, 17, 18, 21, 22, 23, 27, 28, 135, 140
Sustainability 1, 2, 3, 10, 21, 45, 50, 73, 74, 75, 76, 79, 80, 81, 82, 100, 101, 102, 103, 104, 105, 106, 107, 108, 109, 111, 112, 113, 114, 116, 117, 122, 123, 125, 126, 130, 132, 133, 135, 136, 153, 252, 268
Sustainable Development 24, 28, 45, 50, 64, 69, 71, 82, 110, 112, 114, 115, 116, 117, 121, 124, 126, 130, 131, 132, 133, 134, 135, 136, 137, 152, 213, 252

U

Usage 2, 15, 21, 36, 49, 65, 66, 73, 74, 77, 78, 79, 81, 86, 87, 88, 90, 91, 92, 94, 95, 98, 99, 100, 101, 102, 104, 105, 106, 112, 119, 120, 149, 155, 158, 159, 160, 161, 162, 163, 170, 175, 176, 177, 178, 179, 180, 182, 183, 184, 192, 202, 203, 205, 230, 231, 250

V

Virtual Democracy 187, 191, 203, 212

W

Well-Being 74, 76, 114, 137, 251, 268

www.ingramcontent.com/pod-product-compliance
Lightning Source LLC
LaVergne TN
LVHW061546290926
849162LV00004B/928

* 9 7 9 8 3 6 9 3 8 4 7 7 0 *